REBELLION AND REALIGNMENT

REBELLION

— AND —

REALIGNMENT

12-87
Cen

ARKANSAS'S ROAD TO SECESSION

James M. Woods

The University of Arkansas Press

Fayetteville   1987

Designer: Patricia Douglas Crowder
Typeface: Linotron 202 Primer
Typesetter: G&S Typesetters, Inc.
Printer: Thomson-Shore, Inc.
Binder: John H. Dekker & Sons, Inc.

The paper used in this publication meets the minimum requirements of the American
National Standard for Permanence of Paper for Printed Library Materials Z39.48-1984. ∞™

Library of Congress Cataloging-in-Publication Data
Woods, James M., 1952–
 Rebellion and realignment.

 Includes bibliographical references and index.
  1. Arkansas—History. 2. Arkansas—History—
Civil War, 1861–1865. 3. Secession. I. Title.
F411.W63 1987   976.7   85-21024
ISBN 0-938626-59-0

This book is gratefully dedicated to my parents,
Judge Henry and Kathleen Woods.

Acknowledgments

I am indebted to many people for this book. Dr. John B. Boles, now of Rice University, directed this study as a Tulane doctoral dissertation. President Frank Vandiver of Texas A & M University first steered me onto this topic, and oversaw my earliest efforts as my master's thesis director at Rice University. Others in academia who have helped include: Drs. Bill Malone and Lawrence Powell of Tulane University, Dr. Roland Pippin of Northwestern State University, Dr. Walter Brown of the University of Arkansas at Fayetteville, Dr. C. Fred Williams of the University of Arkansas at Little Rock, Dr. Michael Dougan of Arkansas State University. Special thanks to Dr. Richard Beringer of the University of North Dakota and Dr. Daniel Crofts of Trenton State College for their comments and criticisms. Dr. June R. Welch of the University of Dallas and Dr. David Hodgson of Claflin College provided me with strong moral support and encouragement.

Outside of academia, I wish to thank Miller Williams and his staff at the University of Arkansas Press. This book was greatly improved by the hard work of Mr. Ernest Dumas of the *Arkansas Gazette* and of my parents, Judge Henry and Kathleen Woods. Thanks also to Dr. John Ferguson and his patient staff at the Arkansas History Commission. I must include Catherine Catalfamo of the Arkansas Territorial Restoration and Margaret Ross of the Arkansas Gazette Foundation Library. Others in need of recognition include: Thomas Woods, Eileen Harrison, Ray and Diane Hanley, Kathi Schiel, Mrs. Macon Kirkman, Harry and Sue Graham, Joseph and Carolyn Brady, Orlando and Mary Moron, and Eric Wedig. Thanks also to my personal friends who loved and supported me throughout this endeavor, and to the Lord Jesus Christ who gave me the grace to see this book to its completion.

Finally I need to thank my wife, Becky, for without her love, patience, prayers, and encouragement, it would have never been finished.

Contents

REBELLION AND REALIGNMENT

Introduction

After surveying a century of historiography on the secession movement in the South, William Donnelly concluded in 1965 that historians had presented little detailed analysis of the local, class and economic interests that lay behind secession.[1] Five years later, historian William Freehling called for a "fresh look at the sectional and class divisions in the Old South" as a method of explaining tensions within the South before the Civil War.[2] In what seemed to be a direct answer, scholars during the 1970s poured forth monographs on the secession movements in states of the lower South.[3]

Although remarkable studies on secession have been made in most states of the Deep South, current manuscripts have only been concerned with those states in the upper South that joined the Confederacy after the bombardment of Fort Sumter in April 1861.[4] Although Virginia, Arkansas, Tennessee, and North Carolina had major sectional and class divisions, more than other Confederate states, they endured long months of debate and division over breaking up the Federal Union. These states of the upper South experienced similar geographic and economic divisions. Each contained a lowland slaveholding plantation culture like that of the lower South, and a mountain region fostering a mostly non-slaveholding small-farmer society. In Virginia, North Carolina and Tennessee, upland regions are part of the Appalachian mountain chain. In Arkansas, the mountains are part of the Ozark and Ouachita mountain provinces. With their planter and poor white cultures, these four states would seem to be a natural place to begin the search for divisions in Southern society on the eve of the Civil War.[5]

Arkansas especially appears to be ignored. No study of the secession movement in Arkansas has ever been published. One unpublished work was written more than thirty-five years ago by Elsie Mae Lewis, a pioneering black historian from Little Rock, who wrote her dissertation on secession at the University of Chicago under the direction of the venerable historian, Avery Craven.[6] In many ways, Dr. Lewis's study was a remarkable personal achievement, since she was both a woman and black, working in an era that discriminated against her race and sex.

However, like any pioneer study, Dr. Lewis's work contains certain inadequacies. For example, the Arkansas political scene between 1858 and 1861 is described in only about sixty pages of the four-hundred-page dissertation. The important state election of 1860 is mentioned almost in passing.

Since Dr. Lewis's work was completed in 1947, some monographs plus several useful and relevant articles have been published on antebellum Arkansas by both the *Arkansas Historical Quarterly* and the *Journal of Southern History*.[7] With this new scholarship over the past thirty years, the time has come for a fresh interpretation of how and why Arkansas left the Union after less than a quarter-century as a state.

Focusing primarily on the years between 1859 and 1861, a period when major political rebellion and realignment took place, the present political study of Arkansas provides a narrative that will consider strong social, regional and economic differences existing during the antebellum era. For most of this period Arkansas experienced steady but difficult development. Not until the eve of civil war did the state evince material progress and prosperity. Growth, however, was tied to a cotton-slaveholding boom in the southern and eastern lowlands. The new cotton prosperity, along with a large migration from the Deep South, linked Arkansas to the slave states of the lower South. In the mountainous regions, slavery and cotton made only a marginal impact on the society of poor white farmers. Arkansas by 1860 was as divided economically as it was geographically, a division that erupted during the secession crisis of 1861.

Throughout much of the antebellum era geographic and economic differences had little impact on Arkansas politics. From the early 1830s until 1860 the state government was dominated by a few elite families in Little

Rock. The Conway-Sevier-Johnson political clique was often referred to during that time as the "Dynasty" or the "Family." Governed for so long by such a closely knit oligarchy, Arkansas became unique in this respect among states of the Old South.

The last section of this book examines the turbulence prevailing in Arkansas politics from 1859 to 1861, when political upheavals assured Arkansans they would not enter the Civil War united. Thomas C. Hindman, an ambitious and opportunistic schemer, forcefully challenged the Dynasty's rule with an acrimonious campaign lasting more than a year. After the election in August 1860, Hindman joined the Family in carrying Arkansas for Breckinridge in the presidential election that fall. Since Breckinridge was the candidate most closely associated with Southern disunionism, Arkansas's vote represented the state's developing bond with slave states of the lower South.

Within months of Abraham Lincoln's election seven states of the Deep South seceded. The question of how to respond to the election of Lincoln forced another upheaval in Arkansas politics. Old party differences were swept away. In the new alignment southern and eastern lowlands demanded immediate secession and the hill regions called for compromise and national reconciliation. The new alignment emerged in the winter election that called a state convention to consider secession. In March the secession convention repeatedly turned back attempts to have Arkansas leave the Federal Union. It agreed only to call another election in August 1861 in which voters would decide the state's course. Dominant Unionist-Cooperationists at this convention agreed only to call this new referendum because they feared that secessionists might bring about the dismemberment of the state.

Once hostilities commenced between the North and South during April 1861, Arkansas's close ties to the Old South, socially, culturally, and economically, proved too strong. In what appeared to be total unity, the state finally seceded in early May. Unity within the body politic, however, was more apparent than real. Old party factionalism and antagonism once again emerged in Confederate Arkansas. Also, not every area of the state was pleased with secession. In the Ozark regions of northwestern and north central Arkansas, loyalty to the Federal government persisted. Whatever unity existed in Arkansas during the time it seceded from the Union was short-lived.

As in other Southern states, secession in Arkansas was closely tied to the defense of slavery. Yet Arkansas also had a unique heritage as the last frontier of the Old South. Any understanding of the secession movement in Arkansas must begin with the acknowledgment of such local and regional interests as important factors in the state's fateful decision made on May 6, 1861.

I

A Promise Unfulfilled

Settlement of the Arkansas Frontier

At the end of 1860 *DeBow's Review*, a leading magazine of the Old South, quoted a New Orleans newspaper on the growth of Arkansas:

> The Census of 1860 is likely to present the State of Arkansas as one whose progress in the last ten years has been remarkable. For a long period, the soil and climate, and vast resources of the State remained unknown. Rather for a species of savage chivalry and unlettered independence was it celebrated, than for anything which could make it 'specially attractive to emigrants. . . . We rejoice in the evidences of prosperity of our neighbor, and have no fear that she will advance beyond any calculations based upon the past. No State is more rich in fertile soil and genial climate.[1]

Arkansas did in fact have real promise. Although it had been open to American settlement for more than a half-century before 1860, it still lagged behind the rest of the country culturally and in economic development. The New Orleans paper's optimistic forecast about prosperity would have to wait another century to be fully realized. Throughout the antebellum period, Arkansas's promise was slowly emerging from its frontier status. Only at the very end of the antebellum era did Arkansas begin to meet the expectations of regional boosters like J. D. B. DeBow.

The first census taken in Arkansas after it was incorporated into the United States as part of the Louisiana Purchase in 1803, found only three major areas of settlement, all in the eastern part of the state along the White, Arkansas, and Mississippi rivers. The census of 1810 enumerated only 924 whites, 136 slaves, and two persons categorized as free blacks.[2]

Indians, of course, were not counted. Once Louisiana obtained statehood in 1812, Arkansas became a district in the newly created Missouri Territory and remained in this legal status until Missouri applied for statehood in 1819. On March 2, 1819, President James Monroe signed a bill creating the Arkansas Territory, whose government was to begin on the Fourth of July that year.[3]

Boundaries for the new territory on the north, east, and south comprise the present perimeter of Arkansas. At first, the northern boundary was to be 36°30' westward from the Mississippi River, but owing to the influence of the New Madrid township and a wealthy farmer named J. Hardeman Williams, the Missouri territorial legislature let the southern boundary of Missouri dip down to 36° north from the Mississippi River to the St. Francis River, leaving the northern boundary of Arkansas slightly irregular.[4] On the west, the Arkansas Territory once included almost all of Oklahoma, but treaties with the Choctaw in 1825 and with the Cherokee in 1828 reduced it to its present size.[5] After seventeen years as a territory, Arkansas achieved statehood on June 15, 1836, making it the twenty-fifth state in the Federal Union.[6]

Arkansas is almost equally divided between a lowland region known as the Gulf Coastal Plain, and an upland area called the Interior Highlands, a dichotomy that has heavily influenced its social, economic and political development.[7] About 52 percent of the land area is part of the coastal plain, divided into the Mississippi Alluvial Plain and the Gulf Coastal Plain. Slicing through the Mississippi Alluvial Plain is Crowley's Ridge, an uneroded section made up of wind deposited loess that once split the channel of the Mississippi River. The Father of Waters changed its course over time, leaving the St. Francis River Basin and Crowley's Ridge as small remnants of its western channel.[8] The mountain regions are neatly divided into two main provinces, the Ozarks and Ouachitas. The Ozark Mountains extend across the extreme northwestern and north central sections of the state. The Ouachitas run across central western Arkansas. (See numbers 1–7 in Figure 1.) Between these two regions, also part of the Ouachitas, is a plain approximately forty miles wide known as the Arkansas River Valley.[9]

These geophysical features dictated the state's agricultural development, which would determine its economic and political future. Flat and fertile, the eastern and southern sections of the state lured thousands of land-hungry, slaveholding cotton farmers into Arkansas. Cotton commanded high prices on world markets before the Civil War, yet the crop quickly caused soil depletion, sending many farmers from older southern states westward in search of virgin land.[10] The full impact of this out-migration would not strike Arkansas until the last decade of the antebellum era.

Uplands which supported crops besides cotton invited settlers from the mountains of the upper South. Frank I. Owsley, the eminent historian of the plain folk in the Old South, concluded that the average immigrant looked for "a country as nearly as possible like the one in which he formerly lived in matters of soil, rainfall, temperature, and appearance."[11] Thus into the Ozarks and Ouachitas came immigrants from the upland regions of Virginia, Kentucky, North Carolina, and especially Tennessee.[12] Appalachian families moved to the Trans-Mississippi highlands, the Ozark Plateaus and the Ouachitas, where they found a rugged, wooded environment similar to their homeland.[13]

Those who settled in the Arkansas mountains adopted the culture and farming practices of the southern Appalachians, yet they also raised some cotton and owned a few slaves.[14] These upland folk lived isolated, self-sufficient lives. While slavery was never foreign to the hills,[15] it never made the impact there that it did in the lowlands. Although plantation and mountain cultures bore some similarities, differences were real enough to affect the politics of antebellum Arkansas.

Abundant rivers and streams made the interior of Arkansas readily accessible to prospective settlers, even though the rivers were not always dependable for commerce. The Arkansas River runs for more than three hundred miles through the heartland of its state, while the state's eastern boundary is formed by the mighty Mississippi River.[16] A large network of other streams made commercial development easier.[17] One writer has commented that "it would be difficult, indeed, to find another state whose entire surface is so well supplied with natural waterways as is that of Arkansas."[18]

Natural beauty and wild game delighted travelers during frontier times. Henry Schoolcraft, the English adventurer who journeyed down the Buffalo River in early 1819, found it difficult to describe the beautiful Ozarks.[19] German sportsman Frederick Gerstacker visited Arkansas in the late 1830s and found it to be a hunter's paradise: "Game seemed to abound, flocks of wild turkey filled the forests as thick as partridges in Germany, and deer were equally plentiful; in one day, I saw several herds of ten or twelve head each."[20] To many other visitors from Europe and other parts of the United States, Arkansas was a veritable paradise of beauty and ever abundant game.[21]

Natural allurements attracted many settlers to the state and it grew at a rapid rate.[22] (See Table 1a in the Appendix.) Growth between 1810 and 1820 reflected the expansion common to frontier states and territories.[23] After that, Arkansas's population doubled every ten years, and during the 1830s it tripled.[24] This increase greatly outdistanced the national growth rate but was expected of a frontier region.

To obtain a better perspective on Arkansas's population growth, a comparison must be made between the state's expansion and other frontier communities. Table 1b in the Appendix compares the Arkansas population growth with five other states that developed between 1810 and 1860.[25] To be sure, Louisiana was not as underdeveloped as Arkansas or Missouri, but still it was basically a western state whose population was less than a third of Georgia's in 1810.[26] Like Arkansas, Missouri, Mississippi, Michigan, and Illinois developed substantially after 1810. The percentage of population growth in Arkansas exceeded that of the other six states from 1810 to 1860, but largely because Arkansas's base population was so small.

When figures for only the white population are compared, statistics change a bit, and the percentage of population growth drops slightly. Slaves and non-whites did not participate in the politics of antebellum America. When non-whites are excluded, Illinois experienced a slightly higher percentage in population growth than did Arkansas during the 1850s. Arkansas only surpassed the other five states in two decades, 1810–20 and 1840–50. (See Table 1c.)

Percentages can be misleading. While Arkansas's percentage of growth might have exceeded the rates of the other five states, its actual net increase and total population lagged behind them. Arkansas and Michigan, for example, had roughly the same number of people in 1830, but in twenty years the Great Lakes State would have twice the population of its southern counterpart.[27] (See Tables 1b and 1c.) As Tables 1d and 1e illustrate, Arkansas's percentage of growth did not mean that it surpassed the other states in population. Arkansas ranked last in population in 1810, and a half-century of good steady growth did not alter that position. While it is true that Arkansas was much more underdeveloped than the other five states in 1810, the fact that fifty years of substantial growth had not altered the state's relative position indicates that Arkansas had some troubles in attracting and keeping settlers.

An early scholar of antebellum Arkansas once wrote that:

In the chimerical world of the Old South, all southerners were slaveowners, aristocrats, and dueling cavaliers who lived in stately mansions, presided over by jasmine-scented, fragile ladies. The South was no glamour world. Arkansas, on the edge of the frontier . . . was certainly not.[28]

In the years before the Civil War, certain geographic, economic, and cultural conditions combined to make settlement in Arkansas difficult, if not dangerous, and prevented the state from developing as smoothly and as quickly as other states on the western frontier. To many Arkansas settlers even at the end of the antebellum era, the promise of their frontier state remained unfulfilled.

Although waterways blessed the countryside, none of them provided safe and reliable transportation. In one of the earliest guides written for western immigrants, Samuel Brown warned his readers in 1817 that "the Arkansas River is about two-thousand miles in length; the navigation, however, cannot be said to be good; the channel is wide and shallow, and is interrupted by a considerable number of rapids."[29] Ten years later, geographer Timothy Flint reported that "the shore of the Arkansas River, as far up as Little Rock, is decidedly unhealthy. Great tracts on all sides are covered with sleeping lakes and stagnant bayous."[30]

Shallow and swampy, the Arkansas River remained quite hazardous to travelers even after regular steamboat traffic was established in 1840.[31] The *Arkansas Intelligencer,* located in the western river town of Van Buren, reported in the summer of 1845 that "our river is in a deplorable condition for the safe navigation of any kind of craft. . . . In many places, the snags are so numerous that it is almost impossible for a steamer to run between them."[32]

Lady Ida Pfeifer, an Englishwoman, journeyed by steamboat on the Arkansas River in the mid-1850s and noted that the "river is so full of trunks of trees sticking up, or what is still more dangerous only just covered with water, that the greatest caution is required; and, at night, it is only with a bright moonlight and a high water that navigation can be attempted."[33] While all the western rivers could be dangerous, the *Arkansas Gazette* reported in 1859 that insurance rates on the Arkansas and

Red rivers were the highest in the nation.[34] The Red River touched the very southwestern corner of the state.

Almost all rivers flooded periodically and then went through long periods of low water. Lowlands in eastern Arkansas were especially vulnerable to flooding by the Mississippi River. One Poinsett County woman wrote to a friend in 1848 that the river had "overflowed our land for fifty miles."[35] In the summer of 1833, the *Gazette* in Little Rock reported that "all plantations on the north side of the Arkansas for several miles above and below this place [were] under water."[36] Six years later the same newspaper complained, "for the last eight months we have been nearly cut off from all intercourse with the civilized world owing to the river being depended on for the transportation of the mails, while there is scarcely water sufficient to float a dugout."[37] A Union soldier during the Civil War wrote to his wife that the Arkansas River "is one of the changeablest rivers I ever saw, it is rising one day and falling the next, and has been so all of this winter."[38]

A prolonged drought in the early 1850s nearly suspended navigation of the Arkansas and Ouachita rivers for four of five years.[39] In 1855 low water on the Red River stranded 40,000 bales of cotton near Washington.[40] Once a Fort Smith newspaper had to curtail publication for three weeks because the Arkansas River was so low that it could receive neither paper nor news.[41] This unreliable river system isolated the northwestern section of the state until the Civil War. The uncertainty of delivering goods and supplies also discouraged development.[42]

Unreliable rivers were not the only transportation difficulty afflicting antebellum Arkansas. Roads were notoriously difficult, often impassable, particularly in the eastern lowlands. Settlers crossing the Mississippi River at Memphis "heard wonderful stories about Texas and saw only hundreds of miles of formidable swamps in Arkansas."[43]

In 1837, the editor of the *Arkansas Gazette* commented bitterly that "emigrants continue to flock to this part of the country, but they do it at the risk and cost of passing through the most disgraceful bogs, wildernesses, and swamps that can be found."[44] Even though a stagecoach line began running between Arkansas Post and Little Rock in 1826,[45] the trip was hardly comfortable or pleasant. In the late 1850s, northerner Gilbert Hathaway recorded his harrowing experiences on a stagecoach from Helena to Little Rock. The "road" was virtually nonexistent, Hathaway said, and he lost some of his possessions after his coach overturned in a swamp. Hathaway eventually made it to Little Rock, but not on the coach; he was forced to buy a horse in Pine Bluff to complete his journey.[46]

Poor or unsubstantial roads were not restricted to the eastern part of the state. A post rider from Monroe to Little Rock in 1830 had to wade or swim no less than twenty-seven streams. Fifteen miles outside the state capital he had to abandon his horse and carry the mail on his back.[47] Poor roads also meant lack of mail service. At one point in 1835 an editor in Little Rock suggested, in humorous exasperation, that the Federal government send the state's mail quarterly in a balloon.[48] Bishop George W. Freeman, an Episcopal missionary, wrote his superiors in the summer of 1849 that he could not move from Little Rock by land in any direction north or south. To journey to Camden, a distance of 120 miles from the Arkansas capital, the bishop had to take a steamer to New Orleans and then travel by water up the Red and Ouachita rivers. The prelate estimated that he had to journey more than 1,250 miles by water in order to preach at another Arkansas town only 120 miles away.[49] Although conditions on Arkansas roads did improve, as late as 1851, the Fort Smith *Herald* could bemoan:

We have no roads of any kind except a few that are mainly cut out and are not fit to travel over. It does not appear to us that the people of this State manifest more apathy on the improvement of the roads than can be found in any other State in the Union.[50]

Another crucial limitation to Arkansas's growth was the unsettling presence of the Indian territory on its western border. Unlike Missouri, the state would never be a "mother of the West" because the West for Arkansas ended at the 95th meridian. The nearness of an Indian frontier put a damper on development for it tended to steer immigration southwest into Texas. The Ozarks were too formidable to cross, and anyway one could not settle directly west of Arkansas. Many Arkansans were forced to witness what seemed to be a continuous stream of immigrants traveling through their state to Texas. Little Rock was seen by many, in fact, as merely an entrepôt for settlers on their way to the Lone Star State. One Little Rock resident witnessed this scene in the fall of 1851:

The tide of emigration now flowing through our State is immense; the streets of our city are sometimes, in places, blocked up with wagons of ruddy, healthy-looking people, who would be an honor and pride to our State, but, with almost one accord, they say they are "going to Texas."[51]

Texas did outstrip Arkansas by attracting settlers, especially in the 1850s.[52] Since many Arkansans felt they were losing future citizens to Texas, newspapers tried to counter this trend with false bravado or glowingly optimistic accounts about the future of the state, vis-à-vis their larger neighbor. Without citing any evidence, the Fort Smith *Herald* claimed in 1852 that "emigrants east of the Mississippi are finding out that thousands upon thousands of acres of good land [could be acquired] in Arkansas at far cheaper rates than the same quality of land can be purchased in Texas."[53] Unfortunately for Arkansas, these sentiments reflected more hope than reality.

Not all settlers going to Texas were merely passing through Arkansas; others had been residents there before departing for greener pastures. James Neal, an attorney from Fayetteville, wrote to an old lawyer friend who had recently emigrated to Austin, confiding to his correspondent that he intended to move to Texas, for "it has been too laborious [in Arkansas] for the past few years." Neal added that "there is quite a number leaving this county this fall, mostly for Texas."[54] The Lone Star State not only attracted more settlers, it also proved a convenient escape for discontented and restless persons in Arkansas.

Arkansas suffered another population depletion when the news of gold in California was announced. Fort Smith, for a time, served as a major launching point for Forty-Niners enroute to the goldfields. A California Emigration Company was formed in this west Arkansas outpost to aid travelers heading for the Pacific coast.[55] Concerned that many Arkansans might also seek gold in this famous strike, U.S. Senator Solon Borland of Arkansas penned an open letter to constituents asking them to stay and diversify their crops.[56] Fear of population loss was not the only reason to caution against participating in the gold rush. The Fort Smith *Herald* published a letter from a former Arkansan then living in Sacramento, California, warning his old friends and neighbors not to emigrate because "they will be more liable to death and disease, and then will inevitably suffer loss of property, and endure many hardships and privations, than would be bearable at home."[57] The author of these words, William Quesenbury, later reported sardonically that many criminals and gamblers from Arkansas were flourishing in the Sacramento area.[58]

The Indian Territory diverted population from the state and prolonged its frontier conditions. Without an exploitable West, people in western

Arkansas tended to remain where they were, preserving old folkways and traditions long after these had disappeared nationally. Edward Everett Dale, a famous frontier historian, described it as a millpond effect, Arkansas being like a stagnant pool behind the dam of a swift migratory stream flowing across the continent.[59] Alone among western states, Arkansas would have no West, causing the frontier to persist longer than it would have otherwise. As other parts of the country grew more sophisticated, travelers visiting Arkansas reported their observations, sometimes exaggerating them, and from their recollections flowed legends of a backward and provincial region.[60] Legends usually have a basis in fact, and Arkansas was indeed a backward, violent and lawless state until the Civil War.[61] A reputation as one of the least appealing places to live impeded its population growth.

Throughout the antebellum era, travelers returning to the East circulated stories that Arkansas was peopled by a "race of semi-barbarians, who would not hesitate to cut a Christian into shoe strings . . . merely for the amusement it might afford them."[62] Visiting Arkansas in the late 1830s, British geologist Sir George William Featherstonhaugh was on his way to Helena when a fugitive from that river town warned him that the place was where "negur runners, counterfeitors, horse-stealers, murders, and 'sich-like' took shelter 'agin' the law."[63] Featherstonhaugh reported that Helena's fame as a "sink of Crime and Infamy" had spread as far away as Tennessee and other neighboring states.[64] John Monette, an early historian of the Mississippi Valley, wrote in 1846 that the inhabitants of Arkansas "chiefly consisted of the hardy, fearless, and restless spirits of Kentucky and Tennessee, [who] had retired from the wholesome restraints of Law and good Morals."[65] One young Virginia girl wrote a daybook recording a trip taken by her own and two other families by land from Virginia to Texas in the fall of 1851. She reported that everything went well until they reached Arkansas, where the group was robbed of six hundred dollars on the road between Memphis and Little Rock.[66]

Lawlessness flourished not only among river towns and rural roads but in the major towns as well, including the Arkansas capital, Little Rock. Featherstonhaugh probably exaggerated when he claimed that not more than twelve citizens in the Arkansas capital went about without "wearing two pistols and a hunting knife a foot long and an inch broad . . . the Bowie knife."[67] The *Gazette* editor lamented in 1840 that "we are obliged to state that fist fights, and other breaches of the law are becoming more common in this city than at any time since our residence here, and when we first arrived, the place had a name bad enough."[68] Until the very eve of civil war, Little Rock remained a violent little river town. One court term in 1858 brought fifteen indictments, eleven for murder.[69]

Western Arkansas was in a worse predicament. Throughout much of the nineteenth century it was ravaged by brigands and cutthroats who used the Indian Territory as a refuge from local legal authorities.[70] To citizens, the federal government appeared to be unable, or even unwilling, to impose order. After reporting that the Federal government stationed no more than a "corporal guard"[71] at Fort Smith, the *Herald* exclaimed in frustration in 1848, "we are called upon to say something almost daily in regard to the defenselessness of our frontiers . . . and we have, time after time, made remarks on the subject, but our words have fallen heedlessly to the ground. . . ."[72] Towns on the western border were also scenes of much criminal activity. The Fort Smith *Herald* lamented in early 1860 that "murder, vice, and rowdyism stalks our streets by night and by day, with brazen effrontery, confident in the feeling that there is no power to restrain them, or, if there is, it will not be used."[73] Sir George Featherstonhaugh may have best described the prevailing lawlessness of antebellum Arkansas:

Gentlemen who had taken the liberty to imitate the signature of other persons, bankrupts who were not disposed to be plundered by their creditors, homicides, horse stealers, and gamblers, all admired Arkansas on account of the gentle and tolerant state of opinion which prevails there.[74]

Violence, however, was not restricted to the criminal element. In the Ozarks, family feuds erupted with some frequency, and one in the early 1850s grew until the citizens of Marion County were engaged in open civil war. The governor sent the state militia to quell the disturbance.[75] Bloodshed occurred even in the august halls of the Arkansas General Assembly. Offended by remarks of one of the legislators in December, 1837, the Speaker of the House marched down the aisle and stabbed an unarmed House member to death before the startled assembly. A trial acquitted the Speaker of any wrongdoing, even though many witnessed the deed.[76]

Though technically illegal, dueling thrived until the Civil War.[77] Political rivalry often became personal animosity, which in turn could produce personal tragedy. The founder of the state Democratic party lost his life in a duel in 1827.[78] Dueling had respectability, and many ambitious politicians had to prove themselves at the polls and upon the "field of honor." The fine art of personal combat availed itself not only to politicians but to any man who sought to prove to others that he was no coward. Two brothers-in-law shot and killed one another in 1855 over political differences in broad daylight on the streets of Little Rock.[79] Criminal and non-criminal behavior reached such proportions that one man wrote to a friend in Texas in 1857, "if the laws of this State respecting murder are not regarded nor enforced more stringently in the future, no man within the realm of Arkansas can consider his life safe."[80]

What justice was administered was all too often of the vigilante variety. Otherwise law-abiding people were not hesitant to lynch those convicted, or even suspected, of heinous crimes. After a man was robbed and killed on the Memphis-to-Little Rock road in 1835, a posse was organized and soon caught the renegade, who quickly confessed to the deed. Since Crittenden County had no jail, and because the man might escape or be rescued by various outlaw gangs in the area, the confessed murderer was hung without benefit of a formal trial.[81] Six years later, the editor of the *Arkansas Gazette* bemoaned that "Arkansas is a place where no law is recognized except lynch law, and no rights maintained except by brute force."[82] Although vigilante justice lessened a bit in the last two decades before the Civil War, it was by no means eradicated, for frontier lifestyle still prevailed in much of the state.[83] An explanation for such violence ordinarily might rest upon the overabundance of unmarried males between the ages of 18 and 30, but this does not seem to have held true in antebellum Arkansas. From the earliest census records of 1820 to 1860, it is apparent that there was no significantly imbalanced sex ratio. While more males between the ages of 15 and 60 lived during that time, the numerical difference between males and females was not far apart.[84] (See Table 1f in the Appendix.)

Although Arkansas had only been a state for fourteen years, the 1850 census revealed that the ratio between men and women matched that of such states as Mississippi, Missouri and Illinois, all of which were twenty years ahead of Arkansas in maturing to statehood.[85] (See Table 1g in the Appendix.) More likely causes of the high level of violence included proximity to the frontier and the general underdevelopment of the state. However, its violence and lawlessness left little wonder why the state was saddled with such a poor reputation. While traveling on a steamboat on the Mississippi in 1842, the editor of the *Gazette* was told by a man from New England that people from the northeast saw little difference between a man from Arkansas and a Bengal tiger.[86] Arkansans were certainly aware of their poor reputation, yet they felt helpless to do anything about it. In 1849 the *Arkansas Intelligencer* in Van Buren lamented deeply that:

People at a distance easily come to the conclusion that Arkansas is only famous for private brawls and lynchings, and the bloodiest encounters in the annals of border warfare. Consequently, a typical Arkansan is pictured as a person in a semi-barbaric state, half-alligator, half-horse . . . armed to the teeth, bristling with knives and pistols, a rollicking, daredevil type of personage, made up of coarseness, ignorance, and bombast. . . .[87]

No amount of hand wringing or local boasting could alter Arkansas's unfavorable national reputation which has persisted past the Civil War and unfortunately, far beyond.

Possessed of natural beauty, abundant game and rich, alluvial land, Arkansas nevertheless had not fulfilled its promise to the immigrants who settled there. An unreliable river system, miserable or nonexistent roads, together with the unstabilizing and stunting presence of the Indian Territory on the western border, all made living in antebellum Arkansas both difficult and frustrating. Yet these geographical obstacles do not tell the complete story. Arkansas faced serious economic deficiencies until the emergence of the cotton kingdom in the 1850s. On the eve of the Civil War there was cause for hope that Arkansas could discard its earlier doldrums, and was now prepared to enter the new, bright period of prosperity that a New Orleans newspaper had predicted it would enjoy after 1860.

II

A Story of Contrasts

Regional Differences and Economic Development
in Antebellum Arkansas

Arkansas's economic growth is a story of contrasts and delayed development. Divided geographically into two separate regions, there is an obvious contrast between the uplands in the northwest and the lowlands in the southeast. The two intrastate regions attracted different settlers from diverse areas of the Old South. Although a liberal land policy was intended to make it easy for immigrants to obtain homesteads, the harsh reality was that Arkansas was deeply in debt and its state government financially unstable throughout the early decades of development. Other problems, discussed in the previous chapter, also slowed Arkansas's growth. Only late in the antebellum era did the state appear to have emerged from its earlier doldrums. Arkansas evolved from a struggling frontier society into a developing cotton-slaveholding economy. Although by 1860 it had not achieved the flourishing plantation economy of the older Deep South states, it was moving in that direction. Many Arkansans were sure that a cotton-slave economy would be necessary for the state to have a secure and prosperous future. When Arkansas finally began to enjoy an economic boom in the late 1850s, the schism between the northwest and the southeast, owing to their different economies and cultures, was exacerbated. Peopled by upper South and Deep South immigrants, the state previously had no dominant identity, but by the end of the antebellum period much of the state was inexorably pulled toward identification with the Deep South committed to slavery and cotton. The Ozark region became increasingly isolated from the rest of the state.

Economic growth depends on people. To grasp the patterns of economic development in antebellum Arkansas, one must examine where people settled, when they came and from where. Because Congress created the Indian Territory in the 1820s, the Census of 1830 was the first one completed within Arkansas's present boundaries. Only about 30,000 persons inhabited the territory. About 25,000 of them were white. Contrary to the claims of some writers, the upland area did not contain more than two-thirds of the population, or more than three-fifths of the slave population.[1] The northwest and western mountain counties held slightly more than half the population, and about 56 percent of the slaves lived in the lowland counties.[2] (See Table 2a in the Appendix for a presentation of the lowland-upland population of Arkansas Territory in 1830.)

After 1830, Arkansas experienced tremendous immigration. The 1830s would see the largest percentage of population growth in the antebellum period (see Table 1c in the Appendix), the number of inhabitants tripling in that decade. Since much of the lowlands were swampy and disease-infested, early settlers flocked to the milder, less humid mountains. By 1840 about 60 percent of the total inhabitants, and about two-thirds of the whites, lived in the uplands.[3] (For a comparison between the lowland-upland total population and for the white-only inhabitants between 1840 and 1860, see Table 2b in the Appendix.)

During the 1840s the number of residents doubled, reaching more than 200,000. Slavery began to have a greater impact on relative population totals between the uplands and the lowlands after 1840. For example, only 40 percent of the whites lived in the delta in 1850, yet the delta had about 49 percent of the total population.[4] Although most of the whites, about 60 percent, still lived in the uplands, a trend had developed. Soon the delta would have more people than the mountains. During the 1850s, the number of inhabitants doubled again, to more than 400,000. A shift to the lowlands during the 1840s continued in the following decade, yet both regions experienced solid growth in the 1850s. Around 1858, lowlands surpassed the uplands in total population for the first time in the antebellum era.[5] Fifty-two percent of the residents lived in the eastern and southern delta by 1860. Still, the mountain counties contained the solid majority of the whites, roughly 58 percent.[6]

Slavery mainly accounted for this discrepancy in the white population and the total population between the mountains and the delta. According to the census records (see Table 2b in the Appendix), the number of

18

slaves in the lowlands made a 10 percent difference in the population totals in the lowlands and delta by 1860. In 1830, the lowlands had only
about 2,500 slaves; within thirty years that number ballooned to more
than 90,000. While the uplands in 1830 had about 2,000 slaves, fewer
than 20,000 lived there three decades later.[7] This clearly indicates that
while both regions had slaves, the lowlands were developing their agricultural systems upon slave labor. Although the farmers in the hills might
desire slaves, their type of agriculture and lack of cash prevented an easy
acquisition.[8] By the late antebellum period one part of Arkansas, commercial and market-oriented, was increasingly dependent upon slave labor, while another section, still peopled by essentially self-sufficient farmers, relied largely upon labor by free whites.

Most inhabitants of Arkansas were born outside the state. The 1850
census revealed that about 61 percent were born in other states. About 38
percent were born in Arkansas, and about one percent were foreign-
born.[9] Another decade did not alter these percentages.[10] The greatest
number of people were those under ten and between twenty and thirty.[11]
Until the very eve of the Civil War then, Arkansas remained a society of
young people, many of whom had immigrated from other states.

Until the 1850s, Arkansas received most of its in-migration from the
upper South states of Missouri, Kentucky, and especially Tennessee. One
historian of southern migration has called Arkansas the "child of Tennessee."[12] Arkansas not only drew most of its population from the volunteer state, but most of its antebellum political leadership as well.[13] But
while the number of persons from Tennessee coming into Arkansas
doubled between 1850 and 1860, the state increasingly drew its population from Alabama, Georgia, and Mississippi.[14] Immigration from the
lower South was glowingly described by a Helena newspaper in 1857:

Wagon after wagon, in an almost continuous stream are now being put across
daily from the Mississippi side of the River by the Messrs. Weather's Steam Ferry
Boat at this place. The heavy migration into Arkansas this season is marked for
being composed of people who are well-to-do in the way of worldly goods, wooly-
heads [black slaves], and large families of intelligent-looking boys, and bright-
eyed girls.[15]

This shift in migration from the upper to the lower South ultimately
linked the state more closely to the political ideology and cotton economy
of the Deep South.

Indeed, Tennessee supplied more emigrants to Arkansas than any other state, both for the uplands and lowlands, yet beyond this, the migratory patterns of the two regions were very different.[16] (Table 2c shows the half-dozen states providing the highest percentages to the uplands and lowlands from 1834–1850.) Tennessee, Kentucky and Missouri supplied about 38 percent of the settlers to the lowlands. Alabama, Georgia, and Mississippi supplied about 47 percent of the immigrants to the delta between 1834 and 1850. In the uplands, almost three-fourths of the population came from the upper South states and Illinois. Tennesseans alone provided more than 40 percent of the people for the uplands. Although Alabama and Georgia were among the top six states in furnishing settlers for the area, together they accounted for only 12 percent.

The contrast between the uplands and the lowlands became even more pronounced during the last decade of the antebellum era.[17] (See Table 2d in the Appendix for the half-dozen states that offered settlers for the delta and the mountains in Arkansas between 1850 and 1860.) While Tennessee still provided more people for the lowlands than any other state, Deep South states including Mississippi, Alabama, Georgia, and Texas supplied more than half the population for the region. Upper South states including Tennessee and Missouri only supplied about one quarter of the lowland population. Robert Walz, a historian of immigration into Arkansas during most of the nineteenth century, demonstrated that most settlers came into eastern Arkansas because it was so close geographically to their native states. The real lower South concentration of immigrants was in southern and southwestern Arkansas.[18]

In the uplands, during the 1850s, Tennessee, Missouri, and Kentucky furnished about 60 percent of the immigrants. One major difference was that Illinois was no longer in the top half-dozen states providing people for that region, its place having been taken by Georgia. Among the top six states providing population for the mountains, Deep South states now accounted for more than a quarter of the mountain inhabitants.

Walz analyzed this migratory pattern even further when he divided his data into four separate areas comprising the years 1834–1860.[19] (See Table 2e in the Appendix.) In looking at only the top four states providing population in each region, it becomes clear that Deep South immigration in the 1850s was not restricted to eastern and southern Arkansas, but spread as well into the Ouachita region in the west central portion of the state, which was less mountainous than the Ozarks and had broad, fertile river valleys. Only to the Ozarks of northwestern and north central Arkansas did emigrants from the lower South not penetrate in real numbers. There the upper South supplied more than 70 percent of the population. Little wonder, then, that when a question arose over whether to side politically with the lower South, the strongest resistance would come from the Ozarks.

The fundamental dichotomy becomes especially striking when one considers any county in the two portions of the state. Chicot County in the southeastern corner drew over 70 percent of its population from Mississippi, Alabama and Georgia during the 1850s. Marion County in the Ozarks attracted more than 84 percent of its settlers from such upper South states as Tennessee, Missouri and Kentucky.[20] With a substantial majority of its people originating at the border and from the lower South, it would be extremely difficult for Arkansas to reach a consensus over which political camp to follow if ever a dispute should occur between the upper South and the Deep South. Arkansas had a split identity.

Migration into Arkansas was made attractive by a series of liberal land laws passed in the antebellum era. The Arkansas Land Donation Act of 1840 gave tax-forfeited land to anyone who would settle on the property and agree to pay taxes in the future.[21] Ten years later, the legislature enacted one of the most generous homestead laws in United States history. It gave a family as many 160-acre plots of land as there were members of the immediate family, regardless of age or sex. Each family member could claim a tract.[22] This was far more generous than the Homestead Act of 1862, which gave 160-acre plots only to the heads of households over the age of twenty-one. It is not surprising that the state land act of 1850 provoked inquiries to the state land office from places as far away as New York, Massachusetts, Pennsylvania and Virginia.[23]

About the same time, the Federal government bequeathed to the state millions of acres of swampland for farm reclamation. To obtain rich alluvial soil in eastern Arkansas, one had only to build levees to protect overflow and drain the swamps.[24] In addition to this grant from the Federal government, the state exempted from taxation for ten years swampland that had been reclaimed.[25] By 1859 some 3,691,753 acres, about one-tenth of the surface of the state, had been reclaimed.[26] Most of this acreage fell into the hands of the wealthy, for only they could afford to construct dams and levees. Moreover, throughout the 1850s, the process

21

of distribution of the swampland was plagued by fraud, favoritism, and graft.[27] Despite these difficulties, swampland grants were a tremendous boon for Arkansas. According to historians who have studied these land grants, much of eastern Arkansas would never have been settled without them.[28]

The liberal land acts of Arkansas in 1840 and 1850 probably reflected more need than generosity. The development of the state was hindered by a poor national reputation, an unreliable transportation system, and a deep and lasting state debt. Further, Arkansas had neither real hard currency nor stable financial institutions. All of these conditions could hardly be helpful in attracting settlers, despite generous land grants.

Arkansas's massive debt and its lack of sound financial institutions stemmed primarily from the state's ruinous banking policy. Only a month after statehood in 1836, the legislature chartered the Arkansas State Bank, a state institution, and the Real Estate Bank, a private financial operation backed by state funding. Both were to provide loans to businesses and farmers. Headquartered in Little Rock, both banks operated branches throughout the state. To obtain capital for these ventures, the General Assembly borrowed three million dollars. The two institutions opened for business in the fall of 1838, yet both were hampered severely by the fact that they began during the Panic of 1837, a national financial crisis.[29] With a short career marked by "bad luck, folly, and embezzlement," the banks suspended specie payments to their customers by the end of 1839.[30]

A legislative investigation led to the closing of the Arkansas State Bank in 1843, and the Real Estate Bank was assigned to a private trusteeship. It would continue under this arrangement until the state assumed full control in 1855. The state finally closed the Real Estate Bank because it could never obtain good information about how the institution had been run or funded.[31] The fact remained, however, that this antebellum experiment in state banking caused the debt of the state to increase from $9,000 in 1837 to $2.7 million by 1858.[32]

For two decades the banks and the state debt provided a bottomless font of political controversy and haggling. Anti-bank sentiment swept the state and many agreed with state senator Mark Izard of St. Francis County, who declared that any bank "is unequal, unfair, and unjust, calculated to enrich the few at the expense of the many."[33] Responding to such sentiment, the legislature passed laws forbidding future bank charters and the circulation of bank notes. These laws meant that Arkansas would be the only southern state to lack banks just prior to the Civil War.[34] Critics then charged that the millions put into the banks had been embezzled by the political elite. The *Independent Balance* in Batesville claimed in 1856 that the state's political leadership "had eaten up the substance of the state like canker-worms. . . . They had robbed the state through a banking system and protected the thieves."[35] Ted Worley, the historian of these early Arkansas banks, found justification for this charge, yet no one, then or later, could find definitive proof.[36] Though the responsible party for this financial fiasco was unknown, no one doubted the event's crippling effect on economic development. It was clear to the *Southern Shield* in Helena, which evaluated the state's economic progress in 1850:

If we had not established banks when we did, our state would now, in all probability, be in a condition such as would rank her among the first of this glorious Confederacy. But a false step has burdened her with a debt she cannot discharge for a quarter of a century. Her destiny must remain darkened for many years to come, notwithstanding, she had all the elements of greatness scattered in wild profusion about her.[37]

The absence of banks meant Arkansas had little or no fluid currency, and few sources of credit. Citizens were forced to use coonskins, pelts and bank paper from other states.[38] This put a tremendous damper on economic progress. The *Arkansas Gazette* lamented in 1851 that the banking situation was causing "Arkansas to bleed at every pore for the want of money, for the ordinary change necessary to meet the actual demands of society."[39] What little hard currency was available was quickly drained away for the merchants, and the people were usually in debt to merchants in other areas, such as Memphis, New Orleans, Cincinnati, and New York. Only on the western frontier, around government outposts such as Fort Smith, was hard species available.[40]

Lack of hard currency made it almost impossible to accumulate capital to support such ventures as railroad construction. Like other states of the Old South, Arkansas could not accumulate much capital because the little wealth that was acquired was usually invested in land and slaves.[41] While other states in the South had the financial stability to construct railroads, Arkansas did not even have the ordinary currency to meet the demands of its residents. Interest in building railroads arose in the early 1850s. Prominent Arkansans like Absalom Fowler of Little Rock attended a railroad convention in New Orleans in early 1852.[42] Two railroad conventions were held in Camden and Little Rock in late 1851 and early 1852.[43] Unfortunately, not one inch of rail materialized from these assemblies. With little fluid capital and a huge public debt, Arkansas was in no condition to mount a railroad construction campaign.

Confronted by all these difficulties, many grew despondent over Arkansas's economic plight. The concern seemed to be especially prevalent in the early 1850s. "No other state in the Union is without works of internal improvement except, alone, Arkansas," the *Southern Shield* at Helena grieved in 1853, "she [has] no railroads, no canal, no telegraph, no plank or turnpike roads, no deaf, dumb, or insane asylum. No sir, not even a respectable tollbridge, mill dam, spinning jenny, or pork packer."[44] A writer in the *Arkansas Gazette* a year later, gave a more sweeping but no less gloomy analysis:

Poor Arkansas, without navigation, without railroads, deeply in debt, and dependent upon her sister states . . . We have no manufacturing or mining. We are strictly an agricultural people, and yet we purchase from abroad what we could make at home. We import in large quantities of what we should export. No wonder the balance of trade is against us and money is scarce.[45]

Judge John Brown of Camden sounded the most despondent note when he wrote in his diary on New Year's day 1853, "My dissatisfaction with Arkansas has increased. I feel that I am settled and my means invested in and lying comparatively dead in the most hopeless portion of the United States."[46]

All of these dire pronouncements must be leavened by the total economic reality. While the state did have real problems, it also experienced certain growth, especially in the mid-to-late 1850s. In 1838, for example, property value stood at only $15,564,284. Twelve years later it had risen to $34,935,885. Within a decade property value then jumped to $122,455,400.[47] Tax revenues were just over ten thousand dollars at the time of statehood in 1836. A quarter of a century later they had increased to more than one hundred and seventy thousand dollars.[48]

Economic growth can most readily be seen in the increase in agricultural production in the last two decades of the antebellum era. During the 1850s, the number of bushels of wheat grew more than five times, and the number of bushels of corn and pounds of butter quadrupled. The estimated value of livestock tripled. Cotton production increased more than twentyfold between 1840 and 1860.[49] Although overwhelmingly a farming economy, Arkansas also experienced some significant developments in non-agricultural goods. Private capital from lumber, manufacturing, and mining went from only $305,000 in 1850 to $1,316,610 by 1860. The number of small companies operating in the state rose from 261 to 587 between 1850 and 1860. The value of earned wages increased from just over a half-million dollars in 1850 to almost three million dollars by 1860.[50] By the end of the antebellum era, Arkansas ranked second in the United States in the production of magnesium,[51] although admittedly it was a rather insignificant amount. This growth in the non-agricultural economy did not mean that the state was undergoing industrialization or urbanization. By today's standards, indeed, it was almost totally rural. Little Rock, the largest town, had only 3,727 citizens in 1860, and only four other towns—Camden, Fort Smith, Pine Bluff and Fayetteville—had populations near or above 1,000. Only four other places had more than 500 settlers.[52]

A new wave of immigration stimulated economic growth during the last half of the 1850s. The highest immigration numbers occurred between 1855 and 1860.[53] A newspaper in southwestern Arkansas happily noticed this new development: "The tide of immigration, which had come in slowly, has been gradually augmented until now it is a mighty stream, pouring almost incessantly over our borders; our lands are being taken up, not by a few acres, but by thousands of acres."[54] This new surge of settlers raised land values throughout the state. A farm near Little Rock that sold for $600 in 1856 was resold for $2,500 in 1861.[55] Real estate appreciated so much that by 1860 only four states in what became the eleven state Confederacy would outrank Arkansas in value per acre.[56] (See Table 2h in the Appendix.) Prosperity became real in the lowlands immediately preceding the Civil War, and it was inextricably linked to the arrival of the cotton kingdom.

In the last two decades before the war, Arkansas became a major cotton producing state. Only 6 million pounds of cotton were harvested in 1840. Within ten years, that number had risen to 26 million pounds, and in another ten years it had reached almost 150 million pounds. That represented a growth of 2,500 percent in twenty years.[57] Utilizing reclaimed swamplands and liberal homestead laws, settlers poured into the delta after 1854 at a far faster pace than they came to the mountains.[58] Optimism ran high as people contemplated the future wealth of the state. The editor of the *Arkansas Gazette* wrote in 1857, "We consider the fact that the cotton crop in almost all the older states of the Union is diminishing each year by the wearing out and exhaustion of the soil. It does not take a prophet to foretell that 'ere long, Arkansas will be *the* Cotton State of the Union."[59] More than at any time in her history, Arkansas in 1860 was part of the cotton kingdom. It was a regency built on the forced labor of African slaves and a prosperity based upon world demand.

Slavery had been yoked to Arkansas soil since the 1720s, when slaves arrived with French colonists.[60] By 1860, more than 100,000 were in the state, making up about a quarter of the population. (For the number of slaves and their percentage increase decade by decade between 1810 and 1860, see Table 2i in the Appendix.) In every decade after 1820, the percentage increase of slaves was greater than that of whites.[61] (See Table 2j in the Appendix.) While the increase of whites between 1820 and 1860 was 2,500 percent, the number of slaves increased by more than 6,700 percent.[62] The percentage increases in slavery surpassed those of every other Southern state between 1810 and 1850. Texas could claim the dubious honor for the 1850s.[63]

Slavery also provided, increasingly, another distinction between the cultures of the uplands and the lowlands. The 1830 Census revealed that about 56 percent of the slaves resided in the lowlands.[64] (See Table 2a in the Appendix.) In the next three decades, however, slavery became more and more peculiar to the lowlands, and by 1860 almost 82 percent of the slaves lived in those regions.[65]

The contrast between the two geographic areas can be seen even more starkly by comparing counties. For example, Chicot County in the southeastern corner was more than 81 percent slave in 1860, while Newton County in the Ozarks, with only twenty-four slaves, was more than 99 percent white.[66] These two counties are the extremes, yet they illustrate significant regional divergence. While the number of slaves in the upland region doubled during the 1850s, the increase did not begin to keep up with the increase of whites there.[67] The yeoman farmer in the mountains might have desired slaves, but his subsistent toiling at vegetable and cereal-grain crops gave him little capital or opportunity to acquire many.[68]

As slavery increased, it began to have its effect on white society. If having twenty slaves classified someone as a planter, the number of planters rose from 512 in 1850 to 1,363 by 1860. (See Table 2l in the Appendix.) Yet, despite this growth, those who owned slaves or were members of slaveholding families probably comprised no more than 18 percent of the white population.[69] This was the lowest percentage of whites directly involved with slavery in the eleven states of the future Confederacy.[70] (See Table 2m in the Appendix.) Even when the number of slaves is added to the estimate, only about 38 percent of the people were directly involved in slavery.[71] Of the white population, more than 80 percent were not slaveholders or members of slaveholding families. Antebellum Arkansas was not quite the moonlight and magnolia stereotype of the Old South.

Judging by the relatively small number of whites who were directly involved with slavery, it is difficult to perceive antebellum Arkansas as being inextricably bound to a cotton-slave economy. One historian studying Phillips County between 1850 and 1860 found unexpectedly few planters and slaves there on the banks of the Mississippi River. While Phillips County had not reached the level of planter-slave dominance of delta regions of other Deep South states, it was clearly moving in that direction, having already begun to take on the appearance of a planter society by 1860.[72] A correspondent for a Memphis paper reported in spring of the same year that twenty miles from Helena, the county seat, he saw "an almost unbroken column of well-laid plantations, all in a high state of cultivation."[73] Two recent studies indicate that Arkansas County and other lowland counties came under a state of disproportionate planter control as early as 1840.[74]

The cotton kingdom spread not only across the lowlands but into a select group of counties in the southern portion of the uplands, the Ouachita Mountain region and the upper Arkansas River Valley. (See numbers 4−7 in Figure 1 in the Appendix.) The Ouachitas had taken a stream of settlers from the lower South, while the Ozarks remained populated by mostly people from the border South. Another contrast emerges between cotton production and slaveholding among a few counties of these mountain areas. Slaves were more abundant and cotton production much higher in the Ouachitas than in the Ozarks. This is evident when one looks at only a few counties in the two regions.[75] (See Table 2n in the Appendix for a comparison of sample counties in the Ozarks and Ouachitas in cotton production and slaveholding from 1850–1860.) One scholar's detailed study of Yell County in the upper Arkansas River Valley concluded that slaveholding and cotton production had a major impact on the county's economy.[76]

Only the Ozarks remained outside cotton's advancing dominion. A rustic society of slaveless farmers, scratching out a subsistence on hillside farms, the Ozark region found itself more and more economically and culturally isolated.

Another real indication that the state was moving toward a slave society was its treatment of free persons of color during the end of the antebellum era. Free blacks appeared in Arkansas soon after the Louisiana Purchase. The 1810 Census found two in the state, after which time they increased rapidly.[77] Between 1810 and 1840, the percentage increase of free blacks outdistanced that of the white population.[78] (See Table 2j in the Appendix.) Soon after statehood, however, this racial minority became vulnerable to legal harassment. Even though at their greatest number in 1840 free blacks amounted to less than .5 percent of the population;[79] an 1838 law required all who entered the state to present a certificate of freedom within twenty-five days of arrival.[80] A law passed five years later went further and forbade free blacks from coming into the state after March 1, 1843,[81] which diminished the growth of this population. (See Table 2j in the Appendix.) A free black from Little Rock, John Pendleton, challenged the constitutionality of the 1843 law, but the state supreme court ruled that free blacks were not really equal citizens. The court stated: "Differing as they are in complexion, habits, conformations, [and] intellectual endowments, they could not, nor ever will live together upon terms of social or political equality."[82]

Simply forbidding the entrance of free blacks into Arkansas was not enough for some. As early as 1849, editor William Woodruff of the Little Rock *Arkansas State Democrat* started the drumbeat for expelling free blacks from the state.[83] By their very presence they subtly challenged the ideology of slavery, which was that the natural state of blacks as inferior beings was bondage.[84] A widespread opinion in Arkansas and much of the South was that free blacks fomented rebellion among slaves.[85] The El Dorado *Union* expressed this belief in 1849 saying, "the insubordination and disobedience, which are found among the slaves, can be attributed to one cause—that of allowing them to fraternize with free negroes."[86] Al-

28

though no slave insurrection occurred and no free black was ever convicted of trying to start one,[87] their propinquity alone was believed to pose
a silent threat to peace and tranquility. White workers and mechanics in
the towns, moreover, faced economic competition from free blacks, and
thus they were in the vanguard of calling for the expulsion of this racial
minority.[88]

Yielding to increasing pressure, the Arkansas General Assembly in
1859 enacted a law expelling all free blacks as of January 1, 1860. The
legal path for this action was opened by the Dred Scott decision of the
United States Supreme Court in 1857. Since the nation's highest court
had nullified the legal status of free blacks in a wide-ranging judgment,
Arkansas could legally expel and put in bondage any free black within the
state.[89] How vigorously this law was enforced is hard to determine, for the
Census Bureau found 144 free blacks still living in Arkansas in June, 1860.
Most free blacks lived in the Ozarks, yet, surprisingly, Desha County in the
delta still had twenty.[90] In early 1861, the legislature suspended enforcement of the free black expulsion law until January 1, 1863.[91] By that time
Arkansas was in the midst of civil war, and, ironically, President Lincoln's
Emancipation Proclamation took effect on that date. Soon there would
be no need to distinguish between slave and free black, for each would
be free.

In various ways, antebellum Arkansas presented a social and economic
contrast. However blessed with great beauty and a mild climate for much
of the period of the Old South, the state never lived up to its potential.
Liberal land laws attracted settlers to come to Arkansas where the new
inhabitants discovered a rough, unbridled lawlessness, no reliable transportation system, no stable financial institutions, no railroads, and a huge
public debt. Since different regions of the state drew immigrants from diverse areas of the South, it was difficult to discern whether Arkansas belonged to the upper or lower South. For much of the antebellum era,
there remained a struggling frontier society, with an incomplete sense of
identity.

During the decade just prior to the Civil War, Arkansas underwent a
major economic transformation. While agricultural production enjoyed
enormous expansion, even the non-agricultural sector of the economy
also showed signs of progress. The major event of this decade was the
surge of immigration from the lower South into the lowlands, and, to a

29

limited degree, into the Ouachita Mountains. These new settlers intended to grow cotton and own slaves. Only in the Ozarks in the northwestern and north central portion, did the state remain free from this Deep South emigration. That region did not have a major increase in cotton production and slaveholding. It would remain, until the very end of the antebellum era, outside the boundaries of the maturing cotton kingdom in Arkansas. In other portions of the state, optimism ran high as the state experienced its new cotton-based prosperity. By 1860 Arkansas appeared for the first time to be a growing, maturing cotton-slave society. The increased number of planters and slaves, and the increasing intolerance of free blacks, indicated that Arkansas was developing along similar patterns of older southern states.

Although Arkansas emerged from its economic doldrums by 1860, it still remained largely a land of contrasts. Geographical differences eventually became economic divisions which never faded. In fact, as Arkansas moved toward the events of 1860, the upland-lowland contrast became more pronounced. Mountain areas contained most of the white population, while the delta held most of the black slaves. Upland farmers raised vegetables and cereal grains, while the lowland landowner grew cotton. The Deep South emigration of the 1850s only accented the regional division of the state. This new cotton kingdom in the Arkansas delta flowed somewhat into the mountains, causing an increasing difference between the Ozark and Ouachita regions. This new expansion of cotton and slavery in the Arkansas lowlands also served to tie the state more closely to the lower South.

Contrasts in antebellum Arkansas, however, were not just economic; there was also a major divergence between reality and aspiration within the state. While many Arkansans saw their future prosperity based upon forced labor of African slaves, more than 80 percent of the white population were not slaveowners or members of slaveowning families. Although many whites desired to have slaves in order to qualify as planters, the stark reality was that most yeomen in Arkansas could not afford to purchase even a single slave. Society in antebellum Arkansas would remain divided and somewhat frustrated during its economic development until the very eve of the Civil War.

Interestingly, the widening breach between the economies and cultures among the state's principal regions was not all that apparent in the politics of antebellum Arkansas. These socio-economic differences were usually covered over by a political dynasty that controlled the state from its territorial period to the precipice of the Civil War. Although it could not smother all the economic and regional differences, its stranglehold over state politics was so great that it would usually supersede any important divisions. There can be no real understanding of the politics of early Arkansas without a knowledge of the nature of this "family" dynasty that imposed its rule on an economically divided state.

III

The Foundation of a Dynasty

Parties and Politics in Arkansas, 1819–1849

Arkansas political history began when an American officer arrived in March, 1804, at the small trading fort of Arkansas Post to assume control of the area for the United States.[1] The French had founded this outpost on the Arkansas River in 1686, the first white settlement in the lower Mississippi Valley. It predated New Orleans and Natchez by almost three decades.[2] Located thirty miles upstream from the junction of the Arkansas and Mississippi rivers, Arkansas Post continued to be a sleepy French settlement for decades into the American period.[3]

In the same month that the American officer came to Arkansas Post, the United States Congress divided the Louisiana Purchase, which it had obtained the year before. The portion lying south of the thirty-three degree latitude north was to be the Territory of Orleans, while the rest of the purchase was to be the District of Louisiana with its headquarters in St. Louis.[4] For a year this large district was administered as part of the Territory of Indiana, and in 1805 it became the Territory of Louisiana. When the Territory of Orleans entered the Federal Union as the State of Louisiana, the old Territory of Louisiana was renamed the Territory of Missouri. From the Territory of Missouri in 1813 came the District of Arkansas, which within five years was subdivided into five counties.[5]

That part of the Missouri Territory lying between the 36°30′ and 40° parallels south to north, and the Mississippi River and 95° meridian east to west, petitioned Congress in 1818 to be admitted into statehood as Missouri. It became necessary, then, to form a new territory between the state of Louisiana and the proposed new state of Missouri. It is now almost forgotten that the creation of the Arkansas Territory led to a sharp North-South division over slavery in the proposed new territory, a debate that predated a much larger debate over slavery in Missouri.[6]

On February 17, 1819, only two months after a bill had been introduced in the House of Representatives to create the Territory of Arkansas, Representative John Taylor of New York introduced an amendment to have slavery prohibited in Arkansas.[7] Although the motion failed, the New York congressman did succeed in getting an amendment approved granting freedom to all slaves in the proposed territory who had reached the age of twenty-one.[8] Southerners in the House rallied enough support the next day to muster a tie on a motion to pass the Arkansas bill without the Taylor amendment. The tie had to be broken by Speaker of the House Henry Clay of Kentucky, who voted with the South.[9] Senator James Burrill, Jr. of Rhode Island moved in the Senate on March 1, 1819, to forbid slavery in the Arkansas Territory, but he was defeated, 19 to 14. The Arkansas territorial bill was now passed, and President James Monroe signed it the day following Senate approval.[10] Owing to a central southern location, it might seem that Arkansas was destined to be a slave state, and except for a handful of congressional votes, slavery might have ended there much earlier than it did.

Congressional debate over slavery in Arkansas was mild in comparison to the furor concerning Missouri's petition for statehood. Missouri almost broke up the Union it sought to join. A result of the controversy was the Missouri Compromise of 1820, which contended that in all territories south of the 36°30′ line slavery could not be prohibited, yet the area above that line could exclude the institution. This immediately placed Arkansas within the sphere of the slave South. An important social, economic, and, in time, cultural link had been forged between the South and the area that would soon emerge as the state of Arkansas. Long before it achieved statehood, at the very moment of its conception as a territory, Arkansas's future was tethered firmly to slavery and the Old South; but, as we have seen, it was not until the last years before the Civil War that Arkansas really took on the character of the Deep South.

Arkansas remained a territory for seventeen years. At first, its capital was at Arkansas Post, but in 1821, the territorial legislature moved to

Little Rock, where the government would remain.[11] The year Arkansas first became a territory in 1819, William Woodruff arrived at Arkansas Post to establish the territory's first newspaper, the *Arkansas Gazette*.[12] He and his paper followed the government to Little Rock in 1821, and survived to become the oldest continuously published newspaper west of the Mississippi River.[13] Since it was the oldest institution in the state, the *Gazette* served as an important political and cultural vehicle during the antebellum era and beyond.[14]

As a territory, Arkansas was served by four governors, none of whom was a particularly powerful figure. Territorial politics reflected the viciousness and animosity that was prevalent on the American frontier and the violence that was a characteristic of life in Arkansas. Ideologies and issues were less important than personalities and factionalism in antebellum politics.[15]

One man and his faction dominated the territory during its first decade. A native of Kentucky, Robert Crittenden was only twenty-two years old when President Monroe appointed him secretary for the Arkansas Territory. As younger brother of the legendary Kentucky politician, John J. Crittenden, Robert owed his appointment largely to Representative Richard M. Johnson of Kentucky, who would later become U.S. senator and vice-president under Martin Van Buren.[16] Besides being territorial secretary, Crittenden was acting governor on three occasions.[17] Since the first two territorial governors were either too weak, apathetic, or ill to run the government, much of the day-to-day management of the territory was performed by Crittenden,[18] who used his position to increase his own political power, and in the first years of the territory his authority could not be effectively challenged. Crittenden arranged the election of his protégé, James Bates, as the territory's first delegate to Congress.[19]

Owing his position to presidential favor, Crittenden could not be ousted by his enemies as long as he held the support of the national administration. Unfortunately, long years of power had loosely associated him with the administrations of James Monroe, and with John Quincy Adams, who lost the presidency to Andrew Jackson in 1828. Once in office, President Jackson removed Crittenden from power in 1829 and appointed two strong Jackson supporters, John Pope and William Fulton, to the offices of governor and secretary.[20] Governor Pope later severed his ties with Jackson and was replaced by Fulton, who had long schemed and maneuvered to become chief executive for the territory.[21] Fulton was the last territorial governor for Arkansas. (See Table 3a for all the major Arkansas political figures for the period from 1819 to 1861.)

Crittenden and his supporters eventually formed the nucleus of a faction that evolved into the Arkansas branch of the national anti-Jackson Whig party, even though the group did not appropriate the name until the autumn of 1836.[22] Crittenden's fall from power, however, was not complete in 1829, for two years later his faction won control of the legislature. Unfortunately for his own and his supporters' political future, the legislature that year tried to build a statehouse by giving the ten sections of public land granted for that purpose to Crittenden in exchange for Crittenden's own mansion in Little Rock.[23] Whether the bill was passed solely to benefit Crittenden, or was merely a way to obtain a statehouse quickly, territorial Governor John Pope killed the bill with a veto which the Crittenden forces could not override.[24] Now Crittenden and his faction faced a wave of public hostility over the affair.[25] The election of 1833 devastated Crittenden's faction, and the former secretary lost his bid to become the territorial delegate to Congress.[26] A little more than a year later, Crittenden died suddenly at the age of thirty-seven.[27] One early historian of Arkansas gave this explanation for Crittenden's ultimate failure:

His greatest defect was that he mingled too little with the masses of men, and therefore, was without the knowledge of the great mainsprings of human action. He was an inborn aristocrat and a Whig, to the core. To the multitude, he was, therefore, an iceberg; and to him, the multitude was an unthinkable quantity. He was above them, and this feeling of eminence barred his entry into the great domain of human nature.[28]

In a frontier area that prided itself on democracy and equality, Crittenden's pretentious manner never won him or his clique a wide following.

With Crittenden's abrupt death, his political party fell into the hands of a talented, colorful, yet unsuccessful group of politicians. These statesmen of Arkansas Whiggery included William Cummins, Absalom Fowler, Thomas Newton and Albert Pike, all of Little Rock. During its territorial period and throughout the early years of statehood (1836–1850), the Whigs had such capable spokesmen as David Walker of Fayetteville, William Etter of Washington in southwestern Arkansas, Jesse Turner in Van Buren, Benjamin Miles in Chicot County in southeastern Arkansas, and Charles Fenton Mercer Noland of Batesville in the northeastern region.[29] Possessing much natural ability and intelligence, the Whig party lacked only popular support. No Whig ever served as governor or held any other statewide political office.[30] A Whig did capture a seat in the United States Congress once, in a special election in December 1846. Thomas Newton received a plurality of just twenty-three votes in a field of five candidates, but held his seat in the United States House of Representatives for only twenty-five days.[31] In no regular presidential, gubernatorial or congressional election did the Whigs gather more than 45 percent of the vote. Whig power and influence, however, should not be readily dismissed. They could always command at least a third of the vote in any election, and usually they mustered more than 40 percent in national elections.[32] Whig unity and the presence of a solid and faithful constituency forced the Democrats to stay united.

Perennially out of power, the Whigs could not build support through state patronage, so they had to depend upon local issues to gather strength. An issue the Whigs kept before the voters was their opponents' stranglehold on state offices. In presidential contests, the Arkansas Whigs were loyal to their national candidates and platforms, and in elections they incessantly called for internal improvements and a sound financial policy, which meant repaying the state bank debt.[33] The Whigs also had their share of newspapers throughout the state: the *Arkansas Advocate* and later the *Arkansas Whig* in Little Rock; the Helena *Southern Shield*, the Whig voice of the eastern delta for two decades before the Civil War; the *Washington Telegraph* in the southwest; the Batesville *Eagle;* and later the Batesville *Independent Balance* in the northeastern section.[34] In 1843, the Whigs were fortified when the *Arkansas Gazette,* long a Democratic paper, joined their cause and remained opposed to the clique that controlled the Democratic party for the rest of the antebellum era.[35] Never in command of the state legislature after 1833, the Whigs still constituted "an active and vocal minority in both houses of the legislature."[36] They could combine at times with disgruntled and dissident Democrats to influence legislation and elect certain officials.[37]

Traditionally, historians have portrayed the Arkansas Whigs as a party based largely in the towns and in the wealthy southeastern delta.[38] Gene Boyette, the historian of Arkansas Whiggery, compared Whig politicians with their Democratic opponents and found the Whigs to be wealthier, better educated and larger slaveholders, and often leaders in the legal profession.[39] While it is true that the Whigs received their largest percentage of the vote in the commercial townships and delta counties, most of the Whig votes actually flowed from the mountainous northwest since that part of the state held most of the white population.[40] Nevertheless, the uplands remained the bastion of the Democratic party, and the Whigs were never able to cut significantly into that support.[41] Never dominant, yet always undaunted, Arkansas Whigs persisted in their role as the vocal opposition until, like their national counterparts, they dissolved in the early 1850s, only to re-emerge in different political clothing.

Democratic domination for three decades meant domination by one small clique, a situation without parallel in the Old South.[42] The Conway-Sevier-Johnson families headed a dynasty that controlled every branch of state government between 1833 and 1860. Through marriage and blood relations, these three families held public offices for an aggregate of 190 years.[43] This Dynasty—or Family, as it was sometimes called—never lost a major statewide office until the very eve of the Civil War.

Henry W. Conway founded the Dynasty, yet he did not live to see its full development. A native of Tennessee and a veteran of the War of 1812, he arrived in Little Rock in 1820 at the age of 27. Appointed by President Monroe to serve as Receiver of Public Monies for the Arkansas Territory,[44] the energetic and ambitious Conway used his position to launch a political career. Somehow securing Crittenden's blessing, Conway won his bid to become territorial delegate in 1823.[45] Within a few years, however, Crittenden and Conway became the bitterest of enemies. Both were politically ambitious, yet their differences also reflected the growing polarization in national politics. Coming from Kentucky, Crittenden supported the national candidacy of Henry Clay who was also from that state. In this way, he followed in the footsteps of his older brother, John J. Crittenden, who was a long-time Clay partisan. Conway, from Tennessee, had followed that state's favorite son, Andrew Jackson, in his bid for the presidency.[46] During the acrimonious campaign of 1827, Conway trounced his Crittenden-sponsored opposition.[47] The election so sharpened the hostility between the two men that only three months after the election Conway was shot and mortally wounded in a duel with Crittenden.[48] The election, and especially the Conway-Crittenden duel, turned the territory into two warring political factions.

Conway's death ushered in a new period of leadership for the Democratic party. His place was taken by a first cousin, Ambrose Hundley Sevier, who would subsequently attain a much higher political status than that of Conway.[49] Similarly born in Tennessee and capitalizing in part on sympathy for his slain cousin, Sevier was elected as delegate only two months after the duel.[50] Aligning itself nationally with the rise of Andrew Jackson, Sevier's faction evolved into the state Democratic party. With Crittenden's fall from power in 1829, Sevier strengthened his party through the last two Jackson-appointed territorial governors.[51]

As the territorial delegate to the Congress, Sevier was instrumental in securing statehood for Arkansas. When Michigan began preparing for statehood in 1833, the Arkansas delegate believed that unless his state moved soon, Florida would be admitted as the counterbalancing Southern state, which would probably delay Arkansas's entrance into the Union.[52] Sevier prevailed upon the legislature in Little Rock to call a constitutional convention. That body quickly drafted a state constitution, which Sevier presented to Congress in the spring of 1836.[53] After prompt passage by the Senate, and after a long debate (two months) action in the House, President Jackson signed the Arkansas statehood bill on June 15, 1836.[54] Sevier was rewarded when the legislature chose him to be one of the new state's U.S. senators. According to one historian, "Sevier entered the Senate in this, its age of glory, and conquered it. . . . He alone of Arkansas's pre-Civil War senators achieved any prominence in the chamber."[55]

During twelve years in the Senate, Sevier chaired two major committees, including the Foreign Relations Committee from 1845 to 1848, and rose to become one of the inner core of Democratic leaders.[56] He resigned in 1848 in order to serve as a United States peace commissioner implementing the recent treaty with Mexico.[57] While Sevier was making a name for himself among his Senate colleagues, he lost his political grip back home. His near scandalous handling of bonds in a real estate fiasco helped poison his relations with Arkansans. The state legislature censured him for that episode in 1843.[58]

Sevier's abdication of power, however, in no way ended the Dynasty's control. The Family had grown too powerful and extensive to be destroyed by the censure and resignation of one of its leaders.[59] The first governor (1836–1840) was Henry W. Conway's younger brother, James Sevier Conway, the fifth governor (1852–1860) was a still younger brother, Elias Nelson Conway, and every other governor before the war was a member of the Family clique.[60] Every congressman except the Whig Thomas Newton owed his election, to some degree or another, to the Dynasty.[61]

Before 1860, only one Democrat won a significant office by defying a major Family figure. Solon Borland surprisingly defeated Sevier in 1848, and thus earned for himself a full term in the United States Senate. Ironically, Borland had arrived in Little Rock in 1843 to edit the Family's main mouthpiece, the *Arkansas Banner*. With five years of service to the Dynasty behind him, Governor Thomas Drew appointed him to the United States Senate in the spring of 1848 after Sevier had resigned the position to become a peace commissioner to Mexico. In Sevier's absence, Borland gathered support for his own Senate candidacy the next fall by performing needed services for his constituents. He initiated such things as a new Federal court for western Arkansas and the Indian Territory, and he supported swampland reclamation in the eastern delta. When Sevier attempted to regain his seat that fall, he expected that his long years of service and his own Family political organization would be able to put him back in the nation's capital. Borland and his supporters, however, effectively charged Sevier with neglect of duty and political nepotism. The legislature split sectionally as Borland collected enough support among northern and western lawmakers to hand the Dynasty its first major defeat since statehood. Broken by these results, Sevier died on December 31, 1848.[62]

The election proved, however, to be a minor setback for the Family, for Borland never completed his term, resigning his post in the spring of 1853 to become minister plenipotentiary to Central America.[63] Immediately, Governor Elias Conway appointed a new Family leader, the brother-in-law of his first cousin Ambrose Sevier, Congressman Robert W. Johnson, to the Senate seat Borland had vacated. The Dynasty was once again supreme.

Family dominance over state politics was made easy by the method of party nominations. Township and county meetings sent delegates to a state convention that nominated candidates for governor and Congress. Notices of county meetings many times were distributed only a few days before the official conclave, and often the notices were given only to a chosen few. With the slow means of communication in the state, political leaders could easily assure themselves of amenable gatherings. Caucuses before the conventions arranged the chairmanships, drew up the resolutions, picked the candidates, and instructed the chairman as to who should be recognized and allowed to address the assembly.[64] With the Conway-Sevier-Johnson Family directing the proceedings, the Democratic conventions were little more than staged plays. Although the conventions were often referred to as a "caucus of tricksters,"[65] this method of party nomination persisted throughout the nineteenth century.

While the Dynasty dominated politics on a statewide level, its power was far from absolute. It would be wrong to think that the Dynasty was analogous to a later urban political machine because its grip was not equal throughout the state. In Little Rock and in some of the southeastern counties, the Whigs, not the Dynasty, held sway.[66] Moreover, while it may be true that every successful politician belonged to the Family, men like Senator Chester Ashley (1844–1848) and Governor Thomas Drew (1844–1849) could and did have disputes and rivalries with the Dynasty leadership. Archibald Yell was a popular governor (1840–1844) and congressman (1836–1839, 1845–1846) who had his own independent following besides being allied with the regular Democratic organization.[67] As every shrewd elite must do, the Family kept its ranks open to any fresh, talented, and popular political figure who wanted to join.

It might seem difficult to comprehend how the Dynasty could control Arkansas for so long, given the fact that the state had very liberal requirements for voting. Blossoming into statehood in 1836, at the height of the Jacksonian era, the state was known for its relaxed suffrage standards. Historian John Monette wrote in 1846 that Arkansas's first state constitution evidenced "the progress of Democratic principles in the West. . . . By its provisions, every white male citizen of the United States who has been six months resident in the State is a qualified elector, and all votes are given *viva voce*."[68] Twentieth-century historian Lonnie White compared Arkansas's first constitution with several other state constitutions framed between 1819 and 1834. He concluded that the Arkansas charter "neither made any notable innovations nor drew slavishly upon any particular model"; yet "it continued the democratic trends evident in the several state constitutions framed in the previous two or three decades."[69] In addition to the easy voting requirements, representation in the legislature was based upon white population only; there was direct election of governors and legislatures, and, after 1848, judicial officials under the level of the state supreme court were elected directly.[70] All of these measures reflected Jacksonian ideals.

Interest ran high in these state elections. A greater percentage of the electorate turned out for state and local contests than for presidential elections. On an average, state elections between 1840 and 1856 attracted from 75 to 80 percent of the eligible voters, and this was roughly twenty points higher than numbers for presidential elections in the state during the same period.[71]

With such liberal requirements for voting and such a high rate of participation in state and local elections, Arkansas should theoretically never have had a controlling elite. Paradoxically, Jacksonian democracy itself was the convenient and effective popular base for the Conway-Sevier-Johnson Family. In late 1833, Robert Crittenden wrote a merchant friend in New Orleans that he could have "scourged my enemies Sevier and Pope," but "they threw General Jackson upon my shoulders and he bore me down."[72] Crittenden's views are echoed by Absalom Fowler of Little Rock, who wrote a fellow party leader in 1837: "You know what a panacea the name of Jackson presents to a large majority of our people."[73]

Whether the founder of the Arkansas Whig party was correct concerning his own failure as a politician or not, his comment points out how ably the Dynasty could use the popularity of Jackson to attract the common voter. It was a curious feature of antebellum politics. In the "age of the common man" a political clique established "an aristocratic dominance of Arkansas politics from its territorial days to the Civil War."[74] Years after Andrew Jackson left the presidency, the Arkansas electorate reacted easily and passively to an oligarchy that sounded Jacksonian and linked itself, politically and by patronage, to Old Hickory's national Democratic party.

Even at the height of its power, potential for toppling the Dynasty existed. The Family continued to face stubborn, if unsuccessful, opposition from the conservative Whig constituency. Northern and western Arkansas, the real bastion of Democratic voters in the 1830s and 1840s, also felt voiceless in the Dynasty. For a time, Governor Archibald Yell of Fayetteville promised to be the hope of the northwest. The Van Buren *Arkansas Intelligencer* called upon the northern and western parts of the state in the fall of 1845 to unite and put a man in the U.S. Senate, and the paper described Yell as the proper candidate because "he would not bend the knee to the clique and dictatorial set in Little Rock."[75] The dream ended with Yell's premature death in 1847 during the Mexican War.[76] Resentment toward the Dynasty in the northwest, however, did not end with the death of Yell. Just prior to the 1848 election, the *Arkansas Intelli-*

gencer expressed some of the smouldering antagonism of the Democratic northwest when it said that in Arkansas to support the Democrats was:

to support one selected "family" . . . The existence of a clique of office holders, who are banded together at Little Rock, and who pursue one policy, support one set of men, and whose hearts are closed against those of the party who are not classed by them as one of us, is as manifest to the people of this State as the existence of "a nose on a man's face."[77]

The only situation with a potential for frightening the Dynasty was the possible alliance between the conservative, wealthy eastern delta Whigs and the independent Democrats in the northwest. But delta Whigs and mountain Democrats were on different ends of the social scale as well as in different corners of the state, and they had no issue or ideology to unite them, other than a general opposition to the Dynasty. Consequently, the Family felt sure that its opponents could and would never coalesce into a political force that might threaten their rule.[78]

The Compromise Crisis of 1850, however, profoundly shook this confidence. That crisis, the conflict with the Know-Nothings, as well as the social and economic balance of the state, would place a strain on the Conway-Sevier-Johnson clique. Still, the Dynasty managed to stay ahead of its opponents and preserved its power through those turbulent years. Even the Family, however, could not fully comprehend how this last decade of the antebellum era would weaken its grip.

IV

Neither Ready Nor Willing

Arkansas During the Compromise Crisis, 1849–1851

By the middle of the nineteenth century, the Dynasty appeared to be impregnable. Its two main enemies, Whigs in the delta and towns, and Democrats in the northwestern mountains, had never been able to unite sufficiently to deny major state offices to the controlling elite. Its will governed the legislature. Yet, during the great national crisis of 1850, Whigs and Democrats of the northwest did unite briefly to frustrate the Family on a point of major policy: disunion. The man who first introduced the question to Arkansas politics was the new Dynasty leader, Robert Ward Johnson.

With the death of Ambrose Sevier late in 1848, his brother-in-law, Robert W. "Bob" Johnson, took his place of leadership. A native of Kentucky, Johnson descended from a powerful political family. His uncle, Richard Mentor Johnson, had led the Jackson forces in Kentucky and had served as United States senator and vice-president under Martin Van Buren from 1837 to 1841. Robert Johnson's other two uncles were congressmen from Kentucky. Born in 1814, Johnson moved to Little Rock in 1820 after his father, Benjamin Johnson, was appointed to the Superior Court for the Territory of Arkansas. When Arkansas became a state, Benjamin Johnson won appointment as the first federal district judge, a position he held until his death in 1849. Young Bob Johnson had been sent for his education to St. Joseph's Academy in Bardstown, Kentucky, and from there he attended Yale, where he received a law degree in 1835. Return-

43

ing to Little Rock, Johnson married Sarah F. Smith of Kentucky which made him related through marriage to Ambrose Sevier. Such a marital union would practically guarantee Johnson a promising political future. After a term as prosecuting attorney for Pulaski County, and a term as state attorney general, Johnson was elected to Congress as Arkansas's representative-at-large in 1846.[1] In the United States House of Representatives, Johnson at first demonstrated neither leadership nor a willingness stir controversy. Yet once he perceived that the interests of his section were endangered by the potential exclusion of slavery in the newly acquired possessions from Mexico, Johnson became a dynamic and controversial figure.[2]

Until 1850, Arkansans were too preoccupied with growth, the state bank debt, and the lure of California gold to care about a real or supposed threat to slavery. The Dynasty, however, did try to keep the people abreast over this particular issue. At the Family-dominated state Democratic convention in January, 1848, the party had taken a stand for allowing Southerners to take slaves into any lands acquired from Mexico. The assembly also passed resolutions denouncing "fanatical Northern Abolitionists" and upholding state sovereignty concerning the legitimacy of slavery.[3] On the national level, Representative Johnson joined with the states-rights faction of John C. Calhoun. While working with those in Congress sharing his ideas, Johnson sought to awaken his colleagues to what he perceived to be a clear danger to Southern slaveholding.

In early 1850, the Arkansas congressman issued two public letters to constituents through the state's newspapers warning them that their slaveholding rights were about to be restricted. The growing hostility to slavery in the North, Johnson said, was producing sentiment to forbid Southern slaveholders from taking their human chattel into the newly acquired lands of the Southwest. Though Southern blood had been shed in gaining this new territory in the War with Mexico, the North now intended to make these lands available only to non-slaveholders. If this policy was adopted, Johnson warned, Arkansas would be compelled to join her sister states of the South in seceding from the Union.[4] No prominent Arkansas politician had ever before broached the idea of secession to the public. Johnson's appeals landed in the state's political arena like bombshells. But it had been his intention all along to present the issue of slavery and the Union to the voters dramatically. One of Johnson's historians

44

commented: "He had deliberately chosen to shock his constituents because he believed his section was in danger."[5] For the next eighteen months, Johnson's appeals would be the center of an intense controversy.

Johnson planned to gather the people of Arkansas under his banner of disunion, but they refused to give him a consensus. At mid-century the state was simply not prepared for secession. Having been in the Union for only fourteen years, the frontier state still needed federal protection and aid more than it needed to ally with a small but growing slave economy. Slaveowners in 1850 made up less than 4 percent of the white population[6] and much of the eastern delta still awaited the full arrival of the cotton kingdom.

Instead of rallying the state, Johnson's clarion call brought only dissension, reflecting the physiographical division of the state between delta and hills. In the cotton-growing lowlands, where slavery was most prevalent, Johnson was praised at public meetings; in the uplands, the small-farming portion of the state with the most whites, citizens gathered to denounce the congressman and all other sectional extremists and to call upon all politicians to work for national harmony.[7]

Besides the northwest, other areas of the state had their own reasons to avoid secession. In western Arkansas, especially in border towns like Fort Smith, opposition to Johnson was expressed. The presence of Federal troops at this outpost offered some protection, however minor, in a lawless region near the Indian Territory. The loss of Federal troops, moreover, meant a loss of hard currency in a state that had no other stable and secure source of currency. When news came in the early summer of 1850 that the United States government was considering abandoning Fort Smith, citizens and the town press loudly demanded that the troops remain.[8] Even in the delta, where almost 80 percent of the slaves lived (see Table 2k in the Appendix), many whites were reluctant for the state to leave the Union because the Federal government had just started its huge swampland reclamation program, in 1850.[9] Leaving the Union might jeopardize the chances of both large and small property owners to acquire more land.

Arkansas was generally too much of a struggling frontier society in 1850 to consider withdrawing from the Union. Not only did the venture appear risky, but secession might bring on a dreaded civil war. A Fort Smith paper declared that spring that no peaceful separation of the

Union was possible, and then asked rhetorically, "who desires to see anarchy, bloodshed, and civil war, which must be the result if a dissolution of the Union takes place?"[10]

Given Arkansas's social and economic conditions in 1850, Johnson's letters to the public were sure to draw negative responses from many. His own party divided sharply. Generally he had the organizational support of the Dynasty, although prominent Democrats like George Clarke of the Van Buren *Arkansas Intelligencer* and state Representative Thompson Flournoy of Desha County in southeastern Arkansas came out strongly against him. Flournoy even organized a rally in his county in June, praising the Union and calling for national reconciliation.[11] Unionist Democrats received additional help when William Woodruff bought back the *Arkansas Gazette* from Whigs in February, 1850. Woodruff, an old Jacksonian Unionist, would be joined by John Knight of Massachusetts to produce editorials on behalf of compromise and the Union. Now the moderate Democrats would have a statewide paper in which to express their views.[12] In the same issue that Johnson's second letter was printed, the *Gazette* emphatically declared: "Our people do not believe that the time has yet come when they are called upon to assist in dismembering the Confederacy. It is the universal sentiment that the Union must be preserved and the universal belief that it cannot be dissolved."[13]

These moderate pro-Union Democrats would need the assistance of a statewide paper based in Little Rock, for the entire Arkansas delegation comprised of Johnson and Senators William K. Sebastian and Solon Borland was committed to vote against any compromise then before Congress.[14] Arkansas representatives in Washington followed Johnson's lead on disunion without knowing how much this position would hurt them with their constituents. Borland was outspoken to the point of belligerency. The Arkansas senator even physically attacked the moderate Senator Henry S. Foote of Mississippi in the streets of Washington after the latter called him a "servile follower of Calhoun."[15] Borland became so disgusted with events in Washington that he left the capital in June after having made a stirring address before the Senate denouncing the compromise introduced by Henry Clay of Kentucky.[16]

Back in Little Rock, Borland soon caught the wind of popular opinion and began to back away from his stand. His position on the national compromise was particularly ironic since he owed his election in 1848 to

46

heavy support from the northwestern part of the state, the area now most desiring compromise. Speaking in the Arkansas capital on July 19, 1850, Borland attacked abolitionists, reported some difficulties that he had with the compromise, but ended the speech talking about his great love for the Union.[17] He never returned to Washington to vote on the compromise. The Dynasty's main newspaper in Little Rock bitterly attacked him for dereliction of duty while the pro-Union *Gazette* loudly applauded his absence from Congress.[18]

Congress finally worked out a sectional compromise during the summer of 1850 and approved it in a series of votes taken during August and September. The Compromise of 1850 allowed the admission of California to the Union as a free state; the slave trade, but not slavery, was abolished in Washington, D.C.; and the Fugitive Slave Law, giving federal officials more sweeping powers to apprehend fugitive slaves was extended. The compromise also established the Territories of Utah and New Mexico without any stipulation regarding slavery.[19] In the final vote, Congressman Johnson voted for only the new Fugitive Slave Law, and Senator Sebastian voted for all the measures except admitting California into the Union.[20]

While Democrats in Arkansas quarreled over the compromise during spring and summer of 1850, the almost moribund Whig party plotted how best to take political advantage of the situation. While they had never been able to penetrate into the northwest section of the state, Whigs knew that this was where Johnson's radicalism was the most unpopular. The Whigs now decided—like their brothers elsewhere in the South—to identify themselves with moderate or Unionist Democrats in the northwest portion of the state on any major sectional issues or confrontations and to try in that way to forge a moderate and predominantly Whig-controlled statewide majority.[21] By the summer of 1850 almost all Whig papers had joined in the attack on Johnson.[22] Albert Pike, a Whig leader, toured southern Arkansas declaring that he was "for the Union, the whole Union, and nothing less than the Union."[23]

This strategy received its first test during the eighth session of the Arkansas General Assembly, which convened in November 1850. In his opening address, Governor John S. Roane, who owned a plantation near Pine Bluff in Jefferson County, called the national Compromise of 1850 "unjust" and then declared: "I would say dissolve the Union for there is no security in it."[24] But Governor Roane's efforts to have the legislature

47

repudiate the Compromise were blocked by Democrats, including Speaker of the House Thompson Flournoy and Whig state Representative Frederick Trapnall of Little Rock. Moderate or Unionist Democrats had joined with the Whigs by late December to table any motion rejecting the sectional agreement.[25] Democrats in the legislature split geographically, those from the northern and western areas supporting the national compromise and those from the lowlands championing the repudiation efforts of Governor Roane and the Dynasty.[26] Thus, the Whig-Unionist Democratic coalition in the legislature prevented Arkansas from playing a radical role after the Compromise of 1850.

Prior to legislative deadlock, however, the cause of extremism in Arkansas had already been damaged by Congressman Johnson's equivocation during much of 1850. Stung by the unpopularity of his earlier position, Johnson slowly tempered his disunionism as the year wore on. By June, he was saying in the Dynasty's main paper in Little Rock that "no one would have misconstrued me to be a disunionist, *per se*, except one whose appetite was already sharpened by some feeling of prejudice or hostility."[27] Coming to believe that his views on slavery and the sectional question must be out of touch with his fellow Arkansans, Johnson announced in a public letter in early September that he would not seek reelection the next August. He then voted against the Compromise.[28]

The voices of moderation appeared to have achieved a complete triumph by the end of 1850. Southern extremism had raised its head but had produced more dissent than support. Strong Unionism had caught Johnson and the Dynasty off guard. Moderate or Unionist Democrats had access to newpapers like the *Arkansas Intelligencer* in Van Buren and the *Arkansas Gazette* in Little Rock and had used these forums to condemn Johnson's extremism. Moderate Democrats in the northern and western areas of the state, traditional Democratic bastions, had joined the weak Whig party to frustrate any designs of the Dynasty to repudiate the Compromise of 1850, and they had apparently caused Johnson to announce his retirement one year early. Elsewhere in the South, Democrats and Whigs were also joining to win major victories over the radicals during the Compromise controversy.[29]

Moderation's triumph in Arkansas, though, was more apparent than real. Slavery was merely on the threshold of development within the state in 1850. Over the next decade its deeper roots would sink into the economy and culture. Settlers from the lower South would pour into delta areas to generate a greater prosperity built on cotton and slaves. The enforcement of slave labor in 1850 was less important, however, than Arkansas's need to receive federal aid and protection. If slavery were to grow to such importance that the state's entire economic prosperity would be linked with it, many minds would be changed. The prospect of secession could not be completely ruled out as long as slavery was seen as something acceptable and even necessary for the economic well-being of the white community. Since slavery was never questioned by any influential group or political party, the forces of moderation depended upon a perception of the national government's views on slavery. If and when Arkansas came to view the Federal government as a threat to slavery, which promised future prosperity, men would consider secession an option. The perception of most people in Arkansas in 1850 was that the Union was necessary for their economic well-being and security, and they spurned talk of secession even though it came from one of their most respected political leaders.

Conditions rarely remain the same for long in politics, and 1851 saw the comeback of Congressman Johnson and the Dynasty. When the congressman withdrew in September 1850, the Family hoped that another of its spokesmen might come forward to receive the prize, but over the next couple of months a leading candidate appeared to be the Unionist editor from Van Buren, George Clarke. Clarke had little support in the delta, though, and the Dynasty disliked this Democrat who had refused to support the party line during the crisis of 1850.[30] By the spring of 1851 a movement was afoot to renominate Johnson, who "went along with it, if he did not in fact actually instigate it."[31] At the Dynasty's state Democratic convention in April, the assembly "drafted" Johnson on the first ballot. Johnson would run on a pro-Union, pro-Compromise platform![32]

With a candidate who had never actually repudiated his earlier views and who was now running on a platform for the Union, the Family cynically played both sides of the sectional debate. One who happened to be a disunionist Democrat could still vote for Johnson, owing to his earlier stand, while Unionist Democrats could justify voting for him on grounds of the platform on which he was running. This strategy worked because his platform supported the Compromise of 1850 strongly enough to attract Unionist Democrats like Thompson Flournoy and William Wood-

49

ruff. Only the disappointed and disgruntled George Clarke refused to ally with the nominee and backed his Whig opponent.[33] The Dynasty pictured Johnson as a good "conditional" or "modified" Unionist Democrat who now accepted the Compromise of 1850 in order to preserve the peace and harmony of the country.[34]

Johnson's only opposition came from the Whigs, who intended to use his earlier radicalism against him. "If R. W. Johnson expects to run as a Union man," editorialized the *Southern Shield* in Helena, "the People of this State would not be bamboozled by such claptrap."[35] In concentrating upon the disunionist theme, the Whigs planned to attract many Democrats in the northwest. They also hoped to capitalize on divisions within the Democratic party still lingering from the Borland-Sevier Senate contest of 1848. Absalom Fowler of Little Rock wrote another Whig leader in Van Buren that since "the partisans of Borland are open-mouthed for anybody against Johnson," this together with "the distaste for his extreme southern notions tending to disunion, may possibly give us a fair chance for once."[36] Historian Brian Walton believes that since the disunionist theme was a major strategy of the Whigs, the party diminished its chances by nominating John Preston, a wealthy planter from Helena in Phillips County. Unionist voters in the mountains would find it difficult to support a relatively unknown Whig planter and slaveholder from a Mississippi River county.[37]

Actually, the Whig strategy is not mystifying, for it was the same that was employed by the Democrats, running to please both the uplands and the lowlands. Although the Whigs produced no formal platform, if they wanted to run a candidate on the theme of Unionism and national compromise the office-seeker must not appear to be too soft on slavery or they would lose the slaveholding Whigs in the delta. While seeking to gain votes in the northwest, Whigs were guarding against undercutting their lowland base. What better way to do this than by putting into the field a wealthy planter from a Mississippi River county who would never appear lukewarm on slavery and who might yet appeal to northwestern voters by his strong stand for the Union.

While Whigs hoped to turn this election into a referendum on the Union, Democrats wanted voters in a traditionally Democratic state to see the contest as just another between them and the Whigs. The Democrat position was the most convincing, because, with the exception of George Clarke, all the leading party members, including Flournoy and

Woodruff, supported Johnson. The Family organ in Little Rock warned Democrats that the opposition was trying to gain power under the cloak of Unionism.[38] In early July, the paper declared flatly: "There is really no issue between Union or Disunion. The issue is between Whiggery in all its deformity and Democracy in all its attractiveness."[39] Even the Whigs recognized their problem. Their paper in Helena complained near the end of the campaign that "many a white, good, and true . . . Jackson Democrat hesitates to vote for Preston because of the Whig label".[40] Senator Solon Borland, whose personal relations with Johnson were cool, agreed to keep quiet during the election. This was most difficult for him as he confided to a friend in June 1851: "I cannot be encouraging the election of a Whig. My democracy is of the heart as well as the head. But I am still further from desiring the election of such a man as Bob Johnson."[41] Borland's letter indicates that his party loyalty, however, was strong enough to overcome his extreme distaste for Johnson. During the summer of 1851, Johnson and Preston traveled together, spending most of their time in the northwest, where both knew the election would be won or lost.[42]

Johnson received about 57 percent of the vote—a solid majority, although it was five percentage points less than his victory in 1848.[43] The Johnson vote fell only marginally in the northwest, but the key was that Preston did not do well in traditional Whig counties of the south and east. (For the vote in upland and lowland counties in the congressional election of 1851, see Table 4a in the Appendix.) In delta counties where there were many slaveholders, the "modified" radicalism of Johnson had apparently found some support.[44] Such support was noted by Christopher C. Scott of Ouachita County in southwestern Arkansas, who wrote his friend and fellow Whig, David Walker of Fayetteville, that Arkansas voted for the "disunionist" Johnson "out of party will and party habit." However Scott also reported his anger and hurt that "two or three Whigs here voted for Johnson because of his ultra-Southern views."[45] The Conway-Johnson organization had "comfortably weathered the challenge of a moderate Whig strategy without embracing moderation itself."[46] Johnson's re-election at length put controversy over the Compromise of 1850 to rest.

To judge the election of 1851 as only another cunning triumph by the Family elite would not be completely accurate. Lessons learned from the years 1849–1851 must have been most disappointing to the Dynasty's leadership. After all, people had demonstrated convincingly that they were neither ready nor willing to follow Southern extremists into rebellion and disunion over the issue of slavery. The state would not secede in 1850 because it needed the protection and aid of the Federal Union. In that sense, "triumph" of the Dynasty was not complete. Representative Johnson, the titular head of the organization that had run the state since the early 1830s, had been forced to back off from his disunionist rhetoric and had almost been driven from office because he had broached secession. Only temporarily did Whigs and a few Democrats from the northwest coalesce to thwart disunionist designs by the ruling Dynasty.

Fortunately for the Family, this Whig-northwestern Democratic alliance was held together by only one issue: disunion over slavery. Once the national crisis appeared to be settled, old political patterns and suspicions reasserted themselves. Most Arkansans perceived the election of 1851 as merely another contest between Democrats and Whigs and they voted as they always had, for the party of Jefferson and Jackson. Yet the quarrels and controversy over the Compromise of 1850 did have their effect on Johnson. Elsie Mae Lewis, a historian who gave thorough study to Johnson's pre-Civil War career, observed that while Johnson never altered his views on the rights of Southern slaveholders and secession, he nevertheless made no effort to take a lead in Congress again on the subject.[47] This issue would have to await future events and another political figure.

V

Change and Continuity

Family Rule in Arkansas, 1851–1859

Arkansas experienced major social and economic changes in the last decade of the antebellum era. The shift of population to the delta, begun in the 1840s with heavy migration from the lower South, now accelerated to such a degree that, by 1858, most of the population lived in the eastern and southern lowlands. New settlers entrenched the Cotton Kingdom more firmly and strengthened the influence of slavery on the general society. By the decade's end, the change was evident everywhere. In the spring of 1859, a land agent in Desha County in southeast Arkansas wrote to a merchant in Memphis that "this county has changed more this spring than I have seen in any place. . . . Good planters are filling up this country."[1] Many planters were indeed settling in the state, but more typical immigrants were men such as W. E. Coleman. A former overseer from Alabama, Coleman proudly dispatched a letter to his former employer reporting that he and his family now lived on and owned "eighty acres of improved land" only fourteen miles from Camden in Ouachita County.[2] More immigrants from the lower South also settled in the Ouachita Mountains and the Arkansas River Valley. A woman in Pope County wrote to her cousin at home in North Carolina in 1858 that "this country is filling up fast," and further reported that settlers came from both North and South Carolina.[3]

If the 1850s meant internal development and the growth of a cotton-based prosperity, the decade did not witness much political change beyond the rise of a few new politicians—in the Dynasty, of course—and the death of the formal Whig party. Although the Whigs perished as a political party, their constituency continued, in different political clothing. Here and there new faces and new political movements would appear, but the basic framework of Arkansas politics remained. The Family maintained its power against a basically old-line Whig opposition.

With Robert W. Johnson's re-election in 1851, Arkansans turned their attention to "schemes to open the state to markets and prosperity rather than thoughts of disunion or southern independence."[4] The gubernatorial election centered upon the issue of internal improvements. Governor Roane, who had been an intemperate foe of the Compromise of 1850, suddenly and surprisingly announced in December 1851 that he would not be a candidate for re-election the next year.[5] Roane's departure apparently was intended to pave the way for the nomination of Elias Nelson Conway, younger brother of Henry W. and James Sevier Conway.

Born in 1812, Elias grew up with his older brothers in Greene County, Tennessee. He arrived in Little Rock in 1833 to work as deputy surveyor for the northwestern counties. Two years later, Governor William Fulton appointed him auditor for the Territory. With the elevation of his brother to governor when Arkansas achieved statehood in 1836, Elias had no difficulty continuing as auditor, a position he would hold until 1849. Historian John Hallum contended that the Arkansas Land Act of 1840, which gave away tax-forfeited land to prospective settlers, had been the idea of state Auditor Elias Conway, and suggested further that the act formed the basis for the U.S. Homestead Act two decades later.[6] This younger Conway had actually been nominated for governor in December 1843, but was forced to withdraw because of wide belief that he was too young, too inexperienced, and too closely related "to a group of office-seeking relations."[7] His patience and forbearance, as well as strong Family connections, finally prevailed, and he appeared to be the Family's candidate for governor in 1852.

Even before the scheduled state convention in April, independent Democrats who chafed at Family dominance of the party were rallying around the candidacy of Bryan Smithson of Fayetteville, who announced for governor in March of 1852.[8] Despite Smithson's candidacy and the sentiments of many Democrats, however, it was clear that the Family would nominate and run Elias Conway. William Woodruff, a leader of the independent Democrats, wrote to a friend that he was sure Conway's nomination would cause a breach in the party and for this "the Family will have no one to blame but themselves."[9] Knowing that they had little chance in a Dynasty-dominated state convention, delegates from many pro-Smithson counties in the northwest boycotted it. Only twenty-nine of the state's fifty-four counties were represented. Of delegates who attended, Conway won the nomination with approximately 80 percent of the vote.[10] Smithson and his supporters, like editor George Clarke of the Van Buren *Arkansas Intelligencer,* immediately cried foul, and these dissidents were joined shortly by Woodruff of the *Gazette* in Little Rock. Woodruff opted for Smithson because Conway would not endorse a plan for internal improvements and construction of railroads.[11] Smithson and his small cadre of dissenting Democrats focused upon internal improvements as a central issue in their campaign.

Smithson's candidacy posed a real difficulty for the Whigs. If their party decided to run its own candidate, it would only divide the opposition and insure another victory for the Conway-Johnson Dynasty. The Whigs chose reluctantly not to field a candidate and to endorse Smithson.[12] A Whig newspaper justified this action by saying the state "is hopelessly Democratic."[13] Besides, Smithson was at least speaking for one of the Whig party principles: internal improvements and railroad construction. With dissident Democrats in the northwest and a Democratic paper in Little Rock now joined by the Whig press in much of the state, it appeared that the Family would face challenges that were stronger than usual.

The campaign was indeed a spirited affair. Woodruff cleverly nicknamed the Dynasty's candidate "Dirt Road" Conway because the former auditor had publicly declared in a campaign circular that the state did not need any internal improvements but only "a few good dirt roads."[14] The *Arkansas Whig* in Little Rock, a new chief organ for the Whig party, chimed in that the Dynasty had bankrupted the state, pillaged the treasury and levied huge taxes, all in order to supply "innumerable amounts of cousin Eliases and brother Bobs with state offices."[15] The Family relied on its extensive press network throughout the state and its strong organization to pull in the votes. Although Conway was not a strong stump speaker, the Dynasty always claimed to be the true heir of Andrew Jackson's Democratic party.[16]

In the end, the Dynasty did muster about 55 percent of the vote for

Conway.[17] Smithson, however, received more votes against a regular Democratic nominee than did any Whig candidate of the past.[18] He carried sizable territories in the northwest, such as Washington County (Fayetteville) and Crawford County (Van Buren), and eight other counties. Although he did well in that area, he lost in southern and eastern counties.[19] Almost from the day of the election a few of Smithson's Democratic supporters, such as Woodruff, blamed the Whigs for the loss.[20] William Fulton Pope, a contemporary of Woodruff, recalled forty years later that Smithson lost because too many old-time Whigs voted against him.[21] Later studies have agreed with this view.[22] Historian Brian Walton discovered that while most of the Whig vote did go to Smithson, a significant 20 percent crossover vote in some southern and eastern counties went to Conway.[23] A few Whigs in the delta counties apparently found it too repugnant to vote for a candidate coming from the northwestern part of the state.[24]

Regional differences aside, another plausible explanation for the large Whig crossover vote was Conway's financial conservatism. While most Whigs were ideologically committed to internal improvements, on a practical basis a few feared internal improvements would be expensive, as Conway suggested, and since the state already had a huge debt, wealthy Whig planters believed that they would have to bear the real cost of the project in higher land taxes. It is little wonder that a few Whig planters did not vote for an unknown Democrat from the hills who might make the state's already bad financial condition even worse. Smithson, they might have reasoned, was only another Democratic politician who may or may not be open to the counsel of Whig conservatives.

It was not, however, Whig conservatism that placed Conway in the governor's office but the average yeoman farmer who still identified the Dynasty-run state Democratic party with the legacy of Andrew Jackson. Conway won about 80 percent of the regular Democratic vote against a fellow Democrat.[25] As long as the Family could count on such loyalty from the average voter, it would have little to fear from Whigs or anyone else.

In the 1852 presidential election Democrats throughout the state supported the national nominee, Franklin Pierce of New Hampshire. While both Democratic papers in Little Rock, the *Arkansas Gazette* and the *Arkansas Banner,* supported Pierce, they were hostile to one another.[26] In the fall of 1852 the *Arkansas Banner* changed its title to the *True Democrat,*[27] giving as its reason in the first issue: "Democrats immigrating to the State, and desirous to take a newspaper of their own political faith, have been imposed upon by a false beacon."[28] For the next eleven years, the paper would be the official voice of the Conway-Johnson organization.

Whigs generally supported their national candidate, Winfield Scott, but earlier in the year they had enthusiastically endorsed the renomination of President Millard Fillmore.[29] Arkansas Whigs gave Scott about 38 percent of the state vote. Although not a good showing, this surpassed the previous Whig turnout in the presidential contests of 1836 and 1844.[30] Dissatisfaction with Scott was manifested in much of the South, because he was considered unsafe on the slavery issue. In Arkansas, Albert Pike, one of the founders of Arkansas Whiggery, refused to endorse the national ticket.[31] The Whig vote for Scott in Arkansas was much higher than he received in the lower South, but not as high as the national percentage for the Whig candidate.[32] Thus, while most of the Whigs in the lower South were deserting their national nominee, in Arkansas the Whigs polled about their usual percentage. Scott's perceived unreliability on slavery did not greatly damage his standing in that state. He lost Arkansas because it remained staunchly Democratic.

To top off a banner year, the Dynasty re-elected Senator William King Sebastian to a full term, but quarreled again with northwestern Democrats during the Arkansas General Assembly, meeting in November 1852. This time, the northwest supported George Clarke of Van Buren. Since Whigs controlled about one-third of the legislature, they usually decided the victor in a close contest. Forced to choose between westerner George Clarke and Dynasty candidate Sebastian, a wealthy planter from Phillips County, delta Whigs followed their regional and conservative instincts by backing Sebastian, who won easily with their support.[33] Regionalism and rivalries made it easy for the Family to maintain its power and to strengthen its grip during the next few years.

A major triumph in early 1853 was the removal of Senator Borland. The antagonism between Borland and the Dynasty had never really healed since the 1848 Senate race, even though Borland had given a token endorsement to Robert Johnson in 1851. Congressman Johnson did have ambitions to be in the U.S. Senate, and his younger brother, editor Richard Johnson, had once confided to a friend: "Bob's election to the Senate is beyond question. . . . He will be elected by about 85 votes out of 100. The Borland faction cannot get a candidate to take the field openly against him."[34] Borland knew of Johnson's plans and wrote to a friend

57

that he would not serve with Johnson in the Senate: "I prefer his doing so over my head. I don't wish to serve with him. I had rather be beaten by him."[35]

This head-to-head contest between Johnson and Borland never materialized because the latter resigned in April 1853 to become Minister Plenipotentiary to Central America. Although Borland knew Spanish and had been a strong supporter of the Monroe Doctrine, his quick temper and easy belligerence had led him into several well-publicized brawls in Washington and once there had been an attempt to hang him in effigy in the streets. Not a few observers questioned the wisdom of giving such a person an important diplomatic post.[36] Nevertheless, Borland's departure for Central America made it easy for the Dynasty, and Governor Conway appointed Robert W. Johnson to the vacant seat.[37] An old rival and nemesis of the Family had been removed from the Arkansas political scene.

New congressional elections were scheduled for the summer. For the first time, Arkansas was broken into two congressional districts divided by the Arkansas River, which runs diagonally from northwest to south.[38] Each district contained large sections of both uplands and lowlands. Mississippi River towns like Helena found themselves in the same district with such hill communities as Fayetteville and Van Buren in the northwest and west. Fort Smith and Little Rock would be placed in the southern district with the delta counties of southern and eastern Arkansas.

In the northern district, Democrat Alfred Burton Greenwood, from Benton County in the northwestern corner of the state, was unopposed in 1853. Whigs concentrated their efforts in the southern district, backing Little Rock merchant Frederick Trapnall against the Dynasty Democratic nominee, Edward Warren of Camden. Trapnall made a strong effort, perhaps too strong for his health, for he became ill and died in the middle of the campaign. Although the Whigs soon produced a replacement, a Little Rock lawyer named James Curran, much of their early momentum was lost. Warren won easily with 59 percent of the vote.[39] Another congressional election occurred the following year so that subsequent elections could be held in even-numbered years.[40]

The 1854 elections were simply a repetition. Greenwood had no opposition, and the Whigs again concentrated on the southern district, where both candidates were new. Albert Rust of El Dorado in Union County was the Dynasty Democrat, and the Whigs sponsored E. G. Walker of Dardenelle in Yell County. The race had the overtones of an upland-lowland division because Rust was from the border of Louisiana, and Walker was from the Arkansas Valley-Ouachita Mountain region. Walker could muster only 34 percent of the vote and carry three counties, two in the uplands and one in the lowlands.[41] It was a poor showing for the Whigs in an area where they had always been formidable. An indication of the Dynasty's complete dominance came late in 1854 when Robert W. Johnson was unanimously re-elected to the Senate by the Arkansas General Assembly.[42] It seemed as though all organized opposition to the Conway-Johnson-controlled state Democratic party had virtually ceased.

What had ceased was the Arkansas Whig party. Whiggery in the state had never been dominant, but it could always borrow the principles and attract some organizational support from the national party. After the 1852 presidential election, the national Whig party died, hopelessly divided over slavery.[43] When the national party organization no longer appeared safe on the slavery question, the Whig party collapsed throughout the South.[44] A symbol of the demise of the Arkansas party was the death, in May 1855, of its chief organ in Little Rock, the *Arkansas Whig*.[45] Although the Whig party in Arkansas and the South had disappeared by the middle of the 1850s, an old-line Whig constituency remained as a conservative force in the region's politics. It was ready to act under almost any name in opposition to its traditional enemy, the Democrats.[46] Old-line Whigs in Arkansas and the South faced some very difficult choices, because the national parties that arose from Whig ruins had little appeal to Southerners. No self-respecting Southerner could espouse the Republican party, known below the Mason-Dixon as the "Black Republicans." Many Southerners believed the party to be the vehicle of abolition and black equality. Although the Republicans only supported restriction, not abolition of slavery, most Southerners legitimately feared that one would only lead to the other in the not-too-distant future.[47] Joining the Republican party, or promoting some of its doctrines, could lead to expulsion, or worse, in much of the South.[48] As much as the old-line Whigs hated the Democrats, many of them were also slaveholders, and would never promote a political party that might sometime divest them of their property. These old-line Whigs had to look for another political movement if they wanted to oppose the Democrats. Fortunately for this Whig constituency in the Old South, another political movement was available which appeared to gain momentum at mid-century.

Many Americans in the 1850s and 1860s became worried about the number of foreigners entering the country. More immigrants came into the country proportionally from 1845 through 1854 than at any time in the nation's history.[49] Total yearly immigration had never reached 100,000 before 1842, nor 200,000 before 1847, yet it exceeded 400,000 annually in the four years between 1851 and 1854.[50] Newcomers often talked and acted strangely, took jobs away from longtime residents, and caused wages to decrease. An overwhelming proportion of these immigrants, moreover, came from the Roman Catholic southern counties of Ireland, which meant they were members of a faith long held suspect by many Anglo-Saxon Protestant Americans.[51] This anti-foreign and anti-Catholic sentiment erupted into violence as angry mobs rampaged through immigrant neighborhoods attacking and burning Catholic churches and convents.[52] By the early 1850s, this bigotry found its political expression in the new American party, usually referred to in history as the "Know-Nothing" party because its early members were sworn to secrecy and turned away all who inquired into their affairs with the statement "I know nothing."[53]

Based largely in the Northeast where most immigrants settled, the American party did find some pockets of strength in the slaveholding South. Louisiana, Missouri, Maryland and Texas had sizable numbers of foreign-born, and Southern cities like New Orleans, St. Louis, Baltimore, Richmond, and Louisville contained many immigrants. More foreign-born persons lived in New Orleans than Boston in 1850.[54] Within the Old South, however, the percentage of foreign-born was quite small, less than 5 percent, while the national average was 11 percent.[55] If Southern Whigs decided to join the American party, it was not so much because they felt they were being swamped by Papal-directed Irishmen, but because they wanted to continue their battle with the Democrats, and the American party was the only legitimate vehicle.[56]

Democratic opposition was undoubtedly the rationale behind the Know-Nothing movement in Arkansas, for only 1 percent of its population was foreign-born.[57] Know-Nothingism in the state had its beginnings with the ex-Whig, Albert Pike. According to one of Pike's biographers, he promoted this new movement in Arkansas mostly because he hated the state Democratic leadership, and he hoped that concern over foreigners and Catholics would divert the country's attention from slavery. Pike was sure that unless this happened, the Union would dissolve over the issue of slavery.[58] Pike began his activities in the fall of 1854 and apparently found some early support for the new party. Late in the year, the Arkansas General Assembly voted down a resolution condemning the new party, and the Know-Nothing press throughout the nation hailed this as a victory.[59]

At a public rally in Little Rock in August 1855, the American party of Arkansas was formally launched, with ex-Whigs Albert Pike and Absalom Fowler presiding.[60] Although mostly made up of old Whigs, the new party did attract a few dissident Democrats, including Borland, now back in Arkansas after a disastrous stint in Central America, James Yell, the nephew of former governor and Congressman Archibald Yell, and Hugh French Thomason of Van Buren.[61] Another bonus was the addition of Christopher C. Danley, who had taken over the editorship of the *Gazette* from William Woodruff in 1853. Danley joined the Know-Nothings, and by October 1855 the *Gazette* became its official mouthpiece.[62] Former Whig newspapers throughout the state soon endorsed the American party.[63]

After some months of preparation, a state Know-Nothing convention was held at Little Rock in late April 1856 and nominated James Yell of Pine Bluff for governor. Although the platform contained the standard Know-Nothing fare, an attack on Catholics and foreigners, much of the remaining document consisted of standard Whig planks calling for internal improvements, a stable bank system, repayment of the state debt, and a strong pledge to preserve the Union.[64] At congressional district assemblies in May, the Know-Nothings nominated Hugh Thomason for the northern district, and Absalom Fowler for the southern district.[65]

With much of the Whig party and press behind the Know-Nothing party, and with a scattering of disaffected Democrats also participating, the Dynasty knew it could not take the new party too lightly. Evaluating the movement as "old Whigs and here and there a fishy Democrat," the Family's primary paper in Little Rock castigated the Know-Nothings for attempting to seize power by playing upon Protestant prejudices.[66] Party leaders including Governor Conway and Senator Sebastian toured the state denouncing the party as a Northern movement filled with religious bigotry.[67] Democrats derided their opponents as "Sams" or "Sammys" because the Know-Nothings liked to call themselves boys of Uncle Sam.[68]

In this bout with Know-Nothings a political newcomer from Mississippi contributed greatly to the Democratic cause. Thomas Carmichael

Hindman, twenty-seven years old, organized a three-day political festival near his residence in Helena in November 1855. With a theme and accompanying song entitled "Up Salt River Sammy Must Go," Hindman provided participants with food, drink, entertainment by brass bands, and plenty of political rhetoric from leading Democrats in Arkansas, Mississippi and Tennessee.[69] In his own address, Hindman declared it to be his sincere belief that the purpose of any real Southern party was to protect slavery, not to persecute Catholics and rail after the immigrants.[70] After this dramatic entree into the political arena, Hindman did his most effective work for the Dynasty-run Democratic party as a stump speaker. After hearing him at Marion in eastern Arkansas, a Memphis newspaper commented: "He is a young gentleman of ample political information, and he has a brilliancy of intellect which will soon place him in the front ranks of debaters in Arkansas."[71] During the campaign against the Know-Nothings, Hindman's rise among the ranks of the state Democratic party began,[72] and it was clear he was a newcomer to be reckoned with.

Long before the Democratic state convention it was apparent that the Dynasty would run Governor Conway again. A Camden newspaper described him as "the best governor this state has ever had,"[73] and with such accolades flowing from the Family, Governor Conway won easy renomination at the Democratic convention in Little Rock in the spring of 1856.[74]

The real political drama occurred in the Democratic congressional conventions in May. At the northern meeting in Batesville, Representative Alfred Burton Greenwood faced an unusually strong challenge from Thomas Hindman. Hindman drew his support from the delta counties while uplander Greenwood had his strongest support in the Ozarks. Hindman tied up the convention for a week, through 277 ballots, before yielding to Greenwood.[75] It was a moral victory for Hindman because he demonstrated to the Family that he could be an appealing and powerful candidate. At the southern congressional convention at Hot Springs, Warren caught Congressman Rust off guard and seized the nomination. No real ideological or regional difference existed between Rust and Warren, only an intense personal rivalry.[76]

In an age of no-holds-barred, mud-slinging political campaigns, the 1856 elections hit a new low. The Know-Nothing press spent most of its time trying to prove that Catholics could not be trusted with the suffrage and other rights of citizenship because they owed more allegiance to the

Pope in Rome than to any lawful governmental authority in the United States.[77] The *Gazette* attacked Governor Conway for withdrawing from Methodist services in order to attend Catholic Masses,[78] and further attacked him for not being married. The editor even wondered, since Conway had been seen talking to a Catholic priest, that maybe the cleric had sold the governor on his own brand of "connubial felicity."[79] For its part, the Family's newspaper in Little Rock, the *True Democrat,* declared that Solon Borland, now one of the *Gazette*'s editors, had no right to criticize the governor's house of worship, because Borland himself was an "expelled fallen-from-grace backslidden Baptist."[80] The Family newspaper later charged that Borland was living in sin with an "indecent and lewd woman."[81] Other, more legitimate issues were raised, especially the bank debt and the Family's control over state affairs, but were lost in the petty, sectarian insults hurled from the state's newspapers.

The American party received a severe blow in the spring of 1856, when Albert Pike repudiated it, and declared in an open letter that it was unsound on the issue of slavery. Pike had attended the party's national convention where he had become disgusted because it would not say that Congress had no right to forbid slavery in the U.S. territories. Pike was also angered over the choice of Millard Fillmore as presidential nominee, favoring instead the nomination of a former Northern Democrat, in order to counter the charge frequently heard in Arkansas that the "American party was a Whig trick."[82] Although Pike did not return to the state during the rest of the convention and did not openly campaign against the party, his defection crippled the Know-Nothing cause. Democrats were delighted and made good use of his abdication of the American party in the elections.[83]

When votes were counted, the Dynasty and the Democrats triumphed again. Governor Conway defeated Yell with 65 percent of the vote. Yell could carry only six of fifty-four counties.[84] In the congressional races, American party candidate Thomason only won two counties and did not receive a third of the votes. In the southern district, the Know-Nothings made their best showing, but Fowler won only a little more than 40 percent of the ballots.[85] With these abysmal returns, enthusiasm among Know-Nothings for the national presidential election dropped significantly. Almost a quarter of the electorate that had voted in the August state election failed to appear at the November balloting.[86] Arkansas, as usual, voted for the Democratic national ticket. James Buchanan defeated Fillmore by capturing two-thirds of the ballots.[87] Arkansas was the only state in the Old South in which the national American party polled less than 40 percent of the total vote.[88] The Republican candidate, John C. Fremont, was not even on the ticket in Arkansas.[89]

Judging only by the returns, it would seem that the Dynasty must have overreacted to the Know-Nothing challenge. According to the historian of the movement in the Old South, the American party "made less progress in Arkansas than in any other southern state, with the possible exception of South Carolina."[90] Yet in an age devoid of political polls and surveys, the Family could not gauge the full influence of the movement. The Know-Nothings appeared formidable if only because much of the old Whig party and press supported it, as well as a few prominent Democrats like Yell and Borland. For this reason, the Dynasty felt it could not dismiss the party easily.

Even in the best of times, the Know-Nothings in Arkansas faced an uphill battle. The state usually voted Democratic and the ruling party was a tight, cohesive organization. Most of the state's newspapers were attuned to the ruling Democratic Dynasty. In addition, the American party stretched its credibility with many Arkansas voters when it charged that Catholics and foreigners were minorities to be feared. Catholics and foreigners each amounted to about 1 percent of the free population of the state.[91]

The real death blow to the Know-Nothing cause in Arkansas occurred when Pike abandoned the movement, pronouncing it unsafe on the slavery issue. After that, what had been a difficult task became an impossible one. No opposition group could really succeed or even survive if it was tainted ever so little with antislavery.[92] This was pointed out by Thomas Hindman's paper in Helena, the *States Rights Democrat,* which called the Know-Nothings the "Black Sam" party that was really attempting to split the Southern vote against the region's real enemy, the "Black Republicans."[93] Pike's departure left the Know-Nothings unable to effectively counter the charges of the Hindman paper. After that, the Know-Nothings could have no real future in antebellum Arkansas, although traces of the movement lingered until 1858. An Arkansas delegation attended a national convention in Louisville in 1857, but the party ceased to be a real challenge to the ruling Democratic Dynasty after the presidential election of 1856.[94]

With the collapse of the Know-Nothings, the Dynasty could once again feel secure. Even in the turbulent 1850s, no one had come forward to vanquish the dominant elite. But the Conway-Johnson organization did suffer one major disappointment, for it could not rally Arkansas to try to save the Kansas Territory for slavery.

In early 1854 Democratic Senator Stephen A. Douglas of Illinois goaded Congress to abolish the 36°30′ line set during the Missouri Compromise of 1820 to separate prospective free and slave territories. Instead of an arbitrary line set by the national legislature some three decades before, Douglas's proposed Kansas-Nebraska Act allowed the people of a territory to exercise their "popular sovereignty" and to decide for themselves whether they could be a free or slave state. Seeing the Douglas plan as a chance to remove restrictions of the former Missouri Compromise, Arkansas's congressional delegation joined with its fellow Southerners and a few Northern Democrats to pass the Kansas-Nebraska Act in May 1854.[95] Newspapers in Arkansas hailed the new measure because it gave authority concerning slavery back to local communities.[96] The *True Democrat* in Little Rock expressed its delight that "the measure gave the South a chance to have more slave states."[97]

Within a year of the passage of the Kansas-Nebraska Act, Douglas's experiment in "popular sovereignty" was foundering in blood and violence on the plains. Both North and South conceded that Nebraska would be a free state, but a battle developed in Kansas. Both North and South competed in the troubled territory by sending settlers, aid, money and arms. Since Arkansas's northwest corner almost touched the borders of Kansas, one might suspect that, as loyal slaveholding Southerners, its citizens might be galvanized into action on behalf of slavery for the new territory. Yet during most of 1855–56, the state press remained more concerned over Know-Nothingism and the state elections than the events taking place just to the northwest.[98] Only after the state contests were completed did the Family launch a crusade to make the Kansas Territory safe for slavery.

Editor Richard H. Johnson, in September 1856, solemnly warned his fellow Arkansans:

Arkansas has been too lukewarm. She has yet to contribute to the cause, though her interests in the issue are second to those of no State in the Union. Let us do our duty. . . . Kansas is on the very border of Arkansas. With Kansas a Slave State, all will be well. With it a free State, our property will be rendered insecure, and troubles and annoyances the lot of our people.[99]

Eastern and southern Arkansas both responded positively, and immigrant-aid societies were formed.[100] In western Arkansas efforts were made on behalf of the slave cause in Kansas. A broadside in Sebastian County called citizens to Fort Smith in September 1856, declaring such a rally necessary because "Arkansas has already too long been an indifferent spectator of the fearful struggle, Missouri has stood almost alone. . . . Shall not her struggle find an encouraging echo from Arkansas?"[101]

To the disappointment of many, Arkansas did not provide much encouragement on behalf of slavery in Kansas. Most of the immigrant-aid societies did little beyond passing stirring resolutions on Southern rights and raising funds for prospective settlers going to the troubled territory.[102] In the southern and eastern portions of the state, excitement over Kansas was not pervasive. The usually acute observer, Judge John Brown of Camden, did not note any immigrant-aid society meeting in his home county of Ouachita.[103] In the uplands, except for a few meetings in Fort Smith and Van Buren, the clarion call for the salvation of Kansas received virtually no response.[104] Angry over the feeble effort being expended for the plains state, Hindman's paper in Helena pleaded: "We appeal to our political brethren in the press, in all parts of the state, to discard the policy of silence and non-committalism, and boldly range themselves in defense of Southern honor and welfare."[105] Like so many other pleadings of an earlier date, this too seemed to fall on deaf ears.

In searching for explanations why citizens disregarded their political leaders and remained largely indifferent to the "blood of Kansas," historian Allan Nevins summed up the most important reason when he wrote: "Arkansans, with their own State yet half-unsettled, tarried at home."[106] As mentioned before, Arkansas, during the latter half of the 1850s, was in a state of rapid settlement. Many of the older settlers did not want to leave just as prosperity appeared on the horizon. New immigrants did not have the inclination to move their families, and sometimes slave property, to troubled and dangerous Kansas. Why go there when there was a chance of losing your life or your property? It was much better to stay in a stable slave state like Arkansas, which was only now coming into its own. A Camden newspaper was quoted in the summer of 1857 as advising its readers "to forget about Kansas, and rejoice in our glorious wealth, delightful showers, and abundant crops."[107]

Aside from concern over internal development, many thoughtful citizens doubted whether the climate and geography of Kansas were suited for cotton and slavery. Representative Greenwood from Benton County told his fellow members of the U.S. House that Kansas would be fit only for corn, not cotton: "I am perfectly familiar with a portion of the Kansas Territory, and I give as my firm conviction, that slavery will not exist in that territory, even if it is protected by law."[108] Also, a Clarksville resident wrote the *True Democrat* in the fall of 1857 that "the amount of slavery that can be introduced into countries whose climate is more favorable to white labor, is not worth much Southern labor or sacrifice. . . . Kansas, at best, would be a bright mulatto State as Missouri, Kentucky, and Maryland, mere broken reeds to rely on."[109] By the end of 1858, even the Dynasty had given up saving Kansas for slavery. Editor Richard Johnson declared in late September that he was "sick and tired of Kansas, and everything connected with the affair."[110]

Arkansas's lethargy over the whole Kansas question must have been discouraging for the Conway-Johnson Dynasty. For the second time in less than a decade, Arkansas had not responded vigorously to defending slavery on the national scene. The state would not even consider repudiating the Compromise of 1850 and it did almost nothing on behalf of slavery in Kansas. Although the leadership of the Dynasty, in the person of Senator Robert W. Johnson, remained committed to secession to defend slavery, there was no solid evidence before 1860 that Arkansas would follow such a course in a national crisis. If the Family appeared invulnerable to its political foes within the state, it must have worried whether Arkansas would ever make an energetic move to defend Southern rights and slavery.

With the events in Kansas now conveniently shoved into the background, and with the Know-Nothings relegated to a remnant, congressional elections of 1858 were the most peaceful since statehood. In the southern district, Warren and Rust continued their seesaw battle, with Rust coming out on top this time. Rust apparently received some Dynasty backing, for the *True Democrat* openly said that Warren would not follow the party line. An opposition paper in Batesville said Warren was dumped "because he would not bow to the Moguls of the Dynasty."[111] In the northern district, the Dynasty, deciding to recognize Hindman's political ability, rewarded his services to the party by granting him the congressional seat gratuitously relinquished by Greenwood. Hindman won easily at the

Batesville convention over his only opponent, Alfred M. Wilson of Fay-etteville.[112] After Hindman's nomination, the Family's chief newspaper in Little Rock commented that the Helena politician was "a true Democrat, a man of energy and talent, and, if elected, he will prove himself an able and efficient representative of the people of Arkansas."[113] Both Rust and Hindman won easily over token challengers.[114] An opposition paper in northeast Arkansas admitted in the fall that the Know-Nothing party was dead and commented sadly that no group was left to oppose the Dynasty-led Democratic party.[115]

The collapse of inter-party strife in Arkansas clearly paralleled a similar phenomenon occurring at that time in states of the lower South. As recent historians have demonstrated, opposition to the Democrats virtually ceased there, while most of the upper South maintained a vigorous two-party system.[116] Just as Arkansas in the late 1850s was being linked culturally and economically to the Deep South, its political structure was also taking on characteristics of that region. This lower South political resemblance would be altered by a major political rebellion that was just getting underway.

Hindman's rise to office was undoubtedly the most important public event in Arkansas during 1858. The Dynasty hoped by this gift of a congressional nomination to reward him as well as to quench his thirsty ambition. Hindman accepted the reward, and then pursued his ambitions even further. With Greenwood's departure, no uplander now held high public office. Both Hindman and Senator Sebastian resided in Helena, and Governor Conway and Senator Johnson were from Little Rock. Albert Rust, the other congressman, came from El Dorado near the Louisiana border. Traditionally a Democratic bastion, the northwest no longer had one of its own in top political councils of the state.

At this point, the Dynasty felt it could afford to take part of the state for granted. In a decade that had witnessed a national crisis as well as new political parties and massive migration, the Family had always weathered the storms. Little evidence suggested that Arkansas would not continue under the rule of this elite well into the 1860s.

Family leaders had strong grounds for such optimistic predictions, for the common yeomen of the state still voted the regular Democratic ticket. As long as the average voter believed that the Dynasty-run state Democratic party was the true heir of Jacksonian equality for all whites, the

Dynasty was entirely correct about the small likelihood of its defeat. Only if a charismatic figure should arise or a national event occur to break this perception would the Family have something to fear. A politician already living in Arkansas and holding office was prepared to drive that wedge between the yeoman and the elite.

Thomas Carmichael Hindman had already distinguished himself during the Family's battle with the Know-Nothings and had been duly rewarded with a congressional seat. But this did not, as the Family had hoped, satisfy the ambitions of the young Helena upstart. Hindman was infuriated when the Dynasty re-elected Senator Sebastian to another term in a legislative caucus in November 1858, feeling that he deserved the office.[117] Even before he had assumed his seat in Congress, Thomas C. Hindman had already launched his tumultuous election campaign that would not end until it had toppled the thirty-year reign of the Dynasty.

VI

Beyond His Merest and Most Sanguine Hopes

Thomas Hindman and the Defeat of the Dynasty,
1859–1860

For Arkansas and the rest of the nation, 1860 would not just be another election year. Forces within and without the state were pulling apart a political fabric that had grown ragged under tension. America had become, as Lincoln's famous quotation from the Bible said, a "house divided against itself." Over three decades the North had become increasingly hostile to slavery and its expansion into the territories. As northern condemnation grew, the South more vehemently defended its "peculiar institution." During the 1840s and 1850s, mainline Protestant churches had separated and two major political parties, the Whigs and the Know-Nothings, had been torn asunder over the issue. Finally, in the summer of 1860, the last national political organization, the Democratic party, succumbed to a sectional division over slavery.[1]

Even before that fateful summer the Arkansas Democratic establishment had split, but not over slavery and its expansion. The question that destroyed party unity was the continued reign of the Conway-Johnson Dynasty. A rebellion threatened to end its long domination of public affairs.

"Arkansas is a queer place," mused the El Dorado *Times* in the fall of 1859, "but its politics are the queerest."[2] For three decades the Arkansas electorate had voted almost blindly for a Democratic party dominated by a few families in Little Rock that were aligned politically and by patronage to Andrew Jackson's national Democratic party. An average voter thus believed that the state party run by the elite represented the true heritage of Jacksonian equality—common white males. Yet despite the state's having enjoyed remarkable growth during the 1850s, rule by the Dynasty had done little itself to advance Arkansas much beyond a frontier society. One historian has superbly summed up the Family's mismanagement of government:

Family rule had not benefitted the state. Legislature followed legislature without grappling with reality; irresponsible, if not criminal, banking programs had ruined state credit; there was no reliable all-weather transportation system, and the state government had done nothing to establish one; . . . none of the several efforts to establish state colleges and a common school had been successful. Whatever benefits the average Arkansan had enjoyed from the society and the resources of the state, he had gotten from his own efforts, from the local community, or from the Federal government, and only rarely from the state. On the other hand, for decades he would be cursed by the faults of the state's banking enterprises and the almost total lack of an internal improvements program.[3]

Although such were the conditions, the men who led the attack on the Family were not altruistic crusaders seeking the betterment of Arkansas society. Unadulterated ambition motivated them. Ambition ignited combustible resentment and caused a major political conflagration in the state election of 1860.

Opposition to the Family had always been present, and now the rapid influx of immigrants was helping to unsettle the established order. As historian Michael Dougan observed: "The rapidly increasing population brought in men who expected the state government to aid in establishing schools, railroads, levees, and roads. They were not interested in old bank scandals and political obligations. . . . Thus a dangerous situation developed as an increasing percentage of the population owed less and less to the 'Family'."[4] This development presented a grand opportunity for an aggressive schemer like Thomas Hindman.

Thomas Carmichael Hindman, Jr. was born on January 29, 1828, in Knoxville, Tennessee, the younger of two sons of Thomas Carmichael and Salle Holt Hindman. The family had a strong military tradition. Both grandfathers had fought in the American Revolution, and his father had served under General Andrew Jackson in the War of 1812. Appointed by President Jackson as an Indian agent, Thomas Hindman moved his young family to Jacksonville, Alabama, in 1832, to a job which must have been lucrative, since he resigned in 1841 and moved to Tippah County,

Mississippi. Living near Holly Springs, where he had purchased choice cotton land, the elder Hindman acquired enough slaves and land to qualify as a cotton planter by the 1840s.[5]

The youngest son was sent to a classics institute in New Jersey for four years. Upon graduation in 1846, young Thomas Hindman returned home in time to volunteer for a Mississippi regiment then being formed to fight in the Mexican War. He returned from the war two years later with the rank of colonel, a military title he bore proudly until his service in the Confederacy. At Holly Springs, Hindman turned his energies to the study of law and was admitted to the Mississippi bar in 1851. That year, at twenty-three, he had his first real taste of politics. He campaigned earnestly for Jefferson Davis in his race for governor and joined Davis in defending the right of secession by any Southern state. Apparently feeling that greater political opportunities awaited him on the west bank of the Mississippi River, Hindman moved to Helena, Arkansas, in 1854.[6] Although only twenty-six at the time, he had established a reputation as an orator and politician. A Holly Springs paper in early 1855 said: "Colonel Hindman is well known in this State and his friends, who are many, will ever watch, with interest, his career of usefulness as a politician and a private citizen."[7]

His friends back in Mississippi would not have to wait long, for Hindman threw himself into Arkansas politics. His first major political speech was at a Fourth of July rally near Helena in 1854. Hindman volunteered to give a Democratic response to a Whig address by Governor Alcorn of Mississippi.[8] After this impressive beginning, Hindman labored earnestly for the Democratic party in its battle with the Know-Nothings in 1855–1856. He founded a newspaper in Helena—the *States Rights Democrat*—in March 1856.[9] Within a year and a half, his paper received a commendation from the chief Democratic paper in Little Rock: "We regard the *States Rights Democrat* as one of the best papers in the State . . . its course has been soundly democratic."[10] Although Hindman had only turned thirty in 1858, the Dynasty rewarded him for his work by supporting his nomination and election to Congress that year.

As his political career blossomed, so too did Hindman's social and financial status by his marriage to Mollie Watkins Biscoe, daughter of a wealthy planter in Phillips County.[11] An uncle of the bride had served as Arkansas's first secretary of state and another uncle had served as the state's second attorney general and its third chief justice.[12]

Despite such an auspicious beginning, Congressman Hindman was restless for more rapid advancement and more power. A friend later described him as "an ambitious politician, rather overbearing in expression, self-sufficient . . . uncompromising in everything," a man who regarded "Arkansas as an empire of which he should be the emperor."[13] A Republican congressman from Ohio who served with Hindman in the House remembered him as a man "whose personality was dominated by a violent temper, a singlemindedness of purpose, and an intense desire for his own aggrandizement."[14]

Hindman campaigned vigorously during the summer and fall of 1858 for the Senate seat of William King Sebastian.[15] On November 9, the Democrats caucused in the Anthony House in Little Rock to nominate a senator. The assembly consisted of eighty-two Democrats and, surprisingly, thirteen old-line Whigs and Know-Nothings. The caucus waived the usual rule requiring a two-thirds vote for nomination and opted for a simple majority. Senator Sebastian collected fifty-two of the ninety-five votes. Sebastian was declared the Democratic nominee even though he obtained the nomination with the all-important votes of the Whig-Know-Nothing minority.[16] Apparently believing his ambitions too grand, the Family refused to support Hindman. Hindman, of course, immediately cried foul, and his newspaper in Helena denounced the leadership of the party as pretentious "Lords" and "royalists . . . who allow the people to only wag their tails and lick up crumbs from the royal table."[17] The Dynasty later admitted that Whigs and Know-Nothings had been allowed in the Democratic caucus,[18] but its leaders must have felt proud that they could still outmaneuver their opponents. Oldline Whigs and Know-Nothings preferred the conservatism of the wealthy planter, Senator Sebastian, to this upstart from Helena.[19] The Dynasty had confidence in its strong organization and its long tradition of victories over dissidents like Hindman. A few of its supporters openly bragged about how they could easily "crush Hindman in 1860."[20]

Within months, the breach between Hindman and the Dynasty became public. In a Little Rock address in February 1859, Hindman denounced "caucus power" and declared that he considered the re-election of Senator Sebastian to be "null and void" because Whigs and Know-Nothings had taken part in the Democratic process.[21] The Dynasty said Hindman was splitting the Democratic party because, in the words of Editor Richard H. Johnson of the *True Democrat,* "we did not take part to sacrifice Judge Sebastian to Hindman's ambition."[22] A Family newspaper in Fayetteville said that once Hindman had been promoted "beyond his merest and most sanguine hopes, then his inordinate selfishness prompted him to aim at supreme power in Arkansas."[23]

Coinciding with Hindman's rebellion was the development of serious differences between Governor Conway and the General Assembly. Hindman moved quickly into the dispute. In its longest session since statehood, the legislature sat from November 1, 1858, to February 21, 1859, passing the black-expulsion law and setting up the first state-supported school for the blind. Both acts had the support of Governor Conway.[24] What the governor and the General Assembly quarreled over was money. The legislature cut taxes, and Governor Conway vetoed the measure because he said it would mean repudiation of the state banking debt. Another source of friction was the legislature's insistence on taking per diem pay during a short recess, which the parsimonious governor vehemently opposed. Hindman capitalized on the dispute and pulled into his camp such men as state Representative Benjamin DuVal of Fort Smith, which broadened the Helena politician's power base.[25]

Next, Hindman established a second newspaper in Little Rock to combat the Family's main paper, the *True Democrat*. Even during the summer of 1858, rumor had circulated that another Democratic paper would appear in Little Rock.[26] Finally, word came in July 1859 through a Memphis newspaper that a new publication calling itself the *Old Line Democrat* would soon make an appearance in the Arkansas capital.[27] The *True Democrat* sniffed: "It may be called the '*Old Line Democrat*,' but it will be, for all intents and purposes, a disorganizing sheet, supported by and giving aid and comfort to, the opposition, by endeavoring to create a schism in the Democratic party."[28] The *True Democrat*'s editor, Richard Johnson, went on to accuse Christopher Danley of the *Arkansas Gazette* of being behind this new paper. Actually, Danley had burned his bridges with the Democratic party and despised both Hindman and the Dynasty for the way they treated the Know-Nothings.[29] When Johnson continued to accuse the *Gazette* of backing Hindman, Danley responded that the *True Democrat*'s editor had become afflicted with the "mange of meanness and the leprosy of lying."[30]

Finally, on September 15, the *Old Line Democrat* made its appearance in Little Rock. Hindman hired as editor Thomas Peek, a Virginian who had edited a Stephen Douglas paper in Illinois.[31] Peek, an editor for hire, wrote attacks on Douglas as he echoed Hindman's rabid disunionism. The new publication boldly declared that it would be "Southern in tone and character," proudly proclaiming the "right of Secession."[32] On local issues, the paper promised to be "the organ of no one man, faction or clique."[33] That promise rang hollow, as Hindman's name was mentioned no less than thirty-eight times in the first issue "with such effusions as would sicken and disgust an Eastern Sultan."[34]

For the next eleven months, the *True Democrat* and the *Old Line Democrat* waged vicious war upon one another. Both journals allied with papers throughout the state, and soon these publications were drawn into the fray.[35] The *Old Line Democrat* wondered why the people of Arkansas went to the expense of holding county, district, or state conventions when "state offices are bartered and peddled by a little stock-jobbing set of thick-headed politicians whose only distinction is derived from the fact that they live in Little Rock and belong to the Dynasty."[36] Along with these assaults on "the imperious dictations of the Family," Hindman's press needled Governor Conway's administration as inept and lackadaisical and accused the *True Democrat* of overcharging on state printing contracts.[37]

At first, the Family press called Hindman only "a factious disorganizer" with overwhelming ambition and saved most of its fire for the editor of the *Old Line Democrat*. The Family's chief newspaper relished quoting the Douglasite incarnation of Peek vis-à-vis his new role as a rabid secessionist.[38] This initial hands-off policy toward Hindman was understandable, because he was the Democratic representative from the northern district, having obtained the position with the Family's blessing. Behind the scenes, however, the Dynasty searched for a candidate to oppose him. During the fall of 1859 and early 1860, the *True Democrat* tacitly approved such men as Arthur Carroll of Conway County and George Clarke of Van Buren.[39] (Clarke apparently had made his peace with the Family since the early 1850s.)

Heady in the role of insurgent, Hindman announced that he would appear in Little Rock and denounce the leadership of the Family in person on November 24, 1859. Senator Robert W. Johnson made a fifty-mile journey from his plantation in Jefferson County to challenge the first district congressman, but Hindman didn't show up. He later said illness in his family had prevented his appearance, and his father-in-law substantiated the claim, but the Dynasty and its press accused the congressman of cowardice.[40]

Hindman probably avoided the encounter not out of fear but to dodge a major political blunder. His challenge had been made too impetuously. Rebellion against the Family was only getting under way, the paper in Little Rock was barely two months old, and he did not have sufficient public support or endorsement from prominent politicians. Hindman's campaign would look frail compared with the legions the Dynasty could muster for a meeting in Little Rock. Why jeopardize his rebellion at the outset by appearing weak to both his adversary and the public? Hindman conveniently used an actual illness in his family to avert confrontation in which he might not appear formidable. When he failed to show up in Little Rock, Senator Johnson issued a statement calling him a "bully" and "an imposter in the ranks of honor."[41] Hindman would have to suffer for a time with the label of coward but would eventually live that accusation down. Harder to overcome would be an early opinion that his rebellion against the Family was too weak to be taken seriously.

More damaging to Hindman was the Viator letter episode. Elias Boudinot, half-breed Cherokee editor of the Fayetteville *Arkansian*, obtained an envelope containing a letter written by Hindman that was later published in the congressman's newspapers under the signature "Viator." The "Viator" letters always materialized soon after Hindman had made a public appearance, and this series of letters heaped effusive praise and glory upon the Helena congressman. That Hindman wrote these letters himself was verified by witnesses familiar with his handwriting.[42] Hindman's press at first denied the charge, although he later admitted taking part in their composition.[43] The confession delighted the Dynasty, and the *True Democrat* soon scolded its antagonist, saying "He sang his own praises; he wrote his own puffs! Shame! Where is thy blush?"[44] The affair embarrassed the Hindman camp, and even such a staunch supporter as editor J. S. Morrill of the Des Arc *Citizen* put some distance between himself and Hindman during the early months of 1860.[45]

Deflecting debate with Senator Johnson, combined with the "Viator" letter episode, dampened but did not extinguish the fire of Hindman's rebellion. Too much literary and verbal animosity had passed between the factions for either side to let bygones be bygones. Still, Hindman's pride would not let him falter. Personal relations between him and Senator Johnson worsened during the winter. They nearly fought a duel in early January while both were in Congress. Only the intervention of Senator Robert Toombs of Georgia prevented this potentially deadly engagement.[46]

Hindman had another good reason to continue his struggle: he was gathering important support. Albert Rust, the El Dorado congressman, coveted the seat soon to be vacated by Senator Johnson,[47] and although Rust was a strong admirer of Stephen Douglas, whom Hindman's press considered as loathsome as Senator Johnson, the south Arkansas representative received praise and encouragement for his Senate candidacy from the Hindman camp.[48] Hindman also enlisted support from Edward Gantt, who campaigned for Rust's congressional seat in the spring of 1860.[49] While not yet equal to the Dynasty, Hindman's faction was growing.

Dealing with political opposition was nothing new to the Conway-Johnson Dynasty. In Hindman, however, it found an antagonist who had sharpened his political wiles within the organization. Also, the Dynasty had no one to match him as a stump speaker. As historian Dougan has written: "The Family might out-manipulate Hindman, but they had no one who could out-debate him."[50] The Van Buren *Press*, a Democratic paper that stayed neutral in the contest, gave this report on Hindman's speaking ability after hearing him in Van Buren:

As a general thing, his delivery is fluent, smooth, and pleasant; a perfect master of the art, he deals out his argument systematically, and with much energy, and with just enough sarcasm, wit and humor, to keep his hearers in cheerful attendance for hours. His style of oratory is particularly suited in satisfying public assemblages in mass; at times, he is using the most vehement and impassioned language. . . . He has reduced speechmaking to a science; we have seldom seen such a person who could hold the undivided attention of a large concourse for such a lengthy address.[51]

Hindman used his speechmaking abilities to arouse people against the Dynasty. As politicians and demagogues have done throughout the ages, Hindman did not hesitate to fan popular prejudices to advance his personal aims. Gleefully, he returned in kind any abuse received from the Family and its press. The role of a revolutionary suited his overweening pride and bombastic nature.

Though tenacious and talented, Hindman was still without real power,

77

and the Family was doing all it could to keep it that way. It planned to deliver the nomination for governor to Richard H. Johnson, editor of its main paper in Little Rock. Governor Conway would then be elected to Senator Johnson's seat when the legislature met the following November.[52] This convenient rotation of major offices would insure the continuation of the Dynasty well into the 1860s.

Various names were presented by the newspapers during the fall and winter of 1859–1860, but no real candidate emerged to challenge Johnson's impending gubernatorial nomination. While some searchéd for candidates, the Family worked skillfully to secure control of the state Democratic convention. In the first few months of 1860, county conventions chose delegates for the party's assembly. Pitched contests and occasional brawls broke out between Family and Hindman supporters in several places.[53] They raised fears of such scenes at the state convention. The Camden *States Rights Eagle* earnestly implored delegates: "Let there be no wire-working, no packing, no limited expression, but a full attendance, a deliberate consultation, and a just and fair agreement."[54]

Democrats assembled in Little Rock on Monday, April 2, 1860, immediately became embroiled in a fight between contesting delegations.[55] The Johnson faction arranged such representation as it wanted to be sure of controlling the proceedings.[56] With the assembly under Family direction, Johnson was nominated for governor on the second ballot, but the Family had to resort to changing rules again to achieve it. Johnson couldn't get the two-thirds majority normally required for nomination.[57] As with Senator Sebastian's re-election in 1858, Hindman had forced the Family to waive the rules to accomplish its will. And just as Sebastian's re-election failed to quell Hindman's ambitions, Johnson's nomination only sharpened and deepened divisions within the Democratic party.

Near the end of the convention Hindman delegates, led by Benjamin DuVal of Fort Smith and Patrick Cleburne of Helena, protested against irregularities in the proceedings. They maintained that Johnson had been chosen by an illegal majority vote instead of the usual two-thirds and that certain counties had been misrepresented.[58] The latter charge was more serious, for R. S. Yerkes, Johnson's partner at the *True Democrat*, had cast a vote for Van Buren County where he did not live and no county convention had been held there.[59] Although the Dynasty's newspaper later admitted that its opponents voiced a valid case concerning

Yerkes's vote, Johnson was heralded as "the true Democratic nominee" for governor.[60]

Reaction to Johnson's nomination was swift and predictable. Family newspapers like the *True Democrat,* the El Dorado *Times,* the Camden *States Rights Eagle,* the Fayetteville *Arkansian,* the Fort Smith *Times,* and the Napoleon *Planter* immediately endorsed the convention's choice.[61] Hindman's press was furious. Editor Morrill wrote in the Des Arc *Citizen* that the whole assembly had been a "packed and prearranged convention . . . brought to bear in favor of the nomination of R. H. Johnson."[62] The *Jeffersonian Independent* in Pine Bluff solemnly declared: "We feel satisfied that the action in regard to the nomination of governor does not reflect the will of the people of this State."[63] Among citizens as well, the Johnson nomination sparked protests. In Benton County, a petition signed by 821 persons denounced the Family and rejected Johnson's nomination. Meanwhile, Johnson was hung in effigy in Fort Smith.[64]

At first the Hindman faction could not decide how to respond to Johnson's nomination. The *Old Line Democrat* hoisted Johnson's name on its masthead just after the convention's *fait accompli.*[65] Privately, though, Hindman searched frantically for his own gubernatorial candidate. Meanwhile, both Dynasty and insurgent forces prepared for the congressional district conventions in mid-May.

At the northern district meeting in Dover, Hindman assumed authority over the proceedings. Excluding most pro-Dynasty delegations, he arranged his renomination to Congress by acclamation and then moved the assembly to repudiate Johnson's nomination and call for a new state Democratic convention. Hindman was particularly vindictive toward Elias Boudinot, who had exposed his self-aggrandizing "Viator" letters. The convention barred the half-Cherokee editor because, it was said, he did not enjoy full citizenship and thus was no better than the slave Dred Scott.[66]

Neither the Johnson nor the Hindman camp could gain hegemony in the southern district convention at Arkadelphia. Hindman's forces backed E. W. Gantt of Camden for the U.S. House of Representatives while the Family supported Charles Mitchel of Washington in southwest Arkansas. In the noisy and disorderly assembly, neither could gain nomination. The convention could only agree to let voters decide between

Gantt and Mitchel in the August elections. Hindman's faction tried to have the convention repudiate Johnson's nomination, but the Dynasty beat down the motion by a few votes.[67]

When the congressional district conventions lay behind him, Hindman could reveal his own candidate for governor. To the surprise and consternation of the Dynasty, Henry Massie Rector had been chosen, a first cousin of Governor Elias N. Conway![68] Born in Missouri in 1816, Rector and his family emigrated to Arkansas during the 1820s. Owing to his close relation to the Conway clan, Rector had enjoyed a long career with the Dynasty. He had served as U.S. marshal for Arkansas in the 1840s, held office for several terms in the legislature and unsuccessfully sought Democratic nomination for Congress from the southern district in 1854. His years of loyal service, plus his close blood relations with Governor Conway, earned Rector a seat on the state supreme court in 1859.[69] Obviously, the Court did not satisfy Rector's ambition for suddenly, at the age of forty-four, he opportunistically renounced his political heritage and became Hindman's choice for governor.

With exaltation, the Hindman press presented its candidate. Editor Peek of the *Old Line Democrat* was especially eloquent:

Who is Henry M. Rector? A poor, honest farmer of Saline County, who toils at the plow handles to provide bread, meat, and raiment for his wife and children. Do you know him? There are many people who do—who have seen him laboring in the fields, earning his bread with [the] sweat of his brow. But possessing the imprint of manhood from nature, and from nature's God, at this country's greatest need, he arose like Cincinnatus of old and did his duty.[70]

The *True Democrat* responded by asking rhetorically: "Do you know him? For ourselves we answer, 'no sir.' We know a gentleman of that name in Pulaski County who owns quite a bit of property, is a lawyer by profession, and is entirely innocent of plowing."[71] The paper went on to say that although Rector was a clever politician, "even he must sicken when he reads such stuff as the editor plasters him with."[72] While the *True Democrat* continued its formal endorsements of Hindman in the northern congressional race, it castigated him in every edition. Behind the scenes, the Family worked for the election of Jesse Cypert of Searcy, who ran against Hindman as an independent.[73]

In this fratricidal war among the Democrats, the old Whig-Know-Nothing element assumed new importance. The "old opposition" press generally stood on the sidelines as Democrats brawled. Probably the leading spokesman for this constituency was Danley of the *Arkansas Gazette*. Early in June of 1860, Danley surveyed the political field and declared: "Taken altogether, the belligerent Democracy seems to be in a fix, and, as far as the *Gazette* is concerned, we say 'let 'em fight!'"[74] He avowed that neither Johnson nor the Hindman faction would ever receive his endorsement.[75]

It appeared for a time that old-line Whigs would have their own gubernatorial candidate, Judge Thomas Hubbard of Washington. Hubbard opened his candidacy in April and the *True Democrat* welcomed him into the race, hoping he would keep old-line Whigs from supporting "Hindman's disorganizers."[76] For a while, the governor's race was a three-man affair characterized by one early cartoonist as a contest between a Tom, Dick, and Harry.[77] This situation did not last long, for the old Whig opposition was more concerned about the presidential election. A convention of old-line Whigs in Helena in late April selected delegates to the national Constitutional Union party convention which was to be held in Baltimore in mid-May. It also endorsed Hubbard for governor; Hugh F. Thomason, then of Fayetteville, for congressman from the northern district; and Benjamin Askew of Magnolia for congressman from the southern district.[78]

After the national convention in Baltimore the old-line Whigs in Arkansas became the state Constitutional Union party, and the *Gazette* placed the national candidacies of John Bell of Tennessee and Edward Everett on its masthead.[79] At the state convention of the new party in Hot Springs in June, national concerns took precedence. Following a course that Danley described as "good and wise," the assembly pulled Hubbard and the two congressional candidates out of the state election in August so that the party could concentrate on the presidential race in the fall.[80] To individual members of the party would be left the unwelcome task of choosing between the two warring factions in the Democratic party, the traditional enemy.

To call the contest between the Conway-Johnson Family and the Hindman faction an election would do an injustice to reality; it was war. The state may never have witnessed a more rancorous political campaign. While the nation sat anxiously on the eve of its greatest crisis, Arkansas's reigning clique fought tenaciously to preserve its rule. Few ideological differences separated the factions. They agreed on the rightness of slavery and its expansion into the territories; and they advocated secession, if necessary, to protect it. If those issues divided the nation, they at least united Arkansas Democrats. Since the Compromise of 1850, the Conway-Johnson Dynasty had sided with the Southern states' rights wing of the national party, although finding it difficult to motivate Arkansans to make any strong efforts on behalf of slavery. The arguments of this campaign had a familiar ring: the million-dollar bank debt, the fraudulent votes in political assemblies, overcharging on state printing contracts, and the necessity of internal improvements for a rapidly-growing frontier state. But behind all these issues was the central concern: the Family and its dominance of public affairs.

Members of the Dynasty defected to the ranks of their enemies in large numbers, which accounts for much of the bitterness of the election. The Family was not so much directly assaulted; it had grown too powerful for that. It was undermined by the lower echelon of the Dynasty.

Desiring to redeem beyond a doubt the reputation that had been sullied by accusations of cowardice the previous fall, Hindman arrived in Little Rock in late May to denounce the Family on its home ground. He gave an enthusiastic crowd what it wanted to hear—exaggeration: "Of all the unholy alliances and corrupt political influences that ever crushed the energies of a free people, that of Johnsonianism was the most blighting, withering, and corrupting."[81] His attack on the Family soon found an unlikely echo from southern district Congressman Rust. Rust charged the Dynasty with creating "absolute rule" in Arkansas "ever since the admission of this State into the Union."[82] He sought to build support in Hindman's camp for his race for the U.S. Senate; nevertheless, his attacks on the Family showed the secondary role of national affairs in Arkansas politics. In the same statement, Rust reasserted his position as a Union Democrat, warning Arkansas and the South against secession because "it would destroy, perhaps, the last great experiment in free government."[83] For a few months in summertime, Rust and Hindman buried their differences over secession and joined in what they considered to be the more important cause: the struggle against the Conway-Johnson clique.

Other prominent politicians from the Family's ranks joined the insurgency. Edward Warren, the former congressman from the southern district whom the Dynasty had removed in 1858, sought revenge and endorsed the Hindman-Rector-Gantt ticket in mid-June.[84] Former Governor John Seldon Roane denounced the Family in early July for forcing him to retire to make way for Governor "Con-a-way."[85] The Family soon came up with a name for the former governor: John "Seldom Right."[86] The Family press throughout the state dismissed the accusations of Dynasty dominance by Rust, Warren and Roane. According to the *Democratic Sentinel* in Batesville: "This hue and cry of the *Old Line Democrat* against the Johnsons is as worn and thin as the Pharisaical Know-Nothing humbuggery about the Pope of Rome. It is the useless slogan of the Borland dissenters and has been harped on until it makes a decent man sick!"[87]

With his own election secure, which even his enemies admitted,[88] Hindman lowered his profile during the last six weeks of his campaign. He spent the time in Helena or visiting family and friends in Mississippi.[89] The *True Democrat* accused Hindman of coming to regret his support of Rector for governor.[90] No real evidence of this exists, for Hindman's press continued to work earnestly for Rector. Actually, Hindman had played out his major role: he had instigated the rebellion. He no longer had to be in front since it was no longer a one-man revolt. His own candidates, Rector and Gantt, would have to prove themselves to the people. The congressman preferred the appearance of a man who did not desire absolute power but only another term in Congress. While Hindman might have moved to the background, he was directing the show. Contemporaries such as John Hallum, Charles Nash, and Samuel Williams, writing years later, gave Hindman full credit for Rector's victory.[91]

Both Rector and Johnson issued public circulars stating their positions on issues of the day in the final stretch of the campaign. Rector described the Democratic nominating convention as a fraud, attacked Governor Conway's handling of the bank debt, and claimed that the *True Democrat* overcharged on state printing contracts.[92] Johnson replied that Governor Conway's plan for repaying the state bank debt slowly was the only wise and prudent course open to the administration. Even with the fraudulent vote of Van Buren County, Johnson said he still held a majority of votes at the convention. Johnson also repeated the Family line on internal improvements: none until the bank debt was repaid.[93]

Following political custom, Rector and Johnson toured the state together in June and July. In Johnson's absence, his editorial position at the *True Democrat* was taken by Elias Boudinot, whom the Hindman press referred to as that "colored editor."[94] Press reports from the differing Democratic papers throughout the state are totally unreliable, for they always promoted their own candidates. Christopher Danley heard Rector and Johnson speak in late July, and since he refused to endorse either of them, he published perhaps the most evenhanded account of their campaign style in the *Gazette:*

Mr. Johnson's style is slow, dry, and prosy in a painful degree. To form a just appreciation of his oratorical powers, one should hear his style of saying, 'I . . . was . . . born . . . in Arkansas . . . and . . . if you don't elect me Governor . . . I've nowhar to go.' Judge Rector is a fair declaimer, his fault is that he is too wordy— his sentences are crowded with big six syllablers [sic], and that he dilutes his ideas until they are sometimes rather thin. He is an orator of the ka-larruping style, as shown in the following sentence: 'I stand on my pedestal, shorn of the abominations and malpractices whereon they relied to cast the nomination upon the present nominee of the Democratic party.'[95]

A major issue was Rector's plan to pay off the huge state debt. He would delay payment of the debt for twenty-five to fifty years and concentrate on giving state aid to railroads, which, in his view, would produce enough revenue to retire the debt.[96] Many quarters immediately attacked the scheme, and even editor Peek of the *Old Line Democrat* admitted that it might seem impractical. Still, he found merit in the plan because "it opened the doorway for suggestions of other measures."[97] Financial conservatives like Danley were horrified at Rector's proposal, and the *Gazette* said that if it were ever enacted, it would "equal a public calamity."[98] The *True Democrat,* of course, gave the idea nothing but ridicule.[99]

Once the public tired of Rector's fiscal proposal, the *Old Line Democrat* countered in the grand tradition of state politics: personal calumny. Editor Peek wrote that it was common knowledge that R. H. Johnson had been drunk for the past ten years. The *True Democrat* called the charge "base and dastardly," and "an insult to the Democratic party."[100] Both Rector and Johnson knew the ex-Whig vote would be crucial, and both made overtures to this constituency. The Family stressed its sound financial policy, while Rector "appealed to the Whigs with talk of railroads, internal improvements, and good government."[101] Near the end of this very bitter campaign the factions fought over the vote offered by mechanics and laborers in Little Rock. A gunsmith named Jacob Trumpler claimed in the *Old Line Democrat* that he had heard Senator Robert Johnson boast that he could buy every mechanic's vote in the Arkansas capital with a drink of whiskey.[102] The *True Democrat* contended that the story was so groundless that Hindman's newspaper held up publishing Trumpler's accusation for eight hours, until Senator Johnson had left town.[103] Right up to election day, however, Trumpler vigorously maintained that he had spoken the truth.[104]

On August 6, 1860, the long ordeal came to an end and Arkansans went to the polls. When the full returns were tabulated two weeks later, they revealed a stunning defeat for the Conway-Johnson Dynasty. Hindman trounced his opponent in the northern district by more than a two-to-one margin. Edward Gantt received a smaller but solid majority of 54 percent in the southern district. In the governor's race, Rector received 31,948 votes to Johnson's 28,487, a majority of almost 53 percent.[105] The *Old Line Democrat* crowed: "Caesar has had his Brutus, Charles I his Cromwell, and Johnson—has met his Rector."[106] For the first time since statehood Arkansas had rejected a Family-picked candidate, not for one, but for three major offices. Thus the people placed in the governor's chair a maverick, somewhat eccentric, inexperienced politician who would assume and hold office during the greatest crisis of the state and nation.

Was the role of the old-line Whigs, after all, pivotal? A few months after the election, Danley of the *Gazette* said the Whig voters went for Johnson.[107] John Harrell, the editor of the *Old Line Democrat* during the fall of 1860, wrote almost forty years later that Rector owed his election to dissident Democrats and old-line Whigs.[108] Recent scholarship supports that view. Dougan studied twenty-two traditional Whig counties and found that fourteen went for Johnson and eight for Rector, but since the Rector counties were more populous, the result was an 888-vote margin for Rector.[109] Johnson probably enjoyed substantial Whig support at the outset but lost it in the last months of the race. Johnson's ineptitude as a stump speaker may have hurt him. Without endorsing either of the candidates, the former Whig newspaper in Batesville, the *Independent Balance*, commented that "Johnson is the poorest stump speaker we have ever listened to . . . he could save votes by quitting the stump. He loses votes every time he makes a speech, we have no doubt."[110]

Rector's candidacy also gave old-line Whigs the opportunity to defeat their old adversary, the Conway-Johnson regime, without having to vote for someone who might introduce economic radicalism. Many of them saw Rector as a man from a politically prestigious family in Little Rock who was unlikely to be rash. In fact, he seemed to be the perfect conservative candidate to use to defeat the Dynasty. This kind of thinking was exemplified by the ex-Whig Judge John Brown of Camden. Brown wrote in his diary that after hearing both Rector and Johnson he decided to vote for Rector because "he is the right man to use in breaking up . . . what is called the Johnson-party oligarchy." [111]

Other, more financially conservative Whigs, remained hostile to Rector as a result of his plan to delay payment of the banking debt for twenty-five to fifty years. Ex-Whig John Woodward of Little Rock, writing to his friend and former party associate David Walker of Fayetteville, thought it strange that when the Family was finally correct on the debt question it was defeated. Woodward scorned those Whigs who "had laid aside their manhood" and voted for Rector. He doubted that these former Whigs could count on any favors from the next governor. [112]

More intriguing questions surround the personality and appeal of the man who instigated the first successful rebellion against the Dynasty. Early studies characterize Hindman as a romantic and flamboyant figure who was also a states' rights firebrand in the mold of William L. Yancey of Alabama. [113] Hindman fit these descriptions to a degree, but they do not really explain him or his appeal. He possessed great oratorical ability and organizational skill, and sufficient raw opportunism to challenge the Family, but those gifts alone did not grant him success in the election of 1860.

Along with the margin of Whig voters, historian Dougan maintains that Hindman's victory was produced by newcomers who flocked to the state during the 1850s. "Unfamiliar with the older politicians, and vexed by the various unsolved state problems," Dougan wrote, "the new voters had no ties to the family. . . . Such men flocked to the Rector-Hindman-Gantt banner." [114] Although Dougan gave no statistical proof, there is evidence that the new settlers were slightly more likely to support Hindman's candidate for governor. In the counties that voted for Rector, the white population averaged an increase of about 114 percent between 1850 and 1860. In the counties that went for Johnson, the increase of whites was 101 percent. [115] Letters from a few new immigrants indicated their support for Rector. Hugh Brown, a recent immigrant from North Carolina, excitedly wrote from Van Buren to a relative that "the Johnson Family, which have [sic] for so long been *the head* of affairs in Arkansas, are [sic] about to be suspended." [116] A recent arrival from Tennessee who described himself as an ex-Whig wrote to Rector soon after the election that he and his relatives "were your warmest supporters in the late canvass," and said he was pleased that Rector had overthrown "the ruling Dynasty of Arkansas."[117]

Yet literary and statistical evidence does not conclusively prove that Rector and the Hindman ticket won mainly due to the new immigrants. The average increases of white population between the Johnson and Rector counties did not differ dramatically. In fact, the two counties that had the largest percentage of increase of whites between 1850 and 1860 were Ashley and Polk, and both of them voted for Johnson. (See Table 6a in the Appendix.) The small bits of literary evidence also are not enough to account for the appeal of the rebels.

Thomas Hindman was undoubtedly the first successful Arkansas politician to appeal directly to the people over the regular Democratic organization. He turned the last state election of the antebellum era into the kind of contest that later became familiar in political primaries. On this unfamiliar ground the Dynasty was at a clear disadvantage. The Conway-Johnson organization usually could out-manipulate its Democratic opponents and then silence them with favors or appeals for party unity. Although they vigorously attacked the Dynasty, the Whigs usually appeared to be too aristocratic, wealthy and conservative to gain the vote of the average yeoman. When the Dynasty tried to outmaneuver the Helena congressman, Hindman simply went to the people directly and appealed fearlessly to class differences. The Family was caught off guard. In this style of electioneering two historians commented that "state aphorisms gave way to impassioned appeals to class and racial prejudices. Oratorical ability and platform style became important characteristics of the more successful candidates and, unless some deep issue stirred the people, they frequently were decisive."[118] The state election of 1860 reflected these qualities.

Throughout the campaign, Hindman's press had bristled with the rhetoric of revolution, turning the yeoman's suspicion of the aristocracy into political gain. He skillfully used the language of class antagonisms to create popular objection to the "aristocratic" rule of the Family. James Morrill in the Des Arc *Citizen* articulated the theme in an editorial published in August 1859:

The new rank and file of our party, the honest, hard-fisted yeomanry, who do our voting and win our victories, have no mouthpiece in Little Rock. The so-called *True Democrat* makes blind obedience to a clique of office seekers the test of orthodoxy, and denounces as traitors and disorganizers all those who do not kiss the feet of these lordly aristocrats.[119]

Attacks on the Family, its paper and its location in Little Rock provided fuel for the Hindman forces to turn lower-class whites and newcomers against the ruling elite with that magic appeal to political democracy. Hindman's paper in Little Rock once declared in an editorial: "The *True Democrat* may sneer about farmers and plowmen aspiring to high political distinction; that paper may find out that the hard-fisted yeomen think that anyone of their number has as much right to aspire to high position as any of the Johnsons."[120]

The irony of Hindman's triumph was his ability to portray the Dynasty, which had long associated itself with the memory of Andrew Jackson, as another oppressive aristocracy, turning the Family's Jacksonian pretension on its head. Hindman's press frequently referred to the Conway-Johnson regime as "the throne of the Bourbons" who were trying to crush "this uprising among the people."[121] These blatant appeals to the lower classes bewildered the Dynasty, and one of its newspapers in Fort Smith expressed concern in the spring of 1860 that such a tactic might, indeed, succeed:

The honest farmers, mechanics, and laborers, are too often gulled by the gilded pill of this slick-tongued, hypocritical set, and through their smooth talk and plausibility, are often betrayed. Is it not time that some of this class be taught to respect the rights, feelings, and the interests of the whole community?[122]

For all of Hindman's rhetoric about aristocrats and the masses, his objective was not to bring about an economic restructuring of society, but to achieve his own political ambitions. The best evidence of this was that many upper-class Whigs felt comfortable enough with Hindman's aims, despite his class rhetoric, to vote for his gubernatorial candidate, Henry Rector. Since Rector came from an old political family in Little Rock, Whig conservatives felt no real threat. Whigs could vote for a "revolutionary insurgent" ticket because its true aim was to defeat the Dynasty, not economic radicalism. This was Hindman's real genius. He used the bombast of revolution to attract the lower classes while winning substantial Whig backing by choosing a member of Little Rock's elite as his candidate for governor.

As Huey Long was able to achieve in Louisiana three-quarters of a century later, Hindman had to overcome a regional dichotomy. He avoided the lowland-slave vs. upland-slaveless division by appealing to a common denominator: yeoman antipathy to a lordly Dynasty based in Little Rock. Topographical distinctions played no prominent role since Unionist mountaineers and secessionist farmers in the delta could find common ground with Hindman if the election was made to appear to be a battle between aristocracy and democracy. In the gubernatorial race, Rector and Johnson carried counties in both the mountainous northwest and the lowlands of the southeast.[123] (See Figure 6b in the Appendix).

If topographical differences were of little importance in this election, there is some statistical evidence that poor whites identified with this political rebellion. When the election returns are compared with the wealth per capita—the aggregate value of estate, real and personal, per white citizens of each county—they reveal a strong socioeconomic division. Rector carried only six of the top fifteen counties in wealth per capita, while winning the vote of ten of the fifteen poorest counties. Among the middle group of twenty-five counties, Rector swept fourteen, or a little more than half. (See Table 6c in the Appendix.)[124] As Table 6c indicates, there is a statistical correlation between white per capita wealth and this very divisive gubernatorial election. Wealthier counties did tend to vote for Johnson and the poorest ones cast their vote for Rector, with the middle counties giving a slight edge for the insurgent candidate. Apparently Hindman's rhetoric of revolution had some appeal to Arkansas's poor white class.

Hindman also had an uncanny ability to play both sides of the disunionist issue. Secessionist farmers in the delta were gratified by his strong support for slavery and secession. Although the Whig party and press was a conservative force in Arkansas on the issue of disunion, Whig planters in the delta would vote for a disunionist if he strongly supported slavery. This had been evident in the Johnson-Preston congressional race of 1851. While Hindman's views on secession might have won support for his ticket in the delta, the evidence also suggests that some mountain Unionist may have voted for Rector because he opposed a member of the Johnson Family, a name long associated with disunion.[125] One Unionist later claimed to have heard Rector declare in Benton County that even if Seward was elected president, Arkansas should not secede until there had been an overt act of aggression by the North.[126]

Hindman's successful revolt had the effect of shifting Arkansas's political structure into alignment more closely with other upper South states. By the summer of 1860, there was no longer a one-party dominance which prevailed at that time in the lower South.[127] Instead, state politics evolved into fierce competition between three quarreling factions—Hindman, Dynasty Democrats, and the old Whig Know-Nothing opposition. These factions persisted through the presidential election of 1860, only to be replaced later with yet another major political realignment. In all of these events, Representative Hindman would make his influence felt as Arkansas journeyed toward the Civil War.

VII

Arkansas Is With the South

State Politics During the Presidential Election of 1860

In the presidential election of 1860, the dispute over slavery finally sundered the Democratic party, the last remaining political organization that enjoyed substantial support in both the North and South. Upon its disintegration, Abraham Lincoln, a purely Northern candidate of a party no longer recognized in the South, was elected president on a platform that called for barring slavery from the western territories. The South believed this plank could lead only to gradual abolition. For that reason, many Southerners declared that they would never submit to a government headed by any person who desired either the restriction or the abolition of slavery. With the election of such a man in 1860, the dispute over slavery now reached its final crisis.

In Arkansas, the year witnessed culmination of another trend, a metamorphosis of the state toward Deep South culture and economy. For two previous decades, the state had strengthened its ties with the Old South through an increase of cotton production and slaveholding. Moreover, Arkansas had more and more drawn its population from the states of the Deep South, and most of these immigrants settled in the rich alluvial lowlands of the south and east. It was little wonder that Arkansas provided a small but solid majority for the most pro-slavery, pro-Southern of the presidential candidates in 1860. By fall, the state demonstrated that it had become politically, as well as culturally and economically, part of the Old South.

Besides a growing association with slaveholding states, by the late 1850s there were emerging signs that Arkansas might become something more than a struggling frontier society. The Fort Smith *Times* noted, with much satisfaction in late 1859, that "within the last two or three years, the State has increased in population and wealth."[1] This was not mere boosterism, for Arkansas was experiencing a surge of migration and prosperity.

In late 1859, the Memphis-Little Rock railroad line opened operations between Hopefield on the west bank of the Mississippi River and Madison on the east bank of the St. Francis River, a distance of about thirty-eight miles.[2] From late fall until the following spring another part of the line was graded from Little Rock eastward to DeValls Bluff, a distance of about forty-five miles. Rails could not be laid because the private company building the railroad had exhausted its funds by May 1860.[3] Still, efforts at railroad construction reflected Arkansas's emergence from a semi-primitive condition. A Memphis paper made this acknowledgment upon hearing about the completion of grading along the Little Rock-DeValls Bluff branch: "Arkansas is advancing in wealth and population in great strides. . . . It has none of the 'dirt road spirit' so prevalent there some eight or ten years ago."[4]

Rails were not the only lines making their appearance. In May 1860, Fayetteville became the first Arkansas community connected by electric telegraph, by wires run from St. Louis.[5] The line inched southward to Van Buren on the Arkansas River two months later.[6] In Little Rock on July 31, 1860, the Slaughter Gas Works went into operation, bringing welcome illumination to many homes and businesses in the capital.[7] Although the first city to receive this convenience, Little Rock still had no street lighting due to low levels of the Arkansas River which prevented delivery of the iron lampposts.[8]

Major strides in education were made in the last antebellum years. Arkansas College in Fayetteville, a Presbyterian school, and Soulsbury College in Batesville, a Methodist academy, opened their doors in the early 1850s.[9] The first institution of higher learning in Little Rock was St. John's College, a Masonic military academy, opening in the fall of 1859.[10] Although in Arkadelphia the state did establish a school for the blind in early 1859, no state-supported insane asylum or university was founded until after the Civil War.[11] The little education available was provided at log-cabin schools and a few private "academies," numbering about 109 by 1860. Altogether, 168 teachers conducted classes for 4,415 pupils.[12] Free public education would not be offered until decades after the Civil War; consequently, only the wealthier citizens could afford to have their off-spring sufficiently educated.[13] The outlook for education was still quite bleak, as an editor of a Batesville newspaper admitted in 1858: "There is certainly a great amount of ignorance in many portions of our state, and many worthless teachers pretending to instruct a rising generation."[14]

Despite its having no public school system or state-supported university, Arkansas stood on an economic threshold in 1860. Its rising population, wealth, and the appearance of rail and telegraph lines were sure indicators that dawn was breaking across the landscape. On the national horizon, however, clouds of crisis were gathering.

As the most important presidential election in American history approached, local politics receded before the concern over national issues and candidates. From the crisis that produced the Compromise of 1850 to the campaign for the Kansas Territory, the press and politicians of Arkansas focused on growing sectional differences over slavery. Through its leaders and its major press outlet in Little Rock, the state's ruling elite labored to make the state more active in defense of slavery. Until 1860, however, the Dynasty had generally found a lethargic response among the people. Whether they felt they needed aid and protection from the Federal government or because they were too busy with self-development, Arkansans refused to lead or follow any attempt to rock the national ship of state over slavery.

But the recent past proved to be no guide for the future. A profound shift in immigration patterns filled the rich lowlands with settlers from the lower South, carrying with them slaves, or at least a strong desire to become slaveholders, and making Arkansas and Texas the last frontier of the slaveholding South.[15] Immigration even rolled from the lowlands up the valleys of the Ouachita Mountains in west central Arkansas,[16] and would have an impact on the way Arkansas voted in the presidential election of 1860.

Officially, Arkansas's views on national issues closely followed those of Senator Robert W. Johnson. As a co-leader of the ruling Dynasty and a figure with national prominence, Johnson adapted his views to those of the late John C. Calhoun of South Carolina. Johnson arrived at the view that Calhoun had held late in his life, that the Union would inevitably dissolve over slavery and that secession would be the only logical and expedient course open for the South.[17] Although the Arkansas senator had not been particularly vocal during the 1850s, his positions were often stated by his younger brother, Richard H. Johnson, editor of the Dynasty's main newspaper in Little Rock. That paper had been in the vanguard of a crusade to stir Arkansans to work for slaveholding during most of the 1850s. By 1858, the Dynasty had abandoned its efforts to save Kansas for slavery, but it emerged from the controversy feeling betrayed by Senator Stephen Douglas. ·

Arkansas and several other slaveholding states had supported Douglas's Kansas-Nebraska Act in 1854, with high hopes that it would allow additional slave states. When President Buchanan submitted to Congress a bill admitting Kansas to the Union under the fraudulently obtained Lecompton Constitution, (a proslavery document), Senator Douglas rallied Northern Democrats and Republicans to defeat the measure. Douglas maintained that the Kansas constitution drawn up at Lecompton did not really reflect majority opinion. Many Southerners thought that Douglas had betrayed the real purpose of the Kansas-Nebraska Act, which they thought was to make possible more slave states in the western territories.[18] His actions on the Kansas question in early 1858 alienated not only much of the South but also Buchanan's Democratic administration. The president was infuriated that Douglas had challenged his leadership on this important issue, and after the spring of 1858, he openly vied with Douglas for control of the Democratic party.[19] The Arkansas Dynasty sided with Buchanan's administration, declaring in the fall of 1858 that Douglas's re-election to the Senate would be "a calamity to the Democratic party."[20] Until the very eve of the presidential election, the Conway-Johnson Dynasty expressed only contempt for the "traitorous" senator from Illinois.[21]

The Family was not completely in agreement on Stephen Douglas. The "Little Giant" still had a few prominent supporters in the Arkansas political establishment. Among them were Congressman Albert Rust of El Dorado and state Representative Thompson Flourney of Desha County, former Speaker of the House.[22] As Speaker, Flournoy had played a key role in frustrating the attempt by the Dynasty and Governor Roane to have Arkansas repudiate the Compromise of 1850. It was even rumored

94

that Flournoy had strong ambitions to be Douglas's vice-presidential running mate in the election of 1860.[23] What the Douglas forces lacked were
not leaders but strong press support. Douglas enjoyed backing only by
the Van Buren *Press,* the Pine Bluff *Jeffersonian Independent,* and the
Pocahontas *Advertiser* in northeastern Arkansas, publications which
firmly believed that only Douglas could unite both sections of the Democratic party and defeat the notorious "Black Republicans" in 1860.[24] The
Pocahontas *Advertiser* said, in the fall of 1859, that Douglas "is the man
for the North, the man for the South, and he is, emphatically, the Man for
the Union!"[25]

As the presidential contest approached, the split between Buchanan
and Douglas supporters was not the only source of division in the state
Democratic party. Representative Hindman was as usual following a different drummer. Since founding his own newspaper in Helena in 1856,
Hindman was characterized as the "Apostle of dis-union."[26] When his
second paper premiered in Little Rock during fall of 1859, the editor
promulgated the "right of secession."[27] Hindman's *Old Line Democrat* favored the strict enforcement of all national fugitive slave laws, federal
protection of slavery in all U.S. territories, and the reopening of the
foreign slave trade.[28] Although the Conway-Johnson Dynasty had traditionally aligned itself with the secession wing of the national party,
Hindman clearly intended to "out-Southern" them on every major issue.

The Douglas doctrine of popular sovereignty was no better, in Hindman's view, than the odious position of the "Black Republicans." The
Douglas solution gave no absolute guarantee of slave-property rights in
the territories, and according to Hindman, it was nothing more than a
ruse for excluding slavery from all territories in the future. Republicans
at least were clear about their intentions to restrict slavery's expansion.
Since the U.S. Supreme Court had ruled in 1857 that slaves were no
more than human chattel, the South could now legally claim federal protection for slave property in all U.S. possessions. Without such protection, the South's equal property rights would be ignored and it could then
easily justify its withdrawal from the Union.[29] As one of Hindman's back-
ers commented in early 1860: "The people of Arkansas are with the South
on the questions growing out of our national territorial policy."[30]

Since Hindman and the Dynasty shared similar views on slavery in the
territories, neither favored Douglas's nomination in 1860. The Dynasty,

however, expressed its willingness to support the Illinois senator if he became the standard bearer of the national party.[31] As an organization that put much stock in party loyalty and harmony, the Dynasty was leaving a door open in case Douglas could gather the party under his control. Hindman's faction, on the other hand, owed allegiance to nothing except the personal will of its leader and his radical pro-slavery principles. Hindman's paper in Little Rock declared defiantly it would not support Douglas even if he were nominated.[32] As early as December 1859, it assumed an editorial position that the "mere election of a 'Black Republican'" would be justifiable cause and signal for the immediate disruption of the Union."[33] Not even the Dynasty would go that far, for it preferred to decide what to do when and if such an unhappy event should come about.[34] While Family leaders like Senator Johnson might see disunion as something sorrowful and painful, yet nevertheless inevitable, Hindman's camp considered secession advantageous and desirable.[35]

In the national House of Representatives as well as in his own state, Congressman Hindman used the most inflammatory language to promote slavery. He threw the House into disorder during his first term with a two-day address entitled: "That Black Republican Bible: The Helper Book." A native North Carolinian, Hinton Rowan Helper had to flee the South after his book, *The Impending Crisis of the South: How to Meet It,* was published in 1857. Helper had argued in this work that slavery was impoverishing the nonslaveholder of the South, and thus this group should revolt against the planter slavocracy and abolish "the peculiar institution." Helper's book raised the specter of a poor white revolt, and this was indeed ominous to slaveholders as most whites did not own slaves. Since the Republican candidate for the Speaker of the House had once routinely endorsed Helper's work, Hindman accused the Republicans of being traitorous revolutionaries.[36] A Republican congressman from Ohio recalled the Arkansas delegate bitterly as "an irreconcilable man." "No one," he said, "could eat more fire in a given time in connection with southern questions in that Congress. While he was on the floor of the House, it seemed as if he was perpetually anxious for a duel."[37] In the halls of Congress and outside, Hindman would not spurn an opportunity for violence. In a style reminiscent of former Arkansas Senator Solon Borland and reinforcing the state's reputation in the Eastern press, Hindman physically assaulted Republican Congressman Charles Van Wyck of

New York in front of a Washington hotel in March, 1860. For this Hindman received some favorable press coverage back home.[38]

Besides such antics in the nation's capital, Representative Hindman also distinguished himself from the Dynasty by his strenuous demands for the reopening of the foreign slave trade, which had been closed by federal legislation since 1808. More than any other, this issue separated Hindman from the Family on national affairs. His press argued the usual rationale for bringing more slaves from overseas: "The African Negro will be unquestionably benefited morally, religiously, and socially, and the South will assume, then, her position, vouchsafed by heaven, in all walks of life."[39]

Even a few of Hindman's partisans winced at the extremity of this position. The *Jeffersonian Independent* in Pine Bluff called the reopening of the foreign slave trade "a doubtful policy and a dubious experiment."[40] The Conway-Johnson elite, with years of office-holding behind them and a shrewd perception gained from long decades of political power, understood clearly the consequences of such a demand. "The reopening of the slave trade is simply a question of the dissolution of the Union," said the *True Democrat*, ". . . that trade can only be resumed when the Union is broken to pieces."[41]

By comparison with other Southern states, Arkansas was not a major slaveholding state. It was, however, a developing community that needed labor and desired especially slave labor. Most antebellum Southerners, including those in Arkansas, saw slavery as an economic necessity and the ownership of slaves the main vehicle to wealth and social prestige. Whether in the hills or the lowlands, the average yeoman identified his dignity with his white skin and strove to see that Arkansas was a "white folk's democracy."[42] Knowing the pride and prejudice of the common white and his need and desire for black slaves, Hindman held before the Arkansas audience the impossible dream of future African slave importation. Let others, especially the Conway-Johnson Dynasty, quake at the end result of such positions. Hindman knew only that the posture of a swaggering secessionist produced a response that helped his political career.

Curiously, Hindman's demand for new slaves from Africa found support among the state's leading old-line Whig Know-Nothing journal in Little Rock, the *Gazette*. As leading spokesman for the old "opposition," editor Danley blamed the whole sectional dispute on national Democrats, who were "ridden with demagogues and who have appealed to the passions and prejudices of the people rather than their patriotism."[43] Like most of his fellow Southerners, Danley had no moral qualms about slavery, for he felt the institution had been "sanctioned in the Bible and by all other nations, Christian or Heathen . . . since the earliest history of the world."[44] In the same editorial, Danley gave a blunt and racist justification for the institution:

Slavery must exist in some form in all countries, and we prefer that the Negro be the slave rather than the white man. The African is the inferior race, and it is fit that he should serve the superior white man—especially as in this condition of slavery in this country, he advances as far as an African can advance, and when freed, falls back into the habits and status more degrading than that of his savage condition in his native country.[45]

Danley called for a reopening of the slave trade because he believed it would bring Africans to civilization and help a frontier state like Arkansas grow and prosper.[46]

As a conservative, Danley believed an answer to the sectional crisis lay in economic, not political, independence. The *Gazette* editor proposed that the South boycott Northern goods and develop Southern industry. He called for vigorous interstate trade among slaveholding states and more direct trade with England and France, which meant that the cotton South could bypass Yankee merchants and middlemen.[47] If the South became economically and educationally independent of the North, Danley reasoned, it could then stay in the Union without having to worry about Northern attitudes and opinions.[48] Far from being a disunionist, the Little Rock editor planned to keep the states united by having the Old South become more independent of the North. He was cautiously optimistic about the future, for he thought that the American people were "too sagacious, intelligent, and ambitious to suffer the severance of the Union, merely for the sake of appeasing the dismal howl of a handful of harebrained fanatics."[49] For president, Danley suggested Winfield Scott or Sam Houston of Texas, conservatives whom he thought could unite both sections of the country.[50]

Other members of Arkansas's Whiggery were not as sanguine about the future of the Union or the legitimacy of slavery. Judge John Brown of Camden predicted sorrowfully in 1856 that the Union would not last five years longer, that the "Democratic party will be the power," and that the "slavery question the pretext by which traitors of the Ultra-section South as well as the higher law men of the North will use to consummate their traitorous motto of Rule or Ruin."[51] Jesse Turner of Van Buren, an ex-Whig politician and prominent jurist, was less sure than Danley about the rightness of slavery. Writing his fiancée in Pittsburgh, Turner, a devout Methodist, defended slavery on the ground that it brought the blessings of civilization and Christianity to the African Negro. Yet he admitted that "nothing makes it right in the abstract for a superior race to hold an inferior race in bondage simply because they are inferior."[52] Although the state's old opposition might differ on slavery or the prospects for the Federal Union, their views never had any real impact on public policy because they could not obtain political power. Perennial outsiders, the Whigs would have to leave it up to the state Democrats to play a significant role in the presidential election of 1860. That role would begin whenever the Democrats assembled for their quadrennial convention in Little Rock and assumed the task of choosing delegates to the national convention.

When the convention opened in early April, the delegates were already contentious because the Family and Hindman were fighting bitterly over the nomination of Richard H. Johnson for governor. With that unhappy chore behind it, the convention turned to delegate selection for the national convention. The assembly consisted of Douglasites, Dynasty members, and Hindman supporters, all vying to send their own hand-picked politicians to the national convention in Charleston. As one might suspect, a Hindman supporter, Napoleon Burrow, introduced a series of resolutions instructing the state delegates to withdraw from the national convention if it refused to call for federal protection of slavery in the territories.[53] The resolutions were assigned to a platform committee dominated by Family members and Douglasites.[54] When the committee reported back to the full convention, it was clear that the platform had been written by the Conway-Johnson Dynasty. It repudiated Douglas and popular sovereignty and called for no restrictions on the slave-property rights of Southerners in the western territories. Yet the committee's report did not specifically call for a walkout if these demands were not met.[55] The two Hindman members of the committee filed a minority report declaring their support for slave protection in the western territories and stipulating that meaningful support of slavery in the territories must be accepted by the national convention before they could nominate a candidate for the presidency.[56] What the delegates should do in the event the national convention rejected their proposal was left unanswered.[57] Incredibly, the convention adopted the minority report as instructions for the delegates.[58] The Dynasty apparently accepted it on instruction in order to prevent the Hindman faction from carrying the divisions within the state party to the floor of the national convention. Thus, after defeating the Hindman insurgents, the Dynasty turned around and offered them a victory. The Family would reserve to itself the all-important task of naming the delegates. Although the Dynasty must have felt it had outmaneuvered the Hindman faction, the platform represented a real victory for the Helena congressman and his supporters. They had intimidated the Dynasty sufficiently so that Arkansas's delegates were to follow the most extreme Southern position. The only retreat from this radicalism was that delegates were not explicitly ordered to walk out of the convention if it failed to adopt a slave code for the U.S. territories. The Dynasty had been forced to take the more radical ground; in this fight with the Hindman faction it could not afford to appear soft on slavery.

After the Dynasty had conceded on the instructions to delegates, it proceeded to pick a delegation of its own liking. Of eight delegates chosen, only one was a Douglas supporter—a dissenting member of the Family, Thompson Flournoy—and one was a Hindmanite, Napoleon Burrow. Other members of the delegation were all closely related to and allied with the Dynasty.[59] It was not a group that could be described as moderate and open to national reconciliation. They were seven to one against Douglas and armed with instructions to demand the most extreme southern position on slavery in the territories, a plank that the Illinois senator and his Northern Democrats would never accept.

Democrats from around the nation gathered in Charleston, South Carolina, a city long noted for its charm, beauty, and fanatical disunionism, in late April. In such uncongenial surroundings, the "Little Giant" from Illinois hoped to cap his political career with a presidential nomination. Southern radicals, led by William Lowndes Yancey of Alabama, were just as intent on thwarting Douglas's plans even if it meant disrupting the party or the Union. Southern extremists were pushing for adoption of the Alabama platform, a demand that the convention endorse Congressional protection of slavery in the western territories. If the convention failed to adopt this plank, delegates from most of the Deep South would walk out.[60] Senator Douglas was not ignorant of these designs, but he steadfastly refused to yield to any pressure from the South. Months before the convention he had warned his Southern colleagues in the Senate: "I do not believe a Democratic candidate can carry even one of the Democratic states of the North on a platform that makes it the duty of the Federal government to force a people of a territory to have slavery if they do not want it."[61]

Since the Northern Democrats would not and could not accept the Alabama platform, representatives from that state led five other delegations out of the assembly, all cheered by most of Charleston's citizenry. Napoleon Burrow led two other Arkansas delegates from the hall.[62] The Georgia delegation withdrew the next day, along with three more representatives from Arkansas. Of the original eight-man state delegation, only Douglasite Thompson Flournoy and John Stirman of Fayetteville remained.[63]

Stunned by the walkout and knowing that division meant certain defeat in November, the Democrats decided to adjourn and reconvene in Baltimore on June 18. Before the dispirited Charleston assembly dispersed, it heard Flournoy of Arkansas plead with fellow Democrats: "Let us have no more talk of sections. We know no North, no South, no East, no West, . . . where Democrats are concerned."[64] Noble sentiments they were, but the time had passed when such rhetoric reflected reality.

The walkout by six members of the Arkansas delegation was an unprecedented departure from their instructions. Unlike the Alabama contingent and other Southern delegations, the Arkansas representatives were explicitly ordered not to walk out of the convention at any time or for any reason.[65] Moreover, except for about one-third of the Delaware delegation, Arkansas was the only state outside the lower South where most of the contingent joined in a walkout.[66] One might have expected the Hindman radical, Napoleon Burrow, to leave the hall, but not, ordinarily, five members of the Dynasty. It must be recalled, however, that Senator Johnson had always wanted to align Arkansas more closely with the lower South, and his wish would be fulfilled when most of the state's delegation joined with that section in a withdrawal from the national convention. While the Dynasty could tolerate a few Unionist Democrats and Douglas supporters within its ranks—men like Flournoy, Rust, and even Stirman—it still followed the pro-slavery, states' rights line laid down by Senator Johnson. Since two of Senator Johnson's relatives were in the delegation, it was not surprising that most had met with representatives of seven states in the lower South to stage the walkout.[67] Although not strictly authorized to depart, most of the Family-appointed delegates easily followed the lead of other Deep South contingents.

Reactions in the Arkansas press to the breakup of the Charleston convention depended upon each newspaper's particular political stance. Speaking for much of the state's Whig-oriented opposition, Danley declared in the *Gazette* that "The Democratic party has run its course and is too rotten to be held together, even by the cohesive power of public plunder."[68] The Family's paper in Little Rock, the *True Democrat*, treated Stirman and Flournoy with sympathy and blamed the breakup of the convention on "Douglas and his odious doctrine of squatter sovereignty. . . . Until he is out of the way, there will neither be peace nor harmony in our ranks."[69] The Hindman press, of course, gave the most extreme view, calling Stirman and Flournoy "traitors" for not joining the rest of the delegation in the walkout. At the Hindman-dominated congressional district meeting in May at Dover, the convention denounced the two who stayed, and declared that they had forfeited their seats.[70] Hindman's paper in Little Rock reiterated the position that it "would never support Stephen Douglas for the Presidency, whether nominated by a convention or not!"[71] Stirman and Flournoy issued public statements in late May and early June defending their action at Charleston, truthfully maintaining that the delegation had never been authorized to withdraw from that assembly.[72] Most of the newspapers, however, came down on them, with only the Douglasite Van Buren *Press* vigorously remaining in their defense.[73]

As the state Democrats looked forward to the Baltimore convention in June, congressional district assemblies in Dover and Arkadelphia named delegates. A self-appointed Douglas meeting was held at Madison in eastern Arkansas to pick a delegation for the second Democratic convention.[74] The Dynasty tried to bring order out of this confusion when it called for only the original delegates to return to the reconvening national convention.[75] Senator Johnson also issued a conciliatory note: "We are unwilling to take the final step in the dismemberment of that [Democratic] party until the last hope of obtaining justice for the South is destroyed or abandoned."[76] Two weeks later, in late May, Johnson and Arkansas's other senator, William King Sebastian, joined with several other prominent Senate Democrats in calling for party unity and for only the original delegates to attend the Baltimore meeting.[77]

Despite such directives, four Arkansas delegations appeared in Baltimore, each clamoring for recognition, but only the original eight-man contingent was let in.[78] The Douglas forces controlled the credentials committee and they insured that enough of their delegates were allowed in to secure Douglas's nomination. Delegations in some Southern states were replaced with Douglas men. Realizing that the Illinois senator had the votes for nomination, angry Southerners from the lower and upper South, together with a few malcontented western delegations, walked out. Joining the withdrawal were the six Arkansas delegates who had stormed out of the Charleston convention.[79]

Undaunted, the remaining delegates proceeded to nominate Douglas, who won on the first ballot. For his running mate the assembly chose Congressman Herschel Johnson of Georgia. The convention's platform fully endorsed Douglas's much maligned concept of popular sovereignty. Although he had not joined the first walkout, John Stirman left the Baltimore convention before it nominated Douglas. Thompson Flournoy was the only Arkansan who stayed in the assembly to see the nomination of his hero,[80] and returned to his state to campaign vigorously on his behalf.[81] For this, Flournoy was virtually read out of the Dynasty.

Arkansas delegates could later be found in Richmond amid a rump convention comprising mostly Southerners and a few anti-Douglas men from the West and North. In this harmonious gathering, Southern delegates could virtually write their own dream platform of federal protection of slavery in the western territories and strict enforcement of the Fugitive Slave laws. The assembly then nominated the incumbent vice-president, John C. Breckinridge of Kentucky, for the presidency and as his running mate it chose Senator Joseph Lane of Oregon.[82]

The Breckinridge-Lane campaign would have quick support from both the Conway-Johnson Dynasty and the Hindman faction.[83] About a month after the Baltimore convention, the Family admitted that it would have supported Douglas had he a more sound Southern platform.[84] Hindman's fire-breathing on the Dynasty's left gave the Family no real room in which to maneuver. Already embroiled in a tough fight with Hindman in the state election, the Dynasty could ill afford to have itself characterized as soft on slavery's expansion. The Family knew that it would surely lose the state contest if Hindman out-positioned it on the issue of white men's hegemony in life, labor and culture.

Even if the Family wanted to move away from a more radical position, that would have been difficult considering its decade-long association with Southern extremism. This meant that on issues of slavery and union, few real differences separated Hindman from the Dynasty. An ex-Whig at Fayetteville wrote to a compatriot in the same city in May 1860: "Hindman and the Johnsons are at odds, but in this struggle they will come together for they are both disunionists."[85]

While the national Democrats bickered and splintered, another national convention consisting mostly of ex-Whigs and Know-Nothings assembled in Baltimore in mid-May. It styled itself the Constitutional Union party and nominated two elderly former Whig senators for president and vice-president, John Bell of Tennessee and Edward Everett of Massachusetts. Their platform innocuously proclaimed their support for the Constitution and the enforcement of the laws.[86] A handful of Arkansans, led by the editor of the Gazette, Christopher Danley, attended the convention.[87] By the end of May, the Gazette and the rest of the old-line Whig Know-Nothing press endorsed the Bell-Everett ticket.[88] Danley unfurled the banner of the new party: "The Democratic party is denationalized, demoralized, and disintegrated. It is the sectional party of the North against the South and the South against the North. . . . The Constitutional Union party is the only one that can save the country from destruction and the greedy hands of spoilsmen."[89]

In the same month that the Constitutional Union party held its meeting, the six-year-old Republican party had its second national convention in Chicago. In a newly-built structure known as the "Wigwam," front-runner William Seward of New York lost his bid for the presidential nomination to a relatively unknown political newcomer, Abraham Lincoln of Illinois. Lincoln had served a term in Congress as a Whig in the 1840s, but had not been in public office since that time. He had gained some prominence as the unsuccessful Republican opponent of Senator Stephen Douglas in 1858. In a series of well-publicized debates with Douglas, Lincoln had distinguished himself as a sharp orator and a perceptive thinker. The Republicans selected ex-Democrat Hannibal Hamlin of Maine as Lincoln's running mate. While their platform called for internal improvements, a national banking system and a Homestead Act, the plank that the South found the most offensive called upon Congress to restrict slavery from the western territories.[90] Although the Republicans repeatedly insisted that they would not tamper with slavery in the existing states and would even enforce all Fugitive Slave laws, most of the South felt that to restrict slavery's expansion would be nothing short of condemning the institution to gradual extinction. For this reason the South regarded the Republicans as disguised abolitionists, men to be scorned, feared and hated. The Lincoln-Hamlin ticket would not appear on ballots below the Southern boundary of Virginia-Kentucky-Missouri.[91]

Although the Republican ticket was absent on the Arkansas ballot, the *True Democrat* did print the Republican platform on its front page, but an editorial in the same issue warned: "We do not believe that Lincoln or any abolitionist can ever be President of the *United* States. The Fourth of March that sees him inaugurated will see two empires where there is now one Confederacy."[92] Time would make these words prophetic.

During much of the summer, the August state election preoccupied the minds of the voters and the pages of the press. Yet even before the returns were counted, supporters of Douglas, Bell, and Breckinridge were canvassing for votes.

Of the three groups, the Douglas contingent was undoubtedly the weakest. A major Douglas rally was held in the capital on August 15 to choose electors and launch the campaign. On hand to greet the crowd were Congressman Albert Rust and Thompson Flournoy, the real leaders of the Douglas forces in the state.[93] A sorely needed Douglas paper in Little Rock began publication on August 21, calling itself the *National Democrat,* edited by Dr. Cincinnatus V. Meador.[94] The paper and its editor soon came under bitter attack from most of the Breckinridge Democratic papers, which dominated most of the state press. The editor of the pro-Breckinridge paper in Camden referred to Dr. Meador as "a low, contemptible, base-born, heaven-despised, hell-deserving coward" who was also "a filthy, lousy scavenger."[95]

At first it appeared that the Douglas campaign might have real promise. With its new journal and the support of such prominent Democrats as Rust, Flournoy and former Governor Thomas Drew, Douglas forces were ready to push hard for the Illinois senator.[96] Rust without doubt was the most effective weapon in the Douglas arsenal. When he debated Hindman early in the campaign, even the *Old Line Democrat,* which usually gave the Hindman opponents nothing but ridicule, admitted that Rust was a "man of decided talent, a real debater, and, in the advance of a good cause, could make a telling speech." [97] So skilled was the El Dorado congressman as a stump speaker that Senator Johnson refused to debate him. [98] Late in the campaign, the Breckinridge forces made a determined effort to avoid giving him a crowd to address. Judge John Brown of Camden recorded in his diary that Rust was refused permission to speak at a Family-sponsored Breckinridge rally in that city. [99]

Despite Rust's efforts and those by the *National Democrat* in Little Rock and the always-loyal Van Buren *Press,* the Arkansas campaign for Douglas never really had a chance. Unlike the opposition, it did not have much financial support and thus could not sponsor barbecues, parades, or other festivities. Voters were accustomed to such treats, and they probably thought the Douglas forces inadequate for their failure to provide them. [100] Beyond financial imperfections, politicians who supported the "Little Giant" in Arkansas were clearly outside the state's political establishment. Drew was merely a former governor from the 1840s, Flournoy no longer enjoyed the Family's inner circle, and Rust had fallen into disfavor from the Dynasty for his support of Hindman in the state election. The Douglas camp simply did not have money, newspapers, and political backing to win over the people, especially when it also had to fight state Democratic party machinery.

The Bell campaign was not saddled with such limitations. It enjoyed the support of the old-line Whigs' press, which was scattered through much of eastern and southern Arkansas, adding a paper in September 1860: the Des Arc *Constitutional Union.* [101] Many Bell supporters were wealthy former Whigs, so the Constitutional Union party in Arkansas could afford to stage huge rallies and barbecues. One such event in Washington, Arkansas, drew almost a thousand people—a large meeting for that period. [102] Judge John Brown was the honorary chairman of a rally in Camden, his hometown. He left an account of this political festival: "The Bell mass meeting. Beautiful day. The longest, grandest, and most imposing meeting ever seen in Camden. Our own, and Washington's Brass Bands, Barbecue dinner, marches, procession, horseback and carriages at night. The light procession, five hundred transparencies— marched through the whole length of our beautiful young city." [103]

In addition to big rallies, Bell forces enjoyed a good deal of press support in presenting their case to the public. Their newspapers stressed that only the Bell-Everett ticket could unite both sections of the country, thus keeping the "Black Republicans" from obtaining the presidency.[104] Even Solon Borland, that old nemesis of the Dynasty, returned to Arkansas to campaign for Bell.[105] Unlike the Douglas camp, the Bell campaign had the money and enough newspaper support to perhaps carry the state for the Tennessee politician.

That possibility led to bitter tension between the Bell and Breckinridge efforts. A Breckinridge supporter in Clarksville pulled a gun on a Bell elector in the middle of a public debate between the two men.[106] With a perception rare among Arkansas's editors, Danley linked the Breckinridge candidacy with the cause of disunion. He especially tied Breckinridge to William Yancey of Alabama, a man considered to be one of the most extreme Southern radicals. The *Gazette* editor accused the Southern Democrats of being disingenuous secessionists:

They dare not nominate their leader, Yancey, to effect their treasonable ends. They continue to support Mr. Breckinridge in full view of the foregone conclusion of his defeat, with no other end or object than the hope that, by dividing and distracting the South, they may be instrumental in electing Lincoln, the Black Republican candidate, when they intend making another desperate effort to dissolve the Union.[107]

As election day neared, Danley's pleas grew more urgent, as he sensed perhaps the final outcome: "We appeal to every man who is a Union man, who is ready to work for the Union, and who would not follow after the false gods of the Yancey disunionists."[108]

With both the Hindman faction and the Dynasty supporting the Breckinridge campaign, the Kentuckian had the best chance to carry Arkansas. But after an almost eighteen-month-old political war the Dynasty and Hindman camps had a difficult time adjusting to cooperation. More than a month after the state election, the Searcy *Eagle* accused Hindman's followers of being mere "slaves" to "Marse Tom" Hindman.[109] For its part, the Hindman press made it clear it would not tolerate any move by the Family to re-elect Senator Robert Johnson once the legislature convened in November. The *Old Line Democrat* denounced any such effort as "a bold and desperate struggle to retrieve the fortunes of the Johnson family."[110] The paper solemnly warned that "the people of Arkansas had declared that they do not intend to be trammelled any longer by the fetters of an unjust, oppressive, clique government imposed on them by the usurpations of a self-constituted and self-perpetuated Dynasty."[111]

In spite of the lingering antagonism, the Hindman-Dynasty alliance was a formidable political unit. It controlled almost every newspaper in the state. The towns of Fort Smith, Searcy, El Dorado, Napoleon, and Magnolia had only Breckinridge publications.[112] The Family and Hindman differed only in the manner and style of campaigning for the Kentuckian. Hindman's press appeared unabashedly radical, even going so far as to print speeches by William Yancey.[113] It was particularly vicious to Stephen Douglas, portraying him as a traitor, a man who made the constitutionally-sanctioned right of slaveholding dependent upon the whim of a majority in any given territory.[114] Hindman canvassed the state for Breckinridge, relishing another challenge and sensing once again that his cause would be victorious.[115]

The Conway-Johnson Dynasty's approach differed from Hindman's. Its newspapers discreetly downplayed any talk of disunion or any association with such firebreathing radicals as Yancey. The Dynasty's paper stressed that the candidacy of Breckinridge rested on the sound constitutional basis of the Dred Scott case of 1857. If slaves were indeed property, as this famous decision maintained, then Breckinridge and the whole Southern position stood on strong legal ground. According to the *True Democrat* the vice-president was the only man for the Union, the Constitution, and the rights of Southern property owners.[116]

In defending the Breckinridge candidacy and the whole institution of slavery, the Dynasty found welcome support from an old adversary, Albert Pike. The ex-Whig editor and Know-Nothing political leader penned an eloquent and cogently-argued treatise on the rights of states in regard to the Federal government. In the fashion of John C. Calhoun, Pike maintained that the Union was a mere compact of states from which any state could withdraw if its property rights were not protected by the general government.[117] Although it usually tried to avoid any real discussion of disunion when it campaigned for Breckinridge, the Dynasty had always held Pike's view of the Constitution, and his treatise could be used to sway public opinion towards future dissolution of the Union.

Astutely analyzing the state political scene, the Dynasty also understood that Bell, not Douglas, was their greatest adversary. The Bell-

Everett ticket was characterized by the Family's Little Rock newspaper as "headed by an old politician with a dubious record covered in voluminous speeches which no one ever read; and the other is a Fourth of July orator whose splendor has been exhausted in the decoration of commonplace ideas and threadbare aphorisms." [118]

The Breckinridge candidacy received added support from the reports of abolitionist-incited slave arson and rebellion in neighboring Texas. [119] The Searcy *Eagle* said that roads from east Texas were clogged with whites fleeing the slave terror. [120] Accounts like these caused much fear and apprehension, especially in southwestern Arkansas. Since these troubles in Texas were supposed to be inspired by abolitionists and "Black Republicans" posing as ministers and booksellers, [121] many foreigners and strangers found themselves under heavy suspicion in communities in southwestern Arkansas. Henry Lay, the Episcopal Missionary Bishop for the "South-West," wrote his wife from Washington, Arkansas, that his book agent, George Wolfe, had been a victim of harassment and mistrust. In a letter written during late September, Bishop Lay sorrowfully recorded his own concern over the situation: "Such is the excited state of the public mind that he [Wolfe] finds himself suspected everywhere. They have stopped him as an abolitionist, and thrown every obstacle in his way." [122] Lincoln and all the other "Black Republicans" were given indirect blame for the incidents in Texas, and the Family's presses were always quick to remind voters of what might happen if the power of the Federal government did not support the Southern slaveholding system. [123]

Late in the campaign, the Dynasty's papers claimed that the Douglas-Bell factions in Arkansas were going to merge—a way of discrediting the Bell campaign. [124] This prophecy never materialized, largely owing to the traditional antagonism between Douglas Democrats and Bell's old-line Whig supporters. On the very eve of the election, the Fayetteville *Arkansian* made this final appeal for the Southern Democratic ticket: "A vote for Breckinridge-Lane is to show Lincoln and all the Northern Abolitionists that you will resist unto death all approaches against Southern Rights and Privileges, to teach them a lesson they ought long ago to have learned." [125] Judge John Brown of Camden wrote in his diary on election day, November 6, that "This is the most important day to the United States and, perhaps, to mankind since July 4, 1776." [126] Obviously, many other Arkansans were aware of the seriousness of this plebiscite, for a larger percentage of eligible voters showed up at the polls than in any previous presidential election.[127]

Lincoln won the national election, sweeping almost every electoral vote in the North, but received only a little less than 40 percent of the popular vote nationwide. Douglas ran second in the popular vote but could carry only Missouri and a few New Jersey votes in the electoral college. Bell, fourth in the popular vote, won more electoral votes than Douglas. The former Tennessee senator won the votes of Virginia and Kentucky, as well as his own home state. Arkansas and ten other slaveholding states gave their electoral vote to Breckinridge, who ran third in the popular vote and second in the electoral college.[128] In the Arkansas returns, Breckinridge received 28,783 votes to Bell's 20,094 and Douglas's 5,227. There was no recorded vote for Lincoln in Arkansas.[129] The percentage for Breckinridge statewide was a solid 53 percent, highest in the upper South. (For the percentage of Arkansas's vote for Breckinridge as compared with other slaveholding states, see Table 7a.)[130]

When the returns are examined by county, the traditional party alignments of Democrats and Whigs are the dominant political patterns.[131] Douglas carried no county, but he did best in Jefferson and Crawford counties, which were served by newspapers supporting him. Bell found his greatest strength in the traditional Whig counties of eastern and southern Arkansas, but he also did well in the more urban-commercial river towns such as Little Rock, Van Buren, Washington and Fort Smith, all strong centers of Arkansas Whiggery. Bell actually won a plurality in the delta counties of Chicot, Crittenden, Desha, Independence, and St. Francis, yet he carried a majority of the vote only in Mississippi County. The Tennessean almost captured Phillips, Monroe, Jackson, and Prairie counties. Outside of these lowland areas, Bell won Pulaski and Crawford counties, with their respective towns, Little Rock and Van Buren. He came within thirty votes of winning Sebastian County, and its largest community, Fort Smith.[132]

While the old-line Whigs generally voted for the Constitutional Union ticket, yeomen in the northwest, usually the stronghold of the state Democratic party, once again followed their political leaders and voted for the Kentuckian. Most of the region went heavily for Breckinridge, and only in Crawford, Searcy, Washington and White counties did voters return an unfavorable majority. Curiously, of the five northwestern counties that would eventually become centers of mountain Unionism, only Searcy County withheld a majority for Breckinridge. The others voted solidly for him.[133]

It is easy to see that these yeomen were acting out of party loyalty rather than a clear understanding of the issues or the candidates. As Michael Dougan has pointed out, most people in the region could not read and therefore could not grasp the full importance of this election.[134] It was natural that rural, illiterate, somewhat isolated hill farmers would vote more out of party loyalty and political tradition than upon the complex issues of the day. With both Hindman and the Dynasty promoting Breckinridge as the true Democratic nominee, the mountain yeomen found it easy to accept this political advice.

Breckinridge's support was particularly strong within the booming cotton producing counties of southern and southwestern Arkansas, including also the Ouachita mountain counties. He had pluralities in every county in this area and majorities in all of them except for Hempstead and Columbia counties. (For the widespread strength Breckinridge had throughout this area and much of the state see Figure 7b.)[135] It was especially this southern section of the state that was experiencing a strong migration from the lower South. Most people in this part of Arkansas were small slaveholders or lowland farmers who had come to the region in hopes of eventually rising to planter status. To them, the Breckinridge candidacy offered the strongest pro-slavery platform, and slavery provided the symbol for both wealth and prestige.[136]

When these election returns are compared with the per capita wealth for whites of each county, it becomes clear that the poorer voter identified with the candidacy of Vice President Breckinridge. Of the top fifteen counties listed in Table 6c, five voted for Bell, five provided a majority for Breckinridge, and the other five gave the incumbent vice-president only a plurality. Of the middle twenty-five counties listed in the above mentioned table, three went for Bell, six returned anti-Breckinridge majorities, and the remaining sixteen handed the Kentuckian a majority of their votes. Of the fifteen poorest counties, however, all but Searcy County piled up majorities for Breckinridge. While two-thirds of the wealthiest counties either voted for Bell or returned anti-Breckinridge majorities, the Kentucky presidential candidate won majorities from three-fifths of the middle per capita counties and from almost all of the poorest counties.

The election reflected not only a Whig-vs-Democrat pattern but a rich-vs-poor alignment as well.

Nothing seemed really resolved when this long election year was at last over. In both state and nation, what had seemed a political impossibility at the beginning of the year had actually happened. The long-standing Arkansas Dynasty had tasted its first major defeat since statehood. On the national level, a political neophyte from Illinois won the office of the presidency on the ticket of a party that had only existed for six years. The people had spoken on both the state and national levels, but no one could accurately judge the full impact of the elections.

While many might have been puzzled by the events, Congressman Thomas Hindman must have been quite satisfied. After all, he had not reached the age of thirty-three and already he had obtained real power and prestige in his adopted state. In less than two years he had instigated and led the first successful rebellion against the powerful Conway-Johnson Dynasty and then had formed an alliance with his former enemies, carrying Arkansas for John Breckinridge, the candidate most associated with Southern disunionism. It had truly been a remarkable year for the young politician. He had shown a keen ability to arouse the passions and prejudices of the common white yeomen in Arkansas, and to the average white farmer he had become the champion of the cherished ideal of a "White folks democracy" in the Old South.[137]

Hindman's successful revolt against the Dynasty caused Arkansas politics to resemble the competitiveness of other states in the upper South. This action came, however, when the state was most wedded to cotton and slavery. Arkansas virtually acknowledged this new cultural and economic reality when it gave a small yet solid majority vote for John C. Breckinridge in the presidential election of 1860. Ironically, by freeing the state from Family rule, Hindman's rebellion allowed for a new political realignment to take place. The contours of this new arrangement would be the societal and geographical differences within the state. The issue of secession would finally make state politics reflect the true socio-economic contrasts within antebellum Arkansas.

VIII

Division Over Disunion

The Realignment of Arkansas Politics
During the Winter of 1860–1861

On November 11, 1860, Judge John Brown of Camden fretfully inscribed in his diary, "The news of Lincoln's election is confirmed. . . . I am [so] much concerned about the fate of our government, and prospects for individual ruin, that I do not sleep at night more than half my usual time."[1] A perceptive, conservative old-line Whig, Judge Brown understood the crisis facing the nation. Those "designing traitors" who had supported Breckinridge had finally caused the election of that "Black Republican Abraham Lincoln." Now he was sure that "fanatics" in South Carolina and Alabama were preparing to "disrupt our happy government by following the diabolical course of secession."[2] Later, Brown recorded in his diary that "only the activity of the day draws my mind off the gloomy foreboding of the future."[3]

Throughout the winter following the election of Lincoln, Arkansans were finally forced to face the issue of disunion. An issue spurned a decade earlier, the 1850s had produced an economic and cultural bonding between Arkansas and the slaveholding states of the Old South. Now there were rumblings of secession in the lower South even before the president-elect was to assume office on March 4, 1861.[4] Would Arkansas join in this movement out of the Federal Union?

That question caused a fundamental realignment of Arkansas politics during the winter of 1860–61. Older political alignments of Democrat and Whig receded before a geophysical division between uplands and lowlands. The two regions had always had their differences. The hills had settled first with immigrants arriving from farther north, and after the great immigration from the slaveholding South to the delta and plains the hills remained a region of yeoman farmers—slaveless farmers. The low-lands became the final frontier for the slaveholding cotton kingdom, find-ing wealth and prosperity based on cotton production and slave labor. But, however great, the differences had little real effect on the permanent political arrangements prior to the Civil War. The antebellum structure arose from territorial factionalism and evolved into Arkansas's two politi-cal parties—the Democrats and the Whigs. Once the issue of secession was injected into state politics after Lincoln's election, however, the older party structures evaporated before a resurging division between hills and flatlands. By the end of the winter of 1860–61, this division based on a geophysical split seemed to be tearing the state apart.

Such a division could have been foreseen only by the most astute politi-cal observers in November, 1860. Unlike much of the Deep South, the people and press of Arkansas did not react shrilly to the news of Lincoln's election.[5] The reaction was so mild, in fact, it appeared that the state would have little problem adjusting to the incoming administration.

The old-line Whig press that had supported Bell assumed the lead in calling for calm and caution in the wake of Lincoln's victory. Danley of the *Gazette* editorialized, "Lincoln is elected in a manner prescribed by the law and by the majority prescribed by the Constitution. Let him be inaugurated, let not steps be taken against this administration until he has committed an overt act, which cannot be remedied by law."[6] As a le-galistic conservative, Danley felt that secession was not justified except to protect oneself from illegal aggression by the Federal government. Thus he would declare the legality of secession only as a very last resort. The mere election of a man distasteful to the South hardly constituted solid grounds for disunion.[7] Still very much the anti-Democrat partisan, the *Gazette* editor stated flatly, "A Republican administration can be no worse for the South than was done already by Democratic administrations."[8] Danley still hoped that the Constitutional Union party, Bell's running ticket in 1860, could save the country since "it will be the nucleus around which patriotic, conservative, and constitutional elements must gather to form one great opposition to the Republicans and defeat them in 1864."[9] Danley's conservative sentiments were echoed in the Des Arc *Constitu-*

tional Union, which declared that "Lincoln is not as bad as the Disunionists would have us believe." [10]

Even from most of the Democratic papers came no real cry of alarm
over the election of a Republican. The Douglasite Van Buren *Press* ad-
vised "every good citizen to be cool and calm, and to exercise proper reflection, not to be carried away and run wild with excitement. Lincoln,
after all, faces Democratic majorities in both Houses of Congress." [11]
Even the *True Democrat* in Little Rock, the main mouthpiece of the
Conway-Johnson Family Dynasty and a preeminent Breckinridge newspaper, urged caution and patience. Its main comment after the presidential election was that "the South should not secede because Lincoln
had been elected by only a minority of the people." [12] The Fayetteville
Arkansian, another Family-controlled paper in the northwest, counseled
a wait-and-see approach toward the new president:

Well, the majority rules. We should wait until after his inaugural and see what
course he will pursue. . . . If he refuses to recognize our slaves as property, if he
does not aid in bringing to justice . . . those who may make attempts to steal our
slaves, burn our houses, disregard our laws, and murder our citizens; then damn
him, impeach him, damn him forever, but . . . God forbid he should refuse to do
these things; we hope he will make us a good President, and win the praise and
good will of our foes. [13]

Apparently, then, much of the Arkansas press was willing to accept Lincoln so long as he did not tamper directly with slavery. Since the president-
elect and his party were on record for declaring that they did not intend to
challenge slavery where it already existed, [14] it appeared that Arkansas
could accommodate and live under the new administration. Even the
pro-Breckinridge Fayetteville *Arkansian* spoke only of impeachment, not
secession, if Lincoln did try to tamper directly with slavery. Many of the
state's opinion-makers preferred at first to consider the constitutionally
sanctioned process of impeachment rather than disunion as a method
of redress of any grievances that might emerge from the Republican
presidency.

This conservative posture owed much to the fact that Arkansas had
never been a center of fire-eating disunionism. Due to its persistent frontier status, the state was hesitant to undertake any action that might lead
to a breakup of the general government, upon which it was heavily dependent. Once Lincoln's election seemed assured, most of the state's

press reacted with an instinctive conservatism, perhaps sensing then that the Republican victory threatened the Union. Arkansas may have been well enough oriented to the "peculiar institution" by 1860 to vote for the most pro-slavery presidential candidate,[15] but it was still sufficiently an upper South state to back away from the precipice of secession.

Not all political factions were frightened over the possibility of disunion. Congressman Hindman's newspapers led the way in demanding that Arkansas should follow the path of other slaveholding states in the Deep South. Hindman's Little Rock paper declared that "Lincoln has been deliberately flung in our teeth; there is nothing left for Arkansas to do but to follow the lead of the lower South, in secession or not."[16] The Little Rock *Old Line Democrat* went on to observe that "Our destiny is irrevocably linked with that of the other cotton-growing States; we should not falter for one moment to seek that destiny or pause to deliberate the consequences that may follow."[17] Although most newspapers around the state were busy calling for calm in the face of Lincoln's election, Hindman's press beckoned Arkansas toward disunion. With much truth, the *Old Line Democrat* understood that Arkansas had become "irrevocably linked" to the states of the Old South. In the final test, new economic ties would draw Arkansas towards much of the South in secession.

While the state's press debated the significance and consequences of Lincoln's election, the General Assembly convened for its biennial session. The state also awaited the inauguration of its sixth governor, the only chief executive not selected by the Conway-Johnson Dynasty. Sworn into office on November 15, 1860, during the nation's and the state's gravest crisis, Henry Massie Rector was something of a political novice. He had held no prior major administrative post, and he had won the state election in the summer as Hindman's candidate. No one was sure what course this previously obscure and opportunistic politician would take.

Rector's inaugural address has been the most misconstrued speech in Arkansas history. For more than fifty years, historians have chosen to interpret it as a demand for secession.[18] Actually, Rector's first address dealt more with local matters and was quite moderate in tone. He advocated more money for blind and deaf schools and more funding for common schools, and he proposed state aid to the Memphis-Little Rock railroad.[19] Considering the national crisis, Rector perceptively observed that the state, in the end, might have to choose between "the Union without slavery or slavery without the Union."[20] While he thought the South had good reasons to secede, he felt that a convention of states could probably settle the sectional differences.[21] The only possibility for Arkansas's secession foreseen by Rector was if other Deep South states seceded and there followed an effort by the Federal government to coerce them back into the Union. Then Governor Rector felt that the state would be forced to join her Southern sisters. At this point, however, he dismissed the idea of immediate secession, asking instead for the people to await future development.[22]

It was Hindman, not Governor Rector, who initiated efforts for immediate secession. Hindman and Congressman-elect Edward Gantt addressed the General Assembly on November 24 and 25. Editor Danley of the *Gazette* heard these speeches and described them as "the most ultra and the most inflammatory in nature."[23] George Clarke of Van Buren also heard Hindman and Gantt speak and reported to a friend, "Secession is not a popular doctrine in this legislature; although Hindman is certainly a man of many talents—his speeches will do more harm than any other man in this State."[24] After Hindman's discourse, the legislature took up the question of secession. Family member Francis Terry of Little Rock, a member of the Southern walkout at the Charleston convention the previous spring, introduced a resolution calling upon Arkansas to follow the lead of the cotton growing states in secession. Alfred H. Carrigan of Fayetteville introduced a counter-resolution asking for Arkansas to consult with the upper South states or follow no state at all on secession.[25] Outside of the various resolutions, the assembly tried to evade the issue. One observer wrote in early December: "There is strong Union sentiment pervading the legislature, and I am inclined to believe that nothing will be done to precipitate matters."[26] An indication of such conservatism was the legislature's selection of John Stirman, then of Dardanelle, as secretary of state.[27] Stirman was a loyal member of the Conway-Johnson Dynasty, but had dissented from the Family line during the late presidential contest in support of Stephen Douglas.

For almost a month after the news of Lincoln's election, Arkansas seemed to be politically adrift. Except for Hindman and his faction, no one voiced a demand for secession. This changed when Senator Johnson, leader of the Dynasty, published an open letter to his constituents from Washington, D.C., dated December 1, 1860, which did not reach the state until the middle of the month. In it Johnson said he regarded the secession of the several states as a fact and that "Arkansas must go with them for I would not be willing to remain in the Union with just a fragment of the Southern States subject to the overwhelming power of the North."[28] Johnson's letter came as no surprise, for he had been associated with Southern disunionism for more than a decade. With the disruption of the Union a real possibility, Johnson assumed a major role by trying to pull Arkansas into a future Southern confederacy.[29] His letter signalled that the Family would join Hindman in working for secession. It was the same alliance that had carried Arkansas for Breckinridge by a solid majority vote. On December 21, Senator Johnson and Congressman Hindman penned a joint statement calling for a state convention to consider secession because Arkansas needed to consult "the common council of the South for her protection and future safety."[30] That Johnson and Hindman had co-signed this statement was surprising, since only eleven months earlier they had almost fought a duel.

The Family-Hindman alliance would not be long in making its impact felt upon the General Assembly. Hindmanite Benjamin Du Val of Fort Smith introduced a bill calling for a state convention to consider secession.[31] Secessionists received additional support for Governor Rector in the form of a written address to the legislature on December 11. According to him, secession by Mississippi and Louisiana would leave the state in great peril because her economic lifeline, the lower section of the Mississippi River, would no longer provide free access to Arkansas. Rector believed that Arkansas would become a mere border state, a haven for runaway slaves from the lower South. He also speculated that the federally controlled Indian Territory adjacent to the state's western boundary might become peopled with abolitionists who would stir slaves into rebellion. Since the governor believed that peaceful separation had been possible only before Lincoln's inauguration, he advocated a state convention to pull Arkansas out of the Union immediately. He also asked for the General Assembly to appropriate more money for the militia, and called for restrictions on the further importation of slaves into the state. Rector wanted only slave importation with masters who were willing to settle in Arkansas, so that the state would not become a repository for slaves from neighboring areas.[32] He ended his address on a militaristic note: "The Union of States may no longer be regarded as an existing fact, making it imperatively necessary that Arkansas should gird her loins for the conflict, and put her house in order."[33]

Rector's speech was undoubtedly a persuasive case for disunion. He raised fears of economic strangulation and a slave rebellion unless Arkansas began to act in concert with other Southern states. The specter of events outlined by Rector appeared as vital possibilities to thinking men at that time. Secessionist leadership was in place by mid-December. Senator Johnson, Congressman Hindman, and now Governor Rector all worked actively for disunion. Their cause appeared invincible.

Despite this prestigious triumvirate, the secessionists had to convince a reluctant legislature which refused to be railroaded into a revolutionary act without a clear mandate from the people. The General Assembly honored the governor's request for more money for the militia, but refused to forbid further slave importation. In fact, on January 10, 1861, it suspended the controversial free-black expulsion law of 1859 until 1863.[34] Ignoring appeals from disunionists, the legislature also began the task of choosing someone to replace the retiring Senator Johnson. His term would end on March 4, and secessionists argued that a new senator would be superfluous since Arkansas would be out of the Union by that time.[35]

For its selection of a replacement, the legislature would not have to look too hard for candidates. Congressman Albert Rust of the southern district had campaigned for Johnson's seat throughout the past year. During state elections the previous spring and summer, Rust had received some encouragement from the Hindman insurgents in return for which he had openly sided with Hindman in his struggle with the Dynasty. Much had happened since the summer, including a presidential race in which Hindman and Rust endorsed different presidential candidates. Hindman distanced himself from Rust's Senate candidacy during the fall presidential contest.[36] The Dynasty, of course, considered as a traitor the southern district representative by his assistance to Hindman. Its main newspaper in Little Rock declared in October that Rust would never be able to obtain Johnson's Senate seat.[37] Abandoned by Hindman and hated by the Johnson Family, Rust realized his hopes for the Senate were dashed, and in late November formally withdrew.[38]

With Rust out of the way, the Senate contest became a battle of minor candidates each supported by the main political factions. Hindman's press reiterated its opposition to any move by the Dynasty to re-elect Senator Johnson.[39] The Hindman camp endorsed Arkansas River planter Napoleon Burrow of Franklin County, who had led the state delegates from the Democratic convention in Charleston the previous spring. Burrow was considered the most rabid secessionist of all the candidates in the race.[40] The Conway-Johnson group supported Dr. Charles Mitchel of Washington in Hempstead County, who had been the Dynasty's unsuccessful candidate for Congress in the southern district the previous summer. The *True Democrat* affectionately referred to him as "that old warhorse."[41] Mitchel described himself to the General Assembly as a strong states' rights candidate but refused to call outright for immediate secession.[42] Old-line Whigs and a few conservative Democrats rallied around the candidacy of Dynasty member Samuel Hempstead of Little Rock. Scion of an old prestigious family, Hempstead advocated a wait-and-see attitude toward Lincoln and called for caution.[43]

After hearing all the candidates, the legislature met in joint session on December 20. After eight ballots none of the three candidates had a majority, until Burrow withdrew and endorsed Mitchel, breaking the deadlock. Mitchel then defeated Hempstead 56 to 26.[44] Rather than have a conservative like Hempstead in the Senate, Hindman's faction, once its candidate had withdrawn, endorsed Mitchel, perceiving him to be more acceptably radical on secession. The Senate contest revealed the three-way division in Arkansas politics, but it demonstrated once again that Dynasty and Hindman forces together were virtually unstoppable.

On the day that Arkansas elected a new senator, South Carolina formally seceded. Disunion would now no longer be merely a threat widely used by a few Southern radicals. The deed had been done. Secession, an issue Arkansas had tried to ignore for many years, would now fundamentally alter old political allegiances. The realignment was taking shape even before the legislature chose a new senator to send to Washington.

Almost as soon as the news of Lincoln's election reached the state, southern and eastern Arkansas had begun agitating for secession. A South Carolinian wrote to his cousin in Memphis in November that from all he had seen and heard, eastern Arkansas was as ready for secession as Mississippi.[45] Petitions from the delta slaveholding counties, including Chicot, Clark, Desha, Calhoun, and Jefferson, poured into the General Assembly, demanding that a state convention be called to remove Arkansas from the Union.[46] A resolution by a citizens' meeting in Dallas County, southwestern Arkansas, was fairly typical:

If the Congress of the United States now in session, does not by the fourth day of March next, give us a sufficient guarantee for slave protection in the Union, we hereby pledge ourselves to take our chances with such of the slaveholding states as may secede from the Union, and risk the consequences.[47]

The Dynasty's press immediately joined this call for a state convention to detach Arkansas from the Union.[48] Hindman's Little Rock *Old Line Democrat* transformed itself into a daily publication during the legislative session to keep up a drumbeat for secession.[49] The Hindman-Dynasty alliance gave the campaign for disunion such a powerful appearance that Judge Brown of Camden wrote fearfully in his diary on January 10 that "the Demon of Secession is daily growing more powerful and we are in the midst of a revolution."[50]

Not all of the state came under this spell. Petitions from northern and western Arkansas began to trickle into the legislature by late December.[51] A petition from Fort Smith said Lincoln's election provided no grounds for secession and that the "people here are for the Union as it is."[52] Union rallies were held in cities like Fayetteville and Camden, and even the secession-minded Fayetteville *Arkansian* described the rally in that city as "large and enthusiastic."[53]

Forces opposing secession could also count on strong endorsement by Danley of the *Gazette*. Long a leading voice of the conservative old-line Whig constituency, during the secession crisis he became the voice of Unionism in the state. Although Danley held no moral qualms over the legitimacy of slavery, he felt that secession was an improper response to political grievances. In mid-December he told his readers, "I do not think that the State has a right to secede, or that the framers of the Constitution contemplated placing in it an element by which a single State could, at any time and for the most trivial of reasons, destroy the entire fabric of government."[54] The *Gazette* editor rightly feared that disunion would mean civil war and the destruction of lives and property. As a conservative, Danley placed his trust in "the commercial and financial interests" of the country, which should save the Republic "from the hasty and inconsiderate acts of politicians and political communities."[55] What Danley failed to realize was that Arkansas and much of the South had no major "financial and commercial interests" except slaveholding and cotton, and these economic concerns were the actual forces behind secession.

Disunionists received the news of South Carolina's secession in late December with great joy. The Palmetto State had finally been bold enough to act, and it ignited a revolution throughout the lower South during the next few weeks. Demand for a state convention reached a deafening crescendo. The *True Democrat* editorialized in early January 1861: "Arkansas must call a convention. South Carolina is out, and other Southern States are taking the same step. . . . We will soon be left alone if we do not act immediately."[56] Pressure was now too strong for the legislature to resist. The General Assembly could no longer ignore demands that a vote be called, and the House of Representatives passed a measure setting up an election for a state convention on December 22. The Senate at first balked, but finally yielded to pressure and passed the bill on January 15.[57] The measure worked for the benefit of secessionists since it called for an election on February 18, at which time the people would decide for or against a convention, while simultaneously selecting delegates. This meant that a potential Unionist candidate carried the double task of opposing the convention and advocating his own election to it.[58] Anti-secessionist leader David Walker of Fayetteville wrote to a friend that the setup was a "gross outrage."[59]

While disunion occupied the minds of many politicians and editors during December and January, important local issues were dealt with by the legislature and the Rector administration. Driven by a governor anxious to fulfill his campaign pledge, the legislature loaned one hundred thousand dollars, a very small amount actually, to the Memphis-Little Rock railroad company on January 3. The funds came from a Federal grant for state improvements, and work was resumed on the line during the spring.[60] For more than a decade, Whigs and independent Democrats had sought to provide some kind of state aid for railroad construction. It was the state's misfortune that it came during the middle of the secession crisis on the eve of the Civil War. Rector also requested the legislature to appropriate another one hundred thousand dollars to buy munitions for the state militia. Funds were needed, according to the governor, to prepare for any hostilities and to check the lawlessness on the western border.[61] Whether Rector really intended to use weapons for the state's defense, or whether he was preparing for a possible civil war, he appeared at least to be trying to do something about the lawlessness in western Arkansas. By its aid for railroad construction and commitment to police the western border, the Rector administration presented a sharp contrast to former lackadaisical treatment of these concerns by the old Conway-Johnson Dynasty.

To assist his purchase of munitions, Governor Rector headed a three-man commission that included Thomas Churchill and Danley.[62] Since Rector appointed members to this commission, Danley understood his political concerns thus: "The governor for the Hindman wing of the Democratic Party, Captain Churchill for the Johnson wing of the same party, and ourselves for the old opposition."[63] Though Rector acted upon sound perception of older political patterns, the issue of secession was already making former alignments obsolete. The Hindman and Johnson wing of the Democratic party now stood as one on the question of disunion, thereby causing the Helena congressman's paper in Little Rock to go out of existence in early January, although the editor of the *Old Line Democrat* denied that he had sold out "bag and baggage" to the Johnson Dynasty.[64] Hindman no longer needed an independent newspaper in Little Rock, for he now spoke with the Family on the issue of secession. Henceforth it would be geography, not old party labels, that determined political differences in Arkansas. In Fayetteville, Democrat John Stirman and ex-Whig David Walker appeared jointly at a Union rally in late December.[65] In eastern Arkansas, Douglasite Democrat Thompson Flournoy of Desha County and ex-Know-Nothing and Bell elector James Yell of Jefferson County both endorsed immediate secession.[66] The issue of disunion had finally exposed the sharp contrasts between the uplands and lowlands of Arkansas as it altered party alignments within the state and throughout much of the South.[67]

As the state prepared for yet another major election in less than four months, events outside Arkansas were moving at a terrific pace. By the time the legislature had set up the election for the state convention on January 15, three other gulf states had joined South Carolina in secession: Mississippi on January 9, Florida on January 10, and Alabama on January 11. Before January ended, two more states would be added— Georgia on January 19, and Louisiana on January 26. The Texas convention ratified secession on February 1, and the people of the Lone Star State gave their approval to the ordinance later that month. As the wave of disunion swept westward across the lower South, many wondered whether Arkansas would be caught in the tide. Even before Louisiana and Texas seceded, John Wheat of Little Rock wrote to his cousin in Germany that Arkansas would be the next star in the constellation of the Confederacy.[68] To many secessionists, it was only a matter of time before the state would be free of the Federal government and its soon-to-be-inaugurated abolitionist president. Such heady sentiment was especially strong in eastern and southern Arkansas, where the people were either planters or farmers who were "aspiring slaveholders or beneficiaries of a slaveholders world, the only world they knew."[69] To whites in the lowlands, Lincoln's election meant, in the words of Governor Rector, a "union without slavery or slavery without the Union." They already knew which situation they preferred. A citizens' group in Arkadelphia in the southwest part of the state stated quite succinctly: "Arkansas must act with the other Southern States to preserve the right of slavery."[70]

To preserve the "right of slavery," Whig planters and small Democratic farmers put aside past differences and united on secession to preserve the hegemony of the white man in the slaveholder's section of the state. A farmer named A. D. Slavey in Mississippi County in northeastern Arkansas wrote to a planter in his county that as a small farmer and Hindman supporter, he was happy that South Carolina "had fled from Northern Abolitionism and Negre [sic] . . . thieven Tyranny. Amen say I. I hope all the Southern States will follow, we can no longer trust false promises."[71] Planter Frank Peak in Chicot County in southeastern Arkansas described himself as a conservative who supported Bell in the 1860 election, but with the election of Lincoln he had a change of heart. The election of a Republican meant the triumph of abolitionism and, as he put it, "This man is too bitter a pill for the South to swallow."[72] Traditional Whig river counties like Chicot, Crittenden, Phillips and Mississippi, most of them having supported Bell in the presidential contest the previous fall, became the real vanguard of the secession movement during the winter of 1860–61.[73] A state representative from Washington County wrote an open letter to his constituents in mid-December asking for their opinions because "letters and petitions are coming in from the more southern and southeastern counties every day urging upon their members the propriety of a state convention."[74] Disunion sentiment was so strong in Pine Bluff that Episcopal Bishop Henry Lay wrote to his wife in late February that the disposition in the city "is to hang every man who says a word against immediate secession."[75] Secession in order to protect slavery had united the white society of southern and eastern Arkansas.

Anti-secession sentiment found its strongest support from the largely slaveless, subsistence farmers in northern and western Arkansas, an area populated mostly by settlers from Missouri, Kentucky and Tennessee, who "showed a strong attachment to the Unionism of Henry Clay and Andrew Jackson."[76] Although the statement was written in 1863, it was correct in pointing out that most of the people in northern and western Arkansas had come from these upper South states. Settlers felt more kinship with the upper South and border states and were not anxious to withdraw from the Union with no other provocation than the election of a president. Since only 17 percent of the slave population lived in the uplands and the area was overwhelmingly white, there was little pressure on the hill folk to secede in order to preserve white hegemony. It was not that uplanders were abolitionists; on the contrary, there was a strong desire even among these people to own a few slaves to help them in their farm labor. Slavery was simply not a significant enough cause for the community to adopt secession as the only defense of the institution.

A few of the counties in the northwest had supported Hindman in the state election of 1860 and had then voted for Breckinridge for president. The flip-flop in the winter can be explained in terms of the prejudices of the hill yeomen of Arkansas. Many non-slaveholding uplanders were quite willing to vote for Hindman after he turned the election into a battle between aristocracy and democracy. They could also vote for Breckinridge as the candidate of their regular Southern Democratic party, because they were demonstrating their strong backing for the status quo of the slave South. Only after the issue of secession came to the fore did the uplanders revolt against the lowlander farmers and planters. They swung from the Southern right to compromise, by sending delegates to the state convention committed either to oppose secession or to labor with other Southern states for a settlement.[77]

Hill people had a suspicion and even a hatred of the pretentious planters in the delta. The whole disunion movement appeared to them to indicate nothing more than a planter plot to deprive them of their rights and privileges, and especially to curb their power at the ballot box. The Unionists played on these fears and did not fail to point out that the new Confederacy would be dominated by planters. John Smith of Benton County in the Ozarks used this ploy in his broadside printed on election day, February 18:

I ask then, what do we gain by secession?—We abandon our rights in the Union, we create ten offices where now we have one, we assume the privilege to be taxed twenty-fold; we give up our privileges, immunities, and the franchise which we now enjoy and which are secure to us. And for what??? That we form a southern

125

Confederacy!!! Do you know that in that Confederacy your rights will be respected? That you will be allowed a vote unless you are the owner of a negro?!! These things you do not know![78]

Other hill farmers blamed the whole secession movement upon the Conway-Johnson Dynasty in Little Rock. One small farmer in Carroll County in north central Arkansas declared with some truth that the "Johnsons" had been trying to break up the Union since 1850 and he blamed them for the breakup of the national Democratic party and the destruction of the candidacy of Stephen Douglas.[79] Suspicions of a "planter conspiracy" caused many yeomen in the mountains to be unenthusiastic about secession.

Another reason for Unionist sentiment was the concern over the loss of Federal protection regarding the western Arkansas boundary adjacent to the Indian Territory. Although this area was noted for its rough lawlessness, the withdrawal of Federal troops from Fort Smith would probably exacerbate an already bad situation. Since the citizens of that city depended greatly on the presence of the military outpost, the area was reluctant to see the Union dissolved.[80] Across the Arkansas River from Fort Smith was the river town of Van Buren, and here too were many of the same concerns. A group of citizens from the town sent this petition to the legislature in early January: "We infer that your part of the State favors secession. In this section, and all around us, we are decidedly against it. There are not ten secessionists in this county."[81] In Fayetteville, John Stirman published a broadside in early February saying that secession would leave all of western Arkansas open to Indian attacks and further acts of lawlessness.[82] Such concerns about the defense and policing of the boundary caused many residents there to disapprove any steps toward leaving the Union.

By opposing secession, northwestern and western Arkansas would have to rebel against the Dynasty in Little Rock. In 1850, the mountain and western Democrats joined with Whigs in the delta to thwart the disunionist designs of the Family, but Unionists in the northwest could no longer count on much of the Whig party and press. Most of the old-line Whig planters were now firmly in the disunionist ranks. One segment of the old-line Whig constituency, however, was still willing to join with upland Democrats in disapproving secession. They represented commercial interests, merchants and lawyers in the large towns like Little Rock, Van Buren and Camden.

This group of ex-Whig lawyer-business interests included men such as former state Supreme Justice David Walker of Fayetteville, merchant David C. Williams of Van Buren, and two young urban lawyers, William Fishback of Fort Smith and Augustus Garland of Little Rock.[83] Danley, editor of the *Gazette*, was chief spokesman among them. This constituency feared that disunion would lead inevitably to civil war with a loss of lives and private property. Danley painted a terrible picture of secession, describing western Arkansas as being raided by hostile Indians and eastern Arkansas being ravaged by pirates and brigands moving up and down the Mississippi River stealing slaves and attacking plantations.[84] These financial conservatives were mainly concerned about changes in or loss of private property that might occur during a large-scale civil war. They were desperately willing to try any peace plan that might avert a commercially destructive sectional struggle. Several maverick old-line Whigs in the delta opposed secession, most notably Judge John Brown of Camden and the planter James H. Quisenberry of Des Arc. In a letter to the *Gazette*, Quisenberry perceptively asked his fellow citizens, "Suppose we had elected Breckinridge president, and the Northern States, in consequence, had seceded. Would we have thought they were right?"[85] Such examples of Whig Unionism in the lowlands were rare during the winter of 1860–61.

In the middle of the winter campaign calling for a state convention, a potentially explosive situation developed around the Federal arsenal in Little Rock. Late in November, Captain Totten and sixty-five troops of the Second U.S. Artillery Regiment garrisoned the previously unoccupied armory. Presence of the Federal forces stirred no commotion until January,[86] when a new telegraph line linked Little Rock to Memphis. A rumor traveled on the line from Little Rock that the ammunition depot was about to be reinforced. This intelligence quickly made its way from Memphis to Helena, a center of zealous disunionism. Citizens there held a mass meeting demanding that Governor Rector seize the arsenal. Rector received the petition and replied, correctly, that an Arkansas governor had no right to assume control over a Federal outpost while the state was still in the Union. He did say that any reinforcement would be considered an act of war. However, Adjutant General Edmund Burgeven, who was also Rector's brother-in-law, reworded the governor's reply to the Helena citizens, making it sound as if the governor would not take the arsenal outright, but would support any spontaneous action of the people in that regard.[87] Companies were immediately formed in many counties in southern and eastern Arkansas preparing to go to Little Rock and take the "Yankee" armory,[88] believing that the governor would support them in this action.

While these unauthorized military units were being formed in the delta counties, Governor Rector informed Captain Totten on January 28 that he would not permit reinforcement of the arsenal or the removal or destruction of the munitions stored there.[89] Totten replied politely, but firmly, that he had no plans for troop reinforcement, but that he would take orders from the federal government alone.[90] Meanwhile, excitement rose in southern and eastern Arkansas as would-be heroes and adventurers made their way to the capital in anticipation of a showdown. A group of feverish secessionists in Pine Bluff fired on the USS *Tucker*, in a mistaken belief that the vessel was carrying troops to the Little Rock armory.[91] By early February, the streets of the capital were filled with about a thousand armed "volunteers," all of them believing that the governor had called them there to help him seize the arsenal. Rector met these military companies and denied any knowledge of orders for them to appear in Little Rock.[92] The illicit troops were at first disappointed, then angry to have been so misled. They were spoiling for a fight and now it looked as if the fight had been cancelled.

The citizens of Little Rock, meantime, were growing more anxious daily as they witnessed large groups of armed men loitering in the streets. The city council passed a resolution forbidding any unauthorized seizure or attack on the armory.[93] At a citizen's meeting presided over by editor Richard H. Johnson of the *True Democrat*, a petition was adopted asking the governor to request a peaceful transfer of the Federal garrison to state control.[94] Behind the scenes, disunionist politicians such as Senator Johnson were furious with Rector for creating a situation that might cause a hasty or unauthorized attack on a Federal arsenal. Johnson and other secessionist leaders feared that such an assault could backfire politically and cause the state to stay firmly within the Union. Arkansas's U.S. senators sent a terse message to Rector: "The motives which impelled capture of forts in other States do not exist in ours. It is all premature. We implore you to prevent attack upon arsenal if Totten resists."[95]

Despite such cautious advice, Governor Rector proceeded to raise his demands by calling for the surrender of the arsenal to state control on February 7. Heavily outnumbered and having no orders from Washington, Totten agreed to the surrender the next day.[96] On February 9, Federal troops marched out of Little Rock toward St. Louis, having been guaranteed a safe escort from the state by the governor.[97] Senator Johnson in Washington was overjoyed at the news and wired his brother: "Arsenal yours. Thank God. Hold it!"[98]

Although the whole affair blew over peacefully, events around the surrender of the garrison greatly damaged Rector's political reputation. It seemed that the new governor did not know how to control his subordinates, and he almost precipitated a major confrontation with the Federal government. Three months into his term, Rector seemed to be nothing more than a bungler and a major risk to secessionists.

Unionists throughout the state eagerly seized upon the arsenal episode to substantiate their claim that secessionists would stop at nothing in their attempts to disrupt the nation. "There was no earthly reason," stated the Van Buren *Press,* "as we conceive it, to take the arsenal."[99] James Quisenberry of Des Arc spoke of many anti-secessionists when he wrote: "We deem the whole affair to be one gotten up for political effect in order to bring the State into a rash and excited secession attitude, because there exists some fear that the moving of Arkansas out of the Union might not be done precipitately enough."[100] Lame-duck Congressman Albert Rust wrote from the nation's capital his belief that Hindman was the person who pressured Rector to seize the garrison.[101] Whoever may have been behind the episode, it clearly put the secessionists on the defensive during the weeks before the February election.

Additionally, anti-secessionist forces in Arkansas were also cheered by a few events outside the state. Virginia sponsored a peace conference that convened in Washington, D.C., on February 4.[102] On the very day Federal troops marched out of Little Rock, the people of Tennessee refused to call a convention to consider secession. Also, most of the delegates to the proposed Tennessee Convention were elected on the Unionist ticket.[103] Unionists in Arkansas were thrilled with the election news from their neighboring state and now redoubled their efforts to keep Arkansas in the Union.[104]

Sensing that the arsenal affair, the peace conference in Washington and the referendum in Tennessee had damaged the secession movement, Arkansas disunionists began a counter-offensive in mid-February. From Washington, D.C., Senator Johnson wrote an "Address to the People of Arkansas," which appeared in the state just prior to the election. He outlined what he considered to be the true basis for the secession movement in the South, telling his constituents that there were worse things than civil war, such as:

Submission and negro equality, and subversion of our social system which makes the humblest and the poorest white man, a proud man, and the poor equal to the greatest and wealthiest in the land. . . . Arkansas has all the material and requisites to make her a great, prosperous, and powerful State. Secede from this unnatural Union. Unite with thy Sister States and share their fortunes![105]

State Senator Francis Terry of Little Rock, a Family leader, also wrote a perceptive essay in which he argued that Arkansas must secede because her business and commercial interests really linked her to Louisiana and the rest of the lower South. Outside the Southern Confederacy, Arkansas would no longer be able to ship goods easily or freely to New Orleans, the state's gateway to the Gulf of Mexico and the world.[106] Secessionists also took heart from the election on February 6 of Jefferson Davis as president of the Confederacy. Richard Johnson wrote hopefully in the *True Democrat:* "We trust soon to see this glorious Confederacy augmented by the addition of Arkansas."[107] Dynasty newspapers and Hindman's publication kept up a steady drumbeat for disunion, and this included the always loyal Fayetteville *Arkansian,* which supported secession in the difficult area of northwestern Arkansas.[108]

On February 18, the day that Jefferson Davis swore the oath of office as Confederate president, Arkansans straggled to the polls in near-freezing weather.[109] Overwhelmingly, they voted to call a state convention; the totals were 27,412 to 15,826.[110] Yet, most distressing to the secessionists, Unionist delegates won a majority of the seats in the convention. According to the *Gazette,* anti-secessionist candidates received 23,626 votes to their opponents' 17,927.[111] This is especially remarkable considering that in three counties, Johnson, Perry and Clark, Unionists did not even field a candidate.[112]

The election demonstrated the geographic division over disunion. Secessionists carried almost every county in the southern and eastern portions of the state, including those that had voted for Bell in the previous fall's presidential election.[113] Unionists carried almost every county in northern and western Arkansas, and conservative sentiment in Little Rock insured the election of Augustus Garland and Joseph Stillwell as delegates for Pulaski County.[114] Upset by county returns, the Dynasty's publication in the Arkansas capital accused both Garland and Stillwell of being too conservative and of actually acting as friends to that "Black Republican" Abraham Lincoln.[115]

As the election results became known, secessionists sulked and Unionists rejoiced. The victory was especially sweet to the anti-secessionists for, as one of them wrote, "they worked and worked hard" for the results.[116] Even the usually dour and pessimistic Judge Brown from Camden inscribed a cheerful note in this diary: "The secession advocates are sat down for the present. . . . The arrogance of the disruptionists is checked for a time at least."[117] Reaction in the northwest was nothing short of euphoric. David Walker of Fayetteville wrote: "The national flag waves above us. The enthusiasm is great. The vote is [in Washington County] ten to one for the Union ticket! Our success is certain."[118] The Van Buren *Press* was just as pleased: "Western Arkansas has pronounced for the Union and she is determined to stay with the old ship of state as long as the stars and stripes shall wave with honor over our heads."[119] On Washington's birthday, February 22, Unionists staged a huge rally in Fort Smith that attracted a crowd estimated to be about a third of the population of the town.[120] One secessionist in Van Buren confided to a friend that Unionist sentiment was so strong that he had to keep his views to himself.[121] James H. Quisenberry of Des Arc was jubilant and gloating over the Unionists' victory: "I am glad for the display of sentiment by the people, yet I am doubly glad for the discomfort of our enemies."[122]

Actually, the election was not so much a triumph for Unionism as a reflection of the ambiguity in the minds of many voters about the sectional divisions. Arkansans did vote by an almost two-to-one margin to call a convention to consider secession, but by sending mostly Unionist delegates to such an assembly they indicated that they did not want to secede at that time. The fact that a convention won acceptance by the voters was an indication that the people were generally open to the possibility of secession. If the peace conference in Washington formulated a good plan, or if Congress worked out an acceptable compromise, then Unionism in Arkansas would probably prevail. Yet if any compromise plan was not forthcoming from the peace conference or Congress, and if the state was forced to choose between the Union and other seceding slaveholder states, Arkansas's cultural, economic and social ties to the Old South would be too strong to ignore. When Senator Johnson in Washington wired his brother in Little Rock that peace was impossible,[123] editor Richard Johnson confidently predicted in his newspaper that "Arkansas will be with her sister States of the Confederate States of America."[124] According to the Family's leading spokesman, anyone who could not see this fact "is as stupid and ignorant as he is presumptuous and contemptible."[125]

During the crucial winter of 1860–61, the issue of disunion fundamentally realigned Arkansas's politics. Older political divisions between Democrats and Whigs faded before a question that split the state geographically, pitting the uplands against the lowlands. These clear and distinct differences would be reflected in the state convention that assembled in Little Rock on March 4, 1861, the very day Abraham Lincoln was scheduled to assume his duties as president of the United States.

IX

Avoiding Secession and Dismemberment

The State Convention and the Campaign for Cooperation,
March 4–April 15, 1861

In May 1860, the *True Democrat* prophesied that "the day that sees a
Black Republican inaugurated as President, there will be two empires
where there is now one Confederacy."[1] As the Republican president-elect,
Abraham Lincoln prepared to assume his office on March 4, 1861, two
separate governments competed for the loyalty of the American people.
Seven states of the lower South had seceded and proclaimed themselves
the Confederate States of America. The outgoing national administration
of James Buchanan had done little to stop the states from seceding, although he did refuse to recognize their legitimacy.[2] Citizens in both the
old Union and the new Confederacy now awaited Lincoln's inauguration
to see what policy his administration might follow toward the seceded
states.

Arkansas was especially concerned about the policies of the new administration. With other states of the slaveholding upper South, it faced a
real dilemma because some parts of the state held loyalties to the Federal
Union and others to the new Southern Confederacy. The cotton growing,
slaveholding areas of southern and eastern Arkansas viewed Lincoln's
election as a direct threat to slavery and prosperity and eagerly sought
secession, while northwestern Arkansas was more willing to give Lincoln
a chance and to seek some solution that would salvage and restore the
Union. Geographical divisions were manifested sharply at the state convention in March, and the differences became so heated that another

election on secession was scheduled in August to forestall a possible split-up of the state. For a time during the spring it appeared that Arkansas itself might be divided just as the Federal Union was coming apart. From early March to mid-April, Unionists labored desperately to avoid both secession and the dismemberment of the state.

Such efforts by the Unionists undeniably would be dependent to a degree upon the support of the national president. It was the lack of such support that had killed the Crittenden compromise in the national Congress, and even the Washington Peace Conference in February failed to win congressional approval for its recommendations.[3] The fate of the nation quite literally rested on the shoulders of a relatively unknown politician from Illinois, the sixteenth president of the once-United States of America.

Elaborate preparations had already been made by President Buchanan and his military advisors to assure a peaceful transition of presidential duties. On inaugural day, both U.S. Army and District of Columbia militia surrounded the spectators and carefully watched the crowd from rooftops, because there had been rumors of violent plots, including attempts of assassination. Monday morning, March 4, 1861, dawned dark and gloomy, but by noon the sun appeared to warm the spectators who gathered to hear Lincoln give his first speech as president. While Stephen Douglas politely held the incumbent's new stovepipe hat, Lincoln pulled his address from his inside coat pocket, adjusted his spectacles, and began reading in a clear but unmistakably nasal voice.[4] He at first uttered words of conciliation to the South. "I have no purpose," he declared, "directly or indirectly, to interfere with the institution of slavery in the States where it now exists. I believe I have no lawful right to do so."[5] But, after these words, Lincoln emphatically added: "I shall take the course that the Constitution itself expressly enjoins upon me, that the laws of the United States be faithfully executed in all the states. . . . The powers confided in me will be used to hold, occupy, and possess the property and places belonging to the government, and to collect duties and imports."[6] He then finished his address with a call for unity, brotherhood, and reconciliation:

In your hands, my dissatisfied countrymen, and not in mine, is the momentous issue of civil war. The government will not assail you. You can have no conflict without being yourselves the aggressors. You have no oath registered in heaven to destroy the government, while I shall have the most solemn one to 'preserve, protect, and defend it.'[7]

Historian Bruce Catton described Lincoln's inaugural address as containing "soft words of consolation, closely reasoned appeals to forbearance and brotherhood—[which] would have no effect whatsoever."[8] The states of the Confederacy had, irreconcilably, forsaken the Union. The press in the seceded Deep South gave Lincoln's address little but scorn and ridicule.[9] If the new president wanted to restore the Union, he would have to do it by force, not speeches. Backed by sentiment in the North, Lincoln would act on the assumption that states claiming to be out of the Union were eternally in it.[10] Between Lincoln and the seceded South there was no real ground for compromise. Only Arkansas and a few other states in the upper South still clung to the illusion. They persevered in the Union to act as agents of compromise between the North and the Confederacy.

Reaction in the Arkansas press to Lincoln's address reflected the polarization over secession. The leading pro-secession paper in the state, the *True Democrat,* argued that Lincoln's address proved his evil intentions to coerce the seceded states back into a Union under despotism.[11] The editorial ended saying that "Arkansas must join the Confederacy to avoid submitting to Black Republican rule."[12] The Fayetteville *Arkansian* referred to Lincoln as "His Satanic Majesty" and called his inaugural speech a "declaration of war upon the South and its interests."[13] In the same issue, it printed Confederate President Davis's inaugural address adjacent to Lincoln's, showing its readers that they had more in common with the Confederacy than with the old Union.[14] Lincoln's inaugural address and its publication in most of the state's newspapers set off a new round of calls for secession at public meetings in the southern and eastern sections.[15]

Unionists faced the awkward task of praising Lincoln's address for its forbearance while disclaiming any association with the positions of the man who gave it. "Without professing to have admiration for Lincoln as a man or for his inaugural address as a state paper," the Van Buren *Press* commented in an editorial, "we are still at a loss to conceive what he could, as President of the United States, have said that would have been more conciliatory."[16] Danley of the *Gazette* would not even give the speech so weak a compliment, saying only that it was an "objectionable document."[17] Refusing to state his objections, Danley assailed his old enemy, the Democratic party. Lincoln's address, he wrote, "is not as bad as the last acts of the Buchanan administration which preceded it. After living under the Buchanan administration during the whole of its unjust and disgraceful existence, we do not think that our State can be worsened living under Lincoln."[18]

Even before Lincoln's address reached the Arkansas press, attention had already focused upon the state convention called to consider the state's future in the Union. On March 2, after certifying the returns from the February election, Governor Rector issued a formal call for the convention to assemble two days later in Little Rock on Monday, March 4.[19] Already, there was much excitement in the lowlands as the people expected a quick departure from the Union. A man from DeWitt, in eastern Arkansas, wrote to his cousin in North Carolina in late February that men in his area were prepared for secession and ready to defend it with arms if necessary.[20] Episcopal Bishop Henry Lay wrote to his wife on March 3 of his "great consternation that the whole town of Jackson Port on the White River was all astir on the Sabbath with a major secession ball!"[21]

Not all the excitement was confined to the delta. One Unionist delegate later described the feeling in the Arkansas capital as the convention assembled:

Little Rock was filled with politicians of excitable nature who were anxious for secession at any cost; adventurers and would-be soldiers, for all conceded that to take this step meant war and the pressure was intense. The Union men were taunted as 'submissionists' and 'abolitionists' and all kinds of raillery came down from the lobbies. The galleries and the lobbies were always crowded, and it was feared violence would occur, and at times it seemed inevitable.[22]

Much of the fervor was contrived by the secessionist forces, for generally Little Rock was a conservative Whig-oriented city. Most of the people had been upset when Governor Rector seized the arsenal only a month before. One Unionist subsequently recalled how the secessionists manipulated the news from the telegraph offices to help keep the liveliness at fever pitch. One Unionist recalled that the lines from Memphis to Little Rock "were kept busy, as an exciting batch of news was not allowed to become cold before another red-hot item from the electric furnace was thrown upon it. Thus the people were allowed no time to reflect or become cool, but were spurred, whipped and goaded on impetuously."[23] Also, the major secessionist paper, the *True Democrat*, transformed itself into a daily during the convention to try to push that body into disunion.[24] By press and telegraph and by the presence of pro-secessionist spectators in the galleries and lobby of the capitol, the forces for disunion clearly intended to pressure the convention into enacting an ordinance of secession.

A few good reasons existed for the secessionists to feel confident that they could work their will. Ralph Wooster, a historian who has done a comparative study of the secession conventions in all the Confederate states and Kentucky, found the Arkansas assembly most wanting in experience. Although the convention contained no former governors, senators, or congressmen,[25] Wooster failed to mention that the delegates were represented by a few skilled career party politicians who were not ignorant of public affairs or legislative proceedings. David Walker, president of the assembly, had served at the first state constitutional convention in 1836, in the state legislature, and on the supreme court.[26] Among the delegates were several talented young politicians who would lead the state during Reconstruction and afterward. Four became governors: Harris Flanagan (1862–1865), Isaac Murphy (1864–1868), Augustus Garland (1874–1877), and William Fishback (1893–1895).[27] Five members would serve in the Confederate Congress.[28]

Of the seventy-seven men in this state convention, fifty-one were natives of the upper South states of Tennessee, Kentucky and North Carolina. Four were native Arkansans, and the other twenty-two hailed from the lower South states of Georgia, Alabama and South Carolina.[29] All members from the lower South represented counties in the southern and eastern sections of the state except Samuel Griffith of South Carolina who was a Unionist representative from Fort Smith in Sebastian County.[30] The fact that more than two-thirds of the convention delegates were born in the upper South was significant, for they tended to see Arkansas more as a state belonging to that area. They would more easily take as their cue the actions of other states of the upper South. Sixty-one percent of the delegates owned slaves, but the average holding per member numbered only about eleven.[31] Slaveholders had an average holding of about nineteen slaves, but only seventeen delegates qualified as planters by owning twenty or more slaves.[32] As might be expected, secessionist delegates owned many more slaves than did the Unionists.[33]

The question of disunion obliterated the old party alignments of Democrats and Whigs. The new division was between those who favored immediate secession and the Unionist-Cooperationists, who supported some action in cooperation with the upper South and the border states to settle the sectional crisis. Unionist-Cooperationist delegate Alfred Carrigan of Hempstead County recalled the strict polarization saying, "It must be remembered that party lines at all times were strictly drawn between the original secessionists and the original Union men, the latter being more conservative."[34] The Unionist-Cooperationists had experienced leaders among their ranks, including men like Walker of Fayetteville, Jesse Turner of Van Buren and Jesse Cypert of Searcy. According to former delegate Carrigan, the best speakers for this faction were William Fishback, Alfred Dinsmore of Benton County, and Hugh F. Thomason of Van Buren in Crawford County.[35] Unionists also claimed the talents of Little Rock lawyer Augustus Garland. Although Garland was only twenty-nine years old, Carrigan remembered that he was most effective as a debater, for "he did not attempt oratory, but used a colloquial and argumentative style that was most attractive and convincing."[36]

Secessionists too had talent, especially two delegates from Phillips County. Charles Adams, a relative of the famous Massachusetts family, had immigrated from the Bay State to Arkansas in the 1840s and had risen to become a prominent planter and Whig politician. During the recent presidential contest, he had campaigned for Bell and had served as a Bell elector.[37] The other delegate from Phillips County was the able Democratic attorney from Helena, Thomas Hanly. Carrigan described Hanly as the "ablest man in the Convention and the most prominent lawyer in the State."[38] Other secessionist leaders included the Totten brothers: Benjamin, from Prairie County, and James, from Arkansas County, and such able debaters as James Yell from Pine Bluff, Josiah Gould from Bradley County, and George Laughinghouse from St. Francis County.[39] All these secessionist leaders represented counties in southern and eastern Arkansas. Felix Batson of Johnson County was the only delegate from the uplands to support secession.[40] The Conway-Johnson Family had its own personal representative in cousin Jilson Johnson of Desha County.[41]

Unionists had won a narrow majority of seats, and they assumed command of the proceedings at the outset. After selecting Jesse Turner as a temporary chairman, the convention selected David Walker as the permanent presiding officer. Walker defeated secessionist Benjamin Totten forty votes to thirty-five.[42] The next day, William Grace of Jefferson County moved that the convention draw up an ordinance of secession. Unionist-

Cooperationist Rufus Garland of Hempstead County (brother to Augustus Garland of Little Rock) responded with a motion to adjourn for the day, which carried.[43] The Unionist-Cooperationist majority never amounted to more than five votes, yet it was enough to control the assembly, and all the major committees were headed by this political party.[44] Even the permanent secretary of the convention, Elias Boudinot of Fayetteville, despite his long association with the Dynasty, was part of the Unionist coalition.[45]

When the convention reassembled on March 6, real debate over secession began. James Totten said the South had nothing more in common with the North and that sectional divisions could be traced to the English Civil War of the seventeenth century, to the conflict between Puritans and Cavaliers. Jesse Turner responded for the Unionists with a long address on the common heritage of the two sections and made emotional references to the American Revolution. Turner pronounced to his fellow delegates, "Dissolve the Union, and the Earth will send up a moan from the graves of our Revolutionary fathers whose toil, blood, and treasure was vainly expended in establishing our government."[46] Oratory did little to change hearts or votes, but it reflected the polarization. It was evident within days that the convention would not draw up an ordinance of secession. The exasperation of the secessionists grew. Four days into the convention, Jilson Johnson raged that the assembly was wasting time and taxpayer's money; he demanded action on secession.[47] His cousin, editor Richard Johnson, echoed the frustration in the Dynasty paper:

Let us have action. The people are convinced that compromise is at an end. . . . Let us not be the last to join our sister States of the South. Let us take the proud and independent position, and not wait until we are driven out of the Union. For God's sake, give us an ordinance of secession![48]

Augustus Garland interrupted Jilson Johnson's angry speech with the quip that the "gentlemen of the other side" could introduce the issue of secession whenever they wanted, and that he would vote it down "with a light heart and a clear conscience."[49] Optimism was high in the Unionist ranks. Jesse Turner confidently wrote to his wife that "while the Unionist majority is only about five," he believed it to be "totally reliable."[50] The Unionist-Cooperationists effectively used a legislative weapon made famous by later Southern politicians—the filibuster. This tactic exasperated the *True Democrat* which stated, "We are tired of hearing men give us their personal biographies . . . apostrophies to the Stars and Stripes, to the American eagle, and to the g-e-lorious Union!"[51] Disunionists had instigated the convention, but could not move it to draw up and pass an ordinance of secession. Clearly, more outside pressure would have to be brought to bear upon the Unionist majority.

Delegates at first listened to representatives of South Carolina and Georgia, states referred to by Turner in a letter to his wife as "two fallen angels."[52] Not only did they not move any Unionists, but the South Carolina Speaker may have hurt the secessionist cause when he imprudently suggested that Arkansas must secede for it owed its admission into the Union to his state.[53] Governor Rector addressed the convention on March 8 and urged secession, saying that it was essential to preserve slavery and its expansion, as "that is the vital point between the North and South."[54] Slavery was the real reason for the division between North and South, he said, and that difference was not susceptible to compromise:

The South wants practical evidence of good faith from the North, not mere paper agreements and compromises. They believe slavery is sin, and we do not, and there lies the trouble. All confidence is lost and it is too late to repair it. . . . Let us then separate in peace, if possible, if not, let it be in war, for separation must come sooner or later, and our danger increases in magnitude.[55]

Governor Rector made absolutely no impression upon the Unionist majority. It promptly passed a resolution denouncing his seizure of the Little Rock arsenal. The convention then called upon Rector to make a statement concerning the cost of holding the installation.[56] Unionists throughout the state distrusted the governor, and disunionist delegate James Yell believed that "thousands of them would have killed him freely if they only could."[57] When the secessionists attempted to have the convention recognize the Southern Confederacy, the Unionist-Cooperationist majority quickly shoved that motion to a committee, where it died.[58] The first week of the convention had been a complete disaster for the disunionists.

Outside the convention, a newspaper war raged between secessionists and Unionists. In the eastern delta town of Batesville, the *Southern Aurora* declared that "the secession of seven powerful States is an accomplished fact. To think for a moment that these States will be lured into the deadly embrace of Abolitionism by the glittering bauble of a frail and unsafe compromise is absurd!"[59] Editor Johnson of the *True Democrat* attacked the Unionist idea of cooperating with border states to achieve compromise. "In a few weeks," the paper scoffed, "the Union Party will not contain a corporal's guard. Cooperation at this late date is an unmitigated humbug which means nothing."[60] The Fayetteville *Arkansian* claimed to be "fed up with all this useless twaddle about preserving a Union already broken."[61]

The Fayetteville *Arkansian* was the lone voice of secession in a largely Unionist mountain area. To steer mountaineers toward disunion, it raised the specter of Negro equality. The journal warned its mountain readers what they might have to face in a future without slavery:

Think for a moment, and we appeal to the nonslaveholder, how would you like to have a buck negro come up to the polls and tell you to stand back and let him vote? How would you like to sit on a jury with a negro, and how would you like to have a negro give testimony against you?—In a word, how would you like to have him associate with you as an equal? Disgusting beyond description . . . We submit these reflections to you calmly and earnestly entreat you to give them your attention, for they concern your wives and your children.[62]

More forthright than others, the specter raised by the *Arkansian* was never far from the consciousness of many secessionists. Since most of the papers belonged to the Dynasty or were associated with Congressman Hindman, a majority of the presses within the state favored withdrawal from the Union.

To counter this overwhelming disadvantage, Unionists relied heavily upon the pen of editor Danley at the *Gazette*. Danley proclaimed that not only were secessionists misleading the people on disunion but that they were misrepresenting them as well. He referred to Congressman Thomas Hindman as an example. Since his congressional district covered every part of the state north of the Arkansas River, "he stands, by his zeal and ability, as one of the leading secessionists in Congress, and the people in his district are strongly in favor of the Union. The very counties that swelled his majority into thousands, gave more thousands for the Union."[63] Danley failed to acknowledge that Hindman's district also contained a large part of the delta, including the river towns of Batesville and Jacksonport, and the congressman's hometown of Helena. In the congressional election of 1860, moreover, secession was not a major issue. Hindman had turned the contest into a class conflict against the ruling Conway-Johnson Dynasty. Hill farmers who voted for Hindman in the summer of 1860 did so to help him overthrow a political aristocracy in Little Rock. His views on secession did not seem to be so important at that time. Nevertheless, Hindman's upland constituents were probably Unionists in 1861, and in that sense he was not accurately representing them.

In late March, Danley brought a more serious charge against the secessionists. He accused them of trying to dismember the state:

There are gentlemen here, prominent for their social and political positions, and influential for the same reasons, who propose first to force Arkansas out of the Union: and, in failing in that, to divide the State by a revolutionary movement, and join a portion of it to the southern Confederacy, whether the rest go or not.[64]

The Van Buren *Press*, another Unionist-Cooperationist journal, took up the *Gazette*'s charge and provided more detail of the plans: "The secessionists are already discussing the policy of splitting the State, the Baseline [the parallel line which divides Tennessee from Mississippi] and the Arkansas River suggested as the boundaries."[65] While these allegations are difficult to substantiate, their mere assertion emphasized the clear regional dichotomy over secession. Boundaries that were suggested did not truly reflect the diagonal geographic divisions between the delta southeast and the mountainous northwest.[66]

Both secessionists and their opponents knew that carrying the hills was crucial. The Unionist Fayetteville *Democrat*, a paper ironically begun as a Hindman sheet during the summer of 1860, counteracted the Fayetteville *Arkansian*'s appeal to racial prejudice by inciting the hills folk's antagonism toward the planters. "The same mob that can make cotton king and Davis president," the *Democrat* was quoted, "is the same mob that will tell you that only he can be trusted at the ballot box who is a slaveholder, and that a Republican government based upon the universal suffrage of white men is a universal failure."[67] The *Arkansian* responded by accusing its rival of pushing Hinton Helper's "pernicious doctrine of pitting the non-slaveholding white man against the planters."[68] While most press debate over secession generated more heat than light, the exchange between the Fayetteville papers demonstrated the racial and regional class antagonism prevalent in Arkansas during this momentous national crisis.

Upon Lincoln's inauguration, the thirty-sixth Congress formally disbanded without producing national compromise. The next Congress was not scheduled to meet until December. All of Arkansas's congressional delegation, saving Senator Charles Mitchel, Robert W. Johnson's replacement in the Senate, left Washington in early March. Mitchel attended a special Senate session that lasted from the inauguration until the end of March, working vainly to produce a compromise that would restore the Union.[69] With most congressional members no longer in the capital, attention around the country focused on two Federal forts still in government hands within Confederate boundaries: Fort Pickens in Pensacola, Florida, and Fort Sumter in Charleston Harbor, South Carolina. In mid-March, Senator Mitchel telegraphed a widely believed but mistaken rumor that President Lincoln planned to withdraw the government from both installations.[70] The announcement arrived as "news" in the Arkansas convention on the afternoon of March 11, causing much rejoicing among the Unionist-Cooperationists and strengthening their resolve to hold out against immediate secession.

Senator Mitchel's telegraph message could not have come at a more opportune time for the Unionists. Hugh Thomason of Van Buren had just presented a series of resolutions and amendments drawn by Unionists to support the restoration of the nation.[71] While decrying the rise of an anti-slavery party in the North designed to deny protection of slavery in the territories, Thomason's resolutions and proposals resembled Crittenden's compromise in Congress, an extension of the 36°30' line to the Pacific, strict enforcement of the Fugitive Slave laws.[72] This would be the plan on which Arkansas's Unionist-Cooperationists based their hopes for a reconciliation between North and South. That this strategy had failed in Congress only a month earlier appeared to make no impression on them.[73] They were merely holding out, in the hope that such a plan might yet be used to heal the country.

While Unionists proposed, secessionists around the state sulked and grumbled over the inertia of the assembly, that not only refused to secede, but even refused to recognize the government of seceded states, which the *True Democrat* called a disgrace.[74] One frustrated disunionist delegate proposed that the convention adjourn *sine die*.[75] Both parties quickly brushed this aside, but Augustus Garland offered a resolution that passed, declaring that the "people of Arkansas prefer a perpetuity of this Federal Union, rather than its dismemberment or its disruption, provided it can be perpetuated upon a basis recognizing and guaranteeing equal rights and privileges to every State in the Union, South as well as North."[76]

On March 13, two days after Thomason's proposals to restore the Union, secessionists made a desperate effort to turn the convention toward disunion. Hanly of Helena moved that Thomason's proposals be transformed into an ordinance of secession, which would be ratified by the people on the first Saturday in May.[77] For the rest of the week, the debate centered on Hanly's counter-resolutions. The secessionists increased the pressure. Former Senator Robert W. Johnson addressed the Unionist delegates in an effort to urge them toward secession.[78] Although Johnson was the most prestigious political figure in the state, his influence upon the ranks of Unionists was inconsequential. Many anti-disunionists were either former Whigs or hill country Democrats, and both these groups by 1861 had become enemies of the Johnson political Family. Confederate President Jefferson Davis sent his own representative, William S. Oldham of Texas, to the convention. Oldham had been an anti-Family Democrat from Fayetteville in the mid-1840s but had migrated to Texas in 1849 after a failing career in Arkansas. He eventually became a Confederate congressman in his adopted state.[79] Though Oldham had once been an anti-Dynasty Democrat, his abandonment of Arkansas made him less influential with the Unionists.[80]

Outside the assembly, the secessionist press focused on the Unionists' refusal to submit an ordinance to the people for a vote. The *True Democrat* called it a clear act of cowardice.[81] Replying for the Unionists, Danley's *Gazette* decried the "shifting tactics of desperate politicians" who now wanted a secession ordinance submitted to the voters "as if they had not already given an expression which was emphatic enough at the polls, a few days hence, in a returned majority for the Union."[82] Since the people had just had an election on a secession convention, Unionists argued that another contest would be costly and unnecessary.

On March 18, the crucial vote came on Hanly's motion to refer secession to the voters. The Unionist-Cooperationist coalition held firm and defeated the proposal thirty-nine to thirty-five. With only a few exceptions, the vote reflected the diagonal geographic division between southeast and northwest Arkansas.[83] (See Figure 9a in the Appendix.) Immediately after this vote, Yell of Pine Bluff amended Hanly's measure to place before the voters a vote on a secession ordinance upon a later date to be set by the convention. This too failed by three votes.[84] As events stood in mid-March, the Arkansas convention would not approve secession, or even submit the idea to the people for a vote. In the next few days, the convention endorsed an assembly of the border states, sent Thomason's proposals to Congress as suggested constitutional amendments, and selected delegates to attend a border state conference in June at Frankfort, Kentucky.[85]

When the vote on Hanly's motion is analyzed, a clear and distinct pattern emerges connecting slaveholding and wealth with a vote for secession. As Figure 9b outlines, those counties which supported disunion in March, 1961, tended to be those counties with a high slave population. This vote on Hanly's motion makes apparent the lowland-upland division which occurred over disunion. Secession not only divided the state geographically, but along lines of wealth as well. The cumulative per capita wealth for whites in the twenty-four county secession was $31,414.89, almost double that of the thirty-one counties which voted against Hanly's motion. Even though there were seven more Unionist counties, their cumulative per capita wealth amounted to just $15,768.36. Of the top fifteen wealthiest counties listed in Table 6c, all of them voted for secession except for Pulaski, Crittenden, and Hempstead counties. At the opposite end of the scale, all the bottom fifteen counties voted for the Union with the exception of Craighead and Randolph counties, both of them in the eastern delta. Thus a 12 to 3 vote for secession in the wealthiest counties is to be contrasted with a 13 to 2 vote for the Union among the state's poorest counties.

Of the middle twenty-five counties listed in Table 6c, ten voted for secession while fifteen took a Unionist position on Hanly's motion. Yet when the wealth of these counties is all added, the pattern remains consistent. Of the ten disunionist counties, the average per capita wealth for whites equalled 770.03. For the fifteen Unionist counties, their average county's wealth only amounted to 523.11. Prior to Fort Sumter, secessionist sentiment in Arkansas was strongest in those counties which were the wealthiest in per capita land value and where there was the highest concentration of African slaves.

Before the state convention disbanded, secessionists and the Unionist-Cooperationists apparently reached a compromise on submitting the question of the Union to the voters. Prior to March 18, the Unionist-

Cooperationists had successfully resisted a popular vote on secession, yet on the next day, Benjamin Totten proposed that the issue "for secession" or "for cooperation" be put on the ballot for a referendum on the first Monday in August. The convention would meet two weeks afterwards to enact the public's will. This time the Unionist-Cooperationists voted overwhelmingly in favor of Totten's motion[86] apparently because they feared that secessionists would soon use another ploy to separate the state from the Union. A Unionist delegate, John Campbell of Searcy County, wrote to a constituent in June that Unionists agreed to an August election because secessionists planned to have the governor reconvene the legislature and cajole that body into enacting an ordinance of secession. As Campbell wrote, "to prevent that course we made a compromise with them and agreed to refer it to the people for them to vote in August."[87]

Unionists may also have believed that they had to call another election or Arkansas would break apart. Isaac Hilliard, a disunionist delegate from Chicot County, wrote to his constituents that Unionists attending the convention would not have permitted the August election except that the secessionists had warned them that if "they denied this, it would behoove us of the East, and the South, to save our people, by desperate methods if necessary."[88] What these methods might be was openly talked about. A public meeting in Drew County during late March produced the demand that Arkansas either secede or "consult with delegates who are for secession, with regard to a speedy and peaceable division of the State."[89] A man wrote from Napoleon, a Mississippi River town, on March 19 that "the disunionists have, I believe, given Arkansas up as a hard case, and are going on to secede from North Arkansas. Maybe they will."[90] Pro-secession sentiment was so strong in the southeast delta region that many people feared that unless the issue was put before the voters in some form, part of the state would secede on its own.[91]

With the compromise worked out, the convention ended its business in a more amiable mood on March 21.[92] The Unionist-Cooperationists were counting upon some type of national compromise to be worked out at the border state convention in Kentucky during summer. They also placed confidence in the president of the convention, David Walker of Fayetteville.[93] The Unionist-Cooperationists were sure that Walker, an old-line Whig jurist from the northwest, would not easily yield to secessionists' pressure to reassemble the convention before August.

Press reaction to the session depended upon the paper's position on secession. The new mildly secessionist Des Arc *Constitutional Union* was disappointed that the convention did not pass a secession ordinance, but it applauded the decision to submit the choice between secession and cooperation to the people.[94] Johnson of the *True Democrat* was more bitter. He lashed out at the Unionist-Cooperationist leaders of the convention, accusing Walker, Thomason and Jesse Turner of a willingness to submit to Abraham Lincoln "with his Black Republicanism, his negro equality, his hatred of the South. . . . They hate dis-Union more than they love the South."[95]

In the mountains, the men who voted against Hanly's proposal were regarded as heroes, and in Van Buren, a thirty-nine gun salute was fired in their honor, "as a glorious memorial to the Thirty-Nine Men, who, in the defense of their country, stood firm against the ordinance of secession."[96] Two Crawford County delegates returning home to Van Buren found a cheering crowd and a brass band to greet them. Samuel Griffith, delegate from Sebastian County, was welcomed in a similar fashion at Fort Smith.[97] The editor of the Van Buren *Press* was so caught up in celebrating the defeat of secession that "the American flag, the Stars and Stripes, was thrown high into the breeze from the *Press* office in honor of the event."[98] In the lowlands, a few Unionists rejoiced, but mostly in silence. Judge Brown of Camden wrote in his diary how proud he was of the "Unionist men who would not be browbeaten into disunion."[99]

Not all Unionists were completely happy with the outcome of the convention. Perhaps more sagacious than many of his comrades, Danley of the *Gazette* predicted less hope than gloom for the Unionists because they had been pressured into calling for an election in August. He wrote somewhat bitterly, "the Secessionists came into the capital to force the State out of the Union, without referring the matter to the people. If they had had the power, Arkansas would now have been out of the Union despite the wishes of the people."[100] Now that the disunionists had succeeded in getting the issue on the ballot before the people, Danley was too much of an old-line Whig not to believe that the public could be tricked or manipulated into voting for secession.[101] For good or ill, Arkansas would be faced with yet another major election, the fourth one in a year.

By April first, both Unionist-Cooperationists and their opponents were preparing for a four-month campaign over secession. Secessionists knew that the key would be in their ability to sway the mountain folk to their cause. Former Senator Johnson, former Governor John Seldon Roane, and newly elected Congressman Edward Gantt all announced speaking tours in northern and western Arkansas. Congressman Thomas Hindman announced speeches in the same areas and, of course, his itinerary was more extensive than that of any other leading secessionist.[102] Despite having many of the state's leading political figures in their corner, the disunionists anticipated an arduous struggle, for as one of their newspapers declared, "it is hard to convert the bigoted and enlighten the ignorant."[103]

Unionists, of course, had their own strategy and their own coterie of speakers. These included Turner and Walker. Walker had an opportunity to reply to Johnson in the Ozark community of Huntsville in Madison County, and later wrote to a friend that "the Union cause is going well in all the mountain counties."[104] In contrast to Judge Walker's optimism, William Fishback nervously wrote to a Van Buren merchant in early April that "already I have heard good Union men say that the State will secede."[105] Fishback planned to use the Van Buren *Press* as the Unionists' campaign sheet, to paint Senator Johnson as a radical secessionist who voted against the Crittenden compromise, and to organize Union clubs in as many counties as possible.[106] To withstand the predominantly secessionist press and its political leaders, Unionists would have to work hard together.

To preserve their unity, the thirty-nine delegates who voted against Hanly's secession motion published a "Unionist Manifesto" in the *Gazette* during the first week of April. They hoped with this document to launch their campaign and counter many of what they termed lies and deceptions of their opponents.[107] It opened with a strong profession of loyalty to the Old South and slavery by means of rebutting the charge that Unionists were mere agents of Northern abolitionists.[108] On the important issue of hegemony over Southern society, Unionists wanted to clarify that they were not dangerous heretics to racial order. The manifesto went on accurately to declare that before last November's presidential election, "few men in the South took the ground that the election of Mr. Lincoln would justify the destruction of the Union."[109] If secession was not necessary before Lincoln's election, nothing since that moment had happened to justify it now. The only thing that Lincoln had done was to assume an office to which he had been elected in a manner prescribed by the U.S. Constitution. The Unionists also reported as fact that President Lincoln intended to withdraw Federal troops from the forts in Florida and South Carolina, thus averting a sectional confrontation.[110] According to Unionists, the seceded states, not Mr. Lincoln, had acted rashly. The manifesto also declared that it was wrong to judge the entire North by the ravings of a small group of abolitionist fanatics. The South still had many friends in that section of the country. Rather than seceding, Arkansas should be working with the upper South and border states to bring about a peaceful reconstruction of the nation.[111]

Amid words of peace and reconciliation, the manifesto emphasized the Unionists' complete opposition to any action taken by the Federal government to compel a Confederate state to rejoin the Union. "While Arkansas is not committed to the doctrine of secession," it said, "she is against the coercion by the Federal government of any seceded State."[112] While Unionists were not committed to secession, neither were they committed to an enforced union. This was not a new position for Unionist-Cooperationists. During the convention, one of Thomason's resolutions had stated clearly that "any attempt by the Federal Government to coerce the seceding States, by an armed force, will be resisted by Arkansas, to the last extremity."[113] A Unionist delegate recalled later that he and his comrades had believed that "any attempt on the part of the Federal government to coerce the other southern states would be and should be resisted by the state of Arkansas, however anxious the people are to remain in the Union."[114] Opposition to compulsion and secession was not simply the public position assumed by Unionist political leaders. Many of them held this view privately and so, too, did many citizens who were known as Unionists. One Unionist-Cooperationist from an upland county wrote to his delegate in the convention that if Lincoln took possession of the forts "all hope of reconciliation is at an end. I am of the opinion that the citizens of Franklin County, if Lincoln attempted to collect customs, etc., they would vote to ratify an ordinance of secession."[115] A letter signed "H" at Apple Orchard in Benton County appeared in early March in the *Gazette* stating, "Our people are a unit against coercion of a seceded state, and nearly so . . . against being dragooned into secession."[116] The writer was more against coercion than secession.

While this position might seem contradictory a century later, men of that era reconciled their views. A strong Jeffersonian-Jacksonian fear of centralized authority pervaded the antebellum South. This tradition viewed the Union as little more than a just compact between sovereign and independent states. Although they might be dedicated to a strong Federal Union, people in the Old South had felt for several years that a state could secede if it felt threatened severely by a national government. This had been the prevailing ideology of the Old South and also of Arkansas's leading politicians and legal theorists. The Family's main spokesman on national affairs for the previous ten years, Senator Johnson, identified with this states' rights view of the Constitution.[117] When Hindman's first newspaper in Helena called itself the *States Rights Democrat,* he would not have used that masthead if he had not fervently believed in its political doctrine.

Even among the old-line Whig Know-Nothing adherents this attitude prevailed. Albert Pike, ex-Whig editor and Know-Nothing political leader, published a forty-page pamphlet entitled *State or Province? Bond or Free?* two days before the state convention opened. It was a cogently written, well-argued treatise enumerating supposed abuses the South had endured from the North. According to Pike, the only hope for Arkansas and the rest of the South to preserve their independence from the growing anti-slavery Federal monolith was to join their sister slaveholding states in secession. If Arkansas did not secede, then it was merely a bonded province of a United States empire, not a truly independent and sovereign state.[118]

Local autonomy and states' rights were cherished philosophies because they were used to guard against any Federal tampering with slavery. Without these ideologies, the South's peculiar institution would depend on majority rule and the shifting tide of Northern opinion. Lincoln's election signalled to the South that even the Constitution could no longer be relied upon to protect slavery. That document had sanctioned the election of a man who opposed the expansion of slavery beyond its present boundaries. Since Southerners felt that these western territories were held in common by them and the Northerners, they believed that they were not receiving equal justice in the Union. Moreover, the Supreme Court in 1857 had declared that slaves were property, and Southerners considered it to be illegal for Lincoln, Congress, or anyone else to restrict them from carrying their property to any part of the United States. Why restrict slavery, unless the ultimate goal was to bring about its abolition? If the South accepted Lincoln and the Republican's restrictions on the expansion of slavery, within a generation it might be forced to submit to abolition. Since Arkansas was only beginning to enjoy the fruits of a cotton-slave economy, many people were reluctant to remain in a Union hostile to its newly treasured social and economic institution.

By the spring of 1861, most white Arkansans were probably conditional Unionists. This meant, as one historian said, that they were willing "to remain in the Union until the last possible means of compromise had been attempted, and were willing to secede only when they were convinced that the slave states would not be guaranteed equal rights with the free states."[119] There were a few unconditional Unionists who desired to remain in the Union regardless of the fate of slavery. They had to remain quiet, especially if they resided in parts of the state dependent upon slavery.[120]

As much as Unionists wanted reconciliation and peaceful reconstruction of the Old Union, they agreed with their opponents in believing that slavery had to be protected. Hindman's Little Rock paper in December 1860 reflected views later held by Albert Pike in March 1861: "We cannot separate from the Cotton growing States. You might as well expect a limb severed from a human body to live. Sink or swim, persevere or perish, our destiny and theirs must be one."[121] As bitterly as the secessionists and Unionists fought, their positions were not too dissimilar. Secessionists believed with Governor Rector that it was "the Union without slavery, or slavery without the Union." Unionists, as yet unwilling to accept this bleak alternative, still clung to the hope that slavery could be made secure within the Union. In the event of a final break or whenever it appeared that slavery could not be protected, Unionists would not abandon slavery for the sake of the Union. For secessionists and most Unionists slavery had become too important during the 1850s to be disregarded simply to maintain a Union that was no longer convenient and perhaps even hostile to the interests and needs of Arkansas.

Only in the Ozark counties of north central and northwestern Arkansas would Unionism persist even after the break came. Populated by inhabitants born in the upper South who owned few if any slaves, Ozark dwellers tended to view secession as a planter plot to deprive them somehow of their voting rights and privileges. When the attack on Fort Sumter ended most Arkansas Unionists' dreams of national reconciliation, the unconditional Unionists in the Ozarks would find themselves isolated as the only opponents of secession.

During the first six weeks of President Lincoln's administration, in the face of extreme pressure from the press and political establishment, Unionists kept the state in the Union as they pursued reconciliation or compromise. But the state's dependence on slavery and the traditional Southern fear of any centralized authority made it easy for most Arkansans to unite for secession after the bombardment of Fort Sumter. When that event ended all hope for peaceful reconciliation between North and South, Arkansas would make it clear which side she perceived as her own.

X

War and Secession

Consensus and Conflict

The mood of Arkansas citizens changed dramatically in mid-April 1861. President Lincoln declared his intention to use force to maintain the Union. Everyone knew now there would be civil war, and Arkansas had to determine her position. In a real sense, however, a choice had already been made. Since 1819, Arkansas had been reserved for slavery. After a long period of economic doldrums through much of the antebellum era, the state appeared to enter a new period of prosperity brought on by the fact that it was finally becoming a major slaveholding, cotton-growing state. So important had slavery become to Arkansas society that even most Unionists had to make it clear they were willing to leave the general government in order to protect and preserve this "peculiar institution." With President Lincoln's call to arms, Arkansas was forced to choose between the Union and the slaveholding South. Her citizens would not fight against their region and its interests. Within a few weeks after the bombardment at Fort Sumter, the state seceded with what appeared to be near unanimity.

Unity, however, was neither long-lasting nor complete. An Arkansas outside the Union was soon plagued by old rivalries and animosities. New hostility developed between Governor Rector and a conservative alliance of the Family and the old Whigs that formed during the May session of the state convention. This alliance would defeat Rector in 1862, lead the state during the years of the Civil War, recede during Reconstruction, and then form the basis for Bourbon democracy during the post-Reconstruction era. Also, not everyone in Arkansas accepted secession and the state's new place in the Southern Confederacy. Union leagues and anti-Confederate secret societies sprang up in the Ozarks. Other men in the mountains merely paid lip service to the new regime while quietly paying fuller allegiance to the old Union. Fort Sumter, in a sense, inspired both consensus and conflict.

Until mid-April, secession appeared to be at least four months away. The state began a long campaign over the questions of secession or cooperation, and balloting would not take place until early August. The convention would reconvene two weeks later to ratify the people's will. A Unionist in Carroll County in the Ozarks confidently wrote to David Walker on April 4 that "the Union question is safe now. Cooperation is in the wind, and I certainly think that when the question is put to Arkansas . . . that vote will be for cooperation."[1] On April 16, A. H. Hobson of Camden wrote to his fellow Unionist, Jesse Turner, in Van Buren that although he was surrounded by secession counties, he believed that the Union cause would prevail, "unless circumstances change."[2]

Circumstances were changing at that moment. During the first six weeks of President Lincoln's term, both the Union and the new Confederacy focused on the two remaining forts in the seceded South: Fort Pickens in Pensacola, and Fort Sumter in the harbor of Charleston. The latter fort was particularly important, for it stood defiantly facing a city that had been the seedbed of secession. Charleston's white citizenry had witnessed and cheered the breakup of the national Democratic party in April 1860. It was also in Charleston that South Carolina had begun the Southern rebellion when it seceded late in December.

After weeks of vacillation and rumors that he intended to relinquish both Federal forts, Lincoln informed Confederate President Jefferson Davis that his plan was to resupply, with non-military provisions, the installation at Fort Sumter. This triggered the Southern bombardment of the outpost, which was the immediate cause of civil war.[3] Since many in the Confederacy and in upper South states and Arkansas believed that Lincoln had intended to surrender the forts, they now accused him of duplicity.[4] Upon the surrender of Fort Sumter on April 14, Lincoln summoned seventy-five thousand troops to crush this "rebellion." Davis eventually responded with a call for one hundred thousand men to defend his "nation."[5]

Fort Sumter and the call to arms transformed the issue of secession for Arkansas and seven other slaveholding states of the upper South. Now it was not merely whether one found Lincoln's election and inauguration abhorrent but whether one desired to stay in the Union or join with most of the other slaveholding states in the Confederacy.

The impact on sentiment in Arkansas cannot be exaggerated. Former Senator Robert W. Johnson was addressing the Ozark community of Bentonville in mid-April. Just as he was being jeered, news of Fort Sumter and Lincoln's proclamation for troops was announced, and according to an eyewitness account, "all was changed in an instant." The reaction of the people became, "What! Call upon the southern people to shoot down their neighbors, help those from whom we have for years only received injury and wrong . . . No, never!"[6]

Unionism in Arkansas had been primarily of the conditional variety, that the state would persist in the Union to facilitate redress of Southern grievances and to bring about peaceful reunion of the nation. The Unionist party in Arkansas, both during the convention and its short following campaign, always maintained they would resist any effort by the Federal government to impel the seceded states to rejoin the Union. With a Calhounian concept of Federal government being the mere servant to the separate states, both secessionists and Unionists had no problems with the legality of withdrawal.[7] Lincoln's call to arms exposed the "conditionalism" of the Unionist movement. It was merely a sentimental commitment to the Union for most.

After Fort Sumter, the Unionist press capitulated. In an editorial entitled, "Coercion Commenced, Let the People of Arkansas React To It As One Man," Danley of the *Gazette*, formerly the state's leading conservative-Unionist newspaper, announced his support for secession. He recalled his long opposition to coercion and claimed that Lincoln's request for troops represented total war upon the South. Since only Congress could declare war, Danley wrote, the abolitionist-inspired Lincoln clearly usurped his authority, and he must be resisted at all costs.[8] The Van Buren *Press*, the other formerly Unionist paper, also announced its support for secession. The *Press* declared that the people "will fight coercion, defend southern rights, and none will be truer in the day of trial than the Union men of Arkansas."[9] Even the old Unionist, Judge Brown, recorded in his diary on April 20: "This is enough . . . the new administration has been weak enough or wicked enough to afford the pretext to precipitate not only the

Cotton States, but to involve the whole South in a War. Nothing like coercion could or would be bourne [sic] by the South."[10] Almost instantly, Unionist sentiment in the press, and apparently much of the Unionist movement, evaporated like morning mist before a midday sun.

Secessionists were elated at the coming of war. They knew with certainty that Arkansas would secede and join the Confederacy. The *True Democrat* summed up the situation declaring, "We cannot doubt her decision now about whom she will ally herself with . . . the ties of blood and friendship cry aloud for it."[11] In the weeks following the news of Fort Sumter, the pages of the *True Democrat* were filled with petitions from various parts of the state demanding that the convention be recalled to withdraw Arkansas from the Union.[12] In public print and in private letters, many men who had led the fight for the Union during the last few months now announced themselves in favor of secession. S. H. Tucker, a merchant in Little Rock, wrote to his friend, D. C. Williams, in Van Buren, "We fought manfully for the Union, let us fight manfully for the South."[13] Augustus Garland and Joseph Stillwell, Unionist delegates from Pulaski County, publicly asked David Walker to reconvene the convention to bring about a speedy secession.[14] Other leading former Unionists, including former Congressman Rust, former Congressman Edward Warren, William Woodruff, and Samuel Hempstead, declared in favor of secession and for joining the Confederacy.[15] Most of these conservatives had once feared disunion would bring on war; now that civil strife was imminent, they chose to follow the seceding South, demonstrating their greater loyalty to slavery.

Southern and eastern Arkansas, long-time advocates of secession, were thrown into virtual frenzy by the firing on Fort Sumter.[16] Preparations for war began throughout the delta even before the convention actually pulled the state out of the Union. Planter Frank Peak won election as an officer in a volunteer militia company in his home county of Chicot in the southeastern corner of Arkansas.[17] In late April, Judge Brown in Camden grumblingly recorded in his diary that "fanatical companies are mustering, and the sounds of drum and martial music greet me night and day."[18] From the lowlands came one demand to recall the convention in order to withdraw Arkansas from the Union. David Walker alone had the power to recall the convention before the August election. Hanly wrote Walker on April 17 that "the convention must reassemble to speak for the State in the course it would pursue in the ensuing Civil War."[19] Hanly said sentiment in the delta was clear, "In the eastern Arkansas counties, Phillips, Monroe, St. Francis, Poinsett, Craighead, Greene, Crittenden, and Mississippi, the secession sentiment is nearly unanimous since recent events."[20]

As delta leaders pressured Walker to reconvene the convention, Governor Rector dealt with the troop requests from both North and South. Rector replied to the Union request for troops on April 22:

In answer to your requisition for troops from Arkansas to subjugate the Southern States, I have to say that none will be furnished. The demand is only adding insult to injury. The people of this commonwealth are freemen, not slaves, and will defend, to the last extremity, their honor, lives and property against Northern mendacity and usurpation.[21]

To the Confederate request for troops he politely declined one day later, saying that he could not act until the state formally seceded and joined the Confederacy.[22]

The governor then set about the task of seizing all Federal positions in the state. Although Arkansas had not formally withdrawn from the Union, Rector must have felt he had some precedent since he had seized the Little Rock arsenal in February. Placing the Arkansas militia under the command of Solon Borland, the former senator and diplomat to Central America, Rector gave him the task of possessing the U.S. outpost in Fort Smith. When a regiment of militia arrived there on April 23, it discovered Federal troops had already abandoned the installation, taking with them huge quantities of arms and munitions on the previous day.[23] The Federals had escaped northward to Kansas via the Indian Territory.[24] By late April, Arkansas had been cleared of U.S. government forces.

With Federal forces gone from the state, Walker came under increasing pressure to reassemble the convention. Still a Unionist at heart, Walker understood clearly that a convention recalled would probably pass an ordinance of secession. Though reluctant, he felt he had no other choice. Walker and his fellow Unionists had just published the manifesto declaring opposition to Federal coercion of seceded states. How could he hope to justify his refusal to recall the convention in the face of Lincoln's action to raise troops to quell a Southern rebellion? If Walker did not favor secession it might be construed to mean that he was prepared to join Lincoln in taking up arms against the South. Since many in the South believed Lincoln to be an abolitionist, or at least manipulated by abolitionists, why should Walker continue to oppose disunion unless he was also an abolitionist all along? It would now be almost impossible for a Unionist to oppose secession without appearing to be either a traitor to the slaveholding South or the hapless agent of Northern abolitionists.

Walker and other conservative Unionists also kept in mind that even if no convention was ever called, southern and eastern Arkansas might secede on their own and join the Confederacy. Further must have been the fear that unless good conservatives took charge of the state and its affairs, secession might lead to more revolutionary action, such as an assault on private property. On April 15, Danley wrote Walker, his long-time political compatriot, urging him to reconvene the assembly, for "if we take the initiative, the Conservative men of this State will control the movement. If we do not, revolutionaries will take charge, and we will have to blame ourselves for the events that will rise necessary from them."[25] Danley sincerely believed that secession could not be averted, so high-minded conservatives had to take hold of the disunionist movement to prevent more radical change.

Walker still hesitated a bit before finally recalling the convention. Like other Unionists, the Fayetteville jurist believed Arkansas to be an upper South or border state. By late April, it appeared that those areas were also planning to secede and join the Confederacy. Many upland Arkansans were natives of Tennessee, Kentucky, and Missouri, and looked to them for guidance. Walker wrote Missouri Governor Claiborne F. Jackson in mid-April and received the reply that "Missouri will be ready for secession in thirty days, and will secede if Arkansas will get out of the way and give her free passage."[26] The idea of acting with other upper South and border states was common among Unionists. One supporter wrote to Jesse Turner on April 19, "I am for acting in concert with the Border States to unite!"[27] Since newspapers like the formerly Unionist Van Buren *Press* were publishing reports of the imminent withdrawal of North Carolina, Tennessee, and Maryland from the Union,[28] it must have appeared to Walker that all upper South and border slave states were preparing to secede. In late April news arrived that Virginia, the mother of the Old South, had seceded on the seventeenth.[29] Walker succumbed to pressure and issued a call for the convention to reassemble on Monday, May 6.[30]

At ten in the morning on that date, Walker formally opened the second session of the convention. Almost immediately, planter Charles Adams of Phillips County moved that the Committee on Ordinances and Resolutions prepare an ordinance of secession by two o'clock. William Grace of Jefferson County, the committee chairman, amended the motion to three o'clock, claiming his committee needed the extra hour, and the assembly quickly passed Adam's amended motion.[31]

The convention then heard a long letter from Samuel Hempstead of Little Rock, a long-time conservative Family Democrat. Although Hempstead had opposed disunion through much of the secession crisis, he now favored withdrawal. With much truth, Hempstead wrote that "it was only under a peaceful, prudent, and conciliatory course toward the South—the policy of leaving them unmolested and undisturbed—that Arkansas was willing to remain in the Union."[32] Hempstead was quite accurate when he commented that the people of Arkansas "could not be asked to fight our southern brethren."[33]

At three o'clock, the convention came once again to order and the Committee on Ordinances presented its resolution. (This Ordinance of Secession for Arkansas appears on Figure 10a in the Appendix.) Alfred Dinsmore of Benton County in the northwestern corner of the state made a last desperate effort to forestall secession, moving that the ordinance be submitted to the people for a vote on the first Monday in June.[34] His motion failed, fifty-five to fifteen, those supporting votes coming from delegates in western and northwestern Arkansas. (See Figure 10b in the Appendix.) Fort Sumter had, indeed, decimated the once-powerful Unionist vote, which had declined from a majority of thirty-nine to a minority of fifteen. Secession was thus inevitable, and the convention now began to vote on the Ordinance of Secession. Except for an explanatory note requested by a few Unionists, complete silence prevailed during the roll call. Only five votes were cast against secession; sixty-five approved. Four of the five negative votes came from delegates from the Ozark counties in the northwest.[35]

After the vote on secession was completed, Walker stood and addressed the convention saying, "Enough votes have been cast to take us out of the Union. Now since we must go, let us all go together, let the wires carry the news to all the world that Arkansas stands as a unit against coercion."[36] Four of the five remaining Unionists changed their votes to secession. Samuel "Parson" Kelly of Pike County, one of the four delegates, added to his changed vote that he supported the right to revolution, but not the doctrine of secession.[37]

Only one delegate remained recalcitrant, a mountaineer farmer named Isaac Murphy of Madison County. Amid hisses and boos, Murphy declared, "I have cast my vote after mature reflection, and have duly considered the consequences, and I cannot conscientiously change it. I therefore vote no!"[38] As soon as Murphy announced his refusal to change his vote to secession, Mrs. Frederick Trapnall, the widow of a prominent Little Rock merchant and Whig politician, threw a bouquet of roses to him from her seat in the gallery.[39] Alfred Holt Carrigan of Hempstead County in southwestern Arkansas remembered Murphy as "having little cultivation and much information, frequently engaging in debate and bearing himself well."[40] Carrigan later wrote that he believed no other member of the convention could have taken the position Murphy did without being mobbed by the populace. Murphy continued to participate in the convention after it seceded.[41]

The official *Journal* for the convention recorded that "Arkansas completed its vote on secession at ten minutes past four in the afternoon of May 6, 1861."[42] This was only one month and nine days short of Arkansas's twenty-fifth anniversary as a state. Symbolically, it would be Hindman, the man who worked so long and hard for this day, who sent the news of Arkansas's vote to the world. Late that afternoon, Hindman wired this partially incorrect message to Confederate President Jefferson Davis: "Convention passed Ordinance of Secession at 4 P.M. by a unanimous vote."[43] Arkansas had now, for good or ill, cast its fate with the Confederacy.

At the moment in early May when the state finally withdrew from the Union, the body politic appeared totally united. While most of the state supported disunion at that time, once the issue was finally settled Arkansas's politics easily reverted to tradition: factionalism, character assassination, vicious party infighting, and the all too familiar cry of "Family" domination.[44] Nowhere was it more apparent than at the state convention, which continued in session from May 6 through June 3. Historian Michael Dougan has pointed out that "secession did not spell the end to politics, and the passing of an Ordinance of Secession was not the only important act of the convention."[45]

Working on the assumption that secession had obliterated all previous political structures, the convention performed other radical actions. It rewrote the state constitution, legalized state banking, joined the Southern Confederacy, and selected delegates to the Provisional Confederate Congress. The convention also drew up the Confederate congressional districts, moved state elections from August to October, and reduced the governor's term from four to two years. The convention assumed control of the state militia by setting up a military board to oversee its day-to-day actions. It even selected the generals who would oversee the defense of the state.[46] All its actions reflected the strategy of a new political alliance.

This new alliance was a carefully crafted coalition of old-line Whig conservatives and "Family" Democrats. Even before the second session began, Danley wrote to William Mansfield of Ozark that "the Conservative men of the Convention should take charge of the affairs, and prevent the secessionists from leading us to the Devil . . . I think it is of Most Importance that Conservative Men should contrive to control our actions."[47] In early May, ex-Whig merchant David C. Williams of Van Buren wrote to his delegate, Jesse Turner, that "as far as possible, the convention must take control over affairs, especially the appointment of men to places of power."[48] Another Whig merchant in Little Rock, S. H. Tucker, wrote to Williams on May 10 that "our convention delegates are disposed to do things right, and I believe many good changes will be made."[49]

Williams and other Whigs were not disappointed. Many of them were convinced that they must take control of the state so that revolution would not follow closely on the heels of secession.[50] Professing little confidence "in the men who destroyed our Union,"[51] these old-line Whig conservatives used their influence among the old coalition of Unionists in the convention to enact their own agenda. They especially feared Governor Rector, whom they had distrusted since he seized the Little Rock arsenal in February. Many were still irked with Rector because, since the firing on Fort Sumter, "the governor behaves as though the state had already seceded."[52] To these men the governor appeared to have no regard for legality or propriety. They were horrified that secession might place them in the hands of a dangerous man, and decided to take power upon themselves. By challenging Rector, the Whigs found allies among their old adversaries, the Conway-Johnson Dynasty Democrats. Family Democrats refused to forgive the governor for his "treachery" in the state election in 1860. Rector's appointment of Borland, an old anti-Family Democrat, as a commander of the state militia must have irked the Dynasty greatly. The Family was only too willing to join with old-line Whigs to punish the governor and his allies in some way.

This alliance explains many of the actions of the second session of the convention. For example, four of the five men chosen to represent Arkansas in the Confederate Congress had been Unionists before Fort Sumter. Two of them, Augustus Garland and Hugh French Thomason, were old-line Whigs or Know-Nothings who had supported Bell in the past presidential election. The other two were William Wirt Watkins of Carroll County in the Ozarks and former Congressman Albert Rust of El Dorado, both of whom had been Douglas Democrats. The Family's representative in the delegation was former Senator Robert W. Johnson. Even more startling than whom they elected to the Confederate Congress is whom they turned down for the position. The Whig-Family alliance turned down Hindman's bid for the Southern Congress.[53] The Family might be willing to work with Hindman in the cause of secession, but once it was accomplished, they remembered his actions in 1860 and were quick to try and stifle his political career. Also old-line Whigs apparently came to fear and distrust this rabble-rousing secessionist from Helena. The choices for the Confederate Congress angered many early disunionists, and the Des Arc *Citizen* grumbled in late May that "the convention will be long remembered for rewarding submissionists."[54] The Whig-Dynasty leaders simply did not want change to get out of hand, so they took control of the new government. Thus the revolution against the Union would not become a revolution at home.

The new state Constitution also reflected the interests of the new alliance. Here, the ex-Whigs played their most prominent role, for the new Constitution legalized state banks and removed from popular election all judges below the state supreme court. The governor would appoint all state judges with the consent of two-thirds of the state senate.[55] Another manifestation of the alliance was the convention's shearing of Governor Rector's power. It virtually stripped him of all his military authority and reduced his term from four to two years. This was merely the beginning of a sustained conservative-Dynasty attack on Rector. By the fall of 1862, he was forced to resign even before completing his shortened term.[56] The alliance replaced him with Harris Flanagin of Arkadelphia, a loyal Dynasty Democrat who guided Arkansas until the end of the Civil War.[57] The conservative alliance eventually survived the war and resurfaced during Reconstruction as Democratic-Conservatives.[58] The Democratic-Conservatives later formed the basis of Bourbon democracy after Reconstruction, and ruled the state on into the twentieth century.[59]

While old divisions and rivalries still plagued that part of Arkansas that welcomed secession in early May, not everyone accepted the state's new place outside the Federal Union. Loyalty to the old Union continued to prevail in the Ozark plateau, which had enjoyed no major immigration from the lower South during the 1850s and where slavery was incidental to the economy and social life. Taking immense pride in their white skin and their rugged individualism, the hill folks jealously guarded their suffrage privileges, which they believed were threatened by secession, and resented the aristocratic pretensions of the delta planters. They saw little to gain and much to lose in a Southern Confederacy dominated largely by slaveholders. Though old-line Whig Unionists in the delta and river towns finally embraced secession after Fort Sumter, many in the mountains remained loyal to the Union. Protecting slavery mattered little to them.

That secession would not be fully accepted in the Ozarks was apparent soon after the convention disbanded. Unionist delegate John Campbell from the Ozark county of Searcy had to write a letter to angry constituents defending his switch to secession on the second roll call.[60] An angry mountaineer from Carroll County wrote David C. Williams, the former Unionist merchant from Van Buren, that the convention should have referred secession to the people and proclaimed an armed neutrality until the election. He ended his letter expressing his disappointment at being abandoned by merchants like Williams declaring, "I am afraid that like the rest of the Union men, you have been overwhelmed or swept along in the popular tide."[61] Other Unionists in northwestern Arkansas paid lip service to secession and the state's allegiance to the Confederacy but maintained a real loyalty to the Union. One of them was the Democratic lawyer Jonas Tebbetts of Fayetteville. His daughter wrote a journal as a young girl in which she recounted a secret ceremony by her father in their home on July 4. With all the windows and blinds shut, her father ordered the entire family to pledge allegiance to the American flag, telling them that was their real government, and ending the ceremony by reading the Declaration of Independence.[62]

Other Unionists in northwestern and north central areas of the state did more than hold secret ceremonies. In November and December of

1861, the first secret peace society in the Confederacy was uncovered in the Ozark counties.[63] In Searcy, Izard, Carroll, Fulton, Marion and Van Buren counties, an Arkansas Peace Society held secret meetings and sought to resist and to frustrate the war of the state government. The members were captured and carried to Little Rock for trial. After their conviction for treason, they were given the choice of joining the Confederacy or being shot. They all chose the Confederacy.[64] After the breakup of the Arkansas Peace Society, other clandestine anti-Confederate groups were organized in the hills. Thomas Boles, who became a postwar Republican congressman, claimed in 1868 that he and a few others had organized a Union league in Johnson and Pope counties in the spring of 1862. It operated under cover to resist the Confederate draft and aid to the Union army in the northwestern and north central parts of the state.[65]

A greater indication of Unionist sentiment was the number of Arkansans who served with Federal forces. Historian Carl Degler called this the severest test of Unionism in the South, willingness to serve with the invading army.[66] According to the official records, Arkansas provided more troops for the Federal army than any Confederate state except Tennessee.[67] Figures are more remarkable because Arkansas had the third smallest white population among the Confederate states, which was only 39 percent of Tennessee's.[68] Unionism was so strong in northwestern Arkansas that Col. William F. Cloud, a Federal officer who served in the area during the Civil War, wrote to his superiors that he raised six companies for the Northern army in one day.[69] In the same report in September 1863, Col. Cloud made this assessment of Unionist sentiment in much of northwestern Arkansas:

I am convinced that thousands of men stand ready to take arms as soon as they can be furnished, . . . The people come to me by hundreds, and beg of me to stand by them and keep them from being taken by the conscript officers or from being taken back to the rebel army, from which they have deserted, and to show their earnestness they came in with their old guns and joined us.[70]

Unionist sentiment in the Ozarks would later form the basis for the Republican party during Reconstruction, continuing into the twentieth century.[71]

Soon after the news of Fort Sumter arrived in the state, the influential, pro-secessionist *True Democrat* asked for unity saying, "Let us forget all past party distinctions, and bury our past party feuds."[72] As much as this

Conway-Johnson journal might have desired unity at the very outset of a national civil war, it would not be forthcoming. Decades of rancorous and vindictive political infighting could not be buried in one brief moment of euphoria. Such divisions characterized Arkansas's politics even during its life-or-death struggle as part of the Confederacy. Fort Sumter brought some measure of accord to the state, yet this unity was simply too fleeting and incomplete to bind together this fundamentally divided slaveholding society on the Southern frontier.

Conclusion

The role of Arkansas in the Southern secession movement could be dismissed as insignificant. The state does not approach the stereotyped image of the Old South, since it was the region's last frontier. Arkansas had the smallest population of any Confederate state except Florida.[1] Its percentage of slave population (25%) exceeded only that of Tennessee's (24%), and its percentage of whites involved in slavery was below 20%, the lowest in the Confederacy.[2] It is therefore easy to see why Arkansas did not belong to the mainstream antebellum South, but these statistics are only a part of reality.

Much has been made of the fact that by 1861, white Arkansans believed that their future lay with slavery and the cotton economy. The failure of this state to completely succeed in dissolving its bonds with the Union should not cause us to view secession as a sentimental tragedy or a wholly irrational undertaking. It was neither. It was an act accomplished by a political community whose cultural, economic, and social ties to the antebellum South were too strong, even though the state was to some extent out of the mainstream of the slave South.

There has also been some dispute over whether Arkansas belonged to the upper or the lower South. More than fifty years ago historian Lewis Gray allocated Arkansas to the Deep South, and a more recent econometric study has made a similar categorization.[3] Daniel Croft's recent analysis of the upper South does not include Arkansas.[4] Most historians including Ralph Wooster, David Potter, Michael Holt, and William Cooper have all noticed that Arkansas left the Union after bombardment of Fort Sumter and considered the state firmly a part of the upper South.[5]

Geographically speaking, it is easy to see why there is a debate over this question. Arkansas is the northernmost state of the lower South (the only one to reach the 36°30' line), and is the southernmost state of the upper South. Arkansas's southern boundary dips to the 33rd parallel, two full degrees in latitude below that of Tennessee. The state's relationship to the Union reflected this geographic ambiguity. The Arkansas delegation was the only one from the upper South whose majority walked out of the Democratic convention in April, 1860. Arkansas not only gave Breckinridge a majority, but the biggest percentage of any upper South state. Arkansas and Virginia were the only two states of the upper South to call a convention to consider secession in the winter of 1860–1861. In the former, the Unionists had a majority of five; the latter elected only 32 proponents of immediate secession in an assembly of 152 members.[6]

This study is meant to contribute to the growing body of scholarly literature on secession and to the resolution of the dispute over differences between the upper and lower South during the secession crisis of 1860–61. As historian Cooper has commented, "secession remains one of the most vexing questions confronting American historians."[7] While there is not yet a comprehensive treatment dealing with the subject, there have been a number of significant state studies.[8] An analysis of this difficult and complex topic should take into account the unique road to secession followed by Arkansas.

Obviously the state does not completely fit the paradigm outlined by Michael Holt to differentiate between the lower and upper South.[9] In contrast to North Carolina and Tennessee which had strong two-party competition from the 1830s until the secession crisis,[10] Arkansas remained under the iron rule of the Conway-Sevier-Johnson Dynasty from the Jacksonian era to the state election of 1860. According to Holt, this one-party dominance prevailed within the Deep South until the late 1850s.[11] Hindman's successful political revolution of 1860 would do more than shatter Family control over major state offices. By introducing real political competition, Hindman made Arkansas politics resemble those of North Carolina and Tennessee. At a time when the state was becoming economically bonded to the lower South, a secessionist ironically launched a revolt which aligned Arkansas politics with the upper South.

A deeper irony is that by disrupting Family rule, Hindman's rebellion created a new factionalism based upon social, economic, and regional differences. As long as a party dynasty ruled, those divisions could be submerged or suppressed. Prior to 1860 the Family's only disappointment was its failure to arouse the people to a national defense of slavery. After its dominance was successfully challenged in the summer election of 1860, the disunion question that winter brought the state's economic, social, and regional differences into the political arena. These differences became so acute during the secession convention in March 1861, that serious talk of state dismemberment was entertained outside the assembly. A graver specter to the slaveholders was that the yeomen in the mountains or even in the delta regions might be unwilling to defend slavery in secession and civil war. This fear became manifest not only in Arkansas but also in other states of the upper South.

Though such fears had some basis, they did not materialize to a great extent. Most yeomen farmers, especially in the lowlands and many in the hills, loyally supported the Lost Cause, but the Ozark mountaineers, isolated and slaveless, remained unalterably opposed to both secession and the Confederacy. This mountain Unionism would form the basis of the Republican party in the state during Reconstruction and beyond. In Confederate Arkansas, a Whig-Family alliance effectively used the secession convention to undercut and later drive off the governor installed by Hindman's rebellion. This Whig-Family conservative faction survived the war, emerging as Democratic Conservatives during the Reconstruction era. After "redeeming" the state from Carpetbagger control in 1874, it ruled the state for decades as the Bourbon and neo-Bourbon Democrats.

Many antebellum political figures failed to hold center stage during the postbellum period. Ex-Senator Solon Borland and Senator and Confederate Senator Charles Mitchel did not survive the war.[12] Family leader Robert W. Johnson served as a Confederate senator throughout the war. His immense fortune was lost and his political career was ended by the secession he so ardently supported. Failing to regain his wealth and defeated for the U.S. Senate in 1878, Johnson died less than a year later.[13] The Douglas leader Albert Rust served only briefly in the Confederate Congress before embarking on a fairly illustrious career in the Southern army, including a part-time service with General T. J. "Stonewall" Jackson. Rust died five years after the war.[14]

Hindman's career during the Confederacy and after the war would be as colorful and erratic as his antebellum life. When the secession convention refused him a seat in the Provisional Confederate Congress in May, 1861, Hindman decided to pursue glory in the military. He eventually became a Confederate general, and at one point, made himself virtually the military dictator of Arkansas. Refusing to accept Southern defeat, Hindman first fled to Mexico, but eventually returned to Helena in 1867. He threw himself unsuccessfully into politics against the Radical Republicans in the state election of 1867, although he had not received a pardon, and then turned his attention to rebuilding his law practice. Only forty years old, he was mysteriously assassinated as he sat by an open window in his Helena home on the evening of September 27, 1868. According to Hindman's only biographer, his political enemies were too numerous to discover who really killed him, and no arrests were ever made.[15]

Some leaders of the wartime Whig-Family alliance, such as ex-Whig David Walker and former Confederate Governor Harris Flanagan (1862–1865), would continue their leadership roles until late in the century. Flanagan was a prominent delegate to the 1874 Constitutional Convention, and Walker served on the state supreme court from 1874 until shortly before his death in 1879.[16] Other men including Family Democrat Thomas J. Churchill and conservative Unionist William M. Fishback were each elected governor during the era of Bourbon Democracy in the 1880s and 1890s.[17] Even though Henry M. Rector never again held a major state office after 1862, his son Elias Rector became a prominent corporation lawyer after Reconstruction and Speaker of the state House of Representatives in the 1890s. He proved to be the perfect patrician foil for agrarian insurgent Jeff Davis during the gubernatorial campaign of 1902,[18] playing an exactly opposite role to that of his father forty-two years earlier.

Typical of the Whig-Family conservative continuity was Augustus Hill Garland of Little Rock. A Unionist with a Whig Know-Nothing background prior to Fort Sumter, Garland used his role in the secession convention as a springboard into the Confederate Congress where he served in the House and Senate. He was only forty-two when he led the Bourbon Democrats to power in the gubernatorial election of 1874. The state legislature then elected him to the U.S. Senate in 1877 where he served until President Grover Cleveland appointed him attorney general of the United States in 1885. He was the first Arkansan elevated to a Cabinet position.

Garland spent the last decade of his life as a lawyer in Washington, D.C., and died dramatically while arguing a case before the United States Supreme Court on January 26, 1899.[19] Garland's career, spanning the last forty years of the nineteenth century, was launched during the successful wartime alliance of Whigs and Family Democrats, which survived in a slightly mutated form as Bourbon Democracy. To find the roots of postbellum Arkansas politics, one need only look to the secession convention, the last political assembly of the antebellum era.

The Arkansas path to disunion is not without irony. A state with regional and class differences, torn in opposite directions by the upper and lower South, it was fundamentally united behind slavery and appalled by Federal coercion of the seceded states. While those personally involved with slavery never amounted to one-fifth of the total white population during the antebellum era, nevertheless, the influx of immigrants from the Deep South together with the perception and the reality of a new prosperity based upon a cotton economy, caused an overwhelming number of Arkansans to identify with a slaveholding Southern Confederacy. Only the most economically and politically isolated sections of the state remained in opposition to secession after Fort Sumter. The most surprising feature of the secession convention of 1861 is that it not only represented the culmination of the antebellum era, but pointed the way for the state's political future as well.

Arkansas's road to secession bears a striking similarity to disunionism in Texas. These two states, after all, shared a common role as the last western frontier for the Old South. One historian of secession in the Lone Star State has recently observed that "antebellum Texans' vision of their society's future status, stability, and prosperity often came to depend upon slavery. . . . Texans did not cease to be Americans or Texans, but to the degree that a plantation economy dominated their present and their future they became increasingly like the lower southerners."[20] Like Texas, Arkansas was not yet a cotton plantation society, but it was clearly moving along that path. Tasting a new prosperity from both cotton and slavery, this small state was unwilling to part with its new economic success, even for the sake of the Union. Arkansas, only beginning to emerge economically, made a fateful step that retarded its development for another century. This is the final irony of the secession movement.

Appendix

Tables and Figures

PHYSIOGRAPHIC REGIONS OF ARKANSAS
75 COUNTIES   10 REGIONS

Figure 1

COUNTIES				REGIONS
1 Benton	20 Poinsett	39 Polk	58 Sevier	1 Springfield
2 Washington	21 Cross	40 Montgomery	59 Little River	Plateau
3 Carroll	22 Crittenden	41 Garland	60 Hempstead	2 Salem Plateau
4 Madison	23 Jackson	42 Perry	61 Nevada	3 Boston
5 Boone	24 Woodruff	43 Saline	62 Ouachita	Mountains
6 Newton	25 Independence	44 Pulaski	63 Dallas	4 Arkansas Valley
7 Marion	26 White	45 Lonoke	64 Cleveland	5 Fourche
8 Searcy	27 Cleburne	46 Prairie	65 Calhoun	Mountains
9 Baxter	28 Faulkner	47 Monroe	66 Lincoln	6 Central
10 Fulton	29 Van Buren	48 St. Francis	67 Desha	Ouachitas
11 Izard	30 Conway	49 Lee	68 Drew	7 Athens Plateau
12 Stone	31 Pope	50 Phillips	69 Chicot	8 Gulf Coastal
13 Sharp	32 Johnson	51 Arkansas	70 Ashley	Plain
14 Randolph	33 Logan	52 Jefferson	71 Bradley	9 Mississippi
15 Lawrence	34 Yell	53 Grant	72 Union	Alluvial Plain
16 Clay	35 Scott	54 Hot Spring	73 Columbia	10 Crowley's Ridge
17 Greene	36 Sebastian	55 Clark	74 Lafayette	
18 Craighead	37 Franklin	56 Pike	75 Miller	
19 Mississippi	38 Crawford	57 Howard		

TABLE 1a   Arkansas's Population Growth, 1810–1860

	1810	*1820*	*1830*	*1840*	*1850*	*1860*
White	924	12,579	25,671	77,174	162,189	324,191
Slave	136	1,617	4,579	19,935	47,100	111,115
Free Black	2	59	141	465	608	144
Total	1,062	14,255	30,388	97,574	209,897	435,450
% Increase in State	—	1,244%	112%	221%	115.1%	107.5%
% Increase in Nation	—	33.1%	33.5%	32.7%	35.9%	35.6%

TABLE 1b Population Total: Arkansas Compared with Other Frontier States,

	Pop. Total 1810	% of Growth 1810–20	Pop. Total 1820	% of Growth 1820–30	Pop. Total 1830	% of Growth 1830–40
Arkansas	1,062	1,224. %	14,225	112. %	30,388	221. %
Illinois	24,250	349. %	55,161	185.1%	157,455	202.4%
Louisiana	76,556	100.3%	113,872	40.6%	215,739	63.3%
Michigan	4,762	86.8%	8,591	255.6%	31,659	570. %
Mississippi	40,352	86.9%	42,176	81.0%	132,621	174.9%
Missouri	20,845	219.4%	55,988	110.9%	140,455	173.1%
Average % of Growth		344. %		130.5%		242.4%

TABLE 1c Whites Only: Arkansas's Percentage of Growth Compared with

	Pop. Total 1810	% of Growth 1810–20	Pop. Total 1820	% of Growth 1820–30	Pop. Total 1830	% of Growth 1830–40
Arkansas	924	1,261. %	12,579	104.1%	30,388	200.6%
Illinois	11,501	367.6%	53,788	188.5%	155,061	204.5%
Louisiana	34,311	113.8%	73,383	21.5%	89,441	71.6%
Michigan	4,618	86.0%	8,591	264.8%	31,346	574.9%
Mississippi	23,024	83.1%	42,176	67.0%	70,443	154.2%
Missouri	17,224	225.0%	55,988	105.3%	114,795	182.1%
Average % of Growth		356.0%		125.2%		231.3%

TABLE 1d Population of Arkansas and Other Frontier States, 1810 and 1860

	1810		1860	
	White	Total	White	Total
Arkansas	924	1,062	324,143	435,450
Illinois	11,501	12,282	1,704,291	1,711,951
Louisiana	34,311	76,556	357,456	708,002
Michigan	4,618	4,762	736,142	749,113
Mississippi	23,024	40,352	353,899	791,305
Missouri	17,227	20,825	1,063,489	1,182,012

Pop. Total 1840	% of Growth 1840–50	Pop. Total 1850	% of Growth 1850–60	Pop. Total 1860
77,174	115.1%	209,897	107.5%	435,450
456,183	78.8%	851,470	101.9%	1,711,951
352,411	42.9%	517,762	36.7%	708,002
212,297	87.3%	397,654	88.3%	749,113
375,681	61.4%	606,526	30.4%	791,305
383,702	77.7%	682,044	73.7%	1,182,012
	77.2%		71.2%	

Other Frontier States, 1810–1860

Pop. Total 1840	% of Growth 1840–50	Pop. Total 1850	% of Growth 1850–60	Pop. Total 1860
77,174	110.1%	162,109	99.8%	324,143
472,254	79.1%	846,034	101.1%	1,704,291
158,457	61.2%	255,491	39.9%	357,456
211,560	86.7%	395,071	86.3%	736,142
179,074	65.1%	295,718	19.6%	353,899
323,888	82.1%	592,004	79.6%	1,063,489
	77.8%		71.0%	

TABLE 1e   Total Percentage of Growth in Population of Arkansas and Other Frontier States, 1810–1860

	White	Total
Arkansas	38,984.5%	40,902.2%
Illinois	14,718.6%	13,838.7%
Louisiana	941.8%	824.8%
Michigan	15,840.7%	15,631. %
Mississippi	1,381.3%	3,127.1%
Missouri	6,073.3%	5,570.4%

TABLE 1f   Male and Female Population Between Ages 15 and 60 in
Arkansas, 1820–1860

	Age	15–20	20–40		45+	
1820	Male	1,453	1,453		688	
	Female	1,179	934		426	

	Age	15–20	20–30	30–40	40–50	50–60
1830	Male	1,272	2,835	1,820	876	434
	Female	1,225	2,012	1,087	528	301
1840	Male	3,863	8,532	5,129	2,751	1,194
	Female	3,911	5,891	3,317	1,715	805
1850	Male	9,059	15,193	10,043	6,056	3,041
	Female	8,990	13,228	7,420	4,501	2,186
1860	Male	17,810	31,413	19,793	12,164	6,474
	Female	18,252	27,016	15,787	9,307	4,829

TABLE 1g   Ratio of White Females to 100 White Males in Seven Frontier
States, 1850

Age	15–20	20–30	30–40	40–50	50–60	Mean
Arkansas	99.2	87.1	73.8	74.3	71.2	81.12
Missouri	100.1	85.1	75.0	77.1	76.2	82.70
Michigan	100.1	89.7	81.9	76.2	74.4	84.46
Louisiana	117.6	79.9	54.8	54.4	64.4	74.22
Texas	103.0	74.8	60.6	62.9	61.3	72.52
Mississippi	101.9	86.9	74.5	77.1	71.1	82.3
Illinois	97.4	88.8	79.1	80.5	76.9	84.54

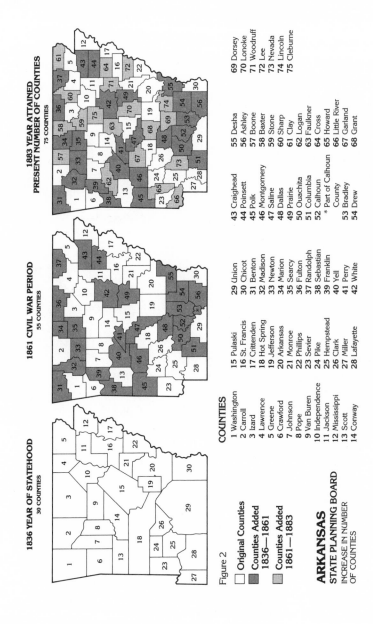

1836 YEAR OF STATEHOOD
30 COUNTIES

1861 CIVIL WAR PERIOD
55 COUNTIES

1883 YEAR ATTAINED
PRESENT NUMBER OF COUNTIES
75 COUNTIES

Figure 2

☐ Original Counties

▨ Counties Added 1836—1861

▨ Counties Added 1861—1883

ARKANSAS
STATE PLANNING BOARD
INCREASE IN NUMBER
OF COUNTIES

COUNTIES

1 Washington	29 Union	43 Craighead	55 Desha
2 Carroll	30 Chicot	44 Poinsett	56 Ashley
3 Izard	31 Benton	45 Polk	57 Boone
4 Lawrence	32 Madison	46 Montgomery	58 Baxter
5 Greene	33 Newton	47 Saline	59 Stone
6 Crawford	34 Marion	48 Dallas	60 Sharp
7 Johnson	35 Searcy	49 Prairie	61 Clay
8 Pope	36 Fulton	50 Ouachita	62 Logan
9 Van Buren	37 Randolph	51 Columbia	63 Faulkner
10 Independence	38 Sebastian	52 Calhoun	64 Cross
11 Jackson	39 Franklin	* Part of Calhoun	65 Howard
12 Mississippi	40 Yell	County	66 Little River
13 Scott	41 Perry	53 Bradley	67 Garland
14 Conway	42 White	54 Drew	68 Grant

69 Dorsey
70 Lonoke
71 Woodruff
72 Lee
73 Nevada
74 Lincoln
75 Cleburne

15 Pulaski
16 St. Francis
17 Crittenden
18 Hot Spring
19 Jefferson
20 Arkansas
21 Monroe
22 Phillips
23 Sevier
24 Pike
25 Hempstead
26 Clark
27 Miller
28 Lafayette

TABLE 2a Population in Lowland and Upland Counties in the Arkansas
Territory, 1830

Lowland Counties	Total Population	Free Population	Slave Population
Crittenden	1,272	1,107	165
St. Francis	1,505	1,369	136
Chicot	1,165	995	270
Arkansas	1,429	1,057	369
Lafayette	748	408	340
Jackson	333	316	17
Monroe	461	386	75
Phillips	1,152	1,026	126
Hempstead	2,512	1,990	522
Union	640	466	174
Sevier	634	568	66
Clark	1,369	1,264	105
Jefferson	772	612	160
Miller	356	301	55
Total	14,345 (47%)	11,755 (46%)	2,580 (56%)
Upland Counties			
Lawrence	2,806	2,481	325
Crawford	2,440	2,089	352
Izard	1,266	1,209	57
Conway	982	895	87
Hot Spring	483	406	52
Pope	1,483	1,272	211
Washington	2,182	2,012	170
Independence	2,031	1,728	303
Pulaski	2,395	1,956	459
Total	16,043 (53%)	14,057 (54%)	1,996 (44%)
Total for all	30,388	25,812	4,576

TABLE 2b Lowland and Upland Population, 1840–1860: Totals and Whites Only

		Totals	Whites Only
1840*	Lowland	38,844 (40%)	25,347 (33%)
	Upland	58,730 (60%)	51,827 (67%)
	Total	97,574	77,174
1850**	Lowland	102,799 (49%)	65,237 (40%)
	Upland	107,898 (51%)	96,952 (60%)
	Total	209,897	162,189
1860***	Lowland	228,244 (52%)	136,351 (42%)
	Upland	207,226 (48%)	187,840 (58%)
	Total	435,450	324,191

*Lowland counties: Arkansas, Chicot, Crittenden, Clark, Desha, Greene, Hempstead, Jackson, Jefferson, Lafayette, Monroe, Mississippi, Phillips, Poinsett, Sevier, St. Francis, Union.
Upland Counties: Benton, Carroll, Conway, Crawford, Franklin, Hot Spring, Independence, Izard, Johnson, Lawrence, Madison, Marion, Pike, Pope, Pulaski, Randolph, Scott, Searcy, Saline, Van Buren, Washington, and White.
**1850 Lowland counties are the above-mentioned, plus: Ashley, Bradley, Dallas, Drew, Ouachita, Prairie. The new upland counties are the above-mentioned, plus: Fulton, Montgomery, Newton, Perry, Polk, and Yell.
***Lowland counties: Calhoun (1850), Columbia (1852), Craighead (1859). Upland county added is Sebastian (1851).

TABLE 2c Birthplace Percentage of Population, Lowlands and Uplands, 1834–1850

Lowlands		Uplands	
Tennessee	28.6%	Tennessee	42.5%
Alabama	21.2%	Missouri	19.1%
Mississippi	20.1%	Alabama	7.1%
Georgia	5.8%	Illinois	7.0%
Missouri	5.0%	Kentucky	5.3%
Kentucky	4.4%	Mississippi	4.9%

TABLE 2d   Birthplace Percentage of Population, Lowlands and Uplands,
1850–1860

Lowlands		Uplands	
Tennessee	24.7%	Tennessee	37.1%
Mississippi	22.0%	Missouri	17.2%
Alabama	16.2%	Mississippi	10.5%
Georgia	10.6%	Alabama	7.7%
Missouri	3.6%	Georgia	6.6%
Texas	3.5%	Kentucky	5.3%

TABLE 2e   Migration Into Sub-Regions of Arkansas, 1834–1860:
States Giving the Largest Percentage of Population

Mississippi Alluvial Plain: East Arkansas

1834–1850:		1850–1860:	
Tennessee	35.9%	Tennessee	38.3%
Mississippi	18.9%	Mississippi	20.1%
Alabama	9.5%	Alabama	9.8%
Missouri	7.5%	Missouri	7.3%

West Gulf Coast Plain: South Arkansas

Alabama	27.6%	Mississippi	23.2%
Tennessee	24.6%	Alabama	20.4%
Mississippi	20.8%	Tennessee	15.7%
Georgia	7.2%	Georgia	15.3%

Ouachita Mountain Province: West Arkansas

Tennessee	36.7%	Tennessee	30.6%
Missouri	17.0%	Missouri	14.4%
Alabama	8.7%	Mississippi	14.3%
Mississippi	7.2%	Alabama	9.3%

Ozark Plateau: Northwest and Northern Arkansas

Tennessee	47.2%	Tennessee	42.7%
Missouri	20.6%	Missouri	19.6%
Illinois	8.6%	Mississippi	7.3%
Alabama	5.8%	Kentucky	6.7%

TABLE 2f   Livestock Values in Arkansas, 1840–1860

	1840	1850	1860
Cattle	$188,786	$ 292,710	$ 567,799
Sheep	$ 42,141	$ 91,256	$ 202,753
Swine	$393,058	$ 836,727	$ 1,171,630
Estimated Value of Total Livestock:	Not given	$6,647,769	$22,096,977

TABLE 2g   Agricultural Production in Arkansas, 1840–1860

	1840	1850	1860
Wheat—No. Bushels:	105,878	199,639	957,601
Corn—No. Bushels:	893,939	4,846,632	17,823,588
Wool—No. Pounds:	64,943	182,595	410,382
Tobacco—No. Pounds:	148,439	218,936	989,980
Butter—No. Pounds:	Not given	1,854,239	4,067,556
Garden Products, Market Value of:	$2,739	$17,150	$37,845

TABLE 2h   Average Farm Value Per Acre in the South, 1850–1860

	1850	1860
Alabama	$ 5.30	$ 9.20
Arkansas	$ 5.88	$ 9.57
Georgia	$ 4.20	$ 5.89
Louisiana	$15.20	$22.04
Mississippi	$ 5.22	$12.04
N. Carolina	$ 3.23	$ 6.03
S. Carolina	$ 5.08	$ 8.62
Tennessee	$ 5.15	$13.13
Texas	$ 1.44	$ 3.48
Virginia	$78.27	$11.95

TABLE 2i Slave and Free Black Population in Arkansas, 1810–1860

	1810	% Increase	1820	% Increase	1830	% Increase	1840	% Increase	1850	% Increase	1860
Slave	136	1,088%	1,617	182.9%	4,576	335.6%	19,935	132.2%	47,100	135.9%	111,115
Free Black	2	2,850%	59	138.9%	141	229.7%	465	30.7%	608	-81.2%	144

TABLE 2j Percentages of Population Increase for Whites, Slaves and Free Blacks in Arkansas, 1810–1860

	1810–1820	1820–1830	1830–1840	1840–1850	1850–1860
White	1,261%	104.1%	200.6%	110.1%	98.8%
Slave	1,088%	182.9%	335.6%	136.2%	135.9%
Free Black	2,850%	138.9%	229.7%	30.6%	-81.2%

TABLE 2k Slave and Free Black Population in Lowlands and Uplands, 1840–1860

	Slave—1840	Free Blacks—1840	Slave—1850	Free Blacks—1850	Slave—1860	Free Blacks—1860
Lowland	13,410 (67.2%)	181 (38.9%)	37,339 (79.2%)	282 (38.1%)	91,815 (82.6%)	59 (40.9%)
Upland	6,525 (32.7%)	284 (61.0%)	9,761 (20.7%)	376 (61.8%)	19,300 (17.3%)	85 (59.1%)
Total	19,935	465	47,100	608	111,115	144

TABLE 2l   Number and Size of Slaveholdings in Arkansas, 1850–1860

Number of Slaves in Slaveholding	Number of Slaveholders	
	1850	1860
1	1,383	2,339
2–5	1,951	3,467
5–10	1,365	2,535
10–20	788	1,777
20–50	382	1,018
50–100	109	279
100–200	19	59
200–300	2	6
300–500	—	—
500–1,000	—	1
1,000 and over	—	—

TABLE 2m   Percentage of Whites Involved in Slavery, 1860 *

Alabama	32. %	Maryland	13.3%
Arkansas	17.7%	Mississippi	43.7%
Delaware	3.2%	Missouri	11.4%
Dist. of Columbia	10.1%	N. Carolina	27.5%
Florida	33.1%	S. Carolina	45.8%
Georgia	34.7%	Tennessee	22.2%
Kentucky	21. %	Texas	25.9%
Louisiana	30.8%	Virginia	24.8%

* This percentage includes slaveholders and their families, whose average size consists of five people. For an explanation of the methodology used in compiling these figures, see page 62, footnote 67.

TABLE 2n A Comparison of the Ozark and Ouachita Mountain Regions in
Production and Number of Slaves: Sample Counties, 1850–1860

Ouachita Counties	1850 No. of Slaves	1850 Cotton lbs. Prod.	1860 No. of Slaves	1860 Cotton lbs. Prod.
Polk	67	8,800	172	36,000
Hot Spring	361	52,000	613	717,200
Montgomery	66	15,600	93	120,000
Scott	146	147,200	215	166,000
Total	640	223,600	1,092	1,040,000
Ozark Counties				
Searcy	29	under 400	94	3,600
Newton	47	under 400	24	2,400
Carroll	213	under 400	330	2,800
Madison	164	1,200	290	4,000
Total	453	2,400	737	12,800

TABLE 3a Major Political Figures in Arkansas, 1819–1861

The Arkansas Territory, 1819–1836

Governor	Secretary	Delegate
James Miller 1819–1825	Robert Crittenden 1819–1829	James W. Bates 1819–1823
George Izard 1825–1828	William Fulton 1829–1835	Henry W. Conway 1823–1827
John Pope 1829–1835	Lewis Randolph 1835–1836	Ambrose Sevier 1827–1836
William Fulton 1835–1836		

TABLE 3a (cont.)   Major Political Figures in Arkansas, 1819–1861

The State of Arkansas, 1836–1861

Governors	U.S. Senators
James S. Conway 1836–1840	Ambrose Sevier 1836–1848
Archibald Yell 1840–1844	Solon Borland 1848–1853
Thomas Drew 1844–1849	Robert W. Johnson 1853–1861
John Roane 1849–1852	Charles Mitchel* 1861
Elias N. Conway 1852–1860	William Fulton 1836–1844
Henry Rector 1860–1862	Chester Ashley 1844–1848
	William Sebastian* 1848–1861

U.S. Representatives, 1836–1853	U.S. Representatives, 1853–1861
Archibald Yell 1836–1839	*First District—Northern*
Edward Cross 1839–1845	Alfred Greenwood 1853–1859
Archibald Yell 1845–1846	Thomas C. Hindman** 1859–1861
Thomas Newton 1847	*Second District—Southern*
Robert W. Johnson 1847–1853	Edward Warren 1853–1855
	Albert Rust 1855–1857
	Edward Warren 1857–1859
	Albert Rust 1859–1861
	Edward Gantt** 1861

*Mitchel and Sebastian were expelled from U.S. Senate, July 11, 1861.
**Hindman was expelled from the House on July 11, 1861. Gnatt never took his seat in Congress.

TABLE 4a   Congressional Vote, 1851

Lowland Counties	Candidates		Highland Counties	Candidates	
	Johnson	Preston		Johnson	Preston
Arkansas	132	122	Benton	301	113
Ashley	103	16	Carroll	400	143
Bradley	156	196	Crawford	114	326
Chicot	123	65	Conway	267	202
Crittenden	72	119	Franklin	235	190
Dallas	215	164	Fulton	129	26
Clark	283	143	Independence	408	422
Desha	136	158	Izard	303	84
Drew	125	107	Johnson	311	220
Green	135	52	Lawrence	291	217
Hempstead	381	389	Madison	378	185
Hot Spring	244	156	Marion	167	81
Jackson	259	184	Montgomery	133	56
Jefferson	331	170	Newton	80	68
Lafayette	111	109	Perry	101	69
Mississippi	not available		Pike	175	65
Ouachita	306	434	Pope	315	247
Phillips	344	443	Randolph	181	81
Poinsett	213	23	Scott	162	122
Prairie	188	113	Searcy	179	100
Pulaski	297	359	Van Buren	154	145
St. Francis	270	174	Washington	378	570
Saline	307	179	Yell	396	252
Sevier	163	67	Polk	92	13
Union	578	442	Sebastian	357	190
White	155	84			
Monroe	103	138			
Calhoun	150	82			

THE GUBERNATORIAL RACE OF 1860
BY COUNTY

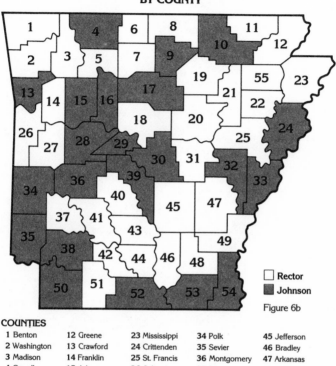

Rector

Johnson

Figure 6b

COUNTIES

1 Benton	12 Greene	23 Mississippi	34 Polk	45 Jefferson
2 Washington	13 Crawford	24 Crittenden	35 Sevier	46 Bradley
3 Madison	14 Franklin	25 St. Francis	36 Montgomery	47 Arkansas
4 Carroll	15 Johnson	26 Sebastian	37 Pike	48 Drew
5 Newton	16 Pope	27 Scott	38 Hempstead	49 Desha
6 Marion	17 Van Buren	28 Yell	39 Saline	50 Lafayette
7 Searcy	18 Conway	29 Perry	40 Hot Spring	51 Columbia
8 Fulton	19 Independence	30 Pulaski	41 Clark	52 Union
9 Izard	20 White	31 Prairie	42 Ouachita	53 Ashley
10 Lawrence	21 Jackson	32 Monroe	43 Dallas	54 Chicot
11 Randolph	22 Poinsett	33 Phillips	44 Calhoun	55 Craighead

TABLE 6a   Percentages of White Population Increases, 1850–1860, and the
Governor's Race of 1860

Counties for Johnson	1850	1860	Percentages of Increases
Crittenden	6,285	8,457	35%
Phillips	4,341	5,932	36%
Monroe	1,651	3,431	107%
Chicot	1,122	1,722	53%
Ashley	1,409	4,829	242%
Lafayette	1,900	4,146	118%
Sevier	2,837	7,150	152%
Polk	1,196	4,090	241%
Yell	2,902	5,335	84%
Perry	957	2,162	125%
Pulaski	4,506	8,187	81%
Saline	3,394	5,891	74%
Montgomery	1,891	3,541	87%
Van Buren	2,761	5,157	88%
Pope	4,231	6,905	63%
Johnson	4,489	6,639	48%
Carroll	4,391	9,053	106%
Lawrence	4,882	8,875	81%
Izard	3,017	6,833	126%
Hempstead	5,189	8,589	66%
(20 counties)			Average 101%

Counties for Rector	1850	1860	Percentages of Increases
Greene	2,530	5,654	123%
Randolph	3,029	5,902	95%
Mississippi	1,496	2,434	63%
St. Francis	3,770	6,051	61%
Jackson	2,517	7,957	216%
Independence	6,927	12,970	87%
Arkansas	1,694	3,923	132%
Jefferson	3,197	7,813	144%
Drew	2,361	5,581	136%
Desha	1,685	2,655	58%
Bradley	2,601	5,698	119%
Pike	1,751	3,798	116%
Hot Spring	5,189	8,589	55%
Clark	3,112	7,516	142%
Scott	2,921	4,930	69%
Franklin	3,497	6,330	81%
Conway	3,339	5,895	77%
Benton	3,508	8,921	154%

Counties for Rector	1850	1860	Percentages of Increases
Washington	8,757	13,133	50%
Marion	2,053	5,923	188%
Madison	4,659	7,444	60%
Newton	1,704	3,369	98%
Searcy	1,950	5,178	165%
Fulton	1,768	3,936	122%
White	2,309	6,881	198%
Prairie	1,812	6,015	231%
Ouachita	6,285	8,457	35%
(27 counties)			Average 114%

TABLE 6c   The Relationship Between Wealth of Arkansas Counties and Specific Voting Frequencies for the Gubernatorial Election of 1860 Using χ^2 Analysis

	Johnson	*Rector*
Top 15 counties*	7,819 vote total	7,434 vote total
Middle 25 counties**	16,341 vote total	17,256 vote total
Bottom 15 counties***	5,708 vote total	7,469 vote total

$\chi^2 - 18.655$ P. < .001

df–2

Arkansas Counties and Their Wealth Per Capita for the White Population

*Top 15 counties: Chicot—4122.29, Desha—3798.48, Phillips—3079.76, Arkansas—2853.40, Jefferson—2150.15, Union—1705.34, Pulaski—1645.58, Mississippi—1612.34, Ashley—1459.52, Hempstead—1420.95, Dallas—1415.40, Lafayette—1335.40, Drew—1306.26, Crittenden—1828.07, Monroe—1188.99.

**Middle 25 counties: Ouachita—1111.33, Prairie—1107.61, Sevier—1037.81, Bradley—1037.80, St. Francis—986.04, Poinsett—817.97, Columbia—801.07, White—684.18, Jackson—660.90, Clark, 601.07, Yell—578.76, Calhoun—577.66, Crawford—537.80, Franklin—508.19, Johnson—481.30, Sebastian—464.02, Conway—463.54, Washington—442.03, Pope—427.29, Independence—416.77, Perry—408.66, Hot Spring—371.54, Saline—368.65, Lawrence—340.41, Benton—314.50.

***Bottom 15 counties: Pike—297.11, Fulton—292.70, Madison—283.70, Scott—269.75, Carroll—269.29, Craighead—266.02, Randolph—256.07, Izard—250.27, Montgomery—237.35, Marion—223.90, Greene—219.74, Polk—218.33, Van Buren—189.66, Searcy—168.69, Newton—106.20.

All counties underlined voted for Rector for governor in 1860.

TABLE 7a   Presidential Election of 1860: Percentage of Votes by Which
Each Candidate Carried the Slaveholding States

Breckinridge	Percentage	Electoral Votes
Alabama	54.4	9
Arkansas	53.7	4
Delaware	43.7	3
Florida	61.5	3
Georgia	48.5	10
Louisiana	45.0	6
Maryland	46.2	8
Mississippi	57.9	7
N. Carolina	51.0	10
S. Carolina*	—	8
Texas	76.1	4
Bell		
Kentucky	45.2	12
Tennessee	47.9	12
Virginia	44.9	15
Douglas		
Missouri	35.7	9

*The people of South Carolina did not vote directly for presidential candidates until 1868.

THE PRESIDENTIAL ELECTION OF 1860

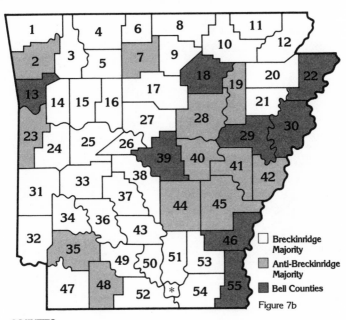

Figure 7b

COUNTIES

1 Benton	13 Crawford	25 Yell	37 Hot Spring	49 Ouachita
2 Washington	14 Franklin	26 Perry	38 Saline	50 Calhoun
3 Madison	15 Johnson	27 Conway	39 Pulaski	* Part of Calhoun
4 Carroll	16 Pope	28 White	40 Prairie	County
5 Newton	17 Van Buren	29 St. Francis	41 Monroe	51 Bradley
6 Marion	18 Independence	30 Crittenden	42 Phillips	52 Union
7 Searcy	19 Jackson	31 Polk	43 Dallas	53 Drew
8 Fulton	20 Craighead	32 Sevier	44 Jefferson	54 Ashley
9 Izard	21 Poinsett	33 Montgomery	45 Arkansas	55 Chicot
10 Lawrence	22 Mississippi	34 Pike	46 Desha	
11 Randolph	23 Sebastian	35 Hempstead	47 Lafayette	
12 Greene	24 Scott	36 Clark	48 Columbia	

HANLY'S SECESSION MOTION
MARCH 18, 1861

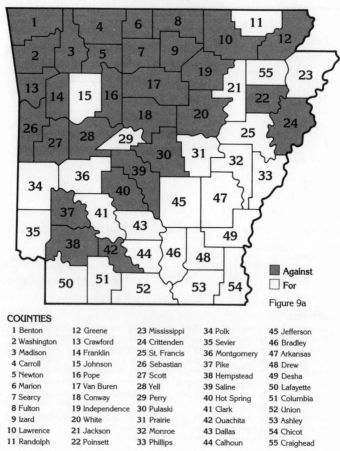

Against

For

Figure 9a

COUNTIES

1 Benton	12 Greene	23 Mississippi	34 Polk	45 Jefferson
2 Washington	13 Crawford	24 Crittenden	35 Sevier	46 Bradley
3 Madison	14 Franklin	25 St. Francis	36 Montgomery	47 Arkansas
4 Carroll	15 Johnson	26 Sebastian	37 Pike	48 Drew
5 Newton	16 Pope	27 Scott	38 Hempstead	49 Desha
6 Marion	17 Van Buren	28 Yell	39 Saline	50 Lafayette
7 Searcy	18 Conway	29 Perry	40 Hot Spring	51 Columbia
8 Fulton	19 Independence	30 Pulaski	41 Clark	52 Union
9 Izard	20 White	31 Prairie	42 Ouachita	53 Ashley
10 Lawrence	21 Jackson	32 Monroe	43 Dallas	54 Chicot
11 Randolph	22 Poinsett	33 Phillips	44 Calhoun	55 Craighead

SLAVE PERCENTAGE OF COUNTY POPULATION—1850 AND 1860

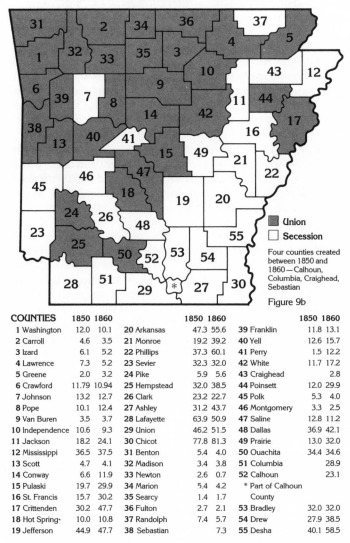

Figure 9b

COUNTIES	1850	1860		1850	1860		1850	1860
1 Washington	12.0	10.1	20 Arkansas	47.3	55.6	39 Franklin	11.8	13.1
2 Carroll	4.6	3.5	21 Monroe	19.2	39.2	40 Yell	12.6	15.7
3 Izard	6.1	5.2	22 Phillips	37.3	60.1	41 Perry	1.5	12.2
4 Lawrence	7.3	5.2	23 Sevier	32.3	32.0	42 White	11.7	17.2
5 Greene	2.0	3.2	24 Pike	5.9	5.6	43 Craighead		2.8
6 Crawford	11.79	10.94	25 Hempstead	32.0	38.5	44 Poinsett	12.0	29.9
7 Johnson	13.2	12.7	26 Clark	23.2	22.7	45 Polk	5.3	4.0
8 Pope	10.1	12.4	27 Ashley	31.2	43.7	46 Montgomery	3.3	2.5
9 Van Buren	3.5	3.7	28 Lafayette	63.9	50.9	47 Saline	12.8	11.2
10 Independence	10.6	9.3	29 Union	46.2	51.5	48 Dallas	36.9	42.1
11 Jackson	18.2	24.1	30 Chicot	77.8	81.3	49 Prairie	13.0	32.0
12 Mississippi	36.5	37.5	31 Benton	5.4	4.0	50 Ouachita	34.4	34.6
13 Scott	4.7	4.1	32 Madison	3.4	3.8	51 Columbia		28.9
14 Conway	6.6	11.9	33 Newton	2.6	0.7	52 Calhoun		23.1
15 Pulaski	19.7	29.9	34 Marion	5.4	4.2	* Part of Calhoun		
16 St. Francis	15.7	30.2	35 Searcy	1.4	1.7	County		
17 Crittenden	30.2	47.7	36 Fulton	2.7	2.1	53 Bradley	32.0	32.0
18 Hot Spring·	10.0	10.8	37 Randolph	7.4	5.7	54 Drew	27.9	38.5
19 Jefferson	44.9	47.7	38 Sebastian		7.3	55 Desha	40.1	58.5

Figure 10a

AN ORDINANCE

To dissolve the Union now existing between the State of Arkansas and the other states united with her under the compact entitled "The Constitution of the United States of America."

WHEREAS, IN addition to the well founded causes of complaint set forth by this convention in resolutions adopted on the 11th March, A.D., 1861, against the sectional party now in power at Washington City, headed by Abraham Lincoln, he has, in the face of resolutions passed by this convention, pledging the State of Arkansas to resist to the last extremity any attempt on the part of such power to coerce any state that had seceded from the old Union, proclaimed to the world that war should be waged against such states, until they should be compelled to submit to their rule, and large forces to accomplish this have by this same power been called out, and are now being marshalled to carry out this inhuman design, and to longer submit to such rule or remain in the old Union of the United States would be disgraceful and ruinous to the State of Arkansas.

Therefore, we the people of the State of Arkansas, in convention assembled, do hereby declare and ordain, and it is hereby declared and ordained, that the "ordinance and acceptance of compact," passed and approved by the General Assembly of the State of Arkansas on the 18th day of October, A.D., 1836, whereby it was by said General Assembly ordained that, by virtue of the authority vested in said General Assembly, by the provisions of the ordinance adopted by the convention of delegates assembled at Little Rock, for the purpose of forming a constitution and system of government for said State, the propositions set forth in "an act supplementary to an act entitled an act for the admission of the State of Arkansas into the Union, and to provide for the due execution of the laws of the United States within the same, and for other purposes, were freely accepted, ratified and irrevocably confirmed articles of compact and union between the State of Arkansas and the United States," and all other laws, and every other law and ordinance, whereby the State of Arkansas became a member of the Federal Union, be, and the same are hereby in all respects and for every purpose herewith consistent, repealed, abrogated and fully set aside; and the union now subsisting between the State of Arkansas and the other states, under the name of the United States of America, is hereby forever dissolved.

And we do further hereby declare and ordain, that the State of Arkansas hereby resumes to herself all rights and powers heretofore delegated to the government of the United States of America—that her citizens are absolved from all allegiance to said government of the United States, and that she is in full possession and exercise of all the rights and sovereignty which appertain to a free and independent State.

We do further ordain and declare, that all rights acquired and vested under the Constitution of the United States of America, or of any act or acts of Congress, or treaty, or under any law of this State, and not incompatible with this ordinance, shall remain in full force and effect, in no wise altered or impaired, and have the same effect as if this ordinance had not been passed.

DAVID WALKER, President of the convention and delegate from the county of Washington.
JAMES L. TOTTEN, Arkansas county.
MARCUS L. HAWKINS, Ashley county.
A. W. DINSMORE, Benton county.
J. GOULD, Bradley county.
PHIL. H. ECHOLS, Calhoun county.
W. W. WATKINS, Carroll county.
BURR H. HOBBS, Carroll county.
I. H. HILLIARD, Chicot county.
H. FLANAGIN, Clark county.
J. C. WALLACE, Columbia county.
GEORGE P. SMOOTE, Columbia county.
S. J. STALLINGS, Conway county.
JESSE TURNER, Crawford county.
H. F. THOMASON, Crawford county.
THOS. H. BRADLEY, Crittenden county.
ROBERT T. FULLER, Dallas county.
J. P. JOHNSON, Desha county.
J. A. RHODES, Drew county.
W. F. SLEMMONS, Drew county.
W. W. MANSFIELD, Franklin county.
S. W. COCHRAN, Fulton county.
JAMES W. BUSH, Greene county.
R. K. GARLAND, Hempstead county.
A. H. CARRIGAN, Hempstead county.
JOSEPH JESTER, Hot Spring county.
F. W. DESHA, Independence county.
URBAN E. FORT, Independence county.
M. SHELBY KENNARD, Independence county.
ALEX. ADAMS, Izard county.
J. H. PATTERSON, Jackson county.
JAS. YELL, Jefferson county.
W. P. GRACE, Jefferson county.
WM. W. FLOYD, Johnson county.
FELIX I. BATSON, Johnson county.
WILEY P. CRYER, Lafayette county.
SAMUEL ROBINSON, Lawrence county.
MILTON D. BABER, Lawrence county.
H. H. BOLINGER, Madison county.
THOS. F. AUSTIN, Marion county.
FELIX R. LANIER, Mississippi county.
WM. M. MAYO, Monroe county.
ALEXANDER M. CLINGMAN, Montgomery county.

ISAIAH DODSON, Newton county.
A. W. HOBSON, Ouachita county.
L. D. HILL, Perry county.
THOMAS B. HANLY, Phillips county.
CHAS. W. ADAMS, Phillips county.
SAMUEL KELLEY, Pike county.
ARCHIBALD RAY, Polk county.
WILLIAM STOUT, Pope county.
BENJAMIN C. TOTTEN, Prairie county.
J. STILLWELL, Pulaski county.
A. H. GARLAND, Pulaski county.
JAMES W. CRENSHAW, Randolph county.
J. M. SMITH, Saline county.
E. T. WALKER, Scott county.
SAML. L. GRIFFITH, Sebastian county.
W. M. FISHBACK, Sebastian county.
BENJ. F. HAWKINS, Sevier county.
JAS. S. DOLLARHIDE, Sevier county.
J. N. SHELTON, St. Francis county.
G. W. LAUGHINGHOUSE, St. Francis county.
H. BUSSEY, Union county.
WM. V. TATUM, Union county.
J. HENRY PATTERSON, Van Buren county.
JOHN P. A. PARKS, Washington county.
T. M. GUNTER, Washington county.
JAMES H. STIRMAN, Washington county.
JESSE N. CYPERT, White county.
W. H. SPIVEY, Yell county.

Adopted and passed in open Convention, on the sixth day of May, Anno Domini 1861.

Attest:

ELIAS C. BOUDINOT, *Secretary of the Arkansas State Convention*

AN ORDINANCE *providing for the signing of the ordinance passed on yesterday, dissolving the political connection theretofore existing between the State of Arkansas and the government known as "The United States of America."*

We, the people of the State of Arkansas, now in convention assembled, do hereby ordain, and it is hereby ordained, that the ordinance adopted by this convention on yesterday, dissolving the political connection theretofore existing between the State of Arkansas and the government known as the "United States of America," be signed by the president and attested by the secretary of this convention, and be also signed by the individual members of this convention, and that in signing the same, there shall be a call of the counties of the state in alphabetical order, and the delegates of each county shall sign the same as their respective counties shall be called by the secretary.

Adopted and passed in open convention, May 7th, A.D., 1861.

DAVID WALKER, *President*
of the Arkansas State Convention.

Attest:

ELIAS C. BOUDINOT, *Secretary of the Convention.*

VOTE TO REFER SECESSION TO THE PEOPLE
MAY 6, 1861

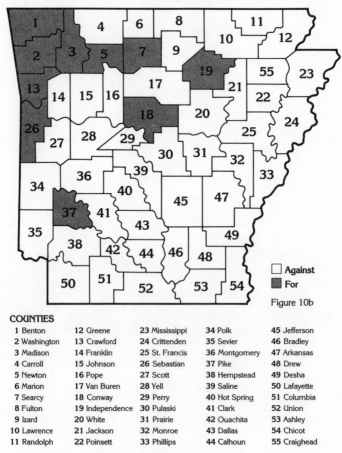

Figure 10b

COUNTIES

1 Benton	12 Greene	23 Mississippi	34 Polk	45 Jefferson
2 Washington	13 Crawford	24 Crittenden	35 Sevier	46 Bradley
3 Madison	14 Franklin	25 St. Francis	36 Montgomery	47 Arkansas
4 Carroll	15 Johnson	26 Sebastian	37 Pike	48 Drew
5 Newton	16 Pope	27 Scott	38 Hempstead	49 Desha
6 Marion	17 Van Buren	28 Yell	39 Saline	50 Lafayette
7 Searcy	18 Conway	29 Perry	40 Hot Spring	51 Columbia
8 Fulton	19 Independence	30 Pulaski	41 Clark	52 Union
9 Izard	20 White	31 Prairie	42 Ouachita	53 Ashley
10 Lawrence	21 Jackson	32 Monroe	43 Dallas	54 Chicot
11 Randolph	22 Poinsett	33 Phillips	44 Calhoun	55 Craighead

Notes

Introduction

1. William S. Donnelly, "Conspiracy or Popular Movement: The Historiography of Southern Support for Secession," *North Carolina Historical Review* 42 (Winter 1965): 83.

2. William W. Freehling, "The Editorial Revolution, Virginia and the Coming of the Civil War: A Review Essay of George Reese's Proceedings of the Virginia State Convention of 1861," *Civil War History* 16 (March 1970): 71.

3. Steven Channing, *Crisis of Fear: Secession in South Carolina* (New York: Simon and Schuster, 1970); Billy Ledbetter, "Slavery, Fear, and Disunion in the Lone Star State: Texans' Attitude Toward the Union, 1846–1861," diss., North Texas State University, 1972; William Barney, *The Secessionist Impulse: Alabama and Mississippi in 1860* (Princeton: Princeton University Press, 1974); Michael P. Johnson, *Toward a Patriarchal Republic: Secession in Georgia* (Baton Rouge: Louisiana State University Press, 1976); J. Mills Thornton, *Politics and Power in a Slave Society: Alabama, 1800–1860* (Baton Rouge: Louisiana State University Press, 1978); Walter L. Buenger, *Secession and Union in Texas* (Austin: University of Texas Press, 1984).

4. Some of the published works on secession in the upper South are almost fifty years old: Henry Shanks, *The Secession Movement in Virginia, 1847–1861* (Chapel Hill: University of North Carolina Press, 1934); Joseph Carlyle Sitterson, *The Secession Movement in North Carolina* (Chapel Hill: University of North Carolina Press, 1939). The most recent published study on Tennessee is over twenty years old; see Mary Campbell, *Attitude of Tennesseans Toward the Union, 1847–1861* (New York: Random House-Vantage Press, 1961). Recently the upper South has received more attention; see Daniel Crofts, "The Union Party of 1861 and the Secession Crisis," *Perspectives in American History* 11 (1977–1978): 325–376; Michael Holt, *The Political Crisis of the 1850s* (New York: John Wiley & Sons, 1978) 219–259. Superseding Sitterson's earlier work is Marc Kruman's *Parties and Politics in North Carolina, 1836–1865* (Baton Rouge: Louisiana State University Press, 1983).

5. Divisions in these upper South states lingered well into the Civil War, bringing a great many problems for the Southern Confederacy; see Georgia Tatum, *Disloyalty in the Confederacy* (Chapel Hill: University of North Carolina Press, 1934); James W. Patton, *Unionism and Reconstruction in Tennessee, 1860–1869* (Chapel Hill: University of North Carolina Press, 1934).

6. Elsie Mae Lewis, "From Nationalism to Disunion: A Study of the Secession Movement in Arkansas, 1849–1861," diss. University of Chicago, 1947. In a recent article on secession in the upper South—Virginia, North Carolina, Tennessee—the author mentions Arkansas only in passing. Crofts, "Union Party of 1861," 329–376.

7. There have been a number of major published and unpublished monographs on antebellum Arkansas since the time of the 1950s. This list is not exhaustive, but it is a basic guide to the major works: Walter L. Brown, "Albert Pike, 1809–1891," diss., University of Texas, 1955; Orville Taylor, *Negro Slavery in Arkansas* (Durham: Duke University Press, 1958); Robert Walz, "Migration into Arkansas, 1834–1880," diss., University of Texas,

1958; Lonnie J. White, *Politics on the Southwestern Frontier: Arkansas Territory, 1819–1836* (Memphis: Memphis State University Press, 1964); Dewey Allen Stokes, "Public Affairs in Arkansas, 1836–1850," diss., University of Texas, 1966; Margaret Ross, *The Arkansas Gazette: The Early Years, 1819–1866* (Little Rock: Arkansas Gazette Foundation Library, 1969); Gene Wills Boyette, "The Whigs of Arkansas, 1836–1856," diss., Louisiana State University, 1972; Michael B. Dougan, *Confederate Arkansas: The People and Policies of a Frontier State in Wartime* (University of Alabama Press, 1976); George H. Thompson, *Arkansas and Reconstruction: The Influence of Geography, Economics, and Personality* (Port Washington, N.Y.: Kennikat Press, 1976); Waddy W. Moore, "Territorial Arkansas, 1819–1836," diss. University of North Carolina, 1963. Relevant articles will be cited in subsequent reference notes.

Chapter I

1. New Orleans *Picayune,* n.d. quoted in *DeBow's Review* 29 (December 1860): 794.
2. *Census of 1810* (Washington, D.C.: Government Printing Office, 1811) 84. The census number quoted excludes the New Madrid Township, which later was to be part of Missouri. A few of the people near that township may have lived in what would later be the very northeastern corner, but it is impossible to be sure. Orville Taylor, *Negro Slavery in Arkansas* (Durham, N.C.: Duke University Press 1958) 20.
3. Fay Hempstead, *A Pictorial History of Arkansas: From the Earliest Times to the Year 1890* (St. Louis: N.D. Thompson & Co., 1890) 164; Dallas Herndon, *A Centennial History of Arkansas,* 3 vols. (Chicago, Ill.: Clarke Publishing Co., 1922) I : 144. Although both these works are old and quite dated, they do contain much useful information about the general history of Arkansas. Herndon is especially good on the prehistoric development of Arkansas. No record of debate in the U.S. Senate concerning the bill for the Arkansas Territory exists, but a heated discussion developed in the House concerning slavery in the Territory. For the best secondary source on this battle over slavery in the soon-to-be-created Arkansas Territory, see Lonnie White, *Politics on the Southwestern Frontier: Arkansas Territory, 1819–1836* (Memphis: Memphis State University Press, 1964) 8–16; William Johnson, "Prelude to the Missouri Compromise," *Arkansas Historical Quarterly* 29 (Spring 1965): 47–66. The Senate passed the Arkansas Territory bill on March 1, 1819, the House on February 20, 1819. *Annals of the Congress of the United States, 15th Congress, 2nd Session* (Washington, D.C.: Cates and Seaton, 1855) 274, 1238.
4. White, *Politics on the Southwestern Frontier* 6–7, footnote 24.
5. Taylor, *Negro Slavery in Arkansas* 21; Harry S. Ashmore, *Arkansas: A History* (New York: W. W. Norton & Co., 1978) 33.
6. White, *Politics on the Southwestern Frontier* 199. White gives a full account of the statehood movement and the efforts on the national level to make Arkansas the twenty-fifth state. This time, not slavery but political considerations were paramount because the Whigs thought the admission of Arkansas would hurt them in the presidential election of 1836, p. 195. White's whole account is found on pp. 164–200.
7. Elsie Mae Lewis, "From Nationalism to Disunion: A Study of the Secession Movement in Arkansas, 1849–1861," diss. University of Chicago, 1947, 4–5. Lewis gives a complete profile of Arkansas's topography and mineral wealth, pp. 1–13.
8. Lewis, "From Nationalism to Disunion," 4.
9. Lewis, "From Nationalism to Disunion," 6–7.
10. William Lynch, "The Westward Flow of Southern Colonists before 1861," *Journal of Southern History* 9 (August 1943): 305–329, especially pp. 313–320. A recent historian has ably documented the development and over-dependence of the Southern economy upon cotton. See Gavin Wright, *The Political Economy of the Cotton South: Households, Markets, and Wealth in the Nineteenth Century* (New York: W. W. Norton & Co., 1978) 1–42.

NOTES

11. Frank Owsley, *Plain Folk in the Old South* (Baton Rouge: Louisiana State University Press, 1949) 52.

12. Owsley, *Plain Folk,* 53. Lynch, "Westward Flow of Southern Colonists," 317. Tennessee did provide most of the settlers for Arkansas. See Robert Walz, "Migration into Arkansas: 1834–1880," diss., University of Texas, 1958, 115.

13. John Solomon Otto and Augustus Marion Burns, "Traditional Agricultural Practices in the Arkansas Highlands," *Journal of American Folklore* 44 (April–June 1981): 166–187. Citation on p. 183.

14. Otto and Burns, "Traditional Agricultural Practices." The authors believe that the slash-and-burn technique of the Southern mountain folk was "a complex synthesis of Native American and British agricultural techniques," p. 182. For a more intensive study of slavery in one upland county of Arkansas in the last two decades of the antebellum era, see John S. Otto, "Slavery in the Mountains: Yell County, 1840–1860," *Arkansas Historical Quarterly* 29 (Spring 1980): 35–53.

15. Otto and Burns maintain that slavery was believed to be of real value because the labor of the slaves meant that mountain wives and daughters would not have to work out in the fields. Drudgery of this nature was the unfortunate lot of too many mountain women. Farmers in the uplands hoped they could afford slaves to help them do manual labor, leaving the women to do household chores. Otto and Burns, "Traditional Agricultural Practices," 177.

16. Lewis, "From Nationalism to Disunion," 11.

17. Lewis, "From Nationalism to Disunion," 13.

18. Mattie Brown, "River Transportation in Arkansas, 1819–1890," *Arkansas Historical Quarterly* 1 (December 1942): 342. On the same page Mrs. Brown writes that "Fifty-one of the present seventy-five counties are watered by navigable streams."

19. Henry Schoolcraft, *Journal of a Tour into the Interior of Missouri and Arkansas: Performed in the Years 1818 and 1819* (London: Sir Richard Phillip and Co., 1820) 65–79. Schoolcraft reported that the settlers he happened to meet in this remote region "were ignorant about affairs in Washington, knew nothing of the President, and cared little whether Missouri might be admitted as a State."

20. Frederick Gerstacker, *Wild Sports in the Far West* (New York: John Lovell, 1858) 83. For a good secondary account of Gerstacker's travels in Arkansas, as well as Arkansas travels taken by Timothy Flint and Washington Irving, see Robert Morris, "Three Arkansas Travelers," *Arkansas Historical Quarterly* 4 (Autumn 1945): 215–230. For a firsthand account of Washington Irving's impression of Arkansas see Little Rock *Arkansas Gazette,* 14 Nov. 1832: 2; 21 Nov. 1832: 3. See also Little Rock *Arkansas Advocate* 21 Nov. 1832: 3.

21. For another account describing the natural beauty of Arkansas, see the work of botanist Thomas Nuttal, *A Journal of Travels into the Arkansas Territory During the Year 1819, With Occasional Observations on the Manners of the Aborigines* (Philadelphia: Thomas A. Palmer, 1821). Nuttal was impressed by the Indians, the mild winters, and the beauty of Arkansas, pp. 54–146.

22. *U.S. Department of the Interior, Eighth Census of the United States, 1860,* 4 vols. (Washington, D.C.: Government Printing Office, 1864–1866) 1:598–599.

23. Between 1850 and 1860, the Minnesota Territory grew from 6,077 to 172,023 for a percentage of 2,730%. Indiana expanded from 4,875 in 1800 to 1,350,481, for a gain of 27,601%. *Census of 1860* 1:598–604.

24. One of the earliest historians of the Mississippi Valley claimed that it was not until the 1830s that Arkansas's population really began to grow and between 1830 and 1835 the population of the Arkansas Territory doubled. John Monette, *History of the Discovery and Settlement of the Valley of the Mississippi by the Three Great European Powers, Spain, France, and Great Britain; and the Subsequent Occupation, Settlement and Extension of the Civil Government by the United States until the Year 1846,* 2 vols. (New York: Harper & Brothers, 1846) 2:555–556.

25. Florida and Iowa did not have a recorded percentage of growth until the 1840s. Texas did not join the Union until 1845. *Census of 1860* 1:598–604.

26. *Census of 1860* 1:601.

27. Lewis, "From Nationalism to Disunion," 13–14, footnote 30.

28. Lewis, "From Nationalism to Disunion," 28.

29. Samuel Brown, *The Western Gazettier; or, an Emigrant's Directory, Containing a Geographical Description of the Western States and Territories* (Auburn, N.Y.: H. C. Southwick, 1817) 174.

30. Timothy Flint, *A Condensed Geography and History of the Western States, or Mississippi Valley*, 2 vols. (Cincinnati: E. A. Flint, 1828) 1:583. Flint thought that the swamps, bayous, and humidity of the lowlands of eastern Arkansas resembled Louisiana lowlands.

31. Brown, "River Transportation in Arkansas," 348.

32. Van Buren *Arkansas Intelligencer* 28 June 1845: 2.

33. Lady Ida Pfeifer, *The Lady's Second Journey Around the World* (New York: Harper & Brothers, 1856) 417.

34. Little Rock *Arkansas Gazette*, 29 September 1859: 2. One newspaper correspondent traveling up the Arkansas River in early 1861 reported that "The Arkansas River is a graveyard of steamboats . . . I should say, from the number of wrecks we passed and places pointed out where others have perished." Quoted from Michael Dougan, *Confederate Arkansas: The People and Policies of a Frontier State in Wartime* (University of Alabama Press, 1976) 3.

35. Nancy Neely, letter to Eliza Bonner, 4 April 1848, Samuel Bonner Papers, Department of Archives and Manuscripts, Louisiana State University, Baton Rouge.

36. Little Rock *Arkansas Gazette* 19 June 1833: 3.

37. *Arkansas Gazette*, 2 January 1839: 2. The immense fluctuations in the Arkansas River frequently caused great inconveniences for the people in the state. A Van Buren paper once claimed that the river was so high it stopped stagecoaches from Little Rock and Fayetteville, and halted regular mail service. Van Buren *Arkansas Intelligencer* 15 March 1845: 2.

38. Letter quoted in Dougan, *Confederate Arkansas* 3.

39. Robert Walz, "Migration in Arkansas: Incentives and Means of Travel" *Arkansas Historical Quarterly* 17 (Winter 1958): 318.

40. Washington *Telegraph* 30 May 1855: 2.

41. Fort Smith *Herald* 28 June 1848: 2. It reappeared as just a single sheet on 19 July 1848, and by early August still no news or paper, (2 August 1848). This issue was a single sheet.

42. The unreliability of the river hurt economic development. For example, a new Slaughter Gas Works began to operate in Little Rock in August, 1860, but the streets remained dark for some time because the low state of the river delayed delivery of the iron posts to be used as street lamps. Little Rock *Arkansas Gazette* 4 August 1860: 2.

43. Dougan, *Confederate Arkansas* 1.

44. Little Rock *Arkansas Gazette* 23 May 1837: 2. One guide for emigrants stated that settlement in Arkansas was hurt by "fear of Indians, fear of illness, and fear of bad roads" and said that roads "have been bad for a long time; no one could venture through the swamps unless he was a Daniel Boone." J. M. Peck, *A New Guide for Emigrants to the West* (Boston: Gould, Kendall, and Lincoln, 1836) 327, 328.

45. Walter Moffatt, "Transportation in Arkansas, 1819–1840," *Arkansas Historical Quarterly* 15 (Autumn 1956): 191.

46. For this harrowing journey see Gilbert Hathaway, "Travels in the South West: Life in Arkansas and Texas," *Travels in Two Hemispheres or, Gleanings from a European Tour* by the Rev. George Duffield, W. P. Isham, Warrens Isham, D. Bethune Duffield, Gilbert Hathaway. 2nd ed. (Detroit: Doughty-Straw, Raymond and Sellneck, 1858) 185–191, 231–239. For another account describing how difficult it was to travel through eastern

Arkansas in the antebellum era, see the troubles of the first Methodist bishop sent to Arkansas in 1836. Moffatt, "Transportation in Arkansas" 189–190.

47. Moffatt, "Transportation in Arkansas" 188.

48. Moffatt, "Transportation in Arkansas." See also Little Rock *Arkansas Advocate* 12 February 1836: 2, for this comment on sending the mail by balloon. The author was Albert Pike, the famed poet, politician and leader of the Masons.

49. Bishop George Freeman, letter to Missionary Board, 19 August 1849, reprinted in Margaret Sims, *White Already to Harvest: The Episcopal Diocese of Arkansas, 1838–1971* (Sewanee, Tenn.: University of the South Press, 1975) 39.

50. Fort Smith *Herald* 22 August 1851: 2.

51. Little Rock *Arkansas Whig* 30 October 1851: 2. In the same article, one migrant was asked why he was going to Texas instead of staying in Arkansas and he replied that "any country with as bad roads as Arkansas wouldn't do him."

52. Although Texas had more overall population than Arkansas in 1850 (Texas had a total of 212,592 to Arkansas's 209,827), Arkansas had more white settlers (Arkansas's total of 162,180 to Texas's 154,034). During the 1850s Arkansas whites increased to 324,143 but whites in Texas grew to a total of 420,891. Arkansas's percentage of increase of whites was 99.6% to Texas's 173.6%. Overall population went to 435,450 in Arkansas, but Texas increased to 604,215. Arkansas's percentage of increase was 107.4%, but Texas's increase was 184.2%. After the 1860 census, Arkansas was to gain only one congressman, while Texas was to receive two. *Eighth Census* 1 : 598–599.

53. Fort Smith *Herald* 21 April 1852: 2.

54. James P. Neal, letter to Sebron G. Sneed, 22 September 1854, Sebron Graham Sneed Papers, University of Texas Archives, Austin. Another significant migrant from Arkansas to Texas was Rev. George Washington Baines, a Baptist minister born in Georgia who settled in Carroll County in the Ozarks of north central Arkansas. After serving for two terms in the Arkansas legislature in the early 1840s, Rev. Baines left for central Texas. He would later become the great-grandfather of President Lyndon Baines Johnson. Ashmore, *Arkansas* 50.

55. Fort Smith *Herald* 12 March 1849: 2.

56. Little Rock *Arkansas Gazette* 26 April 1850: 2.

57. William Quesenbury, 29 January 1851, letter reprinted in the Fort Smith *Herald* 4 April 1851: 2.

58. Ashmore, *Arkansas* 50.

59. Edward E. Dale, "Arkansas: The Myth and the State," *Arkansas Historical Quarterly* 12 (Spring 1953): 20–22.

60. Dale, "Arkansas: The Myth and the State," 22. This poor image of Arkansas persisted throughout the nineteenth century; see C. Fred Williams, "The Bear State Image: Arkansas in the Nineteenth Century," *Arkansas Historical Quarterly* 39 (Summer 1980): 99–112. Mark Twain liked to use the backwardness of Arkansas and its people in his works; see Elmo Howell "Mark Twain's Arkansas," *Arkansas Historical Quarterly* 29 (Autumn 1970): 195–208. For a look at Arkansas's poor image in the twentieth century, see Foy Lisenby, "A Survey of Arkansas's Image Problem," *Arkansas Historical Quarterly* 30 (Spring 1971): 60–71. Lisenby's survey takes it up to 1970. See also Foy Lisenby, "Winthrop Rockefeller. and the Arkansas Image," *Arkansas Historical Quarterly* 43 (Summer 1984): 143–152.

61. Lewis, "From Nationalism to Disunion," 53.

62. Dougan, *Confederate Arkansas* 4.

63. Sir George William Featherstonhaugh, *An Excursion Through the Slave States of North America: From Washington on the Potomac to the Frontier of Mexico* (New York: Harper & Brothers, 1844) 87.

64. Featherstonhaugh, *An Excursion Through the Slave States* 88. A modern historian has confirmed Featherstonhaugh's observations concerning the lawlessness of Helena and eastern Arkansas. See Waddy Moore, "Some Aspects of Crime and Punishment on the Arkansas Frontier," *Arkansas Historical Quarterly* 23 (Spring 1964): 57.

65. Monette, *History of the Discovery and Settlement of the Mississippi Valley* 2:554.

66. Ann Slaughter Page, "Daybook of a Journey from Virginia to Texas by Land, September 4, 1851–November 26, 1851," see October 6, 1851. Typescript, University of Texas archives, Austin, Texas.

67. Featherstonhaugh, *An Excursion Through the Slave States* 97. Arkansas's association with the Bowie knife led to that weapon's fame as the "Arkansas toothpick." This was apparently still talked about late in the nineteenth century, for the historian Fay Hempstead wrote in 1890, "We are called the 'tooth pick state' because it was customary for the people to wear a Bowie knife of a particular pattern, which was absurdly said to be used by the natives as a tooth pick . . . ," Hempstead, *History of Arkansas* 212. In contrast to the picture drawn by Featherstonhaugh, Frederick Gerstacker claimed that "Little Rock is, without flattery, one of the dullest towns in the United States; and I would not have remained two hours in the place if I had not met with some good friends who made [me] forget its dreariness." Gerstacker, *Wild Sports in the Far West* 355.

68. Little Rock *Arkansas Gazette* 20 May 1840: 2.

69. Lewis, "From Nationalism to Disunion," 53.

70. Glenn Shirley, *The Law West of Fort Smith, A History of Frontier Justice in the Indian Territory, 1834–1896* (Lincoln: University of Nebraska Press, 1957) 9–24. This is the standard work on the famous "hanging Judge" Isaac Parker. According to Shirley, it was Parker who ended much of the lawlessness on the western Arkansas border during his years on the bench, 1875–1896.

71. Fort Smith *Herald* 14 June 1848: 2.

72. *Herald* 21 June 1848: 2. Just two years later the same paper reported that "Murder is becoming very frequent and alarming in this region," 14 March 1851: 2.

73. Fort Smith *Herald*, n.d., quoted in Memphis *Weekly Appeal* 29 February 1860: 1.

74. Featherstonhaugh, *An Excursion Through the Slave States* 95.

75. W. P. Flippin, "The Tutt and Everett War in Marion County," *Arkansas Historical Quarterly* 15 (Summer 1958): 155–163.

76. Little Rock *Arkansas Gazette* 10 January 1838: 2. Featherstonhaugh, *An Excursion Through the Slave States* 96–101. In Featherstonhaugh's account, after the jury acquitted the Speaker of any wrongdoing, he then announced to the jurors that he would buy each of them a drink at a nearby saloon, p. 99.

77. Moore, "Some Aspects of Crime and Punishment" 50–51. For general information about dueling in frontier Arkansas, see Diana Sherwood, "The Code Duello in Arkansas," *Arkansas Historical Quarterly* 6 (Summer 1947): 186–197. For an account of the last "official" duel in Arkansas, see Leo Huff, "The Last Duel in Arkansas: The Marmaduke-Walker Duel," *Arkansas Historical Quarterly* 23 (Spring 1964): 34–49. This last duel occurred during the Civil War between two Confederate officers.

78. White, *Politics on the Southwestern Frontier* 50–51. After hearing of the Conway-Crittenden duel in 1827, a Kentucky newspaper commented, "Down in Arkansas, when a man cannot be gotten rid of at the polls, he is immediately killed off in a duel." Quoted in Herndon, *Centennial History of Arkansas* 1:176.

79. Margaret Ross, *The Arkansas Gazette: The Early Years, 1819–1866* (Little Rock: Arkansas Gazette Foundation, 1969) 316. Although this is an account of the early career of the oldest private institution in Arkansas, it is also the best single volume work on the political history of the state before the Civil War.

80. George Smith, letter to H. H. Butler, 2 September 1857, quoted in Lewis, "From Nationalism to Disunion," 54.

81. Moore, "Some Aspects of Crime and Punishment," 56–57.

82. Little Rock *Arkansas Gazette* 29 September 1841: 2.

83. Moore, "Some Aspects of Crime and Punishment," 64. Moore quotes one authority on the frontier, Bryan Latrobe, who said that Arkansas in 1833 resembled Kentucky at the end of the Revolution, 63–64.

84. U.S. Department of the State, *Compendium to the Sixth Census, 1840* (Washington, D.C.: Thomas Allen, Public Printer, 1841) 372–374; U.S. Department of the Interior, *The Seventh Census of the United States, 1850* (Washington, D.C.: Robert Armstrong, Public Printer, 1853) 528–529; *The Eighth Census* 1 : 12–13.

85. James D. B. DeBow, *Statistical View of the United States: A Compendium to the Seventh Census, 1850.* (Washington, D.C.: A. O. P. Nicholson, Public Printer, 1854) 56.

86. Little Rock *Arkansas Gazette* 28 December 1842: 2. The editor was asked about the nature and morality of the Arkansas legislators. The editor replied that they were no better nor worse than others of the frontier. A man whom the *Gazette* editor believed to be from New England was then quoted as saying that the people from his region thought there was little difference between an Arkansas man and a Bengal tiger.

87. Van Buren *Arkansas Intelligencer,* 3 November 1849: 2.

Chapter II

1. Orville W. Taylor, *Negro Slavery in Arkansas* (Durham, N.C.: Duke University Press, 1958) 27; Harry S. Ashmore, *Arkansas: A History* (New York: W. W. Norton & Co., 1978) 52.

2. Figures from the 1830 Census for Arkansas taken from U.S. Congress, House of Representatives, *Abstract of the Fifth Census: The Number of Free People, the Number of Slaves, The Federal or Representative Number, and the Aggregate for Each County of Each State in the United States.* H.R. 263, 22nd Congress, 1st Session. (Washington, D.C.: Duff Greene, 1842) 43. Taylor, in *Negro Slavery in Arkansas* 27, gives his numbers based upon twelve upland counties that he does not identify. Use of county returns in determining upland–lowland population is somewhat problematic, because the boundaries of the counties do not always correspond to geographic divisions. For example, Pulaski County, counted as the uplands, contained large sections of the lowlands until Prairie County split off in 1846. Often, county positions change quite radically over time. Sevier County is now mostly an upland county, yet before the Civil War it contained all of what would later be Little River County along the valley of the Red River. Lawrence County is now a lowland county, yet in the antebellum era it contained all of what would become Sharp County, an Ozark county. (See Figures 1 and 2 in the Appendix.) The county map of Figure 2 was drawn by Mr. Russell Baker of the Arkansas History Commission, Little Rock, Arkansas. Another historian has estimated that the uplands contained about 52% of the population in 1830. S. Charles Bolton, "Economic Inequality in the Arkansas Territory," *Journal of Interdisciplinary History* 14 (Winter 1984): 622.

3. U.S. Department of State, *Compendium of the Inhabitants and Statistics of the United States, as Obtained from the Returns of the Sixth Census, by Counties and by Towns, 1840* (Washington, D.C.: Thomas Allen, Public Printer, 1841) 92–94. Bolton claims that only 57% of the white population lived in the lowlands. Bolton, "Economic Inequality" 622.

4. U.S. Department of the Interior, *The Seventh Census of the United States, 1850* (Washington, D.C.: Robert Armstrong, Public Printer, 1853) 535.

5. Elsie Mae Lewis, "From Nationalism to Disunion: A Study of the Secession Movement in Arkansas, 1849–1861" diss., University of Chicago, 1947, 25, 95–96.

6. U.S. Department of the Interior, *The Eighth Census of the United States, 1860,* 4 vols. (Washington, D.C.: Government Printing Office, 1864–1866) 1 : 18.

7. *Abstract of the Fifth Census, 1830,* 43; *Census of 1860* 1 : 18.

8. John Solomon Otto and Augustus Marion Burns, "Traditional Agricultural Practices in the Arkansas Highlands," *Journal of American Folklore* 44 (April–June, 1981): 177. Bolton claims that by 1840 there was already developing a major difference between the uplands and lowlands over taxable wealth and slaves. Bolton, "Economic Inequality," 624–633.

9. *Census of 1850,* 547. The percentage given in text computed by the author. About

99,247 residents of Arkansas were born in the United States, but outside the state. Approximately 61,289 were actually born in the state and 1,471 were foreign-born, out of a free population of 162,797.

10. *Census of 1860* 1 : 20. 196,551 were born in the United States but outside of the state. 124,043 were born in Arkansas and 3,741 were foreign-born. The author computed the percentages.

11. *Compendium of the Sixth Census, 1840*, 92–94; *Census of 1850*, 528–532; *Census of 1860* 1 : 12–15; Bolton, "Economic Inequality," 629.

12. Migration figures from Robert B. Walz, "Migration into Arkansas, 1834–1880" diss., University of Texas, 1958, 115. The phrase "child of Tennessee" is from William Lynch, "The Westward Flow of Southern Colonists before 1861," *Journal of Southern History* 9 (August 1943): 317.

13. Ralph Wooster has pointed out that the legislators in Arkansas in 1850 and 1860 were mostly from Tennessee, usually over 30 percent, double the percentage born in other states. Wooster, *Politicians, Planters and Plain Folks: Courthouse to Statehouse in the Upper South, 1850–1860* (Knoxville: University of Tennessee Press, 1975) 35, 146. Twenty-four of the seventy-seven members of the Arkansas Secession Convention also came from Tennessee. The next highest numbers came from Kentucky (12), and North Carolina (10). Wooster, "The Arkansas Secession Convention," *Arkansas Historical Quarterly* 13 (Summer 1954): 175, chart insert between pp. 184 and 185. During the Civil War, seven out of the eleven Confederate congressmen from Arkansas were from Tennessee. James M. Woods, "Devotees and Dissenters: Arkansans in the Confederate Congress, 1861–1865," *Arkansas Historical Quarterly* 38 (Autumn 1979): 244. The legislature in Arkansas during the Civil War has yet to be analyzed.

14. Arkansas residents from Tennessee increased from 33,087 in 1850, to 66,609 by 1860. Alabama natives living in Arkansas numbered only 11,250 in 1850, increasing to 24,243 in 1860, and doubling over the previous decade. Former Georgians in Arkansas numbered 6,367 in 1850, and that group almost tripled to 18,081 just ten years later. The number of former Mississippians in Arkansas grew from 4,436 in 1850 to 16,657 in 1860, an almost quadruple increase for these Magnolia State natives. In 1850, Arkansas drew its population from Tennessee, Alabama, North Carolina, Kentucky, Georgia, and Missouri. By 1860 the leading contributors to the state's population came from Tennessee, Alabama, Georgia, North Carolina, Mississippi, and Kentucky. For the exact figures of this migration and the source of all the above figures, see James DeBow, *Statistical View of the United States: A Compendium to the Seventh Census of 1850* (Washington, D.C.: A. O. P. Nicholson, Public Printers, 1854) 116–117. *Census of 1860* 1 : 20.

15. Helena *States Rights Democrat*, 14 August 1857, quoted in Robert Walz, "Migration into Arkansas: Incentives and Means of Travel," *Arkansas Historical Quarterly* 17 (Winter 1958): 322.

16. The breakdown of these migratory figures for the lowlands and uplands are taken from Walz, "Migration into Arkansas, 1834–1880" 67–68.

17. Walz, "Migration into Arkansas, 1834–1880," 67–68.

18. Walz, "Migration into Arkansas, 1834–1880," 71–74. Lower South migrants for the whole state still amounted to only about 24% of the total white population by 1860. *Census of 1860* 4: LXI–LXII. Arkansas, however, did increasingly draw its population from the Deep South.

19. Walz, "Migration into Arkansas, 1834–1880," 71–74.

20. Walz, "Migration into Arkansas, 1834–1880," 77, 111.

21. Robert B. Walz, "Migration into Arkansas, 1820–1880: Incentives and Means of Travel," *Arkansas Historical Quarterly* 17 (Winter 1958): 310.

22. Walz, "Migration into Arkansas: Incentives and Means of Travel," 310.

23. Walz, "Migration into Arkansas: Incentives and Means of Travel," 310.

24. Robert W. Harrison and Walter Kollmorgen, "Land Reclamation in Arkansas under the Swamp Land Grant of 1850," *Arkansas Historical Quarterly* 6 (Winter 1947): 369–

418. The authors claim that by 1880 about 7,686,335 acres had been reclaimed, p. 412. Arkansas ranked third behind Louisiana and Florida in swampland grants by 1880. Lewis Gray, *History of Agriculture in the Southern United States to 1860*, 2 vols. (Gloucester, Mass.: Peter Smith, 1958) 2:635.

25. Harrison and Kollmorgen, "Swamp Land Grant of 1850," 374.

26. Walz, "Migration into Arkansas: Incentives and Means of Travel," 311.

27. Harrison and Kollmorgen, "Swamp Land Grant of 1850," 376–396.

28. Harrison and Kollmorgen, "Swamp Land Grant of 1850," 415–418.

29. Ted R. Worley, "Arkansas and the Money Crisis, 1836–1837," *Journal of Southern History* 15 (May 1949): 178–191.

30. Michael B. Dougan, *Confederate Arkansas: The People and Policies of a Frontier State in Wartime* (University of Alabama Press, 1976) 6. A new work is to appear by Matthew Rothbert on the history of Arkansas banks, banking, and script notes from 1836 to 1900.

31. Ted R. Worley, "The Arkansas State Bank: Antebellum Period," *Arkansas Historical Quarterly* 33 (Spring 1964): 65–73. Ted Worley, "The Control of the Real Estate Bank of the State of Arkansas, 1836–1855," *Mississippi Valley Historical Review* 37 (December 1950): 403–426. Governor John S. Roane (1849–1852) once complained to the Arkansas legislature that the Real Estate Bank and its affairs were "like a sealed book" and a "mystic monument to modern banking." Governor Roane quoted in Worley, "Control of the Real Estate Bank," 421.

32. Lewis, "From Nationalism to Disunion," 18. The debt from the Arkansas State Bank alone stood at $1.3 million by 1848; see Worley, "Arkansas State Bank," 73.

33. State Senator Mark Izard quoted in Worley, "Control of the Real Estate Bank," 408.

34. John L. Ferguson and J. H. Atkinson, *Historic Arkansas* (Little Rock: Arkansas History Commission, 1966) 74. Gray, *History of Southern Agriculture* 2:712. Gray's list excludes Texas, but there were banks operating in Texas prior to the Civil War; see Earl Fornell, *The Galveston Era: The Texas Crescent on the Eve of Secession* (Austin: University of Texas, 1961) 39–57.

35. Batesville *Independent Balance* 14 May 1856, quoted in David Y. Thomas, *Arkansas and Its People: A History*, 4 vols. (New York: American Historical Association, 1930) 1:115.

36. Worley, "Control of the Real Estate Bank," 413–414, 421–422, 425–426. The evidence against this elite is largely circumstantial. David Y. Thomas reported that these families—the Seviers, Conways, Johnsons, Rectors—had all arrived with little; yet by the end of the antebellum era they all "had many slaves, a hundred or more, raised hundreds of bales of cotton, and a great deal of corn and hogs." Thomas, *Arkansas and Its People* 1:115.

37. Helena *Southern Shield* 3 August 1850: 2.

38. Elsie Mae Lewis, "Economic Conditions in Antebellum Arkansas, 1850–1860," *Arkansas Historical Quarterly* 6 (Autumn 1947): 268.

39. Little Rock *Arkansas Gazette* 21 November 1851: 2.

40. Lewis, "Economic Conditions in Arkansas," 268–270.

41. Thomas, *Arkansas and Its People* 1:114. A Yankee traveler in the Old South noted this pattern when he observed in 1835 that "As soon as a young lawyer acquires sufficiently [sic] to purchase a few hundred acres of the rich alluvial lands, and a few slaves, he quits his profession at once, though perhaps just rising into eminence, and turns cotton planter." Rev. Joseph Holt Ingrahams, *The South-West: By a Yankee*, 2 vols. (New York: Harper & Brothers, 1835) 2:85.

42. Helena *Southern Shield* 24 January 1852: 2.

43. *Southern Shield* 13 March 1852: 2. The Camden Convention was held on December 22–23, 1851; see Little Rock *Arkansas Whig* 1 January 1852: 2. The Little Rock convention was held February 9–10, 1852; see the Little Rock *Arkansas Whig* 5 February 1852: 2. The minutes of this Little Rock convention were published in the *Arkansas Whig* on 19 February 1852: 1–3.

44. Helena *Southern Shield* 12 November 1853: 2.

45. Letter from "E" in Little Rock *Arkansas Gazette* 25 August 1854: 2.

46. Diary of Judge John Brown, January 1, 1853, Camden, Arkansas. Manuscript, Arkansas History Commission, Little Rock, Arkansas.

47. Thomas, *Arkansas and Its People* 1:103.

48. Thomas, *Arkansas and Its People* 1:103.

49. *Compendium to the Sixth Census, 1840*, 323–324; *Census of 1850*, 554–556; *Census of 1860*, 2:6–7.

50. Thomas, *Arkansas and Its People* 1:116. The actual figures that Thomas gives on that page are $357,000 in 1850 to $2,880,578 by 1860, of which approximately 50% was from lumber, 30% from milling, and the rest from clothing, shoes, boots and firearms.

51. Lewis, "Economic Conditions in Arkansas," 260.

52. Ashmore, *Arkansas* 69. According to the census records, Little Rock had in 1860 a population of only 3,727, Camden 2,219, Fort Smith, 1,550, Pine Bluff, 1,396, and Fayetteville 967. The four other towns with over 500 people were Van Buren, Arkadelphia, Batesville and Searcy. *Census of 1860* 1:23.

53. Walz, "Migration into Arkansas," 299–300. According to Walz's table (p. 300) migration into Arkansas rarely exceeded 1,000 in any one year. From 1856–60, these were the figures: 1856–57: 1,032; 1857–58: 1,117; 1858–59: 3,461; 1859–60: 1,936.

54. Washington *Democrat*, quoted in Little Rock *True Democrat* 10 March 1857, 2.

55. Dougan, *Confederate Arkansas* 9.

56. Land-value figures compiled by Dr. Walter L. Brown of the University of Arkansas at Fayetteville. By 1860 the true value of real and personal property in the U.S. was $514 per capita; in Arkansas it was $504, showing that the state was developing. Maude Carmichael, "The Plantation System in Arkansas, 1850–1880" diss., Radcliffe College, 1934, 256.

57. *Compendium to the Sixth Census, 1840*, 323–324; *Census of 1850*, 554; *Census of 1860*, 2:6.

58. Walz, "Migration into Arkansas," 300.

59. Little Rock *Arkansas Gazette* 13 June 1857: 2.

60. For a description of the origins of African slavery in Arkansas during the French colonial period and its practice during the Spanish era, see Taylor, *Negro Slavery in Arkansas* 12–27.

61. Figures for Table 2i and 2j are compiled from the *Census of 1860*, 1:598–604.

62. *Census of 1860* 1:599.

63. *Census of 1860* 1:598–604; Taylor, *Negro Slavery in Arkansas* 47, 48. Between 1820 and 1830, the slave population of Arkansas grew by 182.9% to Alabama's 180.9%. Between 1830 and 1840, the percentage of slave population growth was 335.4% to Mississippi's 197.3%. From 1840 to 1850, it was for Arkansas's 136.2% to Mississippi's 58.7%. From 1850 to 1860, Texas's percentage of the slave population was 213.8% to Arkansas's 135.9%.

64. *Abstract of the Fifth Census, 1830*, 43. Orville Taylor states incorrectly that 61% of the slaves lived in the uplands in 1830; see Taylor, *Negro Slavery in Arkansas* 27.

65. *Compendium to the Sixth Census, 1840*, 93–94; *Census of 1850*, 535; *Census of 1860* 1:18.

66. *Census of 1860*, 1:18.

67. Taylor, *Negro Slavery in Arkansas* 52; Walz, "Migration into Arkansas," 45–51.

68. Otto and Burns, "Traditional Agricultural Practices in the Arkansas Highlands," 168–177.

69. Taylor, *Negro Slavery in Arkansas* 56. Taylor's actual figure was 17.7%. He fixed the number of slave-owners at approximately 3.5% of the white population. He presumed that each of these slaveowners was the head of a household five times the size of the average frontier family. He arrived at his figures by multiplying the number of slaveowners by five, which brought him to 57,405, or about 17.7% of the white population.

70. *Census of 1860* 2:223–247. For a slightly different estimate, see Gray, *History of Southern Agriculture* 1:482.

71. The figure Orville Taylor gives is 42.5%; Taylor, *Negro Slavery in Arkansas* 56. Taylor's percentage is inaccurate because his methodology was not computed correctly. To find the number of people involved in slavery, Taylor added the number of whites (17.7%) and the number of slaves, which was 25% of the total population. After these are added together, a total of 42.7% is arrived at. This methodology does not fit when used on other Southern states. For example, South Carolina had a slave percentage of 57.1% and the number of slaveowners and their families amounted to 45.8%. When these percentages are added together they come to the impossible figure of 102.9%. A better method is to take the number of slaves and the number of whites involved in slavery as owners or members of slaveowning families, and then add these two. A new percentage of the total population can then be computed. In the case of South Carolina, that number turns out to be 76.1%. For Arkansas, the number of whites and blacks involved directly with slavery is 38.7%. Taylor's mistake was that he added percentages instead of adding the actual number of people, and then computed the percentage from that number.

72. Carl Moneyhon, "Economic Democracy in Antebellum Arkansas: Phillips County, 1850–1860," *Arkansas Historical Quarterly* 40 (Summer, 1981): 154–172.

73. Memphis *Weekly Appeal,* 18 April 1860: 1.

74. S. Charles Bolton, "Inequality on the Southern Frontier: Arkansas County in the Arkansas Territory," *Arkansas Historical Quarterly* 41 (Spring, 1982): 51–66. Bolton, "Economic Inequality," 619–633.

75. *Census of 1850,* 535; *Census of 1860* 1:18, 2:7.

76. John Solomon Otto, "Slavery in the Mountains: Yell County, 1840–1860," *Arkansas Historical Quarterly* 39 (Spring, 1980): 34–52. Yell County is on the southern shore of the Arkansas River in the Ouachita Mountains in the west central area of the state. This county had a sizeable degree of slavery and cotton production, especially along the river lowlands. Yet, according to Otto, the upland area of the county still grew more than half the cotton crop and "dozens" of upland farmers owned slaves, pp. 50, 51. This small study of one county in upland Arkansas suggests that slavery and the cotton economy may have been more important and substantial to the mountains of the South than earlier historians have often portrayed it.

77. *Census of 1810,* 84.

78. *Census of 1860* 1:598–604. The percentages for the decade 1810–1820 computed by the author.

79. There were 465 free blacks in a population of 97,574, or about 0.4% of the population. *Compendium of the Sixth Census, 1840,* 93–94.

80. Taylor, *Negro Slavery in Arkansas* 244–245.

81. Taylor, *Negro Slavery in Arkansas* 247.

82. Taylor, *Negro Slavery in Arkansas* 249.

83. Little Rock *Arkansas State Democrat* 5 October 1849: 2.

84. For the origin of this Anglo-American concept of the racial inferiority of blacks, see Winthrop Jordan, *White over Black: American Attitude toward the Negro, 1550–1815* (New York: Oxford University Press, 1968).

85. This opinion probably originated from the fact that early in the nineteenth century, two free blacks led a slave rebellion in Richmond, Virginia, in 1800, and in Charleston, South Carolina in 1822. The rebellion in Richmond was led by Gabriel Prosser, and for the most recent treatment see Gerald W. Mullin, *Flight and Rebellion: Slave Resistance in Eighteenth Century Virginia* (New York: Oxford University Press, 1972) 140–163. For a brief survey of the rebellion of Denmark Vesey and how it affected South Carolina society, see William Freehling, *Prelude to Civil War: The Nullification Crisis in South Carolina, 1816–1836* (New York: Harper & Row, 1965) 53–65.

86. El Dorado *Union,* n.d., quoted in Van Buren *Arkansas Intelligencer* 13 October 1849: 2.

87. Taylor, *Negro Slavery in Arkansas* 253.

88. Taylor, *Negro Slavery in Arkansas* 250–251. Paul Lack offers an account of the life of urban slaves in Little Rock and their relationship to whites and free blacks; see "An Urban Slave Community: Little Rock, 1831–1862," *Arkansas Historical Quarterly* 41 (Autumn 1982): 258–287. White workers led the way to expelling free blacks. See Lack's above-cited article, pp. 283–286.
89. Taylor, *Negro Slavery in Arkansas* 256–257.
90. *Census of 1860* 1 : 18.
91. Taylor, *Negro Slavery in Arkansas* 258.

Chapter III

1. David Y. Thomas, *Arkansas and Its People,* 4 vols. (New York: American Historical Association, 1930) 1 : 57.
2. Harry S. Ashmore, *Arkansas: A History* (New York: W. W. Norton, 1978) 6. The founder of the Arkansas Post in 1686 was a Sicilian in the service of the French. For his biography, see Robert Murphy, *Henri de Tonti: Fur Trader of the Mississippi* (Baltimore: Johns Hopkins University Press, 1941).
3. Timothy Flint, a New England traveler in Arkansas and the Mississippi River Valley, wrote about his visit to the Arkansas Post around 1820: "The inhabitants of the Post and its vicinity are chiefly the remains, or the descendants, of the first settlers, and they are, for the most part, of French extract." Timothy Flint, *A Condensed Geography and History of the Western States and the Mississippi Valley,* 2 vols. (Cincinnati: E. H. Flint, 1828) 1 : 584.
4. Dallas Herndon, *A Centennial History of Arkansas,* 3 vols. (Chicago: Clarke Publishing Company, 1922) 1 : 135.
5. Herndon, *A Centennial History* 135–146. In these pages Herndon gives a good general history of the period. The first five counties in the state included Arkansas, 1813; Lawrence, 1815; Pulaski, Clark, and Hempstead in 1818. All of these counties were created by the Missouri territorial legislature; see Lonnie J. White, *Politics on the Southwestern Frontier: Arkansas Territory, 1819–1836* (Memphis: Memphis State University Press, 1964) 5. Another study is by Waddy Moore, "Territorial Arkansas, 1819–1836" diss., University of North Carolina, 1963.
6. The best secondary source for this North-South debate over slavery in the Arkansas Territory is White, *Politics on the Southwestern Frontier* 6–16; see also William Johnson, "Prelude to the Missouri Compromise," *Arkansas Historical Quarterly* 24 (Spring 1965): 47–66.
7. *The Debates and Proceedings in the Congress of the United States: 15th Congress, 2nd Session* (Washington, D.C.: Gales and Seaton, 1855) 1222.
8. *Debates and Proceedings* 1238.
9. *Debates and Proceedings* 1272–1273. The motion to drop Taylor's amendment was proposed by Representative George Robertson of Kentucky, and after a tie vote the record reported, "There being an equal division, the Speaker declared himself in the affirmative, and so the motion was carried." p. 1273. For a North-South breakdown on the vote, see White, *Politics on the Southwestern Frontier* 12.
10. *Debates and Proceedings, 15th Congress, 2nd Session* 274. For a North-South breakdown on the Senate vote, see White, *Politics on the Southwestern Frontier* 15. The text of the Territorial Act is given by Dallas Herndon in *Annals of Arkansas, 1947,* 3 vols. (Little Rock: Historical Record Association, n.d.) 1 : 72–74.
11. For an explanation describing how Little Rock was chosen as the capital, see Ira Richards, *Story of a Rivertown: Little Rock in the Nineteenth Century* (Benton, Arkansas: Private Printing, 1969) 8–10. For an older, but more colorful account describing the choice of Little Rock as capital of the state, see Dallas Herndon, *Why Little Rock Was Born* (Little Rock: Central Printing, 1933). Herndon had claimed in an earlier work that the French explorer Bernard de la Harpe named the area "Le Petit Roche" in the 1730s; Herndon, *Cen-*

tennial History of Arkansas 1 : 819. Ira Richards, in a study of Little Rock, claimed that this story was a complete fabrication; see Richards, *Story of a Rivertown* 3–4, 118; footnotes 8 and 11.

12. For the most complete discussion of William Woodruff's early life and career in territorial Arkansas, see John Lewis Ferguson, "William Woodruff of the Territory of Arkansas, 1819–1836" diss., Tulane University, 1960, 1–76.

13. A good early survey of the *Arkansas Gazette* as well as the best single volume treatment of antebellum Arkansas politics, is by Margaret Ross, *Arkansas Gazette: The Early Years, 1819–1866* (Little Rock: Arkansas *Gazette* Foundation, 1969). Mrs. Ross reports (pp. 41–42) that the *Gazette* had moved from the Arkansas Post to Little Rock by December, 1821.

14. The influence of the *Arkansas Gazette* was traditionally extensive in the state. It is the oldest paper and enjoys a strong statewide circulation. One of its past editors wrote a history of the press in Arkansas; see Fred W. Allsopp, *History of the Arkansas Press for a Hundred Years and More* (Little Rock: Parke-Harper, 1922).

15. White, *Politics on the Southwestern Frontier,* 204.

16. White, *Politics on the Southwestern Frontier* 19; Thomas P. Abernathy, "Richard Mentor Johnson," in *Dictionary of American Biography,* Dumas Malone, ed., 20 vols. (New York: Charles Scribner & Sons, 1928–1936) 10 : 114–116. In the same series, see E. Merton Coulter, "John Jordan Crittenden," 4 : 546–549.

17. Crittenden served as acting governor in 1819, 1823 and 1825. White, *Politics on the Southwestern Frontier* 19, 46–47, 50–55.

18. James Miller, territorial governor from 1819 to 1824, was a hero from the War of 1812 and was too ill, or sometimes too concerned about the Indians in Arkansas, to be able to serve effectively as political leader for the territory. The second territorial governor, George Izard, did attempt to take power away from Crittenden during his three years as governor, and died in late 1828. White, *Politics on the Southwestern Frontier* 18–19, 29, 50–65, 88–89; Fay Hempstead, *History of Arkansas From the Earliest Times to 1890* (St. Louis, Missouri: N. D. Thompson, 1890) 190–192.

19. Ross, *Arkansas Gazette* 23–24, 34, 49. In Bates's first race for territorial delegate in 1819, his strongest challenger was none other than Stephen Austin, the founder of the Texas colony. Austin announced just thirteen days before the election, and his name did not appear on the ballot in Lawrence and Arkansas counties. Even with these disadvantages, the vote was close: Bates 401 to Austin 343. Had Austin won this election, he might have made Arkansas, not Texas, his future destiny. An Arkansas historian feels that if Austin had announced earlier and been on the ballot in those two counties, he would have won. Herndon, *Centennial History of Arkansas* 156–157.

20. White, *Politics on the Southwestern Frontier* 90–91. John Pope came from Kentucky and had helped swing that state for Jackson in 1828. Fulton was from Alabama, a soldier, lawyer and newspaper editor, and quite loyal to Jackson. This information is found in White, *Politics on the Southwestern Frontier* 91, 92.

21. White, *Politics on the Southwestern Frontier* 171–172. Pope would blame his ouster on Fulton; see Little Rock *Arkansas Gazette* 10 March 1835: 2. Lewis Randolph, grandson of Thomas Jefferson, was appointed as the new secretary for the Arkansas territory; Hempstead, *History of Arkansas* 253. Although Pope left the state disgusted, his nephew, William F. Pope, remained in Little Rock and lived to write an interesting account of early development. See William F. Pope, *Early Days in Arkansas: Being for the Most Part the Personal Recollections of an Old Settler* (Little Rock: Fred W. Allsopp, 1895).

22. Gene Wills Boyette, "The Whigs of Arkansas, 1836–1856," diss., Louisiana State University, 1972, 13, 47. This is the best and most thorough work on Arkansas Whiggery. That Crittenden's faction formed the nucleus of the Whig party in Arkansas is confirmed by Mr. Tim Farrell, who wrote to Jesse Turner that the Whigs of 1849 were the same men who followed Crittenden in the days of the territorial government. T. Farrell to Jesse Turner, 14

December 1849, Jesse Turner Papers, Mullins Library, University of Arkansas, Fayetteville.

23. White, *Politics on the Southwestern Frontier* 127–131; Ferguson, "Woodruff of the Territory of Arkansas," 174–181. Ferguson claims that Crittenden's enemies suggested the plan to the former territorial secretary. Crittenden had built a huge house in Little Rock and had gone into debt because of it. According to Ferguson, "the enemies of Crittenden were undoubtedly trying to involve the former secretary in difficulties and for once the astuteness of the latter deserted him. Pressed by financial necessity, he took the bait eagerly and, as soon as the legislature convened, the fateful proposition was made" (p. 175).

24. Governor Pope's veto message printed in Little Rock *Arkansas Gazette* 26 October 1831: 2. For a discussion of the message, see White, *Politics on the Southwestern Frontier* 130–131; Ferguson, "Woodruff of the Territory of Arkansas," 176–177.

25. White, *Politics on the Southwestern Frontier* 140.

26. White, *Politics on the Southwestern Frontier* 141–163. As an example of the bitterness of the election and the violence often associated with frontier politics, Dr. Ferguson described this scene during the campaign of 1833: "When Sevier and Crittenden appeared in Little Rock on the ninth of May, the tension was so great that a threatening gesture by any person would probably have brought a general melee. Editor Charles Bertrand of the *Arkansas Advocate*, with a large pistol prominently displayed, declared that he would shoot Sevier if ever he called him again the damndest liar in Arkansas. Woodruff of the *Gazette* and Sevier both had pistols cocked and ready." Ferguson, "William Woodruff of the Territory of Arkansas," 194.

27. Hempstead, *History of Arkansas* 250.

28. Josiah Shinn, *Pioneers and Makers of Arkansas* (Little Rock: Democrat Printing & Lithograph Co., 1908) 181. Supporting this view, Ferguson writes that "the aloof, aristocratic, coldly brilliant Crittenden was no match at the polls for the witty and gregarious Sevier." Ferguson, "William Woodruff of the Territory of Arkansas," 198.

29. For the best secondary study of these men and the whole organization of the Whig party in Arkansas, see Boyette, "Whigs of Arkansas," 14–103. Boyette says that the Whigs tended to be dominated by the leadership in Little Rock, but this was also true of the Democratic party, p. 35. Perhaps the most colorful Whig was Albert Pike, an editor, poet, political theorist, lawyer, politician, historian, military general, and one of the leading persons of American Masonry. For the definitive biography of this man see Walter L. Brown, "Albert Pike: 1809–1891," diss., University of Texas, 1955.

30. Boyette, "Whigs of Arkansas," 44–46. For another political survey of Arkansas between 1836 and 1850, see Dewey Allen Stokes, "Public Affairs in Arkansas, 1836–1850" diss., University of Texas, 1966.

31. Ross, *Arkansas Gazette* 231–232. Concerning this Whig victory, a Democratic paper in western Arkansas commented, "Well, they are welcome to their rejoicing, as their triumphs are much fewer than angel visits." Van Buren *Arkansas Intelligencer* 23 January 1847: 2.

32. Brian C. Walton, "The Second Party System in Arkansas, 1836–1850," *Arkansas Historical Quarterly* 38 (Summer 1969): 124–125. In the national elections between 1836 and 1852, the vote in Arkansas for Whig presidential candidates was as follows: 1836—32%, 1840—44%, 1844—37%, 1848—44%, 1852—38%. Information from Boyette, "Whigs of Arkansas," 61, 145, 233, 325, 397.

33. Stokes, "Public Affairs in Arkansas," 13–44, 266–296, 323–343. Dr. Boyette feels strongly that the Arkansas Whigs, like their counterparts in other states, suffered from the taint of aristocracy and arrogance. The more they talked about issues, the more arrogant and aristocratic they appeared. Boyette, "Whigs of Arkansas," 189–191. As Boyette put it, "This taint of aristocracy, in fervent egalitarian Arkansas, this charge, if accepted by the voters as valid, would alone bring the defeat of Whiggery" (p. 191).

34. Allsopp, *History of the Press in Arkansas* 178–179, 192, 275, 285; Pope, *Early Days in Arkansas* 127, 130.

35. Ross, *Arkansas Gazette* 191–194. For the *Gazette's* continued opposition to the Democratic leadership in the state, see pp. 195–356.

36. Ralph Wooster, *Politicians, Planters, and Plain Folks: Courthouse to Statehouse in the Upper South, 1850–1860* (Knoxville: University of Tennessee Press, 1975) 46.

37. Walton, "Second Party System in Arkansas," 125–126.

38. The historian of the Whigs in Arkansas categorized them saying, "Whigs were found in the heavily slave populated lowlands of southern and eastern Arkansas and in the more densely populated urban areas like Little Rock, Camden, and Batesville." Boyette, "Whigs of Arkansas," Introduction (a). This view is also confirmed by Stokes; see his "Public Affairs in Arkansas," 1–49. The historian for Little Rock in the nineteenth century confirms the Whigs' dominance, writing, "The city was more Whig than Democrat in its politics; advocates of sound banking, internal improvements, and industrialization, found a ready audience there." Richards, *Story of a Rivertown* 32. This planter and urban base of the Arkansas Whigs was also common in much of the Old South; see the classic work, Arthur C. Cole, *The Whig Party in the South* (Washington, D.C.: American Historical Association, 1913).

39. Boyette, "Whigs of Arkansas," 115–116.

40. Walton, "Second Party System in Arkansas," 124–125.

41. For a good recent article on the socio-economic differences between the Whigs and Democrats in Arkansas, see Gene Boyette, "Quantitative Differences between the Arkansas Whig and Democratic Parties, 1836–1850," *Arkansas Historical Quarterly* 34 (Autumn 1975): 214–226. According to Boyette, the reason the Whigs never penetrated the mountains was that they talked about issues that were not the concerns of the isolated mountain communities. Boyette wrote, "The nationalist economic programs of the Whigs (their support for internal improvements, i.e. roads and canals made at Federal expense) appealed to residents of counties more nearly in the mainstream of the national and world economy. . . . Voters in river counties proved more compatible with Whiggery since such voters were inclined toward an awareness of a way of life beyond their horizons of space and time. The sectional base of Whig strength in Arkansas suggests that this thesis may explain the poor Whig performances in the northern and western regions of Arkansas as contrasted with the more favorable Whig performances in the southern and eastern areas of the state" (p. 221).

42. Wooster, *Politicians, Planters, and Plain Folks* 73; Ralph Wooster, *The People in Power: Courthouse to Statehouse in the Lower South, 1850–1860* (Knoxville: University of Tennessee Press, 1969) 63. Wooster claims in this work on the lower South (pp. 41–47, 62) that only in aristocratic South Carolina and in frontier Texas was there one-party dominance in state politics approaching that of Arkansas.

43. John Hallum, *Biographical and Pictorial History of Arkansas* (Albany, N.Y.: Weed & Parsons & Co., 1889) 42–44. Hallum gives a full account of the names of the people who were members of this "family" in Arkansas politics. As yet there has been no full scholarly study of the Family in antebellum Arkansas. Michael Dougan has written an article on the decline of the Family in Arkansas politics during the Civil War. Michael Dougan, "A Look at the 'Family' in Arkansas Politics, 1858–1865," *Arkansas Historical Quarterly* 29 (Summer 1970): 99–111.

44. Hempstead, *History of Arkansas* 215. In Hempstead's account, Henry Wharton Conway was born in Greene County, Tennessee, on March 18, 1793.

45. Herndon, *Centennial History of Arkansas* 1:164–165; White, *Politics on the Southwestern Frontier* 37–47.

46. Herndon, *Centennial History of Arkansas* 1:165.

47. White, *Politics on the Southwestern Frontier* 66–67. Crittenden's sponsored opposition was Robert Oden of Little Rock, a man Josiah Shinn would later claim was the first lawyer to practice in the city, beginning in 1818. Shinn, *Pioneers and Makers of Arkansas* 188.

48. The date of the election was on August 6, 1827, and the duel was on October 29, 1827. Herndon, *Centennial History of Arkansas* 1:172, 176. Conway died on November 9,

1827; Hallum, *Biographical and Pictorial History of Arkansas* 49–50. For a primary account of the affair, see Little Rock *Arkansas Gazette* 6 November 1827: 1–2; 13 November 1827: 2. For the best modern treatment of the duel see White, *Politics on the Southwestern Frontier* 77–80.

49. White, *Politics on the Southwestern Frontier* 87.

50. White, *Politics on the Southwestern Frontier* 83–86. Ambrose Hundley Sevier was the grand-nephew of John Sevier, revolutionary hero and elected governor of Tennessee six times. Hallum, *Biographical and Pictorial History of Arkansas* 42.

51. White, *Politics on the Southwestern Frontier* 203. For a look at how Sevier secured various offices for his relatives, see his letter to President Andrew Jackson, dated April 4, 1836, reprinted in C. Fred Williams, et al., eds., *A Documentary History of Arkansas* (Fayetteville: University of Arkansas Press, 1984) 79–80.

52. White, *Politics on the Southwestern Frontier* 164.

53. White, *Politics on the Southwestern Frontier* 165–168, 172–191.

54. White, *Politics on the Southwestern Frontier* 192–199. White quotes Senator Thomas Hart Benton of Missouri who said that the knowledge that Arkansas might help the election of Martin Van Buren in the presidential election of 1836 helped to bring the Arkansas statehood bill to a vote quickly in the upper House, p. 198. For another account see Marie Cash, "Arkansas Achieves Statehood," *Arkansas Historical Quarterly*, 1 (December 1943): 392–408.

55. Brian Walton, "Ambrose Hundley Sevier in the United States Senate, 1836–1848," *Arkansas Historical Quarterly* 32 (Spring 1973): 25–60.

56. Walton, "Sevier in the U.S. Senate," 35, 49–50. Walton reported (pp. 31, 39–42) that Sevier succeeded William King of Kentucky in 1845 as manager of party measures on the Senate floor.

57. David Y. Thomas, "Ambrose Hundley Sevier" in Malone, *Dictionary of American Biography* 16:601–602.

58. Ross, *Arkansas Gazette* 247–259. Sevier underwent investigation by the Arkansas legislature in 1843 for mishandling certain bonds in the Real Estate Bank. The usually subservient Arkansas legislature eventually censured the senator for his part in the affair. Sevier sent to the General Assembly afterwards a "series of vituperative letters of incredible arrogance and tastelessness to members who had voted to censure him." Walton, "Sevier in the U.S. Senate," 38. Whether Sevier actually embezzled state funds or not is largely circumstantial, for his family and political associates did have quite a lot of property and slaves; see Thomas, *Arkansas and Its People* 1:115.

59. Ross, *Arkansas Gazette* 252–253.

60. For a good, recent evaluation of the first five governors of Arkansas, see Timothy P. Donovan and Willard B. Gatewood, Jr., eds., *The Governors of Arkansas: Essays in Political Biography* (Fayetteville: University of Arkansas Press, 1981) 1–29.

61. Ross, *Arkansas Gazette* 137, 157–158, 208, 229, 232–233; Boyette, "Whigs of Arkansas," 32–35, 61, 85, 95, 183, 282, 291–294. The Arkansas congressmen for the first twelve years of statehood included Archibald Yell, 1836–1839; Edward Cross, 1839–1845; Archibald Yell, 1845–1846; Thomas Newton, 1847; and Robert W. Johnson, 1847–1853.

62. Hempstead, *History of Arkansas* 780. Herndon, *Centennial History of Arkansas* 1:266. Almost as soon as Borland appeared in Arkansas, he displayed a violent temper. One person witnessed Borland beat a rival editor's face "into jelly" in a street brawl in Little Rock in late 1843. See William Woodruff, letter to U.S. Senator William Fulton, 5 January 1844, reprinted in Hallum, *Biographical and Pictorial History of Arkansas* 210–211. For an account of the election of 1848 and the issues involved between Borland and Sevier see Ross, *Arkansas Gazette* 253–261. For an analysis of the election in the legislature see Brian Walton, "Arkansas Politics in the Compromise Crisis, 1848–1852," *Arkansas Historical Quarterly* 36 (Winter 1977): 319. For editor George Clarke's support of Borland, see Van Buren *Arkansas Intelligencer* 24 June 1848: 2; 16 September 1848: 2.

63. Ross, *Arkansas Gazette* 300. For a brief account of Borland's life and career, see D. Y. Thomas, "Solon Borland," *Dictionary of American Biography* 2:464–465.

64. This presentation of Arkansas political maneuvering is found in Thomas, *Arkansas and Its People* 1:91–92. Thomas explains how conventions were rigged and pre-planned. A Committee on Resolution went into session for five minutes and returned with a well-written report that filled several columns of a newspaper.

65. Batesville *Independent Balance* 11 April 1856, quoted in Thomas, *Arkansas and Its People* 1:92.

66. For a discussion of the relative Family dominance in some local areas of the state, see Walton, "Second Party System in Arkansas," 123; Boyette, "Quantitative Differences between Arkansas Whig and Democratic Parties," 219–221.

67. Walton, "Second Party System in Arkansas," 128. Yell's popularity existed independent of the Family. See Michael Dougan, "Archibald Yell," in Donovan and Gatewood, *Governors of Arkansas* 7. Yell died in February, 1847, during the Mexican War. Drew raised the ire of the Family by appointing Borland to the U.S. Senate in 1848. See Bobby Roberts, "Thomas S. Drew," *Governors of Arkansas* 15. For Ashley's various quarrels with the Family see Susan H. Ruple, "The Life and Times of Chester Ashley of Arkansas, 1791–1848," M.A. thesis, University of Arkansas, 1983.

68. John Monette, *History of the Discovery and Settlement of the Valley of the Mississippi by the Three Great European Powers, Spain, France, and Great Britain, and the Subsequent Occupation, Settlement, and Extension of Civil Government by the United States until the Year, 1846*, 2 vols. (New York: Harper & Brothers, 1846) 2:257. Lonnie White, almost 130 years later, would laud Arkansas's first state charter for its democratic features. White, *Politics on the Southwestern Frontier* 191. White also gives the best secondary account of the Arkansas Constitutional Convention of 1838, pp. 184–191. For a dated but more detailed look at the Constitutional Convention of 1836, see Jesse Turner, Jr., "The Constitution of 1836," *Publications of the Arkansas Historical Association*, 4 vols. (Little Rock: Democrat Printing & Lithograph, 1906–1917) 3:74–166.

69. White, *Politics on the Southwestern Frontier* 191. For two studies on Arkansas's suffrage requirements, see Joseph Taylor Robinson, "Suffrage in Arkansas," *Publications of the Arkansas Historical Association* 4 vols. (Little Rock: Democrat Printing & Lithograph, 1906–1917) 3:167–174; Sidney Crawford, "Arkansas Suffrage Qualifications," *Arkansas Historical Quarterly* 2 (December 1943): 331–339.

70. Arkansas's Constitution of 1836 with amendments to 1861; see Francis Thorpe, ed., *The Federal and State Constitutions: Colonial Charters, and Other Organic Laws of the States, Territories, and Colonies, Now or Heretofore Forming the United States of America* 7 vols. (Washington, D.C.: Government Printing Office, 1909) 1:268–287.

71. Wooster, *Politicians, Planters, and Plain Folks* 74; Walton, "Second Party System in Arkansas," 133–136.

72. Robert Crittenden, letter to Franklin Wharton, 30 November 1833: 3; Clifton Wharton Papers, Department of Manuscripts and Archives, Louisiana State University, Baton Rouge.

73. Absalom Fowler to Jesse Turner, 15 June 1837, quoted in Boyette, "Whigs of Arkansas," 67.

74. George H. Thompson, *Arkansas and Reconstruction: The Influence of Geography, Economics, and Personality* (Port Washington, N.Y.: Kennikat Press, 1976) 20.

75. Van Buren *Arkansas Intelligencer* 1 November 1845: 2. For Yell's address, see the same paper, 25 October 1845: 1. The *Arkansas Intelligencer*, edited by the independent Democrat, George Clarke, who chastised Yell for resigning from Congress and going off to war, thus giving up his bid for the U.S. Senate, 6 June 1846: 2.

76. Ross, *Arkansas Gazette* 235.

77. Van Buren *Arkansas Intelligencer* 9 October 1847: 2. When the *Intelligencer* quoted the El Dorado *Union*, which said that no controlling clique existed in Little Rock, this west-

ern Arkansas paper replied that the editor of the El Dorado publication "was in an enviable state of ignorance." See 4 December 1847: 2. This Van Buren newspaper called upon northern and western Democrats in Arkansas to unite behind a candidate opposed to the Family's congressman, Robert W. Johnson, in the 1848 election; see 16 October 1847: 2; 23 October 1847: 2. Into the next year, George Clarke of the *Arkansas Intelligencer* continued to attack the Dynasty, even backing the unsuccessful candidacy of W. S. Oldham of Fayetteville against Johnson. See 15 April 1848: 2; 27 May 1848: 2. For a time at least, the Van Buren *Arkansas Intelligencer* would serve as the lone voice of independent Democrats in northwestern Arkansas.

78. The Family had good reason to feel that the Whigs and the independent Democrats would never unite. In the 1848 election for the U.S. Senate, while George Clarke was supporting the candidacy of Borland against the Family leader, Sevier, the Whigs stayed aloof from the struggle, backing their candidate to the bitter end. For Clarke's support for Borland, see Van Buren *Intelligencer* 24 June 1848: 2; 16 September 1848: 3. For the Whig nonintervention in what they considered merely an intra-party squabble, see Walton, "Second Party System in Arkansas," 151–153.

Chapter IV

1. David Y. Thomas, "Robert Ward Johnson," in *Dictionary of American Biography,* Dumas Malone, ed., 20 vols. (New York: Charles Scribners & Sons, 1928–1936) 10:117–118. Fay Hempstead, *A Pictorial History of Arkansas from the Earliest Times to the Year 1890* (St. Louis: N. D. Thompson, 1890) 192, 775; Josiah Shinn, *Pioneers and Makers of Arkansas* (Little Rock: Democrat Printing & Lithograph Co., 1908) 197.

2. Elsie Mae Lewis, "Robert W. Johnson: Militant Spokesman of the Old South-West," *Arkansas Historical Quarterly* 13 (Spring 1954): 18. Later in this article, Lewis describes Johnson's role in Arkansas politics: "He was not a great man, but the most outstanding leader of Arkansas in the decade of 1850 to 1860. He ruled the state through a well organized machine composed mostly of his relatives" (p. 30).

3. Fay Hempstead, *Historical Review of Arkansas* 2 vols. (Chicago: Clarke Publishing Co., 1911) 1:173–174.

4. Little Rock *Arkansas Gazette* 29 January 1850: 2; 1 March 1850: 2; Little Rock *Arkansas Banner* 26 February 1850: 2.

5. Lewis, "Robert W. Johnson," 18. In the same article, Lewis discusses more fully the content of Johnson's letters. Also see Elsie Mae Lewis, "From Nationalism to Disunion: A Study of the Secession Movement in Arkansas, 1849–1861," diss., University of Chicago, 1947, 118–122.

6. The number of slaveowners in Arkansas came to 5,999 in 1850. See U.S. Department of the Interior, *The Eighth Census of the United States, 1860,* 4 vols. (Washington, D.C.: Government Printing Office, 1864–1866) 2:248. The white population was 162,109, and this percentage of slaveowners is about 3.7% of the white population. See U.S. Department of the Interior, *The Seventh Census of the United States, 1850* (Washington, D.C.: Robert Armstrong, Public Printer, 1853) 535. Using the methodology described in Chapter 2, footnote 67, the number of whites involved in slavery can be estimated at 18.5%. This is higher than in 1860 when the number of whites involved in slavery in Arkansas is estimated at 17.7%. This figure alone does not take into account the fact that the number of slaveowners and slaves in Arkansas doubled in the years 1850–1860. See Appendix Tables 2i, 2j, and 2l. One must also remember that prices for slaves were increasing, especially during the 1850s. See Clement Eaton, *The Growth of Southern Civilization, 1790–1860* (New York: Harper & Row, 1960) 49, 54.

7. For a description of meetings in southern and eastern Arkansas, comprising such counties as Independence, Jackson, Dallas, Poinsett, and Ouachita, see Little Rock *Arkansas Banner* 5 April 1850: 3; 16 April 1850: 3; 23 April 1850: 2; 21 May 1850: 2; 17 Septem-

ber 1850: 2; 8 October 1850: 2. For a description of the meetings in the northern and western areas of the state, see Little Rock *Arkansas Gazette* 3 May 1850: 2. One meeting in Fayetteville was called the largest public meeting ever held up to that time; see Little Rock *Arkansas Gazette* 9 August 1850: 2. For another look at these meetings, see Dewey Allen Stokes, "Public Affairs in Arkansas, 1836–1850," diss., University of Texas, 1966, 432–434, 435–437.

8. Fort Smith *Herald* 29 June 1850: 2; 6 July 1850: 2. The townspeople sent a protest to the U.S. government and called upon their congressional representatives to stop any troop withdrawal. Edwin Bearss and Arnell Gibson, *Fort Smith: Little Gibraltar on the Arkansas* (Norman: University of Oklahoma Press, 1969) 209–213.

9. Robert Harrison and Walter Kollmorgan, "Land Reclamation under the Swamp Land Grant of 1850," *Arkansas Historical Quarterly* 6 (Winter 1947): 369.

10. Fort Smith *Herald* 30 March 1850: 2.

11. Brian G. Walton, "Arkansas Politics in the Compromise Crisis, 1848–1852," *Arkansas Historical Quarterly* 36 (Winter 1977): 321. This alliance of Flournoy and Clarke was an irony for, as Walton points out, Flournoy led the fight for Sevier's re-election in the Senate race of 1848, while George Clarke was a leading advocate of Solon Borland; see Van Buren *Arkansas Intelligencer* 22 September 1848: 2.

12. William Woodruff actually merged his new paper, *Arkansas Democrat*, with the *Gazette* to become the *Arkansas State Gazette and Democrat*. This title persisted from February 1850 through different editors until July 9, 1859, when it again became *Arkansas State Gazette*. Ross, *Arkansas Gazette* 270, 337. It is subsequently referred to as the *Arkansas Gazette*.

13. Little Rock *Arkansas Gazette* 1 March 1850: 2.

14. Walton, "Politics in the Compromise Crisis," 319.

15. The fight between Borland and Senator Foote of Mississippi occurred in the street in front of the office of the *National Intelligencer* in Washington, D.C. on March 14, 1850. For the exact date of this incident, see Ross, *Arkansas Gazette* (January 1873): 274–275. An unsigned author wrote after the Civil War that "Borland and his colleague in the Congress, known familiarly as Bob Johnson, had a misunderstanding that had the smell of bloodshed at one time, but judicious friends prevented a fight." "Recollections of an Old Stager," *Harper's* 46 (January 1873): 275.

16. On the Compromise of 1850, as it was proposed by Senator Henry Clay of Kentucky, Senator Borland said on May 8, 1850, "I appeal to every one who hears me ask if this plan, comprehensive as it is, contains a single proposition which accords with the views that the Southern States have all along put forth . . ." *Congressional Globe, 31st Congress, 1st Session* (Washington, D.C.: John C. Rives, 1859), 953. Borland's entire address is found on pp. 953–954.

17. Borland's address in Little Rock on July 10th is found in the Little Rock *Arkansas Gazette* 26 July, 1850: 2. For another discussion on Borland's address, see Lewis, "From Nationalism to Disunion," 140–141.

18. The Dynasty's main paper in Little Rock claimed that Borland "loitered" in Little Rock for six weeks and then ran off to be with his family, claiming illness in their midst. The paper terms this excuse "so much humbug." Little Rock *Arkansas Banner* 3 September 1850: 2. The *Gazette* was quite happy with Borland's absence and the Arkansas senator did not leave the state for the nation's capital until November; see Little Rock *Arkansas Gazette* 9 August 1850: 2; 6 September 1850: 2; 27 September 1850: 2; 18 October 1850: 2; 8 November 1850: 2; 15 November 1850: 2. The historian of the Compromise crisis says that Borland's absence from Washington reduced the opposition to the Compromise by one. Holman Hamilton, *Prologue to Conflict: The Crisis and the Compromise of 1850* (New York: W. W. Norton, 1966) 116.

19. For a good recent survey of the Compromise that takes into account all the secondary material and controversy on this subject, see David Potter, *The Impending Crisis, 1848–*

1861 (New York: Harper & Row, 1976) 62–120. Potter sees it as more of a sectional armistice than a real compromise (p. 113).

20. Hamilton, *Prologue to Conflict* 191–192, 198.

21. Walton, "Politics in the Compromise Crisis," 319.

22. Stokes, "Public Affairs in Arkansas," 430–432. The Whigs' papers in 1850 were few, including the Batesville *Eagle*, Camden *Herald*, Helena *Southern Shield*, and Washington *Telegraph*. Not until the spring of 1851 did the Whigs have a paper in the Arkansas capital, the Little Rock *Arkansas Whig*. See Fred W. Allsopp, *History of the Arkansas Press for a Hundred Years and More* (Little Rock: Parke-Harper, 1922) 178–179, 193, 275, 285, 345–346.

23. Walter L. Brown, "Albert Pike, 1809–1891," diss., University of Texas, 1955, 258–259.

24. *Journal of the House of Representatives of the Eighth Session of the General Assembly of the State of Arkansas* (Little Rock: Arkansas Banner Office, 1851) 40. Governor Roane's entire message appears on pp. 20–41, and pp. 37–41, dealing with the Compromise and relations with the Federal government.

25. The vote to table Governor Roane's repudiation came on December 24, 1850, and resulted in a count of 43 to 24 in the House. For a look at this vote and a record of the debate in the House, see *Journal of the House* (as above), pp. 232–235, 294–303, 442–449. The vote in the Senate, on Christmas day, was 12 to 6. For this vote and the debate in the Senate, see *Journal of the Senate of the Eighth Session of the State of Arkansas* (Little Rock: Arkansas Banner Office, 1851) 53–54, 226–227, 245–246, 289–295, 405–407, 422–423, 437–438.

26. Walton, "Politics in the Compromise Crisis," 322.

27. Little Rock *Arkansas Banner* 4 June 1850: 2. Although Johnson did not issue frequent statements, his Dynasty's paper did seem to back off from a call for disunion; see Little Rock *Arkansas Banner* 30 April 1850: 2; 21 May 1850: 2; 28 May 1850: 2; and 2 July 1850: 2. Almost two months after Johnson's second address appeared, the *Arkansas Banner* expressed its disappointment that "the people had not manifested any unusual warmth" when Congressman Johnson "expressed his sentiment with the South;" see 16 April 1850: 2. The Family's paper in Little Rock eventually declared that it would not support the proposed Compromise then being debated in Congress, *Arkansas Banner* 16 July 1850: 2.

28. Johnson's letter dated from Washington on September 2, 1850. See *Arkansas Banner* 17 September 1850: 2; Little Rock *Gazette* 14 October 1850: 2. Arkansas postponed its 1850 congressional election for one year because the new session of Congress would not meet until December of 1851, and Arkansas anticipated that it would be allowed an additional congressman with the new census. Unfortunately, the census was not completed in time, so the state had to wait until 1853 to be eligible for an additional representative. For Johnson's vote against the Compromise, see Hamilton, *Prologue to Conflict* 184–185.

29. Potter, *The Impending Crisis* 126–130; Arthur C. Cole, *The Whig Party in the South* (Washington, D.C.: American Historical Association, 1913) 174–211.

30. Lewis, "From Nationalism to Disunion," 169–174. The Dynasty's newspaper stated publicly that it would never accept Clarke's nomination, Little Rock *Arkansas Banner* 11 March 1851: 2.

31. Ross, *Arkansas Gazette* 280. The Family press in Little Rock announced publicly for Johnson by late March and within the next month printed a report from a whole series of "spontaneous" meetings, mostly in southern and eastern Arkansas, calling for Johnson's nomination. Little Rock *Arkansas Banner* 25 March 1851: 2; 1 April 1851: 2; 8 April 1851: 2; 15 April 1851: 2; 22 April 1851: 2.

32. The Convention was held in Little Rock on Monday, April 28. The platform was written and Johnson was nominated all in one day. The vote on the first ballot was: Johnson 31 and Clarke 24. Little Rock *Arkansas Banner* 29 April 1851: 2. The Family did not believe in wasting time. They had begun a major campaign for Johnson in about a month and secured his nomination in one day.

33. Unfortunately, Clarke's newspaper, the Van Buren *Arkansas Intelligencer*, after December 1849, is lost. For Clarke's support of the opposition to Johnson, see Helena *Southern*

Shield 26 July 1851: 2; Little Rock *Arkansas Whig* 26 June 1851: 2; Little Rock *Arkansas Banner* 24 June 1851: 2; 29 July 1851: 2. For Flournoy and Woodruff's support of Johnson in this election, see Walton, "Politics in the Compromise Crisis," 323; Ross, *Arkansas Gazette* 281.

34. Walton, "Politics in the Compromise Crisis," 321. Actually, the Family had since early 1851 been declaring itself for the Union. In mid-January, its paper in Little Rock said that Johnson was for the Union and the Constitution, yet within the rights of the South. See Little Rock *Arkansas Banner* 14 January 1851: 2. This theme was carried into the summer campaign, for the paper claimed later, "We Democrats are the Union men, not being ashamed to declare and act upon the principles sanctioned by Jefferson and Jackson." 16 July 1851: 2. In a speech at Pine Bluff in early June, Johnson described himself as "the truest and best friend of the Union." Little Rock *Arkansas Banner* 17 June 1851: 2.

35. Helena *Southern Shield* 28 June 1851: 2. For much the same treatment of Johnson's new-found unionism, see Little Rock *Arkansas Whig* 5 June 1851: 2; 12 June 1851: 2; 19 June 1851: 2; 24 July 1851: 2; 31 July 1851: 2.

36. Absalom Fowler, letter to Jesse Turner, 7 June 1851, Jesse Turner Papers, Department of Manuscripts and Archives, Perkins Library, Duke University, Durham, North Carolina.

37. Walton, "Politics in the Compromise Crisis," 324.

38. Little Rock *Arkansas Banner* 17 June 1851: 2. To show the political rhetoric that often filled campaigns in antebellum Arkansas, the *Arkansas Banner* remarked about its opponents, "The Whigs should have a platform so that every time they have a meeting or a convention, we may know what particular invasions of the rights of the people are afoot." 10 June 1851: 2.

39. *Arkansas Banner* 1 July 1851: 2.

40. Helena *Southern Shield* 26 July 1851: 2.

41. Solon Borland, letter to Christopher C. Scott, 6 June 1851, Scott Papers, Arkansas History Commission, Little Rock. In the same document, Borland commented on Johnson and the Dynasty saying, "As long as Bob Johnsonianism is dominant, . . . or even tolerated in the State Democracy, it is not a party, but a faction, unworthy of a poor man's attachment or support."

42. For a study of the campaign, see Lewis, "From Nationalism to Disunion," 181–200; Stokes, "Public Affairs in Arkansas," 436–442; Ross, *Arkansas Gazette* 281.

43. Walton, "Politics in the Compromise Crisis," 325.

44. Walton, "Politics in the Compromise Crisis," 326. Walton says Johnson's vote in the northwest fell off slightly, but he still piled up substantial majorities. In Newton County, Johnson's vote fell off thirty-two percent, yet he still carried the county. The Whigs' Preston carried only six counties in the south and east: Hempstead, Bradley, Crittenden, Phillips, Ouachita, and Monroe. In the uplands, Preston carried only those counties that contained towns: Washington (Fayetteville), Crawford (Van Buren, where Clarke's support may have been important), and Pulaski (Little Rock). See p. 337. Figures for Table 4a on the county vote taken from Little Rock *Arkansas Gazette* 29 August 1851: 2; Little Rock *Arkansas Banner* 9 September 1851: 3. The official tally, as reported in the above cited *Banner* newspaper, gave Johnson 11,979 to Preston 8,876.

45. Christopher C. Scott, letter to David Walker, 11 August 1851, David Walker Papers, Mullins Library, University of Arkansas, Fayetteville.

46. Walton, "Politics in the Compromise Crisis," 326.

47. Lewis, "Robert W. Johnson," 26.

Chapter V

1. David Chevins, letter to Major John H. Bills, 9 May 1859, John H. Bills Papers, Department of Manuscripts and Archives, Louisiana State University, Baton Rouge. This influx also is cited in Gavin Wright, *The Political Economy of the Cotton South: Households, Markets and Wealth in the Nineteenth Century* (New York: W. W. Norton, 1978) 22.

2. W. E. Coleman, letter to Archibald H. Arrington, 13 January 1860, Arrington Papers, Southern Historical Collection, University of North Carolina, Chapel Hill.

3. Emily Torrence, letters to Mary Torrence, 9 February 1858, and 9 April 1858, Leonidas C. Glenn Papers, Southern Historical Collection, University of North Carolina, Chapel Hill.

4. Elsie Mae Lewis, "From Nationalism to Disunion: A Study of the Secession Movement in Arkansas, 1849–1861," diss., University of Chicago, 1947, 197.

5. Governor Roane's letter dated December 18, 1851, reprinted in Little Rock *Arkansas Banner* 23 December 1851: 2. Roane's letter came as a surprise to the Arkansas political scene. See Margaret Ross, *The Arkansas Gazette: The Early Years, 1819–1866* (Little Rock: Arkansas Gazette Foundation, 1969) 290. Roane would later say he was pushed aside by the Family; see Little Rock *Old Line Democrat* 13 July 1860: 2; 6 August 1860: 2.

6. For a brief biography of Conway, see David Y. Thomas, "Elias Nelson Conway" in *Dictionary of American Biography,* Dumas Malone, ed., 20 vols. (New York: Charles Scribner's Sons 1928–1936) 4:361–362. John Hallum's contention that the Arkansas Land Act of 1840 formed the framework of the later U.S. Homestead Act is in Hallum, *Biographical and Pictorial History of Arkansas* (Albany, N.Y.: Weed, Parsons & Co., 1889) 56.

7. William B. Worthen, "Elias Nelson Conway" in *The Governors of Arkansas: Essays in Political Biography,* Timothy P. Donovan and Willard B. Gatewood, Jr., eds. (Fayetteville: University of Arkansas Press, 1981) 24.

8. For a description of Smithson's candidacy and the issues he supported see Little Rock *Arkansas Gazette* 12 March 1851: 2. Smithson's support from the Northwest is discussed by Brian G. Walton in "Arkansas Politics in the Compromise Crisis, 1848–1852," *Arkansas Historical Quarterly* 36 (Winter 1977): 326–327.

9. William Woodruff, letter to Christopher C. Scott, 8 April 1852, Scott Papers, Arkansas History Commission, Little Rock.

10. Walton, "Politics in the Compromise Crisis," 327, footnote 65. The Dynasty's chief paper had earlier promised that the state convention would be the "fullest and fairest ever held." See Little Rock *Arkansas Banner* 30 December 1851: 2. Unfortunately, the *Banner* is lost from that date and so we do not have the official Family viewpoint until the start of the *True Democrat,* beginning in September, 1852. The opposition Democratic paper, the *Arkansas Gazette,* categorized the state convention as the usual event dominated by the Dynasty, conducted by "trick, chicanery, and fraud." See Little Rock *Arkansas Gazette* 7 May 1852: 2.

11. Clarke's and Smithson's views, as well as the reasons Woodruff joined in their efforts, were represented in the Little Rock *Arkansas Gazette* 14 May 1852: 2; 28 May 1852: 2; and 4 June 1852: 2.

12. Walton, "Politics in the Compromise Crisis," 327.

13. Little Rock *Arkansas Whig* 13 May 1852: 2.

14. Little Rock *Arkansas Gazette* 2 July 1852: 2; 9 July 1852: 2; 23 July 1852: 2. A later historian reprinted Conway's own words, which were originally published in a circular addressed to the people of Carroll, Madison, and Izard counties in the Ozarks: "But as Railroads are expensive, perhaps the people in all of these and some other sections of our State would, for the present be contented with establishing a few good dirt, plank, or macadamized roads." See Dallas Herndon, *A Centennial History of Arkansas,* 3 vols. (Chicago: Clarke Publishing Co., 1922) 1:263.

15. Little Rock *Arkansas Whig* 13 May 1852: 2.

16. Worthen, "Elias N. Conway," in Donovan and Gatewood, *The Governors of Arkansas* 25. It is difficult to ascertain the Family coverage of the campaign because its main paper from January to August 1852 is lost. Other Family papers from this period have also disappeared.

17. Little Rock *Arkansas Gazette,* 13 August 1852: 2; 20 August 1852: 3. The official vote tally was Conway 15,442 and Smithson 12,144. See Herndon, *Centennial History of Arkansas* 1:263.

18. Walton, "Politics in the Compromise Crisis," 328; Gene Wills Boyette, "The Whigs of Arkansas, 1836–1856," diss., Louisiana State University, 1972, 379.

19. Walton, "Politics in the Compromise Crisis," 228. Walton provides a chart (p. 337) that shows Smithson carried these counties: Crawford, Franklin, Johnson, Pope, Washington, Madison, Marion, Montgomery, Newton, Scott, and Searcy. These were all in the upland areas. Smithson carried Sevier and Clark counties in the southwest and Pulaski County in the central part of the state.

20. Little Rock *Arkansas Gazette* 13 August 1852: 2.

21. William Fulton Pope, *Early Days in Arkansas: Being For the Most Part the Personal Recollections of an Old Settler* (Little Rock: Frederick W. Allsopp, Publisher, 1895) 302.

22. Lewis, "From Nationalism to Disunion," 231–232.

23. Walton, "Politics in the Compromise Crisis," 339.

24. Boyette, "Whigs of Arkansas," 380.

25. Walton, "Politics in the Compromise Crisis," 329. According to Walton's figures (p. 337) Conway won a majority in both sections of the state, uplands and lowlands, but piled up majorities of seventy-five percent in Calhoun, Chicot, Mississippi, Poinsett, Greene, and Randolph counties in the delta; Conway also polled eighty-seven and eighty-six percent of the vote in small yeoman counties in the uplands like Izard and Perry counties.

26. Little Rock *Arkansas Gazette* 11 June 1852: 2; Little Rock *True Democrat* 7 September 1852: 2. Since the *Banner* issues in that period are lost, it is reasonable to presume it supported Pierce, for the first issue of the *True Democrat* endorsed him.

27. Little Rock *True Democrat* 7 September 1852: 1.

28. *True Democrat* 7 September 1852: 2. The other rival Democratic paper in the city said that if the Johnsons wanted to rename their paper, it should have been called the "Family Pirate Banner." Little Rock *Arkansas Gazette* 10 September 1852: 2.

29. Little Rock *Arkansas Whig* 4 March 1852: 2; Helena *Southern Shield* 1 May 1852: 2; 31 May 1852: 2.

30. Boyette, "Whigs of Arkansas" 397. The Whig vote in the presidential elections of 1836 and 1844 was, according to Boyette, 32 and 37 percent respectively. See pp. 60, 251.

31. Arthur Charles Cole, *The Whig Party in the South* (Washington, D.C.: American Historical Association, 1913) 261–273. Pike's dissatisfaction with the national Whig ticket of 1852 is expressed in Boyette, "Whigs of Arkansas," 378.

32. David Potter, *The Impending Crisis, 1848–1861* (New York: Harper & Row, 1976) 234–237. A more detailed study of the Whig campaign in Arkansas in the presidential election, and the fact that Winfield Scott only carried Bradley and Phillips counties in eastern and southern Arkansas, see Boyette, "Whigs of Arkansas," 379–382.

33. Walton, "Politics in the Compromise Crisis," 336. Sebastian's career is discussed by John Mula, in "The Public Career of William King Sebastian," M.A. thesis, University of Arkansas, 1969.

34. Richard H. Johnson letter to "Dear Ross" 6 July 1852, Samuel W. Williams Papers, Arkansas History Commission, Little Rock.

35. Senator Solon Borland, letter to Elbert H. English, 2 April 1852, English Papers, Arkansas History Commission, Little Rock.

36. Ross, *Arkansas Gazette* 300. Borland's adventures in Central America are contained in James M. Woods, "Expansionism as Diplomacy: The Career of Solon Borland in Central America, 1853–1854," *The Americas* 40 (January 1984): 399–417.

37. The actual appointment by Governor Conway came on July 6, 1853; see Ross, *Arkansas Gazette* 302.

38. A list of counties in each of the two congressional districts is provided by Herndon in the *Centennial History of Arkansas* 1 : 265.

39. Trapnall's death came in early July, and within a few days the Whigs' leadership replaced him with Little Rock lawyer James Curran. Little Rock *Arkansas Gazette* 8 July

1853: 2; 15 July 1853: 2. Curran carried only Pulaski County and the southeastern counties of Bradley, Chicot and Columbia. See Boyette, "Whigs of Arkansas," 387.

40. The reason that Arkansas delayed its congressional elections in 1851 and put them on in 1853 was that the state was hoping to get its new congressional districts in 1851, but the census was not completed until 1853. Once the state was divided into new districts, an election was held which put voting back on even years in 1854. See Harold T. Smith, "Arkansas Politics, 1850–1861," M.A. thesis, Memphis State University, 1964, 21, 47.

41. Little Rock *Arkansas Gazette* 11 August 1854: 2; 13 September 1854: 2. Walker, the Whig, carried only Arkansas County in the southeast, Polk County and his home county of Yell in the uplands. See Boyette, "Whigs of Arkansas," 387.

42. Fay Hempstead, *History of Arkansas From the Earliest Times to 1890* (St. Louis: N. D. Thompson & Co., 1890) 328.

43. A good account of the split in the national Whig party, is given by Potter in *The Impending Crisis* 232–236; and Cole, *Whig Party in the South* 245–259.

44. Cole, *Whig Party in the South* 261–281. In these pages, Cole gives a good rendition of the breakup of the party in Louisiana, Tennessee, Maryland, and Alabama. For specific state studies completed more recently than Cole, see Donald Rawson, "Democratic Resurgence in Mississippi, 1853–1855," *Journal of Mississippi History* 24 (February 1964): 1–27; and James Morrill, "The Presidential Election of 1852: Death Knell of the Whig Party in North Carolina," *North Carolina Historical Review* 44 (October 1967): 342–359.

45. Frederick W. Allsopp, *History of the Arkansas Press For a Hundred Years and More* (Little Rock: Parke-Harper, 1922) 346.

46. Cole, *Whig Party in the South* 281. On the same page, Cole quotes at length from a letter by Whig Senator John Bell of Tennessee after the presidential election of 1852, which says, "The cardinal principles and policies of the Whig party will endure under every vicissitude of fortune, and an organization in some form, and under some denomination, Whig, Conservative or what not—some method of securing a concentrated effort by which these principles can be brought to bear, and have a salutary influence upon, if not the control of public affairs, this must and will be maintained . . . Party divisions will and must ever exist."

47. A good recent monograph discussing the early ideology of the Republican party is offered by Eric Foner in *Free Soil, Free Labor, Free Man: The Ideology of the Republican Party Before the Civil War* (New York: Oxford University Press, 1970).

48. A classic example of intolerance in the Old South is illustrated by Hinton Rowan Helper, who called for the abolition of slavery because it kept the South economically backward and poor whites in subjection to the planters. This North Carolinian had to flee his state and move to New York. For a biography of Helper, see Hugh C. Bailey, *Hinton Rowan Helper: Abolitionist-Racist* (University of Alabama Press, 1965). For the classic study of the restrictions of civil liberties in the Old South, see Clement Eaton, *The Freedom of Thought Struggle in the Old South*, 2nd ed. (New York: Harper, 1964). Historian William J. Cooper believes that politics in the South were determined by slavery, and explores this theory in *The South and the Politics of Slavery, 1828–1856* (Baton Rouge: Louisiana State University Press, 1978).

49. The actual number of immigrants who arrived in the United States was larger in 1905–1914, but the number of immigrants coming into the country in proportion to the actual citizens already in the United States was larger during 1845–1854. The number of immigrants in 1905–1914 equaled about 10.8 percent of the total population while the immigrants during the 1845–1854 period equaled about 14.8 percent of the existing population. See Potter, *The Impending Crisis* 241.

50. Potter, *The Impending Crisis* 241.

51. Potter, *The Impending Crisis* 242. Suspicion of Roman Catholicism in the history of the United States until the Civil War, is discussed by Sister Mary Augustine Ray, in *American Opinion of Roman Catholicism in the Eighteenth Century* (New York: Columbia Uni-

versity Press, 1936); see also Ray Allen Billington, *The Protestant Crusade, 1800–1860: A Study of the Origins of American Nativism* (New York: Macmillan Co., 1938).

52. Billington, *Protestant Crusade* 53–90, 196–198, 220–234, 302–304. Billington has an excellent and extensive chapter discussing the anti-Catholic literature of the period, 1830–1860. (See pp. 344–379).

53. Billington, *Protestant Crusade* 380–397.

54. Information on the foreign-born in Southern states and cities is found in James D. B. DeBow, *Statistical View of the United States: A Compendium to the Seventh Census, 1850* (Washington, D.C.: A. O. P. Nicholson, Public Printer, 1854) 118, 399.

55. DeBow, *Statistical View* 118. In sixteen slave states the foreign-born amounted to 305,286 in a white-free black population of 6,412,605. This equals 4.7 percent of foreign-born in the South in 1850.

56. Cole, *Whig Party in the South* 316; William Darrel Overdyke, *The Know-Nothing Party in the South* (Baton Rouge: Louisiana State University Press, 1950) 51.

57. Foreigners, or those born outside the United States, made up 1.2 percent of the white population in the state. Arkansas contained fewer numbers of foreign-born citizens than any other state of the Old South. DeBow, *Statistical View,* 118.

58. Walter L. Brown, "Albert Pike, 1809–1891," diss., University of Texas, 1955, 449–452. Brown gives full treatment to Pike's role in the Know-Nothing movement in Arkansas (pp. 449–493). Pike was prominent in the national party, served on a national committee, and made major addresses at rallies for the party in Baltimore and New Orleans; see Smith, "Arkansas Politics," 50; Overdyke, *Know-Nothing Party in the South* 73.

59. Overdyke, *Know-Nothing Party in the South* 72.

60. Lewis, "From Nationalism to Disunion," 259–261.

61. Little Rock *Arkansas Gazette* 10 August 1855: 2; 24 August 1855: 2; Harold T. Smith, "The Know-Nothings in Arkansas," *Arkansas Historical Quarterly* 34 (Winter 1975): 296–297. The new party and controversy it engendered did cause one major tragedy. John N. Butler, the old editor of the Little Rock *Arkansas Whig,* planned to start a Know-Nothing journal in Little Rock during the summer of 1855. His brother-in-law, Edward Marcus, a German immigrant, was naturally opposed to the new party. The two men shot it out on the streets of Little Rock and killed each other instantly. Ross, *Arkansas Gazette* 316.

62. Ross, *Arkansas Gazette* 299, 316–317. That the *Gazette* was made the official organ of the new party was particularly ironic. Only a year before, editor Danley had condemned the Know-Nothings for their political and religious intolerance; see Little Rock *Arkansas Gazette* 25 August 1854: 2.

63. Helena *Southern Shield* 26 May 1855: 2; 23 June 1855: 2; 20 October 1855: 2; Batesville *Independent Balance* 9 May 1856: 2; 16 May 1856: 2; Washington *Telegraph* 27 June 1856: 2.

64. Little Rock *Arkansas Gazette* 3 May 1856: 2, 3; Smith, "Know-Nothings in Arkansas," 297.

65. *Arkansas Gazette* 24 May 1856: 2; 31 May 1856: 2; Fort Smith *Herald* 24 May 1856: 2.

66. Little Rock *True Democrat* 14 August 1855: 2; 11 September 1855: 2. This paper likes to quote Danley's early position attacking the Know-Nothings in the *Gazette,* vis-à-vis his new role as spokesman for the movement; 28 August 1855: 2.

67. Smith, "Know-Nothings in Arkansas," 295.

68. Pope, *Early Days in Arkansas* 305.

69. Hindman's rally was held near Helena from Thursday through Saturday, November 22–24, 1855. A verse from the theme song said:

> Not fearing the Pope and the Irish
> So much as Sam's bloody crew
> The people all join in the verdict

Up Salt River Sammy must go!
Helena *Democratic Star* 29 November 1855: 2; 6 December 1855: 2.
70. Hindman's address quoted in Little Rock *True Democrat* 11 December 1855: 2.
71. Memphis *Weekly Appeal*, n.d. quoted in Helena *Democratic Star* 22 November 1855: 2.
72. Smith, "Know-Nothings in Arkansas," 296.
73. Camden *Southern Stamp*, n.d. quoted in Little Rock *True Democrat* 11 September 1855: 2.
74. Little Rock *True Democrat* 13 May 1856: 2.
75. *True Democrat* 20 May 1856: 2; Batesville *Independent Balance* 9 May 1856: 2; 16 May 1856: 2. The convention began on Monday, May 8, and ended the following Saturday.
76. Little Rock *True Democrat* 20 May 1856: 2. For a report of the rivalry between Rust and Warren, see Smith, "Arkansas Politics," 56–57.
77. Little Rock *Arkansas Gazette* 31 August 1855: 2; 7 September 1855: 2; 2 November 1855: 2; Washington *Telegraph* 23 July 1856: 2; Batesville *Independent Balance* 16 May 1856: 2; 27 June 1856: 2; Helena *Southern Shield* 27 October 1855: 2.
78. Little Rock *Arkansas Gazette* 5 October 1855: 2.
79. *Arkansas Gazette* 14 December 1855: 3. For other issues attacking Governor Conway for not being married, see 2 November 1855: 2; and 2 February 1856: 2.
80. Little Rock *True Democrat* 1 January 1856: 2.
81. Editor Johnson of the *True Democrat* made this charge against Borland in early December, 1855. See Little Rock *True Democrat* 11 December 1855: 2; and 18 December 1855: 2. Borland replied that the charge was indecent and refused to discuss it further. See Little Rock *Arkansas Gazette* 14 December 1855: 2; 28 December 1855: 2. Apparently, the charge against him had validity, or Borland, given his violent temper, probably would have shot Johnson. Johnson taunted Borland for refusing to discuss the matter. Little Rock *True Democrat* 1 January 1856: 2.
82. Pike's address entitled "To the American Party, South" was reprinted in the Fort Smith *Herald* 5 April 1856: 2; and Little Rock *True Democrat* 8 April 1856: 2. For a discussion of Pike's withdrawal from the Know-Nothing movement, see Brown, "Albert Pike," 486–492. Overdyke, *Know-Nothing Party in the South* 140.
83. Fort Smith *Herald* 19 April 1856: 2; 23 June 1856: 2; Little Rock *True Democrat* 15 April 1856: 2; 22 April 1856: 2; Smith, "Know-Nothings in Arkansas," 297, 300–301.
84. Conway received 28,158 votes to Yell's 15,346. Yell carried only these counties: Pulaski, Sebastian, Phillips, Lafayette, Columbia and Scott. Scott was the only county not in the delta with a major town within its borders. Washington *Telegraph* 10 September 1856: 1; Fort Smith *Herald* 30 August 1856: 2; Herndon, *Centennial History of Arkansas* 1:270.
85. In the northern district, Greenwood received 15,399 to Thomason's 6,161. This meant that Greenwood received about seventy-one percent of the vote. Thomason could only carry his home county of Crawford (Van Buren) and Phillips County. In the southern district, Warren's vote was 11,835 to Fowler's 8,701. Warren had about fifty-eight percent of the vote. Fowler was the most successful among Know-Nothing candidates for major office. He carried Arkansas, Chicot, Columbia, Lafayette, Pulaski and Sebastian counties. Except for Sebastian and Pulaski which contained major river towns, they were plantation counties in the delta.
86. Smith, "Know-Nothings in Arkansas," 302.
87. Little Rock *True Democrat* 2 December 1856: 3. The vote was Buchanan 21,906 to Fillmore 10,787. Buchanan's total was sixty-seven percent. Fillmore carried essentially the hard core of Arkansas Whiggery, Little Rock's Pulaski County and the very southeastern planter county of Chicot. See Boyette, "Whigs of Arkansas," 396.
88. Potter, *The Impending Crisis* 261, 415.
89. Ross, *Arkansas Gazette* 323.

90. Overdyke, *Know-Nothing Party in the South* 113.

91. There were only 1,600 Catholics in Arkansas among a free population of 162,789, or about 0.98 percent. There were only seven Catholic churches in the state in 1850; and at the same time there were 114 Baptist churches and 168 Methodist churches. See U.S. Department of the Interior, *The Seventh Census of the United States, 1850* (Washington, D.C.: Robert Armstrong, Public Printer, 1853) 535, 560–561.

92. Smith, "Know-Nothings in Arkansas," 302. Cooper, *South and Politics of Slavery,* passim.

93. Helena *States Rights Democrat* 24 April 1856: 2. For other issues which made the same point, see 12 June 1856: 2; and 31 July 1856: 2. The first issue of this new Hindman paper was printed on March 20, 1856.

94. Smith, "Know-Nothings in Arkansas," 303. Information concerning the Arkansas delegation at a national meeting of the Know-Nothings in Louisville in 1857 is provided in Overdyke, *Know-Nothing Party in the South* 271.

95. A good discussion of the development of this act and Douglas's reasons for introducing this ill-fated proposal appears in Potter, *The Impending Crisis* 146–176. For further study on the subject, see Roy Nichols, "The Kansas-Nebraska Act: A Century of Historiography," *Mississippi Valley Historical Review* 43 (September 1856): 187–212. The actual vote on the bill appears in the *Congressional Globe: 33rd Congress, 1st Session* (Washington, D.C.: John C. Rives, 1854) 532, 1254.

96. Granville Davis, "Arkansas and the Blood of Kansas," *Journal of Southern History* 16 (November 1950): 432–435.

97. Little Rock *True Democrat* 27 June 1854: 2.

98. It was not that events in Kansas were totally ignored, but the election campaign and Know-Nothingism took precedent in the Arkansas press from mid-1855 to August, 1856. See Davis, "Arkansas and the Blood of Kansas," 435–439. A very readable account of the events in Kansas in this period is by Alice Nichols. See *Bleeding Kansas* (New York: Oxford University Press, 1954).

99. Little Rock *True Democrat* 2 September 1856: 2.

100. Davis, "Arkansas and the Blood of Kansas," 441–442.

101. "Aid for Kansas: A Public Meeting" Broadside Secession Clippings, University of Texas Archives, Austin. Meetings were held sometime in September, for a Fort Smith paper also mentioned them, but did not give the date. Fort Smith *Herald* 13 September 1856: 2.

102. Davis, "Arkansas and the Blood of Kansas," 442–443.

103. The diary of Judge John Brown does not mention any meetings for Kansas during 1856–1858. See Brown diary in Arkansas History Commission, Little Rock. For further discussion of this diary, see Horace Adams, "The Year 1856 as Viewed by an Arkansas Whig," *Arkansas Historical Quarterly* 1 (June 1942): 124–133.

104. Davis, "Arkansas and the Blood of Kansas," 438–439.

105. Helena *States Rights Democrat,* 9 July 1857: 2. The editorial rebukes Arkansas for not responding to Kansas as had Mississippi and Georgia.

106. Allan Nevins, *The Ordeal of the Union,* 2 vols. (New York: Charles Scribner's Sons, 1945–1947) 2:382.

107. Camden *Southern Stamp,* n.d., quoted in Helena *States Rights Democrat* 16 July 1857: 2.

108. *Congressional Globe, 33rd Congress, 1st Session, Appendix* (Washington, D.C.: John C. Rives, 1854) 844–846. In his speech, Greenwood stated that Kansas was more suited to corn than cotton. Since this speech was made just three days before he voted for the Kansas-Nebraska Act, he said that he would vote in favor of the bill in order to remove "the odious restrictions" of the Missouri Compromise. He also said that he knew slavery would not exist in Kansas because in his area of Arkansas there was very little cotton, and very few slaveholders. The people of his Ozark county grew grains and cereals.

109. Letter quoted in Davis, "Arkansas and the Blood of Kansas," 454.

110. Little Rock *True Democrat,* 22 September 1858: 2.
111. Batesville *Independent Balance,* 12 June 1858: 2. The Family paper in Little Rock had rebuked Warren for not always obeying the party. Little Rock *True Democrat* 8 June 1858: 2. Also see Smith, "Arkansas Politics," 55–56.
112. Hindman's only opposition came from the Fayetteville Democrat, Alfred Wilson. Hindman won easily at the congressional convention with 25 of 32 votes, and captured all the eastern delta counties and a few mountain counties as well; see Batesville *Independent Balance* 6 May 1858: 2; Fort Smith *Times* 19 May 1858: 2. The Family may have indeed forced Greenwood out of his seat, and his willingness to go quietly may have helped the Family to secure him a Federal job. In early 1859, President Buchanan appointed him a commissioner of Indian affairs for the Indian Territory, a position he held for two years. When Buchanan's Secretary of the Interior, Mississippian Jacob Thompson, resigned in early 1861, historian John Hallum claimed that the president offered Greenwood the cabinet post. The former Arkansas congressman felt there was little he could do in office for two months, and turned down the offer. Had he accepted, he would have been the first Arkansas politician to serve in a presidential cabinet. Hallum, *Biographical and Pictorial History of Arkansas,* 274.
113. Little Rock *True Democrat* 11 May 1858: 2.
114. Hindman defeated his Know-Nothing opponent, Dr. William Crosby, by a lopsided vote of 18,255 to 2,853. This meant the Helena politician won with eighty-four percent of the vote. He carried all counties in the district. Rust faced opposition from a Know-Nothing from Little Rock, James Jones, and the independent Democrat, former Governor Thomas Drew. Rust received 16,032 to Drew's 3,452 to Jones' 3,104. Drew carried only his own Bradley County and Jones carried only Little Rock's Pulaski County. Rust polled about seventy-one percent of the vote against his two opponents. Also, the Know-Nothings could now elect only four members to the General Assembly. See Herndon, *Centennial History of Arkansas* 1:271; Ross, *Arkansas Gazette* 333. Dr. Bobby Roberts claims that Drew gave up in this race a month before the balloting. See Bobby Roberts, "Thomas Stevenson Drew" in Donovan and Gatewood, *Governors of Arkansas* 15.
115. Batesville *Independent Balance,* 22 October 1858: 2.
116. William J. Cooper views the death of the two-party system in much of the South by 1856; see *The South and the Politics of Slavery* 362–376. Michael Holt's insightful work points out that while the two-party system died in the lower South, it survived in the upper South, but Arkansas does not really seem to follow his figures for the upper South. See Michael Holt, *The Political Crisis of the 1850s* (New York: John Wiley & Sons, 1978) 219–259, and especially the charts, pp. 232, 234, 235. Marc Kruman's work on North Carolina substantiates Holt's point about a vigorous two-party tradition in North Carolina after 1856 and even into the Confederacy. Marc Kruman, *Parties and Politics in North Carolina, 1836–1865* (Baton Rouge: Louisiana State University Press, 1983) 181–279. For Tennessee's two-party system to 1859, see Paul Bergeron, *Antebellum Politics in Tennessee* (Lexington: University Press of Kentucky, 1982).
117. John Mula, "Public Career of William Sebastian," 55; Bobby Roberts, "Thomas Carmichael Hindman: Secessionist and Confederate General," M.A. thesis, University of Arkansas, 1972, 13–14.

Chapter VI

1. The literature on the split in America over slavery and the growth of the antebellum Southern civilization is large. Several general studies include those by Charles Snyder, *The Development of Southern Sectionalism, 1819–1849* (Baton Rouge: Louisiana State University Press, 1949); Avery Craven, *The Growth of Southern Nationalism, 1849–1861* (Baton Rouge: Louisiana State University Press, 1953); Clement Eaton, *The Growth of Southern Civilization, 1790–1860* (New York: Harper & Row, 1963); and William Taylor, *Cavalier*

and Yankee: The Old South and American National Character (New York: Harper & Row, 1969). Two general studies of events leading up to the Civil War during the 1850s are those by Avery Craven, *The Coming of the Civil War* (New York: Charles Scribner's & Sons, 1942) and David Potter, *The Impending Crisis, 1848–1861* (New York: Harper & Row, 1976). A good general account of the growing hostility to slavery in the North is by Louis Filler, *The Crusade Against Slavery, 1830–1860* (New York: Harper & Row, 1960).

2. El Dorado *Times* n.d., quoted in Batesville *Democratic Sentinel* 6 September 1859: 2.

3. Dewey Allen Stokes, "Public Affairs in Arkansas, 1836–1850," diss., University of Texas, 1966, 448.

4. Michael B. Dougan, *Confederate Arkansas: The People and Policies of a Frontier State in Wartime* (University of Alabama Press, 1976) 21; Michael B. Dougan, "A Look at the Family in Arkansas Politics, 1858–1865," *Arkansas Historical Quarterly* 29 (Summer 1970): 99–111.

5. Biscoe Hindman, "Thomas Carmichael Hindman," *Confederate Veteran* 38 (March 1930) 97.

6. Hindman, "Thomas Carmichael Hindman," 97–99; David Y. Thomas, "Thomas C. Hindman," in *Dictionary of American Biography*, Dumas Malone, ed., 20 vols. (New York: Charles Scribners & Sons, 1928–1936) 9:61. Thomas was inaccurate when he said Hindman came in 1856. Other sources show him to have made speeches in 1855; see Chapter 5.

7. Holly Springs *Democrat*, n.d., quoted in Helena *Democratic Star* 1 March 1855: 3.

8. Hindman, "Thomas C. Hindman," 98. Hindman held a formal debate the next day with Governor Alcorn in Helena, which was said to have been a draw.

9. Helena *States Rights Democrat* 20 March 1856: 1. This paper described Hindman on its front page as "brilliant, powerful, energetic, he is a worthy champion of a good cause." The paper had many editors after Hindman departed in 1858. One of the later ones, A. J. Rogers, was once convicted of stealing slaves. Fayetteville *Arkansian* 23 March 1860: 2.

10. Little Rock *True Democrat* 15 December 1857: 2; in the same editorial, this paper denied that the *States Rights Democrat* was a "disorganizing sheet."

11. The wedding was held on November 11, 1856. See Charles Edward Nash, *Biographical Sketches of Gen. Pat C. Cleburne and Gen. T. C. Hindman, Together with Humorous Anecdotes and Reminiscences of the Late Civil War* (Little Rock: Tunnah & Pittard, Printers, 1898) 78.

12. An uncle of Mollie Watkins Biscoe was Robert Watkins, the first Arkansas secretary of state, 1836–1840. Her other uncle, George Watkins, served as Arkansas's second attorney general, 1841–1851, and third chief justice, 1852–1854. See Fay Hempstead, *History of Arkansas From the Earliest Times to 1890* (St. Louis: N. C. Thompson & Co., 1890) 764–765, 1188–1189.

13. Nash, *Biographical Sketches* 54, 56.

14. Congressman Samuel Cox from Ohio quoted in Bobby Roberts, "Thomas C. Hindman: Secessionist and Confederate General," M.A. thesis, University of Arkansas, 1972, 12.

15. Roberts, "Thomas C. Hindman," 15.

16. For a primary account given by Hindman of these events, see Thomas C. Hindman, *Federal and State Politics: Speech Delivered in Little Rock, Arkansas, February 15, 1859*, (Little Rock: James Butter, Printer, 1859) 3–17; Thomas C. Hindman, *Speech of the Honorable Thomas C. Hindman at Helena, Arkansas, November 28, 1859*, (Washington, D.C.: Lionel Towers, Printers, 1860) 1–18.

17. Helena *States Rights Democrat*, n.d., quoted in Batesville *Independent Balance* 21 January 1859: 2.

18. Little Rock *True Democrat* 28 December 1859: 3.

19. Roberts, "Thomas C. Hindman," 16. A Whig Know-Nothing paper in Batesville commented on Sebastian in early 1858 how favorably "he never interferes in debate, except

when imperative duty calls." Batesville *Independent Balance* 31 March 1858: 2. For Sebastian's career, see John Mula, "The Public Career of William King Sebastian," M.A. thesis, University of Arkansas, 1969.

20. A. H. McKissack to Thomas C. Hindman, 3 October 1859, quoted in Thomas Hindman, *Speech at Helena, November 28, 1859,* 11. McKissack tells Hindman that a swamp land agent told him on November 15, 1858, that "he and Dick Johnson" would "put their heads together . . . to crush Hindman in 1860."

21. Thomas C. Hindman, *Speech at Little Rock, February 15, 1859,* 15–17.

22. Little Rock *True Democrat* 22 June 1859: 2. In the same editorial, Richard H. Johnson claimed that Hindman had told the leaders of the state Democratic party that "it was now war to the knife."

23. Fayetteville *Arkansian* 30 July 1859: 2. Another Family paper in Batesville called Hindman a "disappointed Senator seeker." Batesville *Democratic Sentinel* 23 August 1859: 2.

24. The establishment of a blind school in Arkadelphia is studied by Hempstead; see *History of Arkansas* 336–338. The expulsion law is discussed in chapter 2, or see Orville Taylor, *Negro Slavery in Arkansas* (Durham: Duke University Press, 1958) 256–258.

25. Dougan, *Confederate Arkansas* 13.

26. Batesville *Independent Balance* 8 July 1858: 2. This Whig Know-Nothing editor then asked the Democratic leaders what was wrong, "Are the faithful falling out by the way?" Also see Little Rock *Arkansas Gazette* 3 July 1858: 2.

27. Margaret Ross, *The Arkansas Gazette: The Early Years, 1819–1866* (Little Rock: Arkansas Gazette Foundation, 1969) 342.

28. Little Rock *True Democrat* 6 July 1859: 2. The Family paper in Batesville said that the Democrats "don't need another Democratic voice in Little Rock." Batesville *Democratic Sentinel* 19 July 1859: 2.

29. Ross, *Arkansas Gazette* 342.

30. Little Rock *Arkansas Gazette* 23 July 1859: 2. In the same editorial, Danley said whoever was the editor of this new *Old Line Democrat,* he would be a better writer than R. H. Johnson of the *True Democrat,* and that that wouldn't be very difficult to do.

31. Dougan, *Confederate Arkansas* 13.

32. Little Rock *Old Line Democrat* 15 September 1859: 2.

33. *Old Line Democrat* 15 September 1859: 2.

34. Dougan, *Confederate Arkansas* 13. Although the Family press blasted this new publication, a more or less neutral Democratic paper in Van Buren called the *Old Line Democrat* "one of the finest papers in the State, and its editorials show a high degree of talent." Van Buren *Press* 30 September 1859: 2.

35. Democratic papers that were allied with the Family included: Little Rock *True Democrat,* Fayetteville *Arkansian,* Helena *Weekly Notebook,* Batesville *Democratic Sentinel,* Camden *States Rights Eagle,* Washington *South Arkansas Democrat,* El Dorado *Times,* Fort Smith *Times,* Bentonville *Northwest Appeal,* (after February 1860) Bentonville *Democrat,* and the Huntsville *Madison Journal,* Napoleon *Planter.* Papers supporting Hindman included the Little Rock *Old Line Democrat,* Helena *States Rights Democrat,* Des Arc *Citizen,* Fort Smith *Herald* (after January 1860), Pine Bluff *Jeffersonian Independent,* and (after July 1860) the Fayetteville *Democrat.* See Dougan, *Confederate Arkansas* 16; and the Little Rock *True Democrat* 30 November 1859: 2. Information on the change of the Bentonville paper from *True Democrat* 22 February 1860: 2. For the changeover at the Fort Smith *Herald,* see Fayetteville *Arkansian* 20 January 1860: 2. For the announcement of the Hindman paper in Fayetteville, see Little Rock *Old Line Democrat* 3 July 1860: 2. The neutral Democratic papers were the Searcy *Eagle* and Van Buren *Press;* see Dougan, *Confederate Arkansas* 16; Van Buren *Press* 2 December 1859: 2.

36. Little Rock *Old Line Democrat* 17 November 1859: 2.

37. *Old Line Democrat* 22 September 1859: 2; 6 October 1859: 2; 27 October 1859: 2; 10 November 1859: 2; 24 November 1859: 2.

38. Little Rock *True Democrat* 9 November 1859: 2. For other issues with much the same treatment, see 19 October 1859: 2; 16 November 1859: 2.

39. *True Democrat* 14 September 1859: 2; 26 October 1859: 2; 28 December 1859: 2; 1 February 1860: 2. The Hindman press was not unaware of these attempts by the Family to recruit a candidate against Hindman in 1860; see Little Rock *Old Line Democrat,* 29 September 1859: 2; 13 October 1859: 2; 24 November 1859: 2.

40. Editor Richard Johnson said Hindman had been in Helena on November 19, 1859, and could easily have traveled to Little Rock in five days, Little Rock *True Democrat* 30 November 1859: 2. Hindman's father-in-law, Henry Biscoe, defended Hindman in a letter in the Helena *States Rights Democrat;* the letter reprinted in the Des Arc *Citizen* 21 December 1859: 1.

41. Little Rock *True Democrat* 7 December 1859: 2.

42. *True Democrat* 30 November 1859: 2; 14 December 1859: 2; Fayetteville *Arkansian* 25 November 1859: 2; 9 December 1859: 2.

43. At first, the Hindman press claimed that W. L. Martin wrote these "Viator" letters; see Little Rock *Old Line Democrat* 11 December 1859: 2; 29 December 1859: 2. The admission by Hindman that he had taken part in their writing appeared in the above cited newspaper, 9 February 1860: 2.

44. Little Rock *True Democrat* 15 February 1860: 2.

45. Dougan, *Confederate Arkansas* 14. The paper began speaking more favorably of Hindman by late March. See Des Arc *Citizen* 23 March 1860: 1.

46. Little Rock *True Democrat* 18 January 1860: 2.

47. There was speculation that Johnson would not run again in early 1859. See Little Rock *Arkansas Gazette* 19 February 1859: 2. Johnson made a formal announcement later that year, and by mid-1860 Rust said he sought this seat. See Fayetteville *Arkansian* 30 December 1859: 2; 1 June 1860: 1.

48. Little Rock *Old Line Democrat,* 6 October 1859: 2; 26 January 1860: 2.

49. *Old Line Democrat* 2 February 1860: 2.

50. Dougan, *Confederate Arkansas* 14.

51. Van Buren *Press* 30 September 1859: 2. The Family press had a different view of Hindman's speaking ability, stating that "his powers of declamation are, by no means, superior, though he is fluent and flippant in debate and he appears to the casual observer as potent and strong. We have never seen him as a man of sense and judgement." See Helena *Weekly Notebook* 18 October 1860: 2.

52. Ross, *Arkansas Gazette* 342; Little Rock *Arkansas Gazette* 19 February 1859: 2; 17 March 1859: 2; Harold T. Smith, "Arkansas Politics, 1859–1861," M.A. thesis, Memphis State University, 1964, 72.

53. Dougan, *Confederate Arkansas* 15.

54. Camden *States Rights Eagle,* n.d. quoted in Little Rock *True Democrat* 22 February 1860: 2.

55. The minutes from this short convention's proceedings fit upon one page of a newspaper; see Little Rock *True Democrat* 14 April 1860: 4.

56. Smith, "Arkansas Politics," 73.

57. Little Rock *True Democrat* 14 April 1860: 4; Des Arc *Citizen* 21 April 1860: 2.

58. Des Arc *Citizen* 21 April 1860: 2. Other complaints of the Hindman delegates were that the candidate was chosen before the platform and that the county vote distribution was inconsistent with the 1856 gubernatorial election.

59. Little Rock *True Democrat* 14 April 1860: 4.

60. *True Democrat* 5 May 1860: 2.

61. Napoleon *Planter,* n.d., quoted in Little Rock *True Democrat* 14 April 1860: 3; El Dorado *Times* n.d., quoted in *True Democrat* 23 April 1860: 3; Camden *States Rights Eagle,* n.d., quoted in *True Democrat* 19 May 1860: 2; Fort Smith *Times* 12 April 1860: 2.

62. Des Arc *Citizen* 28 April 1860: 2.

63. Pine Bluff *Jeffersonian Independent*, n.d., quoted in Des Arc *Citizen* 12 May 1860: 2.

64. The account of this citizens' meeting in Benton County in Van Buren *Press* 17 May 1860: 1. Johnson hung in effigy. See Fort Smith *Times* 26 April 1860: 2.

65. Little Rock *Old Line Democrat* 12 April 1860: 2.

66. An account of the events at Dover, appears in the Little Rock *Old Line Democrat* 17 May 1860: 2; and 24 May 1860: 2. The situation in which Boudinot would be excluded from the convention because he was a half-breed, is examined in the Fayetteville *Arkansian* 11 May 1860: 2; 18 May 1860: 2; and 25 May 1860: 2. A good short biography of Elias Boudinot appears in John Hallum's *Biographical and Pictorial History* (Albany, N.Y.: Weed, Parsons, and Co., 1889) 349–359.

67. An account of the southern convention in Arkadelphia is mentioned in the Little Rock *True Democrat* 19 May 1860: 2; and 26 May 1860: 2; and in the Little Rock *Old Line Democrat* 17 May 1860: 2; and 24 May 1860: 2.

68. Elias Conway's mother was Ann Rector Conway. Henry Rector's aunt was the mother of the leader of the Dynasty, Governor Conway. See Hallum, *Biographical and Pictorial History of Arkansas* 45, 405.

69. Hallum, *Biographical and Pictorial History* 404–408; Waddy Moore, "Henry Massie Rector," in *The Governors of Arkansas: Essays in Political Biography,* Timothy P. Donovan and Willard B. Gatewood, Jr., eds. (Fayetteville: University of Arkansas Press, 1981) 30–31.

70. Little Rock *Old Line Democrat* 24 May 1860: 2.

71. Little Rock *True Democrat* 26 May 1860: 2.

72. *True Democrat* 26 May 1860: 2.

73. The *Old Line Democrat* began attacking the Family for supporting Cypert in June of 1860; see Little Rock *Old Line Democrat* 21 June 1860: 2; 28 June 1860: 2; and 17 July 1860: 2. The Family always denied the charge but spoke highly of Cypert and his candidacy; see Little Rock *True Democrat* 30 June 1860: 2; 14 July 1860: 2; and 21 July 1860: 2. At the end of the campaign this paper gave an assessment of the race in the northern district, saying "Hindman has estranged many good Democrats . . . and has well secured the election of Cypert, the independent candidate." See *True Democrat* 4 August 1860: 1.

74. Little Rock *Arkansas Gazette* 2 June 1860: 2.

75. *Arkansas Gazette* 9 June 1860: 2; 16 June 1860: 2.

76. Hubbard's announcement in the Washington *Telegraph* n.d., quoted in the Little Rock *True Democrat* 28 April 1860: 2. The praise of this candidacy is in the same issue on the same page. Hubbard did for some time appear to be the old line Whig-opposition's candidate, see Little Rock *Arkansas Gazette* 26 May 1860: 2; 2 June 1860: 2.

77. William Quesenbury's cartoon appeared in Little Rock *Arkansas Gazette* 2 June 1860: 2, as one of the earliest political cartoons in the state.

78. A discussion of the old line Whig opposition convention in Helena on April 30, 1860, appears in the Van Buren *Press* 25 May 1860: 1. Thomason was a Democrat turned Know-Nothing who ran as that party's candidate for the northern district in 1856. (See chapter 5.) Benjamin Askew had been a Whig from Magnolia in Columbia County in southwestern Arkansas. His career is outlined in Hallum, *Biographical and Pictorial History* 252–253; Hempstead, *History of Arkansas* 1111, 1112.

79. Little Rock *Arkansas Gazette* 19 May 1860: 2.

80. *Arkansas Gazette* 23 June 1860: 2.

81. Des Arc *Citizen* 2 June 1860: 2; Little Rock *Old Line Democrat* 31 May 1860: 2.

82. Little Rock *Old Line Democrat* 7 June 1860: 1.

83. *Old Line Democrat* 7 June 1860: 1.

84. *Old Line Democrat* 14 July 1860: 2. Warren was attacked by the Family; see Little Rock *True Democrat* 7 July 1860: 2.

85. Former Governor Roane's attack on the Dynasty is mentioned in the Little Rock *Old Line Democrat* 21 June 1860: 1; 13 July 1860: 2; and 6 August 1860: 2.

86. Little Rock *True Democrat* 7 July 1860: 2; 21 July 1860: 2; 28 July 1860: 2.

87. Batesville *Democratic Sentinel*, n.d., quoted in *True Democrat* 28 July 1860: 1.

88. Danley said there was little proof that Hindman could be beaten in the northern district; see Little Rock *Arkansas Gazette* 16 June 1860: 2.

89. Nash, *Biographical Sketches of Cleburne and Hindman* 153; Dougan, *Confederate Arkansas* 18.

90. Little Rock *True Democrat* 21 July 1860: 3; 28 July 1860: 2.

91. There is some controversy about whether Hindman abandoned Rector and regretted having chosen him to be his candidate. Both Dougan and Roberts take this view. See Dougan, *Confederate Arkansas* 18, 132, footnote 23; and Roberts, "Thomas C. Hindman" 15–19. Both base their ideas on the charges brought up by editor Elias Boudinot. Since Hindman left no papers, it is hard to discern the truth. I choose to believe contemporaries like Charles Nash, Samuel Williams and John Hallum. Years later, Williams claimed he heard Hindman speak up for Rector: "so brilliant was his oratory and so formidable was his argument that he turned many followers of the Johnsons to Rector." Nash, *Biographical Sketches* 62–63. Nash in the same work (p. 153) says Rector owed his election to Hindman. John Hallum lived in Memphis at that time, but wrote years after these events that Hindman "moulded, led, and crystallized public opinion in Arkansas at that time." See Hallum, *Biographical and Pictorial History* 369, 408. To say Hindman left center stage of the campaign did not mean he abandoned Rector or his struggle with the Dynasty. The Family still viewed him as the central leader of the rebellion, considering the abuse the paper *True Democrat* gave him throughout the summer of 1860.

92. Rector's circular printed in Little Rock *Arkansas Gazette* 9 June 1860: 2.

93. Governor Conway's circular printed in the *Arkansas Gazette* 16 June 1860: 1. In an editorial of the same issue, Danley says that Governor Conway's plan to repay the bank debt was a myth, while the only reality was the Dynasty's mismanagement of public affairs since statehood. The Family had "made the banks, then broke them."

94. Little Rock *True Democrat* 2 June 1860: 2; 9 June 1860: 2; Little Rock *Old Line Democrat* 17 July 1860: 1.

95. Little Rock *Arkansas Gazette* 28 July 1860: 2.

96. *Arkansas Gazette* 9 June 1860: 2.

97. Little Rock *Old Line Democrat* 28 June 1860: 2.

98. Little Rock *Arkansas Gazette* 9 June 1860: 2.

99. Little Rock *True Democrat* 9 June 1860: 2; 16 June 1860: 2.

100. Little Rock *Old Line Democrat* 20 July 1860: 2; Little Rock *True Democrat* 21 July 1860: 2.

101. Dougan, *Confederate Arkansas* 20.

102. Little Rock *Old Line Democrat* 20 July 1860: 2.

103. Little Rock *True Democrat* 28 July 1860: 2. The Family attempted to mitigate the damage of the Trumpler allegations by holding a rally for mechanics in the Arkansas capital on Saturday, August 4, 1860. Little Rock *True Democrat* 4 August 1860: 2.

104. Little Rock *Old Line Democrat* 27 July 1860: 2; 6 August 1860: 2.

105. Hindman defeated Cypert by a vote of 20,051 (67%) to 9,696 (33%). In the southern district, Gantt garnered 16,369 to Mitchel's 13,007. Askew's name appeared on the ballot even after he withdrew from the race, and he won 891 votes. Gantt received 54 percent to Mitchel's 43 percent. Askew received approximately 3%. Hubbard's name also appeared on the ballot and he received 274 votes, or a little less than ½%. These returns compiled by Dallas Herndon, *A Centennial History of Arkansas*, 3 vols. (Chicago: Clarke Publishing Co., 1922) 1:273.

106. Little Rock *Old Line Democrat* 16 August 1860: 2.

107. Little Rock *Arkansas Gazette* 11 October 1860: 2.

108. General Clement A. Evans, gen. ed., *Confederate Military History*, 12 vols. (Atlanta: Confederate Publishing House, 1899) vol. 10: *Arkansas* by John Harrell, 3.

109. Dougan, *Confederate Arkansas* 21–22.

110. Batesville *Independent Balance*, n.d., quoted in Little Rock *Arkansas Gazette* 28 July 1860: 2.

111. Diary of Judge John Brown, 4 August 1860, Arkansas History Commission, Little Rock.

112. John W. Woodward, letter to David Walker, 19 August 1860, Arkansas Gazette Foundation Library, Little Rock. David Walker held much the same views as Woodward. As a conservative old-line Whig, Walker wrote to a friend in April of 1860 that he considered the dispute between Hindman and the Johnsons to be purely personal. Walker admired Hindman's energy and intelligence, yet he thought the Helena congressman was immoral and politically unsound. David Walker, letter to "Dear Sir," 3 April 1860, Walker Papers, Mullins Library, University of Arkansas, Fayetteville, Arkansas.

113. This view of Hindman found in Nash, *Biographical Sketches;* Dougan, *Confederate Arkansas;* Roberts, "Thomas C. Hindman."

114. Dougan, *Confederate Arkansas* 22.

115. Records for Rector and Johnson counties compiled from the official count printed in Fayetteville *Arkansian* 24 November 1860: 2. All the counties presented in Figure 6a in the Appendix are those that had a sizeable increase of whites from 1850–1860. During the 1850s, some counties were divided to make new ones. For example, Sebastian County was mostly a parcel taken from Crawford County in 1851 and Craighead County was taken from Poinsett County in 1859. Of the counties not counted, Rector carried six: Columbia, Sebastian, Craighead, Poinsett, Dallas, and Calhoun. Johnson carried only Crawford and Union counties. These counties were not included either because they were created during the 1850s or had significant portions of their areas detached to form new counties.

116. Hugh Thomas Brown, letter to Mrs. Carrie Hackett, 11 June 1860, Gordon-Hackett Papers, Southern Historical Collection, University of North Carolina, Chapel Hill. Hugh Brown writes at great length about politics in his newly adopted state saying, "Late developments have shown that they [the Family] have enriched themselves by plundering the treasury. Always crying out against internal improvements, they, by their plundering, have brought the State to the brink of repudiation . . . Since the Johnsons and their adherents have commenced going down the political hill, every one seems disposed to give them a kick. Every newspaper contains a letter from some small politician giving his reasons for withdrawing support. From the glance of politics and politicians which I have seen in Arkansas, I have come to the conclusion that the private station is the post of honor."

117. James Ward, letter to Henry M. Rector, 8 October 1860, W. S. Oldham Collection, Arkansas History Commission, Little Rock.

118. Thomas D. Clark and Albert Kirwan, *The South Since Appomattox: A Century of Regional Change* (New York: Oxford University Press, 1967) 110.

119. Des Arc *Citizen* 3 August 1859: 1.

120. Little Rock *Old Line Democrat* 2 August 1860: 2.

121. These terms taken from *Old Line Democrat* 10 July 1860: 2; Des Arc *Citizen* 9 June 1860: 2.

122. Fort Smith *Thirty-Fifth Parallel* 26 March 1860: 2.

123. Even the early returns given by the papers show that the votes for Rector and Johnson did not follow the state's geopolitical division. See Little Rock *Arkansas Gazette* 11 August 1860: 2.

124. To find the wealth per capita for whites you take the aggregate value of real and personal estate and divide that by the white population of that particular county. To see which counties were placed in which category, see Table 6c in the Appendix. Population and wealth statistics are found in the population tables and the miscellaneous statistics in the 1860 census. U.S. Department of the Interior, *The Eighth Census of the United States, 1860* (Washington: Government Printing Office, 1864–1866) 1: 18; 3: 296. The official election returns for each county in the 1860 gubernatorial election were found in Fayetteville *Arkansian*, 24 November 1860: 2.

125. Dougan, *Confederate Arkansas*, 22.

126. James M. Demby, *The War in Arkansas; or a Treatise on the Great Rebellion of 1861: Its Progress and Ultimate Results Upon the Destinies of the State. A Defense of the Loyalty of the People, Their Wretched Condition Considered, A Review of the Policy of the Government toward the Union People and the Rebels* (Little Rock: Eghart Press, 1864) 56. Demby also claims that many Unionists did vote for Rector because of the Johnsons' long association with secession (pp. 51–52).

127. Michael Holt, *The Political Crisis of the 1850s* (New York: John Wiley & Sons, 1978) 219–259. For a contrary view of Holt's thesis see William J. Cooper, "The New Political History Faces Southward," *Reviews in American History* 12 (September 1984): 383–387.

Chapter VII

1. Fort Smith *Times* 1 December 1859: 2.

2. Stephen Wood, "The Development of the Arkansas Railroads: Part II, Period of Land Grants and the Civil War," *Arkansas Historical Quarterly* 7 (Summer 1948): 121.

3. Leo Huff, "The Memphis to Little Rock Railroad During the Civil War," *Arkansas Historical Quarterly* 23 (Autumn 1964): 260. In the same article, Huff provides a small map of the Hopefield–Madison line and the Little Rock–DeValls Bluff branch of the Memphis–Little Rock railroad.

4. Memphis *Weekly Appeal* 18 April 1860: 1. The reporter who signed the article "J. P. P." wrote that a woman in Clarendon, Arkansas, told him that Little Rock, which by this reporter was understood to be the controlling powers of the state—the Conway-Johnson Dynasty, would not care if a railroad was ever built between Memphis and the Arkansas capital.

5. Fayetteville *Arkansian* 11 May 1860: 2.

6. Van Buren *Press* 13 July 1860: 2.

7. Little Rock *Arkansas Gazette* 4 August 1860: 2.

8. Margaret Ross, *The Arkansas Gazette: The Early Years, 1819–1866* (Little Rock: Arkansas Gazette Foundation Library, 1969) 347.

9. John L. Ferguson and James H. Atkinson, *Historic Arkansas* (Little Rock: Arkansas History Commission, 1966) 96–97; Clyde McGinnis, "Arkansas College," *Arkansas Historical Quarterly* 31 (Autumn 1972): 234–35.

10. Little Rock *Old Line Democrat* 15 September 1859: 2.

11. Fay Hempstead, *History of Arkansas From the Earliest Times till 1890* (St. Louis: N. D. Thompson & Co., 1890) 336–38. A state-supported college was not founded in Arkansas until 1871. Early history of the University of Arkansas at Fayetteville, especially the institute's oldest building, is provided by Thomas Rothrock in "The University of Arkansas's Old Main," *Arkansas Historical Quarterly* 30 (Spring 1971) 1: 52.

12. U.S. Department of the Interior, *The Eighth Census of the United States, 1860*, 4 vols. (Washington, D.C.: Government Printing Office, 1864–1866) 4: 506. Ten years earlier, the state had 126 teachers with 2,407 students. U.S. Department of the Interior, *The Seventh Census of the United States, 1850* (Washington, D.C.: Robert Armstrong, 1853) 551.

13. Ferguson and Atkinson, *Historic Arkansas* 90; Michael Dougan, *Confederate Arkansas: The People and Policies of a Frontier State in Wartime* (University of Alabama Press, 1967) 9.

14. Batesville *Independent Balance* 30 September 1858: 2. The editor went on to say in the same article, "There is not a single good reason why we should not have as good schools in Arkansas as anywhere else."

15. Gavin Wright, *The Political Economy of the Cotton South: Households, Markets and Wealth in the Nineteenth Century* (New York: W. W. Norton & Co., 1978) 17, 22. The states of Arkansas and Texas had the greatest percentage of increase between 1850–60 in cotton production and slave-holding, *Census of 1860* 1: 599; 2: 185, 189.

16. For a recently published article on slavery in the Ouachita Mountains, see John

Solomon Otto, "Slavery in the Mountains: Yell County, Arkansas, 1840–1860," *Arkansas Historical Quarterly* 39 (Spring 1980): 35–52. See also Gaven Wright's book with his map showing cotton production in the Arkansas Valley in the Ouachita region: Wright, *Political Economy of the Cotton South* 16.

17. Elsie Mae Lewis, "Robert W. Johnson: Militant Spokesman of the Old South-West," *Arkansas Historical Quarterly* 13 (Spring 1954): 19, 28.

18. For the controversy surrounding the pro-slavery Constitution in the Kansas Territory, see David Potter, *The Impending Crisis, 1848–1861* (New York: Harper and Row, 1976) 297–323. The Southern reaction to the defeat in Congress of the pro-slavery LeCompton Constitution is studied by Avery Craven in *The Coming of the Civil War*, 2nd ed. rev. (Chicago: University of Chicago Press, 1956) 397–98.

19. Potter, *The Impending Crisis* 393–95. The Buchanan-Douglas battle for control of the Democratic party is discussed by Philip Auchampaugh in "The Buchanan-Douglas Feud," *Journal of the Illinois State Historical Society* 25 (April 1932): 5–48; and Reinhard H. Luthin, "The Democratic Split During Buchanan's Administration," *Pennsylvania History* 9 (January 1944): 13–35.

20. Little Rock *True Democrat* 27 October 1858: 2.

21. *True Democrat* 23 June 1859: 2; 5 October 1859: 2; 19 October 1859: 2; 7 March 1860: 2.

22. Albert Rust was described by a friend in 1858 as "a follower of Douglas, not Buchanan." Thomas Drew, letter to Christopher C. Scott, 22 June 1858, Scott Papers, Arkansas History Commission, Little Rock. For Flournoy's support of Douglas, see Dougan, *Confederate Arkansas* 24–25.

23. Dougan, *Confederate Arkansas* 25.

24. Support of Douglas is documented in the Van Buren *Press* 3 August 1859: 2; 14 September 1859: 2; 30 September 1859: 2; 7 October 1859: 2; 18 November 1859: 2; and 16 March 1860: 2. For the support of Douglas by the Pine Bluff *Jeffersonian Independent*, see Dougan, *Confederate Arkansas* 30.

25. Pocahontas *Advertiser*, n.d., quoted in Little Rock *True Democrat* 19 October 1859: 2.

26. This title was given to Hindman by the Dynasty's main newspaper in Little Rock in late 1858. Little Rock *True Democrat* 28 October 1858: 2. Although the issues of the Hindman sheet in Helena are lost after August 1857, early issues showed the radicalism of this Arkansas politician; see Helena *States Rights Democrat* 3 April 1856: 2; 24 April 1856: 2; 12 June 1856: 2; 24 June 1856: 2; 16 July 1856: 2; 30 July 1856: 2.

27. Little Rock *Old Line Democrat* 15 September 1859: 2.

28. Little Rock *Old Line Democrat* 22 September 1859: 2; 29 September 1859: 2; 19 January 1860: 2; 22 March 1860: 2.

29. Craven, *The Coming of the Civil War* 381–87. Hindman outlined his views on national politics in a printed speech he gave in Little Rock in February 1859. See Thomas C. Hindman, *Federal and State Politics: Speech at Little Rock, February 15, 1859* (Little Rock: James Butter, 1859) 13–17.

30. Des Arc *Citizen* 15 February 1860: 2.

31. Little Rock *True Democrat* 24 March 1860: 2.

32. Little Rock *Old Line Democrat* 19 January 1860: 2.

33. *Old Line Democrat* 29 December 1859: 2.

34. Little Rock *True Democrat* 4 January 1860: 2.

35. Dougan, *Confederate Arkansas* 24.

36. Hindman's address before the House of Representatives given on January 19–20, 1860, printed in the *Congressional Globe, 33rd Congress, 1st Session, Appendix* (Washington, D.C.: John C. Rives, 1860) 81–88. John Sherman of Ohio was the Republican candidate for Speaker who had endorsed Helper's book. The contest over the election of a Speaker tied up the House from December 6, 1859 to February 1, 1860. *Congressional Globe, 33rd Congress, 1st Session* (Washington, D.C.: John C. Rives, 1860) 12–645. For a secondary

account of this battle see Ollinger Crenshaw, "The Speakership Contest of 1859–1860," *Mississippi Valley Historical Review* 29 (December 1942): 323–38. William Pennington of New Jersey, another Republican, eventually won the contest. Potter, *Impending Crisis*, 386–88. See also Hinton Rowan Helper, *The Impending Crisis of the South; How to Meet It* (New York: Burdick Brothers, 1857). Helper (1829–1909) cared little for the slave, just for the impact of slavery upon the nonslaveholder. See also Helper's life and thought in Hugh Bailey, *Hinton Rowan Helper: Abolitionist-Racist* (University of Alabama Press, 1965). For the southern response to Helper's book see Jack Cardoso, "Southern Reaction to the *Impending Crisis*," *Civil War History* 16 (March 1970): 5–17.

37. Samuel Sullivan Cox, *Three Decades of Federal Legislation 1855–1885: Personal and Historical Memories of Events Preceding, During, and Since the American Civil War, Involving Slavery and Secession, with Sketches of Prominent Actors During These Periods* (Providence, R.I.: J. H. and R. A. Reid, Publishers, 1885) 96. Cox was an Ohio congressman 1855–1865, a New York congressman 1868–1885, p. 6.

38. The entire Hindman-Van Wyck dispute was reported in Des Arc *Citizen* 4 April 1860: 2; 11 April 1860: 2.

39. Des Arc *Citizen* 4 April 1860: 2. More of the same sentiments are expressed in the Little Rock *Old Line Democrat* 29 March 1860: 2. For the most thorough treatment of the attempt by many in the Old South to reopen the slave trade directly with Africa, see Ronald Takaki, *A Pro-Slavery Crusade: The Agitation to Re-Open the African Slave Trade* (New York: Free Press, 1971).

40. Pine Bluff *Jeffersonian Independent,* n.d. quoted in Des Arc *Citizen* 22 February 1860: 2. The Pine Bluff paper seemed to be increasingly fearful of the importation of more blacks into the South than of the inhumanity of the foreign slave trade. In a later issue, the *Jeffersonian Independent* was quoted as saying that it opposed the further importation of African blacks because "it would introduce a swarm of savages, who would be fit tools of abolitionist vengeance." Pine Bluff *Jeffersonian Independent,* n.d. quoted in Des Arc *Citizen* 28 March 1860: 2.

41. Little Rock *True Democrat* 24 March 1860: 2.

42. Eugene Genovese, "Southern Yeomen in a Slaveholders' Democracy," *Agricultural History* 49 (April 1975): 331–342. This "white folks democracy" theme is credited with the ironic growth of both freedom and slavery in colonial Virginia, which would have a subsequent impact upon the history of the Old South. Edmund Morgan, *American Slavery, American Freedom: The Ordeal of Colonial Virginia* (New York: W. W. Norton & Co., 1975). This attempt to keep the hegemony of the white race in the South has played a central role in Southern history and in forming the collective mind of the region. Ulrich B. Phillips, "The Central Theme of Southern History," *American Historical Review* 34 (October 1928): 12; W. J. Cash, *The Mind of the South* (New York: Alfred A. Knopf, 1941).

43. Little Rock *Arkansas Gazette* 29 December 1859: 2.

44. *Arkansas Gazette* 21 January 1860: 2.

45. *Arkansas Gazette* 21 January 1860: 2.

46. *Arkansas Gazette* 14 January 1860: 2; 4 February 1860: 2.

47. *Arkansas Gazette* 17 December 1859: 2.

48. *Arkansas Gazette* 24 December 1859: 2; 4 February 1860: 2; 14 January 1860: 2.

49. *Arkansas Gazette* 25 February 1860: 2.

50. *Arkansas Gazette* 11 February 1860: 2; 3 March 1860: 2.

51. Diary of Judge John Brown of Camden, 4 August 1856, 8 November 1856, Arkansas History Commission, Little Rock.

52. Jesse Turner, letter to Rebecca Allen, 9 November 1853, Turner Papers, Perkins Library, Duke University, Durham, North Carolina. John Hallum offers a good study of the life of this distinguished Arkansas jurist in *Biographical and Pictorial History of Arkansas* (Albany, N.Y.: Weed, Parsons & Co., 1889) 895–96.

53. Little Rock *True Democrat* 14 April 1860: 4.

54. *True Democrat* 14 April 1860: 4; Dougan, *Confederate Arkansas* 26.
55. Dougan, *Confederate Arkansas* 27.
56. Little Rock *True Democrat* 14 April 1860: 4.
57. Dougan, *Confederate Arkansas* 28.
58. Little Rock *True Democrat* 14 April 1860: 4.
59. *True Democrat* 14 April 1860: 4. The other six men who belonged to the Family were Jilson Johnson, cousin of Senator Robert W. Johnson and editor Richard H. Johnson, who was the Dynasty's nominee for governor. Dr. John Jordan of Little Rock, another delegate, was Senator Johnson's brother-in-law. The rest included Col. Francis Terry, Van H. Manning, F. W. Hoadley, and John I. Stirman. Dougan, *Confederate Arkansas* 28.
60. Bruce Catton, *A Centennial History of the Civil War*, vol. 1: *The Coming Fury* (New York: Doubleday & Co., 1961) 1–12, 24–36.
61. Douglas quoted in January 1860 in Catton, *A Centennial History* 27. The battle between Yancey and Douglas had been brewing since 1857, and culminated at the Democratic convention in Charleston. See Austin L. Venable, "The Conflict between the Douglas and Yancey Forces in the Charleston Convention," *Journal of Southern History* 8 (May 1942): 226–241. The historiography surrounding William Yancey, the famed fire-eater from Alabama, is offered by Malcolm McMillan in "William I. Yancey and the Historians: One Hundred Years Later," *Alabama Review* 20 (July 1967): 163–187. The best written account of the Charleston Democratic convention, is by Roy Nichols, *The Disruption of American Democracy* (New York: Macmillan Co., 1948) 288–306.
62. Potter, *The Impending Crisis* 410. On the first day of the walkout, Potter describes the withdrawal of the delegates from Alabama, Mississippi, Louisiana, Texas, South Carolina, and Florida. On the first day the Arkansas delegates who joined in the walkout were Burrow and Dr. John Jordan, Senator Johnson's brother-in-law, and Van Manning. Jack Scroggs, "Arkansas in the Secession Crisis," *Arkansas Historical Quarterly* 12 (Autumn 1953): 184.
63. Little Rock *True Democrat* 3 May 1860: 2; 12 May 1860: 2. On the second day of the walkout, the three Arkansas delegates who left the hall were Jilson Johnson, Francis Terry and F. W. Hoadley. Scroggs, "Arkansas in the Secession Crisis," 185.
64. Little Rock *True Democrat* 12 May 1860: 2.
65. Nichols, *The Disruption of American Democracy* 279.
66. Potter, *The Impending Crisis* 410.
67. Nichols, *The Disruption of American Democracy* 295.
68. Little Rock *Arkansas Gazette* 19 May 1860: 2.
69. Little Rock *True Democrat* 12 May 1860: 2.
70. Des Arc *Citizen* 19 May 1860: 2; 26 May 1860: 2.
71. Little Rock *Old Line Democrat* 24 May 1860: 2.
72. Flournoy's letter appeared in the Little Rock *True Democrat* 26 May 1860: 2. Flournoy asked why the Arkansas Democrats could not support the national platform of the 1860 Charleston convention when it was basically the same document of the 1852 and 1856 Democratic conventions. Flournoy's logical appeal ignored the fact that the controversy over the Kansas Territory and the Dred Scott decision of 1857 had greatly exacerbated national tensions. Stirman's letter appeared in the Fayetteville *Arkansian* 1 June 1860: 1.
73. Van Buren *Press* 25 May 1860: 2; 17 May 1860: 1; 11 May 1860: 2; Dougan, *Confederate Arkansas* 29.
74. Dougan, *Confederate Arkansas* 29.
75. Little Rock *True Democrat* 19 May 1860: 2.
76. *True Democrat* 19 May 1860: 2.
77. *True Democrat* 2 June 1860: 3. This call for unity came from such prominent Southern senators as Robert Toombs and Benjamin Hill of Georgia, Robert Hunter of Virginia, John Slidell and Judah P. Benjamin of Louisiana, and Jefferson Davis of Mississippi.
78. Dougan, *Confederate Arkansas* 30.

79. Catton, *The Coming Fury* 49–67; Nichols, *Disruption of American Democracy* 314–18.

80. Dougan, *Confederate Arkansas* 30. Flournoy even addressed the Baltimore convention after the walkout and following the nomination of Douglas. Dwight I. Dumond, *The Secession Movement, 1860–1861* (New York: Macmillan, 1931) 89.

81. Little Rock *True Democrat* 14 July 1860: 2; 11 August 1860: 2.

82. Potter, *The Impending Crisis* 412–14.

83. The Family papers that supported the Breckinridge-Lane ticket included Little Rock *True Democrat* 30 June 1860: 2; 14 July 1860: 2; Fayetteville *Arkansian* 21 July 1860: 2; the Hindman press endorsements were the Little Rock *Old Line Democrat* 3 July 1860: 2; 10 July 1860: 2; Des Arc *Citizen* 11 July 1860: 2; 18 July 1860: 2.

84. Little Rock *True Democrat* 14 July 1860: 2.

85. James Walker, letter to David Walker, 9 May 1860, David Walker Papers, Mullins Library, University of Arkansas, Fayetteville. James Walker would later be a United States senator from Arkansas after Reconstruction. He was writing to his father-in-law, Judge David Walker; see John I. Smith, *The Courage of a Southern Unionist: A Biography of Isaac Murphy, Governor of Arkansas, 1864–1868* (Little Rock: Rose Publishing Company, 1979) 19.

86. Potter, *The Impending Crisis* 416–17.

87. Ross, *Arkansas Gazette* 341.

88. These papers included the Helena *Southern Shield*, Camden *Ouachita Herald*, Washington *Telegraph*, and the Batesville *Independent Balance*. See Donald E. Reynolds, *Editors Make War: Southern Newspapers in the Secession Crisis* (Nashville, Tenn.: Vanderbilt University Press, 1970) 222. All of these papers are in southern and eastern Arkansas.

89. Little Rock *Arkansas Gazette* 2 June 1860: 21. The Family's main paper dismissed the Constitutional Union party's choice of Bell as "just an old Whig." The editorial speculated that the party might have carried Arkansas with a candidate like Sam Houston of Texas, but an old Whig like Bell did not have a chance. Little Rock *True Democrat* 19 May 1860: 2. This political assessment by the Dynasty was probably quite accurate.

90. Potter, *The Impending Crisis* 418–30. The works on Lincoln are too numerous to mention here, but an excellent and recent one-volume account of his life is by Stephen B. Oates, *With Malice Toward None: The Life of Abraham Lincoln* (New York: Harper & Row, 1977).

91. The attack on Lincoln in the South is discussed by Avery Craven, in *The Coming of the Civil War* 423–24. The Republican ticket did not appear below the Southern boundaries of Virginia, Missouri, and Kentucky. See William Learner, ed. and comp., *Historical Statistics of the United States: Colonial Times to 1970*, 2 vols. (Washington, D.C.: Government Printing Office, 1975) 2:1080.

92. Little Rock *True Democrat* 26 May 1860: 1, 2.

93. *True Democrat* 18 August 1860: 2; Van Buren *Press* 24 August 1860: 2; 31 August 1860: 2.

94. Ross, *Arkansas Gazette* 347.

95. Camden *Southern Star*, n.d., quoted in Memphis *Weekly Appeal* 21 November 1860: 1. After that comment, the Memphis paper said, "The Arkansas Press, just like the Arkansas Toothpick, can do some pretty rough work."

96. Elsie Mae Lewis, "From Nationalism to Disunion: A Study of the Secession Movement in Arkansas, 1849–1861," diss., University of Chicago, 1947, 355.

97. Little Rock *Old Line Democrat* 18 August 1860: 2.

98. Dougan, *Confederate Arkansas* 30.

99. Diary of Judge John Brown, 27 October 1860, Arkansas History Commission, Little Rock.

100. Dougan, *Confederate Arkansas* 31.

101. Des Arc *Citizen* 5 September 1860: 2.

102. Little Rock *Arkansas Gazette* 27 October 1860: 2.

103. Diary of Judge John Brown, 23 October 1860, Arkansas History Commission, Little Rock.

104. Little Rock *Arkansas Gazette* 21 July 1860: 2; 4 August 1860: 2; 1 September 1860: 2; 15 September 1860: 2; 13 October 1860: 2; 27 October 1860: 2.

105. *Arkansas Gazette* 8 September 1860: 2.

106. Van Buren *Press* 31 August 1860: 2.

107. Little Rock *Arkansas Gazette* 15 September 1860: 2.

108. *Arkansas Gazette* 20 October 1860: 2.

109. Searcy *Eagle*, n.d. quoted in Des Arc *Citizen* 19 September 1860: 2. In the same issue and on the same page, this Hindman paper called the Helena congressman "the ablest man of his age in the Southwest."

110. Little Rock *Old Line Democrat* 25 October 1860: 2. For similar anti-Johnson and anti-Family remarks by this Hindman paper, see the issues of 6 September 1860: 2; 1 November 1860: 2.

111. *Old Line Democrat* 11 October 1860: 2.

112. Reynolds, "Editors Make War" 72, 222.

113. Little Rock *Old Line Democrat* 20 September 1860: 2; 4 October 1860: 2.

114. *Old Line Democrat* 18 August 1860: 2; 20 September 1860: 2; 18 October 1860: 2; Des Arc *Citizen* 5 September 1860: 2; 19 September 1860: 2.

115. Bobby Roberts, "Thomas C. Hindman: Secessionist and Confederate General," M.A. thesis, University of Arkansas, 1972, 27.

116. Little Rock *True Democrat* 18 August 1860: 2; 25 August 1860: 2; Fayetteville *Arkansian* 7 July 1860: 2; 4 August 1860: 2; 7 September 1860: 2.

117. Fayetteville *Arkansian* 31 August 1860: 2. Calhoun's theory on nullification is discussed by Margaret Coit, *John C. Calhoun: American Portrait* (Boston: Houghton Mifflin & Co., 1950) 230–256; William Freehling, *Prelude to Civil War: The Nullification Controversy in South Carolina, 1816–1836* (New York: Harper-Torchback Edition, 1966) 154–176, 354–355. For the most complete biography of Calhoun and the many changes in his thought and career, see Charles Wiltse, *John C. Calhoun,* 3 vols. (Indianapolis: Bobbs-Merrill, 1944–1951).

118. Little Rock *True Democrat* 13 October 1860: 2.

119. *True Democrat* 8 September 1860: 2; Fayetteville *Arkansian* 31 August 1860: 1; 28 September 1860: 2; 5 October 1860: 2. For a look at what is called the "Texas Troubles" in the late summer of 1860, see Ollinger Crenshaw, "The Slave States in the Presidential Election of 1860," *Johns Hopkins University Studies in Historical and Political Science* 63 (Baltimore: Johns Hopkins University Press, 1954) 92–98. For other studies of this possible slave insurrection in Texas, see William White, "The Texas Slave Insurrection in 1860," *Southwestern Historical Quarterly* 52 (January 1949): 259–288; Wendall Addington, "Slave Insurrection in Texas," *Journal of Negro History* 35 (October 1950): 408–434.

120. Searcy *Eagle*, n.d. quoted in Little Rock *True Democrat* 15 September 1860: 2.

121. White, "Texas Insurrection in 1860" 259–293; Reynolds, *Editors Make War* 97–117.

122. Bishop Henry C. Lay, letter to Mrs. Henry C. Lay, 23 September 1860, Lay Papers, Southern Historical Collection, University of North Carolina, Chapel Hill, N.C. Despite great fear, no slave insurrection occurred in Arkansas. See Orville Taylor, *Negro Slavery in Arkansas* (Durham, N.C.: Duke University Press, 1958) 223–225, 253; and Paul Lack, "An Urban Slave Community, Little Rock, 1831–1862," *Arkansas Historical Quarterly* 41 (Autumn, 1982): 279–280.

123. Fayetteville *Arkansian* 31 August 1860: 2; 21 September 1860: 2.

124. Little Rock *True Democrat* 3 November 1860: 2.

125. Fayetteville *Arkansian* 2 November 1860: 2.

126. Diary of Judge John Brown, 6 November 1860, Arkansas History Commission, Little Rock.

127. Learner, *Historical Statistics of the United States* 2: 1071–1072. According to this

work, the actual percentage of voters in this election was 79.5%, the highest in Arkansas's history for presidential elections.

128. Potter, *The Impending Crisis* 442–45; Crenshaw, "Slave States in the Presidential Election of 1860," 193–97, 295–98.

129. Dallas Herndon, *A Centennial History of Arkansas,* 3 vols. (Chicago: Clarke Publishing Co., 1922) 1 : 273. There is some evidence which might contradict this no-vote tally for Lincoln in Arkansas. A letter from a Dr. Z. Wales of Van Buren in Crawford County to President-Elect Lincoln stated that he had voted for him. Wales claimed to be from Illinois. What makes Wales' letter somewhat suspect is that he wrote Lincoln in order to ask to be appointed U.S. Marshal for the western district of Arkansas. See Dr. Z. Wales, letter to Abraham Lincoln, 24 November 1860, Arkansas Gazette Foundation Library, Little Rock.

130. Crenshaw, "Slave States in the Presidential Election of 1860," 197, 298.

131. As one recent close observer of this election has pointed out: "The large number of voters for Bell and Douglas came from counties which had a history of supporting the non-Democratic presidential candidate." An election map at the end of this article illustrates the point. See also Lenette Sengel Taylor, "Polemics and Partisanship: The Arkansas Press in the 1860 Election," *Arkansas Historical Quarterly* 44 (Winter 1985): 333, 335.

132. The county election returns taken from Little Rock *Arkansas Gazette* 8 December 1860: 3.

133. Ted R. Worley, "The Arkansas Peace Society of 1861: A Study in Mountain Unionism," *Journal of Southern History* 24 (November 1958): 445. For the returns from each of these counties see Little Rock *Arkansas Gazette* 8 December 1860: 3.

134. Dougan, *Confederate Arkansas* 34. Some seventy-five years ago, David Y. Thomas, an Arkansas historian, wrote that Breckinridge, the more radical pro-Southern-slavery candidate, owed much of his support to non-slaveholders. John Bell, the more moderate candidate, gathered much of his support from large planters. See David Y. Thomas, "Southern Non-Slaveholders in the Election of 1860," *Political Science Quarterly* 26 (June 1911): 222–237. What Thomas failed to note was that the old political structures of Democrats vs. Whigs still held sway in Arkansas and much of the South as well. Wealthy Whig planters voted for Bell, an old-line Whig, while yeomen non-slaveholding Democrats voted for Breckinridge, the man who was touted as the regular candidate for the real (i.e., Southern) Democratic party.

135. The source for Figure 7b is found in Little Rock *Arkansas Gazette* 8 December 1860: 3; Lewis, "From Nationalism to Disunion," 358. Although these two sources generally agree, I was unable to confirm in the primary source material Lewis's presentation that Randolph County gave a majority vote for Breckinridge, although that is highly plausible since thirty-four other Arkansas counties voted likewise. In the table of the *Gazette* cited above, the Searcy County vote for Breckinridge is listed as 076. This I believe is a misprint. In all other numbers below a hundred, there are no other zeros in front of the two digits. Also if this vote is accurate, the Bell and Douglas vote was 198 to 117 respectively, giving Bell a majority vote for this small Ozark county. In fact, this would be the highest percent Bell would ever receive in any other Arkansas county. I tend to believe Lewis's contention, although unsubstantiated, that Searcy County gave its vote for Breckinridge by plurality, yet returned an anti-Breckinridge majority.

136. This pattern of small slaveholders as the vanguard of the Breckinridge vote was found to be true in Mississippi and Alabama according to William Barney in *The Secessionist Impulse: Alabama and Mississippi in 1860* (Princeton: Princeton University Press, 1974).

137. Thomas, "Southern Non-slaveholders in 1860," 235–237; Genovese, "Southern Yeomen in a Slaveholders' Democracy," 331–342.

Chapter VIII

1. Judge John Brown, Diary, 11 November 1860, Arkansas History Commission, Little Rock.
2. Brown, Diary, 18 November 1860.
3. Brown, Diary, 26 November 1860.
4. Dwight L. Dumond, *The Secession Movement, 1860–1861* (New York: Macmillan Co., 1931) 113. Dumond is an established, though somewhat dated writer on the secession movement in the South. There have been a number of studies in the last twelve years dealing with the secession movements in the various Southern states. These include: Steven Channing, *Crisis of Fear: Secession in South Carolina* (New York: Simon and Schuster, 1970); William Barney, *The Secessionist Impulse: Alabama and Mississippi in 1860* (Princeton: Princeton University Press, 1974); Michael Johnson, *Toward a Patriarchal Republic: Secession in Georgia* (Baton Rouge: Louisiana State University Press, 1976); Walter L. Buenger, *Secession and Union in Texas* (Austin: University of Texas Press, 1984).For a quantitative analysis of voting in Alabama, Mississippi, and Louisiana, see Peyton, McCrary, Clark Miller, and Dale Baum, "Class and Party Politics in the Secession Crisis: Voting Behavior in the Deep South," *Journal of Interdisciplinary History* 8 (Winter 1978): 429–457.
5. Donald Reynolds, *Editors Make War: Southern Editorials During the Secession Crisis, 1860–1861* (Nashville, Tenn.: Vanderbilt University Press, 1968) 140–143; Dumond, *Secession Movement* 204–209, 113–145, 189–212.
6. Little Rock *Arkansas Gazette* 17 November 1860: 2.
7. *Arkansas Gazette* 17 November 1860: 2.
8. *Arkansas Gazette* 17 November 1860: 2. In the same editorial, Danley shrewdly points out that Thomas Jefferson, the founder of the Democratic party, first restricted slavery from the territory of the old Northwest in 1787. Danley noted the irony of Southern Democrats, claiming devotion to Jefferson, being ready to secede just because Lincoln and his Republican party intended to do for the Western territories what Jefferson did for the old Northwest—prohibit slavery.
9. *Arkansas Gazette* 10 November 1860: 2. In a later issue Danley hoped that Arkansas and the South as a whole would not listen "to a few restless and reckless political adventurers, whose whole ambition of their lives is to destroy the best government the world has ever seen." *Arkansas Gazette* 24 November 1860: 2.
10. Des Arc *Constitutional Union* 30 November 1860: 2.
11. Van Buren *Press* 16 November 1860: 2. For much the same sentiments, see the issues of 9 November 1860: 2; 23 November 1860: 2.
12. Little Rock *True Democrat* 24 November 1860: 2.
13. Fayetteville *Arkansian* 24 November 1860: 2.
14. David Potter, *The Impending Crisis, 1848–1861* (New York: Harper & Row, 1976) 338–355, 421–422, 445.
15. Historian Avery Craven says that many voted for Breckinridge because they "felt they must stand by their section in the face of the Republican threat." Avery Craven, *The Coming of the Civil War*, 2nd rev. ed. (Chicago: University of Chicago Press, 1957) 430.
16. Little Rock *Old Line Democrat* 13 December 1860: 2.
17. *Old Line Democrat* 13 December 1860: 2. These same ideas can be found in other issues of Hindman's Little Rock paper: 22 November 1860: 2; 29 November 1860: 2.
18. The question of whether Rector's address was "secessionist" has a curious history. An early historian of Arkansas correctly says that Rector's address was quite moderate in tone on the issue of secession. Fay Hempstead, *A History of Arkansas From the Earliest Times to 1890* (St. Louis: N. D. Thompson & Co., 1890) 343. Thirty years later, Dallas Herndon reaches the same interpretation and quotes at length from the address. Dallas Herndon, *A Centennial History of Arkansas,* 3 vols. (Chicago: Clarke Publishing Co., 1922) 1:277–278. Apparently, it was David Y. Thomas who first inaccurately characterized

Rector's address as a major call for secession. See David Y. Thomas, *Arkansas in War and Reconstruction* (Little Rock: United Daughters of the Confederacy, 1926) 41. His error has been passed on by the historiography of Arkansas; see Elsie Mae Lewis "From Nationalism to Disunion: A Study of the Secession Movement in Arkansas 1849–1861," diss., University of Chicago, 1947, 361; Jack Scroggs, "Arkansas in the Secession Crisis," *Arkansas Historical Quarterly* 12 (Summer 1953): 194; Margaret Ross, *The Arkansas Gazette: The Early Years, 1819–1866* (Little Rock: Arkansas Gazette Foundation, 1969) 349; Michael Dougan, *Confederate Arkansas: The People and Policies of a Frontier State in Wartime* (University of Alabama Press, 1976) 35; Harry S. Ashmore, *Arkansas: A History* (New York: W. W. Norton & Co., 1978) 75.

19. Little Rock *Arkansas Gazette* 24 November 1860: 1.
20. *Arkansas Gazette* 24 November 1860: 1.
21. *Arkansas Gazette* 24 November 1860: 1.
22. *Arkansas Gazette* 24 November 1860: 1.
23. *Arkansas Gazette* 1 December 1860: 2.
24. George Clarke, letter to Jesse Turner, 29 November 1860, Turner Papers, Mullins Library, University of Arkansas, Fayetteville.
25. Little Rock *Arkansas Gazette* 1 December 1860: 2.
26. James Haney, letter to Jesse Turner, 13 December 1860, Turner Papers, William Perkins Library, Duke University, Durham, North Carolina.
27. Fayetteville *Arkansian*, 24 November 1860: 2.
28. Little Rock *Arkansas Gazette* 22 December 1860: 2.
29. Elsie Mae Lewis, "Robert W. Johnson: Militant Spokesman of the Old South-West," *Arkansas Historical Quarterly* 13 (Spring 1954): 28–31.
30. Little Rock *Arkansas Gazette* 22 December 1860: 2; Lewis, "From Nationalism to Disunion," 363–364.
31. *The Journal of the House of Representatives: The Thirteenth Session of the General Assembly of the State of Arkansas* (Little Rock: Johnson & Yerkes, Public Printers, 1861) 290–309; Scroggs, "Arkansas in the Secession Crisis," 198.
32. *Journal of the House: Thirteenth General Assembly* 301–305; Little Rock *Arkansas Gazette* 22 December 1860: 1.
33. Little Rock *Arkansas Gazette* 22 December 1860: 1.
34. Orville Taylor, *Negro Slavery in Arkansas* (Durham, N.C.: Duke University Press, 1958) 257–258.
35. Dougan, *Confederate Arkansas* 37.
36. Dougan, *Confederate Arkansas* 37. It was not that Hindman's paper in Little Rock attacked Rust; rather, the paper just no longer supported him or mentioned his candidacy. See the various fall issues of the Little Rock *Old Line Democrat*.
37. Little Rock *True Democrat* 13 October 1860: 2.
38. Van Buren *Press* 30 November 1860: 2.
39. Little Rock *Old Line Democrat* 1 November 1860: 2; 15 November 1860: 2; 29 November 1860: 2.
40. Little Rock *True Democrat* 24 November 1860: 2; Little Rock *Arkansas Gazette* 22 December 1860: 2.
41. Little Rock *True Democrat* 24 November 1860: 2.
42. Little Rock *Arkansas Gazette* 22 December 1860: 2.
43. *Arkansas Gazette* 22 December 1860: 2.
44. *Arkansas Gazette* 29 December 1860: 2; Herndon, *Centennial History of Arkansas* 1:278. Dumond, *Secession Movement* 217.
45. John Cantey, letter to "cousin John," 25 November 1860, Cantey Papers, Perkins Library, Duke University, Durham, North Carolina.
46. Jack Scroggs, "The Secession Movement in Arkansas," M.A. thesis, University of Arkansas, 1948, 73–74.

47. Little Rock *Arkansas Gazette* 5 January 1861: 3.

48. Little Rock *True Democrat* 8 December 1860: 2; 2 January 1861: 2; Fayetteville *Arkansian* 22 December 1860: 2; 5 January 1861: 2.

49. Little Rock *Old Line Democrat* 22 November 1860: 2. Although this paper announced that it was to be a daily paper, no copies seem to be in existence. For another record of this paper, see Ross, *Arkansas Gazette* 349.

50. Judge John Brown, Diary, 10 January 1860.

51. Scroggs, "Secession Movement in Arkansas," 74.

52. Little Rock *Arkansas Gazette* 5 January 1861: 3.

53. For the rally in Camden, see *Arkansas Gazette* 15 December 1860: 2.

54. Little Rock *Arkansas Gazette* 15 December 1860: 2.

55. *Arkansas Gazette* 15 December 1860: 2.

56. Little Rock *True Democrat* 5 January 1861: 2.

57. The House of Representatives had passed the convention bill on December 22, 1860, yet the Senate stalled until January 15, 1861. *Journal of the House: Thirteenth General Assembly* 410; *Acts Passed at the Thirteenth Session of the General Assembly of the State of Arkansas, Which Was Begun in the Capitol, in the City of Little Rock, on Monday the Fifth Day of November, One Thousand Eight Hundred and Sixty, and Ended on Monday, the Twenty-First Day of January, One Thousand Eight Hundred and Sixty-one* (Little Rock: Johnson & Yerkes, State Printers, 1861) 214–216.

58. Dougan, *Confederate Arkansas* 39.

59. David Walker, letter to David C. Williams, 29 January 1861, Williams Papers, Arkansas History Commission, Little Rock.

60. *Acts of the General Assembly, 1860–1861* 136–137. Des Arc *Constitutional Union* 11 January 1861: 2; Leo Huff, "The Memphis to Little Rock Railroad During the Civil War," *Arkansas Historical Quarterly* 23 (Autumn 1964): 260–261. For Rector's strong support for the railroad bill, see J. H. Haney, letters to Jesse Turner, 13 December 1860, and 12 January 1861, Turner Papers, William Perkins Library, Duke University, Durham, North Carolina.

61. Hempstead, *History of Arkansas* 345. Money was appropriated on January 21, 1861. *Acts of the General Assembly, 1860–1861* 368–369.

62. For the Commission members' appointments in the bill, see *Acts of the General Assembly, 1860–1861* 368. Captain Thomas Churchill was born in Kentucky, settling in Arkansas after the Mexican War. Churchill later served as governor of Arkansas, 1881–1883. See F. Clark Elkins, "Thomas James Churchill," in Timothy P. Donovan and Willard B. Gatewood, Jr., eds., *The Governors of Arkansas: Essays in Political Biography* (Fayetteville: University of Arkansas Press, 1981) 68–72.

63. Little Rock *Arkansas Gazette* 26 January 1861: 2.

64. Little Rock *Old Line Democrat* 3 January 1861: 2. Hindman did keep control over his paper in Helena, the *States Right Democrat*. Fred W. Allsopp, *History of the Arkansas Press for a Hundred Years and More* (Little Rock: Parke-Harper, 1922) 286.

65. Fayetteville *Arkansian* 22 December 1860: 2. To show the shifting ground of Arkansas politics, the Pine Bluff *Jeffersonian Independent* stood with Hindman against the Dynasty in the summer of 1860, and then stood for the Union in the secessionist delta of eastern Arkansas. The Hindman/Family secessionists were forced to found a disunionist paper in Pine Bluff, the *True Southerner*, in early 1861; Fayetteville *Arkansian* 5 January 1861: 2.

66. Flournoy's letter supported secession in the Memphis *Weekly Appeal* 2 January 1861: 2; Yell addressed the legislature and expressed his opinion for disunion. Little Rock *Arkansas Gazette* 5 January 1861: 2.

67. This realignment between the slaveholders and non-slaveholding areas happened in other states of the upper South; see Daniel Crofts, "The Union Party of 1861 and the Secession Crisis," *Perspectives in American History* 11 (1977–1978): 327–376. The issue of secession so altered party structures in the South that one historian has stated: "The fact is that neither the Constitutional Democracy nor the Democrats functioned as recognizable

political entities during the secession winter." John V. Mering, "The Slave-State Constitutional Unionists and the Politics of Consensus," *Journal of Southern History* 43 (August 1977): 407.

68. John T. Wheat, letter to Leo Wheat, 23 January 1861, Wheat Papers, University of North Carolina, Chapel Hill.

69. Eugene Genovese, "Yeomen Farmers in a Slaveholders' Democracy," *Agricultural History* 49 (April 1975): 340.

70. Citizens' meeting quoted in Scroggs, "Secession Movement in Arkansas," 77.

71. A. D. Slavey, letter to Eliot Fletcher, 25 December 1860, Eliot Fletcher Papers, Arkansas History Commission, Little Rock.

72. Frank Peak, "A Southern Soldier Views the Civil War," unpublished typescript, Louisiana State University, Baton Rouge. This account was written while Peak was in a Union prison in Alleghany City, Pennsylvania, in December, 1863. Peak's full comment was, "The moment I became convinced that the flag she carried was no longer friendly, but hostile to me and my Section, [then] did I turn to the protection of a flag more congenial to the feelings of the people of my Section."

73. Of all the counties mentioned, only Chicot voted in favor of Breckinridge, while the rest voted for Bell. Yet all of these counties sent delegates to the convention committed to vote for disunion. Dougan, *Confederate Arkansas* 39; Little Rock *True Democrat* 21 February 1861: 2.

74. State Representative John Crawford wrote this open letter to his constituents of Washington County, and it was published in the Fayetteville *Arkansian* 15 December 1860: 2. Some of the petitions from southern and eastern Arkansas were published in the Little Rock *True Democrat* 11 January 1861: 3; Scroggs, "Arkansas in the Secession Crisis," 194–195.

75. Bishop Henry C. Lay, letter to Mrs. Henry C. Lay; 20 February 1861, Lay papers, University of North Carolina, Chapel Hill.

76. Albert Webb Bishop, *Loyalty on the Frontier, or Sketches of Union-Men of the Southwest; with Incidents and Adventures During the Rebellion on the Border* (St. Louis: B. P. Studley and Co., 1863) 141.

77. A statistical analysis of Virginia, North Carolina, and Tennessee illustrates a polarization between high and low slaveholding areas during the secession crisis. See Daniel Crofts, "The Political and Social Origins of Opposition to Secession in the Upper South," 11. This paper presented at the Southern Historical Association in Louisville, Ky., November 2, 1984. Manuscript in possession of the author.

78. John Smith, "To the Voters of Benton County, February 18, 1861," Broadside, Arkansas History Commission, Little Rock.

79. T. Denton, letter to David C. Williams, 21 February 1861, D. C. Williams Papers, Arkansas History Commission, Little Rock.

80. Edwin Bearss and Arnell Gibson, *Fort Smith: Little Gibraltar on the Arkansas, 1817–1896* (Norman: University of Oklahoma Press, 1969) 239.

81. The petition printed in Little Rock *Arkansas Gazette* 12 January 1861: 2.

82. John Stirman, "To the People of Washington County, February 5, 1861." Broadside, Arkansas History Commission, Little Rock.

83. For evidence of David C. Williams' work on behalf of the Union, his papers may. be studied in the Clara Eno Collection, Arkansas History Commission, at Little Rock. Garland's support for the Union is explored by Beverly Watkins, "Augustus Hill Garland" in Donovan and Gatewood's *Governors of Arkansas* 61. Little Rock was known for its conservative views on disunion, and one Unionist later recalled that secessionists referred to it as "that damn abolitionist hole." See James William Demby, *The War in Arkansas, or a Treatise on the Great Rebellion of 1861; Its Progress, and Ultimate Results Upon the Destinies of the State, A Defense of the Loyalty of the People, Their Wretched Condition Considered; A Review of the Policy of the Government Toward the Union People and the*

Rebels (Little Rock: E. G. Hart, 1864) 54. For the work of William M. Fishback, see Harry Readnour, "William Meade Fishback" in Donovan and Gatewood's *Governors of Arkansas* 92.

84. Little Rock *Arkansas Gazette* 12 January 1861: 2; 19 January 1861: 2; 26 January 1861: 2. In an earlier issue, Danley dismissed all claims that secession will be peaceful, for he pointed out "they show their lack of faith in their own professions by recommending the strictest and fullest military expenditures . . . They cry peace when there is no peace." 5 January 1861: 2.

85. Quisenberry's letter in *Arkansas Gazette*, 23 January 1861, 2. Judge John Brown's Unionist sentiments are recorded in his diary in the Arkansas History Commission, Little Rock.

86. Dougan, *Confederate Arkansas*, 41. According to Margaret Ross, the commander James Totten had spent some of his childhood years in Little Rock. Ross, *Arkansas Gazette*, 352.

87. Margaret Ross gives the best synopsis of these events in *Arkansas Gazette*, 352–353.

88. Dougan, *Confederate Arkansas*, 41.

89. *The War of the Rebellion: A Compilation of the Official Records of the Union and Confederate Armies*, 4 series, 70 vols. in 128 books and index. (Washington, D.C.: Government Printing Office, 1880–1901) series 1, 1:638–639. Hereinafter these documents will be cited as *Official Records*.

90. *Official Records*, series 1, 1:639.

91. Scroggs, "Secession Movement in Arkansas," 83.

92. Dougan, *Confederate Arkansas*, 41. The counties which sent militia were Phillips, Jefferson, Monroe, White, Prairie, Montgomery, Hot Spring, St. Francis, and Saline, all in eastern and southern Arkansas. See Ross, *Arkansas Gazette*, 353.

93. *Official Records*, series 1, 1:641–642.

94. *Official Records*, series 1, 1:642.

95. *Official Records*, series 1, 1:681. Senator Johnson was even more direct to his brother Richard: "If Totten resists, for God's sake, deliberate and go stop the assault" (p. 682).

96. *Official Records*, series 1, 1:640, 644–645.

97. *Official Records*, series 1, 1:643–645. The ladies of Little Rock showed their appreciation to Totten by giving him a sword. One lady regretted this gift later when she found out that Totten was serving in the Union army in Missouri during the War, and she wrote during the summer of 1861: "Totten is in Missouri, wielding the sword we gave him against us." See Dougan, *Confederate Arkansas*, 42, 136, footnote 28.

98. *Official Records*, series 1, 1:683.

99. Van Buren *Press* 15 February 1861, 2.

100. Quisenberry's letter in Des Arc *Constitutional Union*, 9 February 1861, 2.

101. Albert Rust letter to David Williams, 7 February 1861, Williams Papers, Arkansas History Commission, Little Rock.

102. The Washington Peace Conference was reported by L. H. Chittenden in *A Report of the Debates and Proceedings in the Secret Sessions of the Conference Convention for Proposing Amendments to the Constitution, Held at Washington, D.C. February A.D. 1861* (New York: D. Appleton & Company, 1864). For a secondary account of this convention, see Robert G. Gunderson, *Old Gentlemen's Convention: The Washington Peace Conference of 1861* (Madison: University of Wisconsin, 1961).

103. Potter, *The Impending Crisis* 509.

104. H. Welden, letter to Jesse Turner, 11 February 1861, Turner Papers, William Perkins Library, Duke University, Durham, North Carolina. Also see William F. Holtzmann, letter to David Williams, 10 February 1861, D. C. Williams Papers, Arkansas History Commission, Little Rock.

105. Senator Robert W. Johnson, *Address to the People of Arkansas, February 7, 1861* (Washington, D.C.: A. Polkinghorn, Printer, 1861) 8.

106. Francis Terry's essay appeared in the Little Rock *True Democrat* 7 February 1861: 2.

107. *True Democrat* 14 February 1861: 2.

108. Fayetteville *Arkansian* 22 December 1860: 2; 5 January 1861: 2; 25 January 1861: 2; 8 February 1861: 2.

109. Dougan, *Confederate Arkansas* 45.

110. The official returns were not released or even certified until Saturday, March 2, 1861. They were printed in the Little Rock *Arkansas Gazette* 9 March 1861: 2.

111. *Arkansas Gazette* 9 March 1861: 2.

112. Dougan, *Confederate Arkansas* 46.

113. Little Rock *True Democrat* 21 February 1861: 2; Lewis, "From Nationalism to Disunion," 372.

114. Lewis, "From Nationalism to Disunion," 373.

115. Little Rock *True Democrat* 21 February 1861: 2.

116. John Smith, letter to David C. Williams, 18 February 1861, D. C. Williams Papers, Arkansas History Commission, Little Rock.

117. Judge John Brown, Diary, 21 February 1861.

118. David C. Walker, letter to David C. Williams, 18 February 1861, Williams Papers, Arkansas History Commission, Little Rock.

119. Van Buren *Press* 22 February 1861: 2.

120. Little Rock *True Democrat* 28 February 1861: 3. The crowd numbered about five hundred and the population of Fort Smith in 1860 was only 1,530. See Ashmore, *Arkansas* 69.

121. Hugh Thomas Brown, letter to Carrie L. Hackett, 25 February 1861, Gordon-Hackett Papers, University of North Carolina, Chapel Hill.

122. James H. Quisenberry, letter to David C. Williams, 21 February 1861, Williams Papers, Arkansas History Commission, Little Rock.

123. *Official Records*, series 1, 1:683.

124. Little Rock *True Democrat* 28 February 1861: 2.

125. *True Democrat* 28 February 1861: 2.

Chapter IX

1. Little Rock *True Democrat* 26 May 1860: 2.

2. David M. Potter, *The Impending Crisis, 1848–1861* (New York: Harper & Row, 1976) 514–545.

3. Potter, *The Impending Crisis* 548–554; Roy Franklin Nichols, *The Disruption of American Democracy* (New York: Macmillan Co. 1948) 474–491. For a primary account of the U.S. Congress which met from December 16, 1860 to March 3, 1861, see John C. Rives, *Congressional Globe, 36th, 2nd Session* (Washington, D.C.: Congressional Globe Office, 1861); *Congressional Globe, 36th Congress, 2nd Session, Appendix* (Washington, D.C.: Congressional Globe Office, 1861). The Washington Peace Conference is discussed by Robert G. Gunderson, *Old Gentleman's Convention: The Washington Peace Conference* (Madison: University of Wisconsin Press, 1957); Lucius Eugene Chittenden, *A Report of the Debates and Proceedings in the Secret Session of the Conference Convention for Proposing Amendment to the Constitution of the United States, Held at Washington, D.C. in February A.D. 1861* (New York: D. Appleton & Company, 1864).

4. Bruce Catton, *A Centennial History of the Civil War*, vol. 1: *The Coming Fury* (New York: Doubleday & Co., 1961) 268–273; Shelby Foote, *The Civil War: A Narrative History*, 3 vols. (New York: Random House, 1958–1974) 1:39.

5. Lincoln's address printed in the Little Rock *True Democrat* 7 March 1861: 2. For a more contemporary presentation of Lincoln's speech and its preparation, see Potter, *The Impending Crisis* 560–570; Stephen Oates, *With Malice Toward None: The Life of Abraham Lincoln* (New York: New American Library, 1977) 235–237.

6. Little Rock *True Democrat* 7 March 1861: 2.

7. *True Democrat* 7 March 1861: 2.
8. Catton, *The Coming Fury* 265.
9. Donald L. Reynolds, *Editors Make War: Southern Newspapers in the Secession Crisis* (Nashville, Tenn.: Vanderbilt University Press, 1968) 190.
10. Catton, *The Coming Fury* 265. For the growth of the idea on the indissolubility of the Union in the mind of the North between 1787–1830, see a recent perceptive article by Kenneth Stampp: "The Concept of a Perpetual Union," *Journal of American History* 65 (June 1978): 5–33. Stampp ends the article with a quotation by John Quincy Adams in 1831 as to whether the Union can be dissolved, "It is the odious nature of the question that it can be settled only at the cannon's mouth."
11. Little Rock *True Democrat* 13 March 1961: 2.
12. *True Democrat* 13 March 1861: 2.
13. Fayetteville *Arkansian* 15 March 1861: 2.
14. *Arkansian* 15 March 1861: 4.
15. Michael B. Dougan, *Confederate Arkansas: The People and Policies of a Frontier State in Wartime* (University of Alabama Press, 1976) 49.
16. Van Buren *Press* 8 March 1861: 2.
17. Little Rock *Arkansas Gazette* 9 March 1861: 2.
18. *Arkansas Gazette* 9 March 1861: 2.
19. Dallas T. Herndon, *The Centennial History of Arkansas*, 3 vols. (Chicago: Clarke Publishing Co., 1922) 1:278–279.
20. William Willcox, letter to G. Willcox, 26 February 1861, Willcox Papers, Perkins Library, Duke University, Durham, North Carolina.
21. Bishop Henry C. Lay, letter to Mrs. Henry C. Lay, 3 March 1861, Lay Papers, University of North Carolina, Chapel Hill, North Carolina.
22. Alfred Holt Carrigan, "Reminiscences of the Secession Convention," Part I, *Publications of the Arkansas Historical Association*, 4 vols. (Little Rock: Democrat Printing & Lithograph Co., 1906–1917) 1:306.
23. James William Demby, *The War in Arkansas, or A Treatise on the Great Rebellion of 1861; Its Progress and Ultimate Result upon the Destiny of Our State. A Defense of the Loyalty of the People, Their Wretched Condition Considered: A Review of the Policy of the Government Towards the Union People and the Rebels* (Little Rock: Eghart, Printer, 1964) 45.
24. Demby, *The War in Arkansas* 44; Little Rock *True Democrat* 4 March 1861: 2. There were also other influences used upon the Unionist delegates. The correspondent for the *True Democrat* once apologized to readers for missing a few words of the convention because his eyes had been distracted by the "patriotic beauties thrilled with noble zeal for the cause of the South. The heroines of the Revolution were neither braver nor more self-sacrificing than the fair women of Arkansas who thronged the gallery of the convention and showered down lovely flowers and approving smiles upon the advocates of secession and southern rights. We can offer no better apology for our sins of omission." *True Democrat* 16 March 1861: 2.
25. Ralph Wooster, "The Arkansas Secession Convention," *Arkansas Historical Quarterly* 13 (Summer 1954): 174. For another treatment of the Arkansas convention as well as the other secession conventions in the South, see Ralph Wooster, *The Secession Conventions of the South* (Princeton: Princeton University Press, 1962) 155–172.
26. John Hallum, *Biographical and Pictorial History of Arkansas* (Albany, N.Y.: Weed, Parsons & Co., 1889) 103.
27. For a look at these men and their careers as governors, see Timothy P. Donovan and Willard B. Gatewood, Jr., eds., *The Governors of Arkansas: Essays in Political Biography* (Fayetteville: University of Arkansas Press, 1981) 33–42, 61–64, 91–96.
28. The five men were Augustus Garland of Pulaski County, William Wirt Watkins of Carroll County, Felix Batson of Johnson County, Thomas Hanly of Phillips County, and

Hugh French Thomason of Crawford County. For a look at these men's careers in the Confederate Congress, see James M. Woods, "Devotees and Dissenters: Arkansans in the Confederate Congress, 1861–1865," *Arkansas Historical Quarterly* 38 (Autumn 1979): 227–247.

29. For a profile of the delegates, see chart in Wooster, "Arkansas Secession Convention," 184–185. In Wooster's chart he could not identify Jilson Johnson of Desha County, the cousin of Senator Robert W. Johnson and editor Richard H. Johnson; Dougan, *Confederate Arkansas* 138, footnote no. 5. Elsie Mae Lewis also has a list of the delegates and how they voted, in her study "From Nationalism to Disunion: A Study of the Secession Movement in Arkansas, 1849–1861," diss., University of Chicago, 1947, 395–97.

30. Wooster, "Arkansas Secession Convention," 177–78.

31. Wooster, "Arkansas Secession Convention," 178; Wooster, *Secession Conventions of the South* 160.

32. Wooster, "Arkansas Secession Convention," 177–78. Wooster's book says that there were only four Arkansas delegates who could be called great planters, that is, who owned more than fifty slaves. See Wooster, *Secession Conventions of the South* 160–61.

33. Wooster, "Arkansas Secession Convention," 179–180, 181, 187–195.

34. Carrigan, "Reminiscences of the Secession Convention," 311.

35. Carrigan, "Reminiscences of the Secession Convention," 305–313. See also Jesse Cypert, "Reminiscences of the Secession Convention," Part II. *Publications of the Arkansas Historical Association* (Little Rock: Democrat Printing and Lithograph Co., 1906–1917) I : 316.

36. Carrigan, "Reminiscences of the Secession Convention," 307.

37. Carrigan, "Reminiscences of the Secession Convention," 307–308. According to the author, nothing delighted Adams more than to "engage Fishback in a debate." Adams' background and his career in Arkansas as a Whig planter and a Bell supporter appear in Hallum, *Biographical and Pictorial History* 306–311.

38. Carrigan, "Reminiscences of the Secession Convention," 308. Hanley would also play a competent role in the Confederate Congress; see Woods, "Devotees and Dissenters," 235–236, 239–240.

39. Carrigan, "Reminiscences of the Secession Convention," 306–311; Cypert, "Reminiscences of the Secession Convention," 316; Lewis, "From Nationalism to Disunion," 395–397.

40. Cypert, "Reminiscences of the Secession Convention," 315. Batson also would have a somewhat erratic career in the Confederate Congress; see Woods, "Devotees and Dissenters," 234, 241.

41. Dougan, *Confederate Arkansas* 138, footnote no. 5.

42. *Journal of Both Sessions of the Convention of the State of Arkansas, Which Was Begun and Held in the Capitol, in the City of Little Rock* (Little Rock: Johnson and Yerkes, 1861) 10–11; Cypert, "Reminiscences of the Secession Convention," 315.

43. *Journal of Both Sessions* 16–17.

44. The major committees of the convention and their chairmen included: Federal Relations—Jesse Turner of Van Buren; State Affairs—William Mansfield of Ozark; Resolutions and Ordinances—William Grace of Pine Bluff; Militia—James Yell of Pine Bluff; Ways and Means—Thomas Gunter of Fayetteville; and Publications—M. S. Kennard of Batesville. Four of the six committees were controlled by the Unionist-Cooperationists, including the ones on Federal and State Relations, Ways and Means, and State Affairs. The two committees controlled by the secessionists were Militia and Ordinances and Resolutions. This list was compiled from a letter by Hugh French Thomason to David C. Williams, 7 March 1861, Williams Papers, Arkansas History Commission, Little Rock. A list of the delegates and the positions they assumed at the time of secession can be found in Lewis's "From Nationalism to Disunion," 395–397.

45. Carrigan, "Reminiscences of the Secession Convention," 306; Dougan, *Confederate*

Arkansas 49. Boudinot edited the Family's main newspaper in Little Rock while the regular editor, Richard H. Johnson, ran for governor in the spring and summer of 1860.

46. Both Totten's and Turner's speeches were recorded in a long letter that Jesse Turner wrote to his wife; see Jesse Turner, letter to Rebecca Turner, 7 March 1861, Turner Papers, William Perkins Library, Duke University, Durham, North Carolina.

47. *Journal of Both Sessions* 33.

48. Little Rock *True Democrat* 9 March 1861: 2.

49. *True Democrat* 9 March 1861: 2; *Journal of Both Sessions* 33; Dougan, *Confederate Arkansas* 51.

50. Jesse Turner, letter to Rebecca Turner, 7 March 1861.

51. Little Rock *True Democrat* 15 March 1861: 2.

52. Jesse Turner, letter to Rebecca Turner, 7 March 1861.

53. Dougan, *Confederate Arkansas* 50.

54. *Journal of Both Sessions* 45. Rector's address printed in the convention's journal; see pp. 39–49. At one point, Governor Rector states his belief that "God, in his omnipotent wisdom, . . . created the cotton plant, the African Negro, and the lower Mississippi Valley, to clothe, and feed the world, and a gallant race of men and women produced upon its soil to defend it and execute that decree." In other words, in holding slaves and planting cotton, the Southerner was not only himself prosperous, but really carrying out the mysterious plan of God.

55. *Journal of Both Sessions* 46.

56. *Journal of Both Sessions* 36–38, 47–49, 56–57, 70.

57. James Yell quoted in Dougan, *Confederate Arkansas* 51.

58. *Journal of Both Sessions* 38–39.

59. Batesville *Southern Aurora*, n.d., quoted in Little Rock *True Democrat* 28 February 1861: 2.

60. Little Rock *True Democrat* 12 March 1861: 2.

61. Fayetteville *Arkansian* 8 March 1861: 2.

62. *Arkansian* 8 March 1861: 2.

63. Little Rock *Arkansas Gazette* 9 March 1861: 2.

64. *Arkansas Gazette* 9 March 1861: 2.

65. Van Buren *Press* 13 March 1861: 2.

66. The Arkansas River would not be reliable as a division of the state. The congressional districts of the state already used that as a dividing line. Both districts contained the uplands and the lowlands. Since 1858, congressmen—Hindman, Rust and Gantt—were all from the lowlands. The Baseline is the survey boundary between Mississippi and Tennessee, which would run across Arkansas. That, too, would not work because even in the northern section it would contain a good deal of land in the lowlands, including such towns as Batesville and Jacksonport on the White River. The secessionist press never responded to these charges, and thus never denied them. This gives credence to a position that the secessionists might, indeed, have talked about splitting up the state.

67. Fayetteville *Democrat*, n.d., quoted in Fayetteville *Arkansian* 8 March 1861: 2.

68. Fayetteville *Arkansian* 8 March 1861: 2.

69. John Rives, *Congressional Globe, 36th Congress, 2nd Session* 1433–1526. This session lasted from March 4, 1861 to March 28, 1861. A review of this session reveals that Arkansas's new senator, Charles Mitchel, did not engage in debate, but voted with the upper South and border state Democrats.

70. Senator Mitchel sent this telegraph from Washington, D.C. on March 11, 1861. See Little Rock *Arkansas Gazette* 16 March 1861: 2. This rumor had been widely circulated and even printed in major eastern newspapers; see Catton, *The Coming Fury* 277–78. Lincoln did appear in March to give conflicting signals as to whether he would hold or abandon the forts; see Potter, *The Impending Crisis* 572–74.

71. *Journal of Both Sessions* 51–54.

72. *Journal of Both Sessions*, 51–54; Lewis, "From Nationalism to Disunion," 380.

73. James G. Randall and David Donald, *Civil War and Reconstruction*, 2nd ed. (Lexington: D. C. Heath & Co., 1961) 148–149. Randall and Donald give a brief synopsis of the Crittenden compromise and its fate.

74. Little Rock *Daily True Democrat* 15 March 1861: 2.

75. The delegate who proposed this was Dr. Philip Echols of Calhoun County in southeastern Arkansas. *Journal of Both Sessions* 62.

76. *Journal of Both Sessions* 63.

77. *Journal of Both Sessions* 64–67.

78. Dougan, *Confederate Arkansas* 53.

79. *Journal of Both Sessions* 73–75. For Oldham's early career in Arkansas, see chapter 3; for his career in Texas, consult Ezra Warner and Buck Yearns, *Biographical Register of the Confederate Congress* (Baton Rouge: Louisiana State University Press, 1975) 187–188.

80. Dougan, *Confederate Arkansas* 54.

81. Little Rock *True Democrat* 10 March 1861: 1.

82. Little Rock *Arkansas Gazette* 16 March 1861: 2.

83. Jesse Turner wrote his wife, "As soon as I voted 'no!' a lady in the gallery threw me a bouquet of flowers, which, of course, was highly appreciated. . . . That most foul sheet, the *True Democrat,* is stimulating the reckless disunionists to violence, bloodshed, and revolution; but the Union phalanx stood like a rock on the Ocean, unmoved by the dashing waves of faction and treason." Jesse Turner, letter to Rebecca Turner, 19 March 1861, Turner Papers, William Perkins Library, Duke University, Durham, North Carolina.

84. *Journal of Both Sessions* 82.

85. *Journal of Both Sessions* 90–93. The delegates chosen to go to Kentucky were former Congressmen Edward Warren and Albert Rust. Other men included Unionists like Samuel Hempstead of Little Rock, Thomas Bradley of Crittenden County, and James P. Spring of Carroll County.

86. *Journal of Both Sessions* 93.

87. John Campbell, letter to Neal Walters, 10 June 1861, reprinted in James E. Johnston, "Letter of John Campbell, Unionist," *Arkansas Historical Quarterly* 29 (Summer 1970): 178.

88. Isaac Hilliard of Chicot County quoted in Jack E. Scroggs, "Arkansas in the Secession Crisis," *Arkansas Historical Quarterly* 12 (Summer 1953): 317.

89. Little Rock *Arkansas Gazette* 20 April 1861: 3; Scroggs, "Arkansas in the Secession Crisis," 217.

90. F. J. Lane to David C. Williams, 19 March 1861, D. C. Williams Papers, Arkansas History Commission, Little Rock.

91. Scroggs, "Arkansas in the Secession Crisis," 217.

92. *Journal of Both Sessions* 109.

93. *Journal of Both Sessions* 102.

94. Des Arc *Constitutional Union* 5 April 1861: 2.

95. Little Rock *True Democrat* 11 April 1861: 2.

96. Philip Pennywit to Honorable Jesse Turner and Honorable Hugh Thomason, telegram dated 19 March 1861, Turner Papers, Mullins Library, University of Arkansas, Fayetteville.

97. Van Buren *Press* 27 March 1861: 2; 3 April 1861: 2; Lewis, "From Nationalism to Disunion," 383.

98. Van Buren *Press* 20 March 1861: 2.

99. Judge John Brown, Diary, 22 March 1861, Arkansas History Commission, Little Rock.

100. Little Rock *Arkansas Gazette* 6 April 1861; 2.

101. *Arkansas Gazette* 6 April 1861: 2. A Unionist paper in Searcy had made this charge earlier, stating that the secessionists planned to take Arkansas out of the Union "by appealing to the passions and prejudices of the people." Searcy *Eagle*, n.d., quoted in Little Rock *Arkansas Gazette* 23 March 1861: 3.

102. Little Rock *True Democrat* 11 April 1861: 2; Little Rock *Arkansas Gazette* 30 March 1861; 2; 6 April 1861: 2.

103. Lake Village *Chicot Press,* n.d., quoted in Little Rock *Arkansas Gazette* 13 April 1861: 2. There is some indication that the secessionist anticipated difficulty in northern and western Arkansas. In his county of Franklin, in the upper Arkansas River valley, Napoleon Burrow sponsored a disunionist rally in early March. One Unionist attended the rally and he said the whole affair reminded him "of some camp meeting where the good parson sung loud and long, whist [sic] the mourners were coming up . . . In my opinion, Col. Burrow's visit to this place has, by no means, advanced the cause he advocates." John J. Walker, letter to William Mansfield, 17 March 1861, Mansfield Papers, Arkansas History Commission, Little Rock.

104. William Mansfield, letter to Jesse Turner, 13 April 1861, Turner Papers, Perkins Library, Duke University, Durham, North Carolina.

105. William Fishback, letter to David C. Williams, 10 April 1861, Williams Papers, Arkansas History Commission, Little Rock.

106. Fishback to Williams, 10 April 1861.

107. Little Rock *Arkansas Gazette* 6 April 1861: 2. Concerning the attacks by the secessionist press, Samuel Griffith, Unionist delegate from Fort Smith's county of Sebastian, wrote in late March, that "the minds of the people must be protected from the poisonous influence of the lying secessionist papers, and the foul speeches from men, reckless and desperate gamblers, who would stake the destiny of the Union upon a game of cards, and play that game upon the graves of their fathers. . . . You have heard the foul attacks upon me by the *Times* and *Herald.*" These two papers were in Fort Smith. Samuel Griffith, letter to David C. Williams, 30 March 1861, William Papers, Arkansas History Commission, Little Rock.

108. Little Rock *Arkansas Gazette* 6 April 1861: 2.

109. *Arkansas Gazette* 6 April 1861: 2.

110. *Arkansas Gazette* 6 April 1861: 2.

111. *Arkansas Gazette* 6 April 1861: 2.

112. *Arkansas Gazette* 6 April 1861: 2.

113. *Journal of Both Sessions* 55.

114. Cypert, "Reminiscences of the Secession Convention," 317.

115. Dr. W. Fillengens, letter to William W. Mansfield, 10 March 1861, Mansfield Papers, Arkansas History Commission, Little Rock.

116. This letter appeared in Little Rock *Arkansas Gazette* 8 March 1861: 2.

117. For a study of Senator Johnson's views on the Union between 1849–1861, see especially Lewis, "From Nationalism to Disunion," 118–122; Elsie Mae Lewis, "Robert W. Johnson: Militant Spokesman of the Old South-West," *Arkansas Historical Quarterly* 13 (Spring 1954): 16–30.

118. Albert Pike, *State or Province? Bond or Free? Addressed Particularly to the People of Arkansas* (Little Rock: n.p. 1861) 7–37. Pike's view of the Federal Union was vigorously maintained after the Civil War by the Vice-President of the Confederacy. See Alexander Hamilton Stephens, *A Constitutional View of the Late War Between the States,* 2 vols. (Philadelphia: National Publishing Co., 1868–70). The difference between Pike and Stephens is that Stephens opposed secession until his state of Georgia seceded in January 1861. Alexander Stephen's life and career, outlined by Rudolph Van Abele, appears in *Alexander H. Stephens: A Biography* (New York: Alfred A. Knopf, 1946).

119. Margaret Ross, *The Arkansas Gazette: The Early Years, 1819–1866* (Little Rock: Arkansas Gazette Foundation Library, 1969) 348.

120. Ross, *Gazette: Early Years* 349.

121. Pike, *State or Province? Bond or Free?* 40.

Chapter X

1. James D. Spring, letter to David Walker, 4 April 1861; Walker Papers, Mullins Library, University of Arkansas, Fayetteville.

2. A. H. Hobson, letter to Jesse Turner, 16 April 1861, Turner Papers, Perkins Library, Duke University, Durham, North Carolina. In the same letter, Hobson mentions some hint of change, saying, "We have been startled by telegraph dispatches indicating war, but others, or later ones do not confirm them."

3. The whole question of who maneuvered whom into firing the first shot of the Civil War has provided a dispute among historians for over one hundred years. Professor Charles Ramsdell argues that Lincoln maneuvered Davis into firing the first shot in order to make it appear that the Confederate president was the aggressor. Lincoln supposedly did this intentionally. See Charles Ramsdell, "Lincoln and Fort Sumter," *Journal of Southern History* 3 (August 1937): 259–288. His thesis became the basis of a book written by the Alabama attorney John Shipley Tilley, *Lincoln Takes Command* (Chapel Hill: University of North Carolina, 1941). The view was first disputed by David M. Potter, who said that Lincoln sought peace and did not try to preserve the unity of his party by initiating a civil war; see David Potter, *Lincoln and His Party in the Secession Crisis* (New Haven: Yale University Press, 1942). The Ramsdell-Tilley thesis was dispatched by Kenneth Stampp, who said that Lincoln hoped to preserve peace and the Union by a strategy of defense. See Kenneth M. Stampp, "Lincoln and the Strategy of Defense in the Crisis of 1861," *Journal of Southern History* 11 (August 1945): 297–323. For a book-length discussion of this question, see Richard N. Current, *Lincoln and the First Shot* (Philadelphia: J. B. Lippincott & Co., 1963). Grady McWhinney studies this question from the Confederate point of departure and produces evidence that Jefferson Davis wanted war and tried to start it at Fort Pickens, yet was dissuaded by his general, Braxton Bragg. See Grady McWhinney, "The Confederacy's First Shot," *Civil War History* 14 (March 1968): 5–14.

4. *The War of the Rebellion: A Compilation of the Official Records of the Union and Confederate Armies,* 4 series, 70 vols. in 128 books and index. (Washington, D.C.: Government Printing Office, 1880–1901) series 1, 1:208–209, 222–223, 281, 282. Hereinafter these documents will be cited as *Official Records*. Current, *Lincoln and the First Shot,* 71–74; David M. Potter, *The Impending Crisis, 1848–1861* (New York: Harper & Row, 1976) 572–578.

5. In an address on April 29, 1861, President Davis told the Confederate Congress that the South had 19,000 men under arms, was going to send 16,000 to Virginia, and he "proposed to organize and hold in readiness for instant action, . . . an army of 100,000 men." *Official Records,* series 4, 1:266.

6. N. Bartlett Pearce, "Price's Campaign of 1861, *Publications of the Arkansas Historical Association,* 4 vols. (Little Rock: Democrat Printing and Lithograph Co., 1906–1917) 4:332–333.

7. This view of the constitution was outlined well for the people of Arkansas by the ex-Whig, Know-Nothing lawyer-editor from Little Rock, Albert Pike. Albert Pike, *State or Province? Bond or Free? Addressed Particularly to the People of Arkansas* (Little Rock: n.p. 1861) 3–40.

8. Little Rock *Arkansas Gazette* 20 April 1861: 2.

9. Van Buren *Press* 17 April 1861: 2.

10. Judge John Brown, Diary, 20 April 1861, Arkansas History Commission, Little Rock, Arkansas.

11. Little Rock *True Democrat* 18 April 1861: 2.

12. *True Democrat* 25 April 1861: 2; 2 May 1861: 2.

13. S. H. Tucker, letter to David C. Williams, 9 May 1861, Williams Papers, Arkansas History Commission, Little Rock.

14. Little Rock *Arkansas Gazette* 27 April 1861: 2.

15. Little Rock *True Democrat* 18 April 1861: 2. For the turn to secession by William Woodruff, founder of the *Gazette*, see his signature on a secessionist broadside dated 18 April 1861. Arkansas History Commission, Little Rock.

16. Michael Dougan, *Confederate Arkansas: The People and Policies of a Frontier State in Wartime* (University of Alabama Press, 1976) 63.

17. Frank Peak, "A Southern Soldier Views the Civil War," typescript, Louisiana State University Library, Baton Rouge.

18. Judge John Brown, Diary, 22 April 1861.

19. Thomas Hanly, letter to David Walker, 17 April 1861, Walker Papers, Mullins Library, University of Arkansas, Fayetteville.

20. Hanly to Walker, 17 April 1861.

21. *Official Records* series 1, 1:687.

22. *Official Records,* series 1, 1:687. In this letter dated April 23, Rector wrote to the Confederate Secretary of War, "You may be assured of the immediate action of Arkansas in joining the Southern Confederacy; but I have no power to act, I regret to comply with your request. Our convention assembles on the sixth of May."

23. David Yancy Thomas, *Arkansas in War and Reconstruction* (Little Rock: United Daughters of the Confederacy, 1926) 79. On the same page Thomas wrote, "On the return trip down the river from this 'lark' the members of the militia company were so hilarious that, according to the owner, they damaged the boat transporting them to the extent of five hundred dollars."

24. Edwin Bearss and Arnell Gibson, *Fort Smith: Little Gibraltar on the Arkansas* (Norman: University of Oklahoma Press, 1969) 239–242.

25. Christopher C. Danley, letter to David Walker, 15 April 1861; letter in the Arkansas Gazette Foundation Library, Little Rock. Danley repeated many of these sentiments in an editorial in early May; see Little Rock *Arkansas Gazette* 4 May 1861: 2.

26. Claiborne F. Jackson, letter of David Walker, 19 April 1861, quoted in Dougan, *Confederate Arkansas* 60.

27. G. I. Stallings to Jesse Turner, 19 April 1861, Turner Papers, Perkins Library, Duke University, Durham, North Carolina.

28. Van Buren *Press* 24 April 1861: 2; 1 May 1861: 2.

29. Little Rock *Arkansas Gazette* 20 April 1861: 2.

30. Walker's proclamation recalling the state convention printed in Little Rock *True Democrat* 25 April 1861: 2.

31. *Journal of Both Sessions of the Convention of the State of Arkansas, Which Were Begun and Held in the Capitol, in the City of Little Rock* (Little Rock: Johnson and Yerkes, 1861) 113–116.

32. *Journal of Both Sessions* 119. Samuel Hempstead's entire letter printed in the *Journal* of the convention, pp. 117–120.

33. *Journal of Both Sessions* 118.

34. *Journal of Both Sessions* 121–122.

35. *Journal of Both Sessions* 123. The five men were Isaac Murphy and H. H. Bolinger of Madison County, John Campbell of Searcy County, Thomas Gunter of Washington County, and Samuel "Parson" Kelley of Pike County. For Campbell's story on his vote, see John Campbell to Neal Walters, 10 June 1861. Letter reprinted in James E. Johnson, ed., "Letters of John Campbell, Unionist," *Arkansas Historical Quarterly* 29 (Summer 1970): 178–182.

36. Cypert, "Reminiscences of the Secession Convention," 318–19.

37. *Journal of Both Sessions* 124.

38. Cypert, "Reminiscences of the Secession Convention," 319. Another version of Murphy's vote is found in Albert W. Bishop's small treatise, written during the Civil War on the Unionist movement in the southwest. Bishop claimed to have met Murphy in the spring of 1862, and his rendition of the vote sounds a little too flamboyant, and geared to the reading consumption of the Northern public during the war. His account of Murphy's vote said:

As the President sat down, four of the members who had voted 'no' rose one after one another, asking leave to change their votes. As before, the crowd was uproarious in their applause, and now, Isaac Murphy, alone in the negative was expected to swing easily into the popular current. His name was called by the chair. For a moment there was another deathlike stillness. 'Murphy!'—This was shouted from the gallery, and, at last, from the very floor of the Convention rose the noisy call. He stood up calmly and clearly spoke of his southern life. 'My principles are all southern,' said he, 'if necessary, I would lay down my life for the benefit of the Southern States, but I would rather lose a thousand lives than aid in bringing about the untold evils that would assuredly follow in the train of secession. Again I say to the passage of this ordinance, 'No!' He resumed his seat. Storms of hisses instantly burst forth. 'Traitor!' 'Traitor!' 'Shoot him!' 'Kill him!' This resounded throughout the hall, but no personal violence was attempted.—Albert Webb Bishop, *Loyalty on the Frontier; or Sketches of Union Men of the South-West, with Incidents and Adventures in the Rebellion on the Border* (St. Louis: R. P. Studley, Printer, 1863) 25–26.

39. Cypert, "Reminiscences of the Secession Convention," 319.

40. Alfred Holt Carrigan, "Reminiscences of the Secession Convention," Part I. *Publications of the Arkansas Historical Association,* 4 vols. (Little Rock: Democrat Printing and Lithograph Co., 1906–1917) 1:312.

41. Carrigan, "Reminiscences" 1:32. Murphy's career before, during and after the Civil War, is described in John I. Smith, *The Courage of a Southern Unionist: A Biography of Isaac Murphy, Governor of Arkansas, 1864–1868* (Little Rock: Rose Publishing, 1979).

42. *Journal of Both Sessions* 124.

43. *Official Records,* series 1, 1:690.

44. Dougan, *Confederate Arkansas* 63–67, 81–83, 94, 96, 122–25.

45. Dougan, *Confederate Arkansas* 66–67.

46. *Journal of Both Sessions* 125–473. Justification for the actions came from C. C. Danley of the *Gazette:* "The convention can do anything which the legislature can do and many [things] which the legislature cannot do." Little Rock *Arkansas Gazette* 20 April 1861: 2.

47. Christopher C. Danley, letter to William W. Mansfield, 23 April 1861, Mansfield Papers, Arkansas History Commission, Little Rock.

48. David C. Williams, letter to Jesse Turner, 7 May 1861; Turner Papers, Perkins Library, Duke University, Durham, North Carolina.

49. S. H. Tucker, letter to David C. Williams, 10 May 1861, D. C. Williams Papers, Arkansas History Commission, Little Rock, Arkansas.

50. Jesse Turner wrote to his wife, "God knows what will become of our unhappy country. All is darkness and gloom ahead. Our people are imbued with a revolutionary spirit. Madness and folly rules, I fear. The Conservative man who cares for his times cannot stay the rush of revolution. I fear it can only be quenched in blood." Jesse Turner, letter to Rebecca Turner, 8 May 1861, Turner Papers, Perkins Library, Duke University, Durham, North Carolina.

51. Jesse Turner, letter to David C. Williams, 19 May 1861, Williams Papers, Arkansas History Commission, Little Rock.

52. Dougan, *Confederate Arkansas* 64.

53. A brief profile of the men the convention chose for the confederate Congress, is contained in James M. Woods, "Devotees and Dissenters: Arkansans in the Confederate Congress, 1861–1865," *Arkansas Historical Quarterly* 38 (Autumn 1979): 227–233. For Hindman's failure to win a seat in the Provisional Confederate Congress, see Dougan, *Confederate Arkansas* 66.

54. Des Arc *Citizen* 31 May 1861: 2.

55. Dougan, *Confederate Arkansas* 64. Arkansas's first state constitution of 1836 and its amendments regarding banks and the popular election of the judiciary below the state supreme court, is contained in Francis Thorpe, ed., *The Federal and State Constitutions: Colonial Charters, and other Organic Laws of the States, Territories, and Colonies, Now or*

Heretofore Forming the United States of America, 20 vols. (Washington, D.C.: Government Printing Office, 1909) 1 : 268–287. A few old-line Whigs were quite pleased with the actions of the state convention in its May session. Judge John Brown of Camden wrote that the body "was a step in advance of any we have had in the State heretofore." Judge John Brown, Diary, 6 July 1861, Arkansas History Commission, Little Rock.

56. Dougan, *Confederate Arkansas* 94–95.

57. Former delegates Alfred Carrigan and Jesse Cypert recall Harris Flanagin as one of the most conservative delegates at the convention who favored secession; see Carrigan, "Reminiscences of the Secession Convention," 310; Cypert, "Reminiscences of the Secession Convention," 321. For a look at Flanagin's career, especially his career as Arkansas's Confederate governor from 1862–1865, see Farrah Newberry, "Harris Flanagin," *Arkansas Historical Quarterly* 17 (Spring 1958): 3–20; Michael B. Dougan, "Harris Flanagin," in Timothy P. Donovan and Willard B. Gatewood, Jr., eds., *The Governors of Arkansas: Essays in Political Biography* (Fayetteville: University of Arkansas Press, 1981) 33–37.

58. In George H. Thompson's recent work on Reconstruction in Arkansas, he notes that the opposition to the Republicans came from an alliance of former Whigs and Democrats. He calls them, for want of a better term, "Democratic Conservatives." They were led by the old Conway-Johnson Democrat, Harris Flanagin, and the old-line Whig, Augustus Garland. See George H. Thompson, *Arkansas and Reconstruction: The Influence of Geography, Economics, and Personality* (Port Washington, N.Y.: Kennikat Press, 1976) 91–93, 124–158.

59. C. Vann Woodward, *Origins of the New South, 1877–1913* (Baton Rouge: Louisiana State University Press, 1951) 1–22. For a look at a recent critique of this "Whig thesis" of Woodward, see James T. Moore, "Redeemers Reconsidered: Change and Continuity in the Democratic South, 1870–1900," *Journal of Southern History* 44 (August 1978): 359–378. Moore claims that the old-line Whig influence among the Bourbon Democrats was not substantially pervasive.

60. John Campbell, letter to Neal Walters, 10 June 1861, in Johnston, "Letters of John Campbell," 178–182.

61. James D. Grieg, letter to David C. Williams, 9 May 1861; D. C. Williams Papers, Arkansas History Commission, Little Rock.

62. Mary Tebbetts Banes, Journal, n.d., William S. Campbell, *One Hundred Years of Fayetteville, 1828–1928* (Fayetteville: Washington County Historical Society, 1977) 89–90. An attorney active in Democratic politics during the 1850s, Jonas Tebbetts was a strong supporter of Congressman Alfred Greenwood of the northern congressional district, 1853–1859. When Hindman challenged Greenwood's renomination at the congressional Democratic convention in Batesville in May 1856, Tebbetts led the victorious Greenwood forces. For this action, Tebbetts earned the bitter antagonism of Hindman. Mary Tebbetts Banes recalled that her mother feared for her father because Mrs. Tebbetts "always pictured Hindman with a bowie knife, or pistol, or two fists hidden somewhere for Father's special benefit," p. 83.

63. Georgia Tatum, *Disloyalty in the Confederacy* (Chapel Hill: University of North Carolina Press, 1934) 36.

64. For the best articles on the Arkansas Peace Society, see the work of the late Arkansas historian Ted R. Worley, in "The Arkansas Peace Society of 1861: A Study in Mountain Unionism," *Journal of Southern History* 24 (November 1958): 445–456; and Ted R. Worley, "Documents Relating to the Arkansas Peace Society of 1861," *Arkansas Historical Quarterly* 17 (Summer 1958): 82–111.

65. Congressman Thomas Boles, letter to Charles Lanham, 26 March 1868, Lanham Papers, Arkansas History Commission, Little Rock.

66. Carl Degler, *The Other South: Southern Dissenters in the Nineteenth Century* (New York: Harper & Row, 1974) 174.

67. The number of men who were from the Confederate states, yet served with the Union army were as follows: Tennessee–31,092; Arkansas–8,289; Louisiana–5,224;

North Carolina–3,156; Alabama–2,578; Texas–1,965; Florida–1,290; Mississippi–545. List taken from Frederick Henry Dyer, *A Compendium of the War of the Rebellion*, 3 vols., 1909 (New York: Thomas Yoseloff, 1959) 1:11. Three Confederate states, South Carolina, Georgia and Virginia, were not included in this list provided by Dyer. There might have been too few recruits from these states to record officially in the Federal Army records.

68. U.S. Department of the Interior, *The Eighth Census of the United States, 1860*, 4 vols. (Washington, D.C.: Government Printing Office, 1864–1866) 1:598. Only two states had a smaller white population than Arkansas—South Carolina and Florida. South Carolina had more people owing to its large slave population. Florida had the least number of people in all the Confederacy. Even with its small population, Arkansas came in second in the number of men who served with the Union armies. Arkansas's white population was about 324,143 to Tennessee's 826,722.

69. *Official Records* series 1, 22; Pt. 1, 603.

70. *Official Records* series 1, 22; Pt. 1, 603.

71. Thompson, *Arkansas and Reconstruction* 59–123. For a classic look at the place of this mountain Republicanism in the bourbon democratic South, 1877–1945, see V. O. Key Jr., *Southern Politics in State and Nation* (New York: Alfred A. Knopf-Vintage Paperback Edition, 1949) 280–285. Key points out that two former Unionist counties in the Ozarks, Newton and Searcy, still elected local Republicans during the first half of the twentieth century. This mountain Republicanism would form the core for the resurgence of the Republican party in the South after World War II. See Jack Bass and Walter DeVries, *The Transformation of Southern Politics: Social Change and Political Consequence Since 1945* (New York: New American Library, 1977) 25.

72. Little Rock *True Democrat* 18 April 1861: 2.

Conclusion

1. U.S. Department of the Interior, *The Census of 1860*, 4 vols. (Washington, D.C.: Government Printing Office, 1864–1866) 1:599–604.

2. Lewis Gray, *History of Agriculture in the Southern United States to 1860*, 2 vols., 1932 (Gloucester, Mass.: Peter Smith, 1958) 1:482.

3. Gray, *History of Agriculture* 2:656. Gavin Wright treats Arkansas as basically a lower South cotton state. Gavin Wright, *The Political Economy of the Cotton South: Households, Markets, and Wealth in the Nineteenth Century* (New York: W. W. Norton, 1978) 15–37.

4. Daniel Crofts, "The Union Party of 1861 and the Secession Crisis," *Perspectives in American History* 11 (1977–1978): 327–376; Daniel Crofts, "The Political and Social Origins of Opposition to Secession in the Upper South," Southern Historical Association Convention, Louisville, Kentucky, November 2, 1984.

5. Wooster considered Arkansas part of the upper South. Ralph Wooster, *Politicians, Planters, and Plain Folks: Courthouse to Statehouse in Upper South, 1850–1860* (Knoxville: University of Tennessee Press, 1975); David Potter, *The Impending Crisis 1848, 1861* (New York: Harper & Row, 1976) 505–509; William J. Cooper, *Liberty & Slavery: Southern Politics until 1860* (New York: Alfred A. Knopf, 1984) 276–281. Michael Holt identifies Arkansas as part of the upper South, yet it does not completely fit his categorization of that area. Michael Holt, *The Political Crisis of the 1850s* (New York: John Wiley & Sons, 1978) 219–259, especially 234–35.

6. Potter, *The Impending Crisis* 507–508.

7. Cooper, *Liberty and Slavery* 302.

8. Steven Channing, *Crisis of Fear: Secession in South Carolina* (New York: Simon & Schuster, 1970); William Barney, *The Secessionist Impulse: Alabama and Mississippi in 1860* (Princeton: Princeton University Press, 1974); Michael P. Johnson, *Toward a Patriarchal Republic: Secession in Georgia* (Baton Rouge: Louisiana State University Press, 1976); J. Mills Thornton, *Politics and Power in a Slave Society: Alabama, 1800–1860*

(Baton Rouge: Louisiana State University Press, 1978); Harry Votz, "Party, State, and Nation: Kentucky and the Coming of the American Civil War," diss., University of Virginia, 1982; Walter L. Buenger, *Secession and Union in Texas* (Austin: University of Texas Press, 1984).

9. Holt, *Political Crisis of the 1850s*, 219–59.

10. Paul Bergeron, *Antebellum Politics in Tennessee* (Lexington: University Press of Kentucky, 1983); Marc Kruman, *Parties and Politics in North Carolina, 1836–1865* (Baton Rouge: Louisiana State University Press, 1983). Both studies outline the strong two-party systems in these states.

11. Holt, *The Political Crisis of the 1850s*, 219–59; William J. Cooper, *The South and the Politics of Slavery, 1828–1856* (Baton Rouge: Louisiana State University Press, 1978) 362–76.

12. For a look at Borland's demise, see James M. Woods, "Expansionism as Diplomacy: The Career of Solon Borland in Central America, 1853–1854," *The Americas: A Quarterly Review of Inter-American Cultural History* 40 (January 1984): 314. For Mitchel's career in the Confederate Senate and his death, see James M. Woods, "Devotees and Dissenters: Arkansans in the Confederate Congress, 1861–1865," *Arkansas Historical Quarterly* 38 (Autumn 1979): 237–38, 240.

13. Woods, "Devotees and Dissenters," 229, 236, 240, 247.

14. Woods, "Devotees and Dissenters," 231–232.

15. For a look at Hindman's "military rule" in Arkansas during 1862–1863, see Michael Dougan, *Confederate Arkansas: The People and Policies of a Frontier State in Wartime* (University of Alabama Press, 1976) 89–99. For the most thorough treatment of Hindman's military career and his postbellum activity and assassination, see Bobby Roberts, "Thomas C. Hindman: Secessionist and Confederate General," M.A. thesis, University of Arkansas, 1972, 40–168.

16. Harris Flanagin's life and political career is briefly outlined by Michael Dougan, "Harris Flanagin" in *The Governors of Arkansas: Essays in Political Biography*, Timothy P. Donovan and Willard B. Gatewood, Jr., eds. (Fayetteville: University of Arkansas Press, 1981) 3–37. George H. Thompson, *Arkansas and Reconstruction: The Influence of Geography, Economics and Personality* (Port Washington, N.Y.: Kennikat Press, 1976) 95–96. For Walker's post-Reconstruction seat on the state supreme court and his death, see John Hallum, *Biographical and Pictorial History of Arkansas* (Albany, N.Y.: Weed, Parsons & Co., 1887) 104–105.

17. F. Clark Elkins, "Thomas James Churchill," and Harry Readnor, "William Meade Fishback," in Donovan and Gatewood, *The Governors of Arkansas* 68–72, 91–96.

18. For Rector's political history after resigning the governorship, see Waddy W. Moore, "Henry Massie Rector," in Donovan and Gatewood, *The Governors of Arkansas* 32. For the political career of Elias Rector and his ill-fated match with Jeff Davis, see Raymond Arsenault, *The Wild Ass of the Ozarks: Jeff Davis and the Social Bases of Southern Politics* (Philadelphia: Temple University Press, 1984) 64, 68, 72, 141–149.

19. Beverly Watkins, "Augustus Hill Garland," in Donovan and Gatewood, *The Governors of Arkansas* 61–64. This is a fine, short summary of Garland's long career.

20. Buenger, *Secession and the Union in Texas*, 10.

Bibliography

Primary Sources: Manuscripts

"A Call for Unity, April 18, 1861." Broadside, Arkansas History Commission, Little Rock.

"Aid for Kansas: A Public Meeting." University of Texas Archives, Austin.

Arrington, Archibald. Papers. Southern Historical Collection, University of North Carolina, Chapel Hill.

Bills, John H. Papers. Department of Manuscripts and Archives, Louisiana State University, Baton Rouge.

Bonner, Samuel. Papers. Department of Manuscripts and Archives, Louisiana State University, Baton Rouge.

Brown, John. Diary. Arkansas History Commission, Little Rock.

Cantey, John, to "Cousin John," 25 November 1860, John Cantey Papers, Department of Manuscripts and Archives, Perkins Library, Duke University, Durham, North Carolina.

Danley, Christopher C., to David Walker, 15 April 1861. Arkansas Gazette Foundation Library, Little Rock.

English, Elbert H. Papers. Arkansas History Commission, Little Rock.

Fletcher, Eliot. Papers. Arkansas History Commission, Little Rock.

Glenn, Leonidas. Papers. Southern Historical Collection, University of North Carolina, Chapel Hill.

Gordon-Hackett Papers. Southern Historical Collection, University of North Carolina, Chapel Hill.

Gulley, L. C., Collection. Arkansas History Commission, Little Rock.

Lanham, Charles. Papers. Arkansas History Commission, Little Rock.

Lay, Henry. Papers. Southern Historical Collection, University of North Carolina, Chapel Hill.

Mansfield, William. Papers. Arkansas History Commission, Little Rock.

Oldham, W. S., Collection. Arkansas History Commission, Little Rock.

Page, Ann Slaughter. "Daybook of a Journey from Virginia to Texas. September 4, 1851 to November 26, 1851." University of Texas Archives, Austin.

Peak, Frank. "A Southern Soldier Views the Civil War." Unpublished ms., 1863. Department of Manuscripts and Archives, Louisiana State University, Baton Rouge.

Scott, Christopher C. Papers. Arkansas History Commission, Little Rock.

Smith, John. "To the Voters of Benton County, 18 February 1861." Broadside, Arkansas History Commission, Little Rock.

Sneed, Sebron Graham. Papers. University of Texas Archives, Austin.

Stirman, John. "To the People of Washington County, February 5, 1861." Broadside, Arkansas History Commission, Little Rock.

Turner, Jesse. Papers. Department of Manuscripts and Archives, Perkins Library, Duke University, Durham, North Carolina.

————. Papers. Mullins Library, University of Arkansas, Fayetteville.

Wales, Z., Letter to Abraham Lincoln, 24 November 1860. Arkansas Gazette Foundation Library, Little Rock.

Walker, David. Papers. Mullins Library, University of Arkansas, Fayetteville.

Wharton, Edward C. Papers. Department of Manuscripts and Archives, Louisiana State University, Baton Rouge.

Wheat, John T. Papers. Southern Historical Collection, University of North Carolina, Chapel Hill, North Carolina.

Wilcox, William. Papers. Department of Manuscripts and Archives, Perkins Library, Duke University, Durham, North Carolina.

Williams, David C., Clara Eno Collection. Arkansas History Commission, Little Rock.

Williams, Samuel W. Papers. Arkansas History Commission, Little Rock.

Primary Sources: Arkansas Newspapers

Batesville *Democratic Sentinel* 1858–59.

Batesville *Independent Balance* 1856–59.

Des Arc *Constitutional Union* 1860–61.

Fayetteville *Arkansian* 1859–61.

Fort Smith *Herald* 1847–52, 1856.

Fort Smith *Thirty-Fifth Parallel* 1860.

Fort Smith *Times* 1858–60.

Helena *Democratic Star* 1854–55.

Helena *Southern Shield* 1840–60.

Helena *States Rights Democrat* 1856–57.

Helena *Weekly Note Book* 1860.

Little Rock *Arkansas Advocate* 1835–36.

Little Rock *Arkansas Banner* 1844–51.

Little Rock *Arkansas Gazette* 1819–61.

Little Rock *Arkansas State Democrat* 1849.

Little Rock *Arkansas Whig* 1851–52.

Little Rock *Old Line Democrat* 1859–61.

Little Rock *True Democrat* 1852–61.

Memphis, [Tennessee] *Weekly Appeal* 1859–61.

Van Buren *Arkansas Intelligencer* 1845–49.
Van Buren *Press* 1859–61.
Washington *Telegraph* 1843–59.

Primary Sources: Books and Articles

Banes, Mary Tebbetts. "Journal." In William S. Campbell, *One Hundred Years of Fayetteville, 1828–1928.* 1928. Fayetteville, Ark.: Washington County Historical Society, 1977.

Bishop, Albert Webb. *Loyalty on the Frontier; or, Sketches of Union Men of the South-West, with Incidents and Adventures in the Rebellion on the Border.* St. Louis: R. P. Studley, Printer, 1863.

Brown, Samuel. *The Western Gazettier; or, an Emigrant's Directory, Containing a Geographical Description of the Western Territories.* Auburn, N.Y.: H. C. Southwick, 1817.

Carrigan, Alfred Holt. "Reminiscences of the Secession Convention." *Publications of the Arkansas Historical Association.* 4 vols. Little Rock: Democrat Printing & Lithograph Co., 1906–1917.

Chittenden, Lucius Eugene. *A Report of the Secret Session of the Conference Convention, for Proposing Amendments to the Constitution, Held at Washington, D.C. February, A.D. 1861.* New York: Appleton & Co., 1864.

Cox, Samuel Sullivan. *Three Decades of Federal Legislation, 1855–1885; Personal and Historical Memories of Events Preceeding, During, and Since the American Civil War, Involving Slavery and Secession, With Sketches of Prominent Actors During these Periods.* Providence, Rhode Island: J. H. and R. A. Reid, Publishers, 1885.

Cypert, Jesse. "Reminiscences of the Secession Convention." *Publications of the Arkansas Historical Association.* 4 vols. Little Rock: Democrat Printing & Lithograph Co., 1906–1917.

Demby, James M. *The War in Arkansas; or, A Treatise on the Great Rebellion of 1861: Its Progress and Ultimate Results upon the Destiny of the State. A Defense of the Loyalty of the People, Their Wretched Condition Considered, A Review of the Policy of the Government Toward the Union People and the Rebels.* Little Rock: Eghart, Printer 1864.

Dyer, Frederick. *A Compendium of the War of the Rebellion.* 3 vols. New York: Thomas Yoseloff, 1959.

Evans, Clement, gen. ed. *Confederate Military History.* 12 vols. Atlanta: Confederate Publishing House, 1899. Vol. 10: *Arkansas* by John Harrell.

Featherstonhaugh, Sir George William. *An Excursion Through the Slave States of North America: From Washington on the Potomac, to the Frontiers of Mexico.* New York: Harper & Brothers, 1844.

Flint, Timothy. *A Condensed Geography and History of the Western States, or Mississippi Valley.* 2 vols. Cincinnati: E. A. Flint, 1828.

Gerstacker, Frederick. *Wild Sports in the Far West*. New York: John Lovell, 1858.

"Growth of Arkansas." *DeBow's Review* 29 (December 1860): 754.

Hathaway, Gilbert. "Travels in the South-West: Life in Arkansas and Texas." Printed in Rev. George Duffield, W. P. Isham, Warrens Isham, D. Bethune Duffield, Gilbert Hathaway, *Travels in Two Hemispheres: or, Gleanings From a European Tour*. 2nd ed. Detroit: Doughty, Straw, Raymond, and Sellneck, 1858.

Helper, Hinton Rowan. *The Impending Crisis of the South: How to Meet It*. New York: Burdick Brothers, 1857.

Hindman, Thomas Carmichael. *Federal and State Relations: A Speech Delivered in Little Rock, Arkansas, February 15, 1859*. Little Rock: James Butter, Printer, 1859.

———. *Speech of the Honorable Thomas C. Hindman, Delivered at Helena, Arkansas, November 28, 1859*. Washington: Lionel Towers, Printer, 1860.

Ingraham, Joseph Holt. *The South-West: By a Yankee*. 2 vols. New York: Harper & Brothers, 1835.

Johnson, Robert Ward. *Address to the People of Arkansas, February 7, 1861*. Washington: A. Polkington, Printer, 1861.

Monette, John. *History of the Discovery and Settlement of the Valley of the Mississippi by the Three Great European Powers, Spain, France, and Great Britain, and the Subsequent Occupation, Settlement, and Extension of the Civil Government by the United States Until the Year, 1846*. 2 vols. New York: Harper & Brothers, 1846.

Nash, Charles Edward. *Biographical Sketches of Gen. P. C. Cleburne and Gen. T. C. Hindman, Together with Humorous Anecdotes and Reminiscences of the Late Civil War*. Little Rock: Tunnah & Pittard, Printers, 1895.

Nuttal, Thomas. *A Journey of Travels into the Arkansas Territory During the Year 1819, With Occasional Observations on the Manners of the Aborigines*. Philadelphia: Thomas Palmer, 1821.

Pearce, N. Bartlett. "Price's Campaign of 1861." *Publications of the Arkansas Historical Association*. 4 vols. Little Rock: Democrat Printing & Lithograph Co., 1906–1917.

Peck, J. M. *A New Guide for Emigrants to the West*. Boston: Gould, Kendall, and Lincoln, 1836.

Pfeifer, Lady Ida. *The Lady's Second Journey Around the World*. New York: Harper & Brothers, 1856.

Pike, Albert. *State or Province? Bond or Free? Addressed Particularly to the People of Arkansas*. Little Rock: n.p., 1861.

Pope, William Fulton. *Early Days in Arkansas: Being For the Most Part the Personal Recollections of an Old Settler*.

"Recollections of an Old Stager." *Harper's New Monthly Magazine* 46 (January 1873).

Schoolcraft, Henry. *Journal of a Tour into the Interior of Missouri and Arkansas: Performed in the Years 1818 and 1819*. London: Sir Richard Phillips, 1821.

Stephens, Alexander Hamilton. *A Constitutional View of the Late War Between the States.* 2 vols. Philadelphia: National Publishing Co., 1868–1870.

Primary Sources: Public Documents

Acts Passed at the Thirteenth Session of the General Assembly of the State of Arkansas; Which was Begun in the Capitol, in the City of Little Rock, on Monday, the Fifth Day of November, One Thousand Eight Hundred and Sixty, and Ended on Monday, the Twenty-First Day of January, One Thousand Eight Hundred and Sixty-One. Little Rock: Johnson and Yerkes, State Printers, 1861.

Congressional Globe, 31st Congress, 1st Session. Washington: John C. Rives, 1850.

Congressional Globe, 33rd Congress, 1st Session. Washington: John C. Rives, 1854.

Congressional Globe, 36th Congress, 1st Session. Washington: John C. Rives, 1860.

Debates and Proceedings in the Congress of the United States: 15th Congress, 2nd Session. Washington: Gales Seaton, 1855.

DeBow, James D. B. *Statistical View of the United States: A Compendium to the Seventh Census, 1850.* Washington: A. O. P. Nicholson, Public Printer, 1854.

Greenwood, Alfred Burton. "Nebraska and Kansas." Speech printed in *Congressional Globe, 33rd Congress, 1st Session, Appendix.* Washington: John C. Rives, 1854.

Hindman, Thomas Carmichael. "That Black Republican Bible—The Helper Book." *Congressional Globe, 36th Congress, 1st Session, Appendix.* Washington: John C. Rives, 1860.

Journal of Both Sessions of the Convention of the State of Arkansas, Which was Begun and Held in the Capitol, in the City of Little Rock. Little Rock: Johnson & Yerkes, State Printers, 1861.

Journal of the House of Representatives of the Eighth Session of the General Assembly of the State of Arkansas. Little Rock: Arkansas Banner Office, 1851.

Journal of the Senate of the Eighth Session of the General Assembly of the State of Arkansas. Little Rock: Arkansas Banner Office, 1851.

Learner, William. *Historical Statistics of the United States: Colonial Times to 1970.* 2 vols. Washington: Government Printing Office, 1975.

Thorpe, Francis., ed. *The Federal and State Constitutions: Colonial Charters, and Other Organic Laws of the States, Territories, and Colonies, Now, or Heretofore Forming the United States of America.* 20 vols. Washington: Government Printing Office, 1909.

U.S. Congress., House. *Abstract to the Fifth Census: The Number of Free People, The Number of Slaves, The Federal or Representative Number, and the Aggregate For Each County of Each State in the United States.* H.R. no. 263, 22nd Congress, 1st Session. Washington: Duff Greene, Public Printer, 1832.

U.S. Department of the Interior. *The Eighth Census of the United States, 1860.* 4 vols. Washington: Government Printing Office, 1864–1866.

U.S. Department of the Interior. *The Seventh Census of the United States, 1850.* Washington: Robert Armstrong, 1853.

U.S. Department of State. *The Third Census of the United States, 1810.* Washington: Government Printing Office, 1811.

U.S. Department of State. *A Compendium of the Inhabitants and Statistics of the United States, as Obtained from the Returns of the Sixth Census, by Counties and by Towns.* Washington: Thomas Allen, 1841.

The War of the Rebellion: A Compilation of the Official Records of the Union and Confederate Armies 4 series, 70 vols. in 128 books and index. Washington: Government Printing Office, 1880–1901.

Secondary Sources: Books and Published Monographs

Allsopp, Frederick. *History of the Arkansas Press For a Hundred Years and More.* Little Rock: Parke-Harper, 1922.

Arsenault, Raymond. *The Wild Ass of the Ozarks: Jeff Davis and the Social Bases of Southern Politics.* Philadelphia: Temple University Press, 1984.

Ashmore, Harry S. *Arkansas: A History.* New York: W. W. Norton & Co., 1978.

Bailey, Hugh C. *Hilton Rowan Helper: Abolitionist-Racist.* Tuscaloosa: University of Alabama Press, 1965.

Barney, William L. *The Secessionist Impulse: Alabama and Mississippi in 1860.* Princeton: Princeton University Press, 1974.

Bass, Jack, and Walter DeVries. *The Transformation of Southern Politics: Social Change and Political Consequence Since 1945.* New York: New American Library, 1977.

Bearss, Edwin, and Arnell Gibson. *Fort Smith: Little Gibraltar on the Arkansas.* Norman: University of Oklahoma Press, 1969.

Bergeron, Paul. *Antebellum Politics in Tennessee.* Lexington: University Press of Kentucky, 1982.

Billington, Ray Allen. *The Protestant Crusade, 1800–1860: A Study of the Origins of American Nativism.* New York: Macmillan Publishing Co., 1938.

Buenger, Walter L. *Secession and Union in Texas.* Austin: University of Texas Press, 1984.

Campbell, Mary. *Attitude of Tennessians Toward the Union, 1847–1861.* New York: Random House, 1961.

Cash, W. J. *The Mind of the South.* New York: Alfred A. Knopf, 1941.

Catton, Bruce. *A Centennial History of the Civil War.* Vol. 1, *The Coming Fury.* New York: Doubleday & Co., 1961.

Channing, Steven. *Crisis of Fear: Secession in South Carolina.* New York: Simon & Schuster, 1970.

Clark, Thomas, and Albert Kirwan. *The South Since Appomattox: A Century of Regional Change*. New York: Oxford University Press, 1967.

Coit, Margaret. *John C. Calhoun: American Portrait*. Boston: Houghton, Mifflin Co., 1950.

Cole, Arthur Charles. *The Whig Party in the South*. Washington: American Historical Association, 1913.

Cooper, William J. *The South and the Politics of Slavery, 1828–1856*. Baton Rouge: Louisiana State University Press, 1978.

———. *Liberty and Slavery: Southern Politics to 1860*. New York: Alfred A. Knopf, 1983.

Craven, Avery. *The Coming of the Civil War*. 2nd ed. Chicago: University of Chicago Press, 1957.

———. *The Growth of Southern Nationalism, 1847–1861*. Baton Rouge: Louisiana State University Press, 1953.

Crenshaw, Ollinger. *The Slave States in the Presidential Election of 1860*. Baltimore: Johns Hopkins University Press, 1945.

Current, Richard. *Lincoln and the First Shot*. Philadelphia: J. B. Lippincott Co., 1963.

Degler, Carl. *The Other South: Southern Dissenters in the Nineteenth Century*. New York: Harper & Row, 1974.

Donovan, Timothy P., and Willard B. Gatewood, Jr., eds. *The Governors of Arkansas: Essays in Political Biography*. Fayetteville: University of Arkansas Press, 1981.

Dougan, Michael B. *Confederate Arkansas: The People and Policies of a Frontier State in Wartime*. University of Alabama Press, 1976.

Dumond, Dwight L. *The Secession Movement, 1860–1861*. New York: Macmillan, 1931.

Eaton, Clement. *The Freedom of Thought Struggle in the Old South*. 2nd ed. New York: Harper & Row, 1964.

———. *The Growth of Southern Civilization, 1790–1860*. New York: Harper & Row, 1960.

Ferguson, John L., and James H. Atkinson. *Historic Arkansas*. Little Rock: Arkansas History Commission, 1966.

Filler, Louis. *The Crusade Against Slavery, 1830–1860*. New York: Harper & Row, 1960.

Foner, Eric. *Free Soil, Free Labor, Free Men: The Ideology of the Republican Party Before the Civil War, 1854–1861*. New York: Oxford University Press, 1970.

Foote, Shelby. *The Civil War: A Narrative History*. 3 vols. New York: Random House, 1958–1974.

Fornell, Earl. *The Galveston Era: The Texas Crescent on the Eve of Secession*. Austin: University of Texas Press, 1961.

Freehling, William. *Prelude to Civil War: The Nullification Crisis in South Carolina, 1816–1836*. New York: Harper & Row, 1965.

Gray, Lewis. *History of Agriculture in the Southern United States to 1860.* 2 vols. Washington: 1933. Gloucester, Mass.: Peter Smith, 1958.

Gunderson, Robert G. *Old Gentlemen's Convention: The Washington Peace Conference of 1861.* Madison: University of Wisconsin Press, 1961.

Hallum, John. *Biographical and Pictorial History of Arkansas.* Albany, N.Y.: Weed & Parsons, 1889.

Hamilton, Holman. *Prologue to Conflict: The Crisis and Compromise of 1850.* New York: W. W. Norton, 1966.

Hempstead, Fay. *History of Arkansas From the Earliest Times Till 1890.* St. Louis: N. D. Thompson & Co., 1890.

———. *Historical Review of Arkansas.* 2 vols. Chicago: Clarke Publishing Co., 1911.

Herndon, Dallas. *A Centennial History of Arkansas.* 3 vols. Chicago: Clarke Publishing Co., 1922.

———. *Annals of Arkansas, 1947.* 4 vols. Little Rock: Arkansas Historical Association, 1947.

———. *Why Little Rock Was Born.* Little Rock: Central Printing, 1933.

Holt, Michael. *The Political Crisis of the 1850s.* New York: John Wiley & Sons, 1978.

Johnson, Michael. *Toward a Patriarchal Republic: Secession in Georgia.* Baton Rouge: Louisiana State University Press, 1976.

Jordan, Winthrop. *White Over Black: American Attitudes Toward the Negro, 1550–1815.* New York: Oxford University Press, 1968.

Key, V. O., Jr. *Southern Politics in State and Nation.* New York: Random House, 1949.

Kruman, Marc. *Parties and Politics in North Carolina, 1836–1865.* Baton Rouge: Louisiana State University Press, 1983.

Morgan, Edmund. *American Slavery, American Freedom: The Ordeal of Colonial Virginia.* New York: W. W. Norton, 1975.

Mullen, Gerald. *Flight and Rebellion: Slave Resistance in Eighteenth Century Virginia.* New York: Oxford University Press, 1972.

Murphy, Robert. *Henri DeTonti: Fur Trader of the Mississippi.* Baltimore: Johns Hopkins University Press, 1941.

Nevins, Allan. *The Ordeal of the Union.* 2 vols. New York: Charles Scribner's Sons, 1945–1947.

Nichols, Alice. *Bleeding Kansas.* New York: Oxford University Press, 1954.

Nichols, Roy. *The Disruption of American Democracy.* New York: Macmillan Co., 1948.

Oates, Stephen. *With Malice Toward None: The Life of Abraham Lincoln.* New York: New American Library, 1977.

Overdyke, William Darrell. *The Know-Nothing Party in the South.* Baton Rouge: Louisiana State University Press, 1950.

Owsley, Frank. *Plain Folk in the Old South.* Baton Rouge: Louisiana State University Press, 1949.

Patton, James. *Unionism and Reconstruction in Tennessee, 1860–1869*. Chapel Hill: University of North Carolina Press, 1934.

Potter, David M. *The Impending Crisis, 1847–1861*. New York: Harper & Row, 1976.

Randall, James G., and David Donald. *Civil War and Reconstruction*. 2nd ed. Lexington, Mass.: D. C. Heath & Co., 1969.

Ray, Sister Mary Augustine. *American Opinion of Roman Catholicism in the Eigthteenth Century*. New York: Columbia University Press, 1936.

Reynolds, Donald. *Editors Make War: Southern Editorials During the Secession Crisis*. Nashville: Vanderbilt University Press, 1968.

Richards, Ira Don. *Story of a Rivertown: Little Rock During the Nineteenth Century*. Benton: Private Printing, 1969.

Ross, Margaret. *The Arkansas Gazette: The Early Years, 1819–1866*. Little Rock: Arkansas Gazette Foundation Library, 1969.

Shanks, Henry. *The Secession Movement in Virginia*. Chapel Hill: University of North Carolina Press, 1934.

Shinn, Josiah. *Pioneers and Makers of Arkansas*. Little Rock: Democrat Printing & Lithograph Co., 1908.

Shirley, Glenn. *Law West of Fort Smith: A History of Frontier Justice in the Indian Territory, 1834–1896*. Lincoln: University of Nebraska Press, 1957.

Sims, Margaret. *White Already to Harvest: The Episcopal Diocese of Arkansas, 1838–1971*. Sewanee, Tenn.: University of the South Press, 1975.

Sitterson, Joseph Carlyle. *The Secession Movement in North Carolina*. Chapel Hill: University of North Carolina Press, 1939.

Smith, John I. *The Courage of a Southern Unionist: A Biography of Isaac Murphy, Governor of Arkansas, 1864–1868*. Little Rock: Rose Publishing Co., 1979.

Sydnor, Charles. *The Development of Southern Sectionalism, 1819–1848*. Baton Rouge: Louisiana State University Press, 1947.

Takaki, Ronald. *A Pro-Slavery Crusade: The Agitation to Reopen the African Slave Trade*. New York: Free Press, 1971.

Tatum, Georgia. *Disloyalty in the Confederacy*. Chapel Hill: University of North Carolina Press, 1934.

Taylor, Orville. *Negro Slavery in Arkansas*. Durham, N.C.: Duke University Press, 1958.

Taylor, William. *Cavalier and Yankee: The Old South and the American National Character*. New York: Harper & Row, 1960.

Thomas, David Y. *Arkansas and Its People: A History*. 4 vols. New York: American Historical Association, 1930.

———. *Arkansas in War and Reconstruction*. Little Rock: United Daughters of the Confederacy, 1926.

Thompson, George H. *Arkansas and Reconstruction: The Influence of Geography, Economics, and Personality*. Port Washington, N.Y.: Kennikat Press, 1976.

Thornton, J. Mills. *Politics and Power in a Slave Society: Alabama, 1800–1860*. Baton Rouge: Louisiana State University Press, 1978.

Tilley, John. *Lincoln Takes Command*. Chapel Hill: University of North Carolina Press, 1941.

Van Abele, Rudolph. *Alexander H. Stephens: A Biography*. New York: Alfred A. Knopf, 1946.

Warner, Ezra J., and W. Buck Yearns. *The Biographical Registrar of the Confederate Congress*. Baton Rouge: Louisiana State University Press, 1975.

White, Lonnie J. *Politics in the Southwestern Frontier, Arkansas Territory, 1819–1836*. Memphis: Memphis State University Press, 1964.

Williams, C. Fred, S. Charles Bolton, Carl Moneyhon, and LeRoy Williams, eds. *A Documentary History of Arkansas*. Fayetteville: University of Arkansas Press, 1984.

Wiltse, Charles. *John C. Calhoun*. 3 vols. Indianapolis: The Bobbs-Merrill Co., 1944–1951.

Woodward, C. Vann. *Origins of the New South, 1877–1913*. Baton Rouge: Louisiana State University Press, 1951.

Wooster, Ralph. *The Secession Conventions of the South*. Westport, Conn.: Greenwood Press, 1962.

———. *The People in Power: Courthouse to Statehouse in the Lower South, 1850–1860*. Knoxville: University of Tennessee Press, 1969.

———. *Politicians, Planters, and Plain Folks: Courthouse to Statehouse in the Upper South, 1850–1860*. Knoxville: University of Tennessee Press, 1975.

Wright, Gavin. *The Political Economy of the Cotton South: Households, Markets, and Wealth in the Nineteenth Century*. New York: W. W. Norton & Co., 1978.

Secondary Sources: Published Articles

Adams, Horace. "The Year 1856 as Viewed by an Arkansas Whig." *Arkansas Historical Quarterly* 1 (June 1942): 124–133.

Addington, Wendall. "Slave Insurrection in Texas." *Journal of Negro History* 35 (October 1950): 408–434.

Auchampaugh, Phillip. "The Buchanan-Douglas Feud." *Journal of the Illinois State Historical Society* 25 (April 1932): 5–48.

Bolton, S. Charles. "Inequality on the Southern Frontier: Arkansas County in the Arkansas Territory." *Arkansas Historical Quarterly* 41 (Spring 1982): 51–66.

———. "Economic Inequality in the Arkansas Territory." *Journal of Interdisciplinary History* 14 (Winter 1984): 619–633.

Boyette, Gene W. "Quantitative Differences Between the Arkansas Whig and Democratic Parties, 1836–1850." *Arkansas Historical Quarterly* 34 (Autumn 1975): 214–226.

Brown, Mattie. "River Transportation in Arkansas, 1819–1890." *Arkansas Historical Quarterly* 1 (December 1942): 292–308.

Cardoso, Jack. "Southern Reaction to the *Impending Crisis*." *Civil War History* 16 (March 1970): 5–17.

Cash, Marie. "Arkansas Achieves Statehood." *Arkansas Historical Quarterly* 2 (December 1943): 292–308.

Cooper, William J. "The New Political History Faces Southward." *Reviews in American History* 12 (September 1984): 383–387.

Crawford, Sidney. "Arkansas Suffrage Qualifications." *Arkansas Historical Quarterly* 2 (December 1943): 331–339.

Crenshaw, Ollinger. "The Speakership Contest of 1859–1860." *Mississippi Valley Historical Review* 29 (December 1942): 323–338.

Crofts, Daniel W. "The Union Party of 1861 and the Secession Crisis." *Perspectives in American History* 11 (1977–1978): 327–376.

Dale, Edward Everett. "Arkansas: The Myth and the State." *Arkansas Historical Quarterly* 12 (Spring 1953): 8–29.

Davis, Granville. "Arkansas and the Blood of Kansas." *Journal of Southern History* 16 (November 1950): 431–456.

Donnelly, William S. "Conspiracy or Popular Movement: The Historiography of Southern Support for Secession." *North Carolina Historical Review* 42 (Winter 1965): 70–84.

Dougan, Michael. "A Look at the Family in Arkansas Politics, 1858–1865." *Arkansas Historical Quarterly* 29 (Summer 1970): 99–111.

Escott, Paul. "Southern Yeomen and the Confederacy." *South Atlantic Quarterly* 77 (Spring 1978): 146–158.

Freehling, William W. "The Editorial Revolution, Virginia and the Coming of the Civil War. Review Essay of George M. Reese's Proceedings of the Virginia State Convention of 1861." *Civil War History* 16 (March 1970): 64–72.

Genovese, Eugene. "Yeomen Farmers in a Slaveholders' Democracy." *Agricultural History* 49 (April 1975): 331–342.

Harrison, Robert and Walter Kollmorgen. "Land Reclamation in Arkansas Under the Swamp Land Grant of 1850." *Arkansas Historical Quarterly* 6 (Winter 1947): 369–418.

Hindman, Biscoe. "Thomas Carmichael Hindman." *Confederate Veteran* 38 (March 1930): 97–104.

Howell, Elmo. "Mark Twain's Arkansas." *Arkansas Historical Quarterly* 29 (Autumn 1970): 195–208.

Huff, Leo. "The Last Duel in Arkansas: The Marmaduke-Walker Duel." *Arkansas Historical Quarterly* 23 (Spring 1964): 34–49.

———. "The Memphis to Little Rock Railroad During the Civil War." *Arkansas Historical Quarterly* 23 (Autumn 1964): 260–270.

Johnson, William. "Prelude to the Missouri Compromise." *Arkansas Historical Quarterly* 24 (Spring 1965): 47–66.

Johnston, James, ed. "Letter of John Campbell, Unionist." *Arkansas Historical Quarterly* 29 (Summer 1970): 170–182.

Lack, Paul D. "An Urban Slave Community: Little Rock, 1831–1862." *Arkansas Historical Quarterly* 41 (Autumn 1982): 258–287.

Lewis, Elsie Mae. "Economic Conditions in Antebellum Arkansas, 1850–1860." *Arkansas Historical Quarterly* 6 (Autumn 1947): 256–274.

———. "Robert Ward Johnson: Militant Spokesman of the Old South-West." *Arkansas Historical Quarterly* 13 (Spring 1954): 16–30.

Lisenby, Foy. "A Survey of Arkansas's Image Problem." *Arkansas Historical Quarterly* 30 (Spring 1971): 60–71.

———. "Winthrop Rockefeller and the Arkansas Image." *Arkansas Historical Quarterly* 43 (Summer 1984): 143–152.

Luthin, Reinhard. "The Democratic Split During Buchanan's Administration." *Pennsylvania History* 11 (January 1944): 13–35.

Lynch, William. "The Westward Flow of Southern Colonists Before 1861." *Journal of Southern History* 9 (August 1943): 305–327.

Malone, Dumas. *Dictionary of American Biography.* 20 vols. New York: Charles Scribner's Sons, 1928–1936. "Elias Nelson Conway," by David Y. Thomas.

———. *Dictionary of American Biography,* "Thomas Carmichael Hindman," by David Y. Thomas.

———. *Dictionary of American Biography,* "Richard Mentor Johnson," by Thomas P. Abernathy.

———. *Dictionary of American Biography,* "Ambrose Hundley Sevier," by David Y. Thomas.

MacMillan, Malcolm. "William Yancey and the Historians: One Hundred Years Later." *Alabama Review* 20 (July 1967): 163–186.

McCrary, Peyton, Clark Miller, and Dale Baum. "Class and Party in the Secession Crisis: Voting Behavior in the Deep South, 1856–1861." *Journal of Interdisciplinary History* 8 (Winter 1978): 429–457.

McGinnis, Clyde. "Arkansas College." *Arkansas Historical Quarterly* 31 (Autumn 1972): 234–245.

McWhinney, Grady. "The Confederacy's First Shot." *Civil War History* 14 (March 1968): 5–14.

Mering, John V. "The Slave-State Constitutional Unionists and the Politics of Consensus." *Journal of Southern History* 43 (August 1977): 395–410.

Moffatt, Walter. "Transportation in Arkansas, 1819–1840." *Arkansas Historical Quarterly* 15 (Autumn 1956): 187–201.

Moneyhon, Carl. "Economic Democracy in Antebellum Arkansas: Phillips County, 1850–1860." *Arkansas Historical Quarterly* 40 (Summer 1981): 154–172.

Moore, James. "Redeemers Reconsidered: Change and Continuity in the Democratic South, 1870–1900." *Journal of Southern History* 44 (August 1978): 359–378.

Moore, Waddy. "Some Aspects of Crime and Punishment on the Arkansas Frontier." *Arkansas Historical Quarterly* 23 (Spring 1964): 50–64.

Morrill, James. "The Presidential Election of 1852: Death Knell of the Whig Party in North Carolina." *North Carolina Historical Review* 44 (October 1967): 342–359.

Morris, Robert. "Three Arkansas Travelers." *Arkansas Historical Quarterly* 4 (Autumn 1945): 215–230.

Newberry, Farrah. "Harris Flanagin." *Arkansas Historical Quarterly* 17 (Spring 1958): 3–20.

Nichols, Roy. "The Kansas-Nebraska Act: A Century of Historiography." *Mississippi Valley Historical Review* 43 (September 1956): 187–212.

Otto, John S. "Slavery in the Mountains: Yell County, Arkansas, 1840–1860." *Arkansas Historical Quarterly* 39 (Spring 1980): 35–52.

Otto, John S., and Augustus Marion Burns. "Traditional Agricultural Practices in the Arkansas Highlands." *Journal of American Folklore* 44 (April-June 1981): 167–187.

Ramsdell, Charles. "Lincoln and Fort Sumter." *Journal of Southern History* 3 (August 1937): 259–288.

Rawson, Donald. "Democratic Resurgence in Mississippi, 1853–1855." *Journal of Mississippi History* 24 (February 1964): 1–27.

Robinson, Joseph Taylor. "Suffrage in Arkansas." *Publications of the Arkansas Historical Association*. 4 vols. Little Rock: Democrat Printing & Lithograph Co., 1906–1917. 3: 167–174.

Rothrock, Thomas. "The University of Arkansas's Old Main." *Arkansas Historical Quarterly* 30 (Spring 1971): 3–52.

Scroggs, Jack. "Arkansas in the Secession Crisis." *Arkansas Historical Quarterly* 12 (Autumn 1953): 179–224.

Sherwood, Diana. "The Code Duello in Arkansas." *Arkansas Historical Quarterly* 6 (Summer 1947): 186–197.

Smith, Harold T. "The Know-Nothing Party in Arkansas." *Arkansas Historical Quarterly* 34 (Winter 1975): 291–303.

Stampp, Kenneth. "The Concept of a Perpetual Union." *Journal of American History* 65 (June 1978): 5–33.

———. "Lincoln and the Strategy of Defense in the Crisis of 1861." *Journal of Southern History* 11 (August 1945): 297–323.

Taylor, Lennette Sengel. "Polemics and Partisanship: The Arkansas Press in the 1860 Election." *Arkansas Historical Quarterly* 44 (Winter 1985): 314–335.

Thomas, David Y. "Southern Non-Slaveholders in the Election of 1860." *Political Science Quarterly* 26 (June 1911): 222–237.

Turner, Jesse. "The Constitution of 1836." *Publications of the Arkansas Historical Association* 4 vols. Little Rock: Democrat Printing & Lithograph Co., 1906–1917. 3: 74–116.

Venable, Austin. "The Conflict Between the Douglas and Yancey Forces in the Charleston Convention." *Journal of Southern History* 8 (May 1942): 226–241.

Walton, Brian. "The Second Party System in Arkansas, 1836–1850." *Arkansas Historical Quarterly* 28 (Summer 1969): 120–155.

———. "Ambrose Hundley Sevier in the United States Senate, 1836–1848." *Arkansas Historical Quarterly* 32 (Spring 1973): 25–60.

———. "Arkansas Politics During the Compromise Crisis, 1848–1852." *Arkansas Historical Quarterly* 36 (Winter 1977): 307–337.

Walz, Robert. "Migration into Arkansas, 1820–1880: Incentives and Means of Travel." *Arkansas Historical Quarterly* 17 (Winter 1958): 309–324.

White, William. "The Texas Slave Insurrection of 1860." *Southwestern Historical Quarterly* 52 (January 1949): 259–285.

Williams, C. Fred. "The Bear State Image: Arkansas in the Nineteenth Century." *Arkansas Historical Quarterly* 39 (Summer 1980): 99–111.

Wood, Stephen. "The Development of the Arkansas Railroads: Part II, Period of Land Grants and the Civil War." *Arkansas Historical Quarterly* 7 (Summer 1948): 119–140.

Woods, James M. "Devotees and Dissenters: Arkansans in the Confederate Congress, 1861–1865." *Arkansas Historical Quarterly* 38 (Autumn 1979): 227–247.

———. "Expansionism As Diplomacy: The Career of Solon Borland in Central America, 1853–1854." *The Americas: A Quarterly Review of Inter-American Cultural History* 40 (January 1984): 399–417.

Wooster, Ralph. "The Arkansas Secession Convention." *Arkansas Historical Quarterly* 13 (Autumn 1954): 172–195.

Worley, Ted R. "Control of the Real Estate Bank of the State of Arkansas." *Mississippi Valley Historical Review* 37 (December 1950): 403–426.

———. "The Arkansas Peace Society of 1861: A Study in Mountain Unionism." *Journal of Southern History* 24 (November 1958): 445–456.

———. "Documents Relating to the Arkansas Peace Society of 1861." *Arkansas Historical Quarterly* 17 (Spring 1958): 82–111.

———. "The Arkansas State Bank: Antebellum Period." *Arkansas Historical Quarterly* 23 (Spring 1964): 65–73.

Secondary Sources: Unpublished Material

Boyette, Gene Wills. "The Whigs of Arkansas, 1836–1856." Ph.D. diss., Louisiana State University, 1972.

Brown, Walter L. "Albert Pike, 1809–1891." Ph.D. diss., University of Texas, 1955.

Carmichael, Maude. "The Plantation System in Arkansas, 1850–1880." Ph.D. diss., Radcliffe College, 1934.

Crofts, Daniel. "The Political and Social Origins of Opposition to Secession in the Upper South." Paper in Typescript, Southern Historical Association, Louisville, Ky., November 2, 1984.

Ferguson, John Lewis. "William Woodruff of the Territory of Arkansas, 1819–1836." Ph.D. diss., Tulane University, 1960.

Ledbetter, Billy. "Slavery, Fear, and Disunion in the Lone Star State: Texans' Attitude Toward the Union, 1846–1861." Ph.D. diss., North Texas State University, 1972.

Lewis, Elsie Mae. "From Nationalism to Disunion: A Study of the Secession Movement in Arkansas, 1849–1861." Ph.D. diss., University of Chicago, 1947.

Moore, Waddy W. "Territorial Arkansas, 1819–1836." Ph.D. diss., University of North Carolina, 1963.

Mula, John. "The Public Career of William King Sebastian." M.A. thesis, University of Arkansas, 1969.

Roberts, Bobby. "Thomas Carmichael Hindman: Secessionist and Confederate General." M.A. thesis, University of Arkansas, 1972.

Ruple, Susan H. "The Life and Times of Chester Ashley of Arkansas, 1791–1848." M.A. thesis, University of Arkansas, 1983.

Scroggs, Jack. "The Secession Movement in Arkansas." M.A. thesis, University of Arkansas, 1948.

Smith, Harold T. "Arkansas Politics, 1850–1861." M.A. thesis, Memphis State University, 1964.

Stokes, Dewey Allen. "Public Affairs in Arkansas, 1836–1850." Ph.D. diss., University of Texas, 1966.

Walz, Robert. "Migration into Arkansas, 1834–1880." Ph.D. diss., University of Texas, 1958.

Index

General Assembly (Arkansas), see Arkansas General Assembly
Georgia, 19, 20, 21, 77, 103, 123, 137, 140
Gerstacker, Frederick, 7
Gould, Josiah, 138
Grace, William, 138, 159, 245n.44
Gray, Lewis, 166
Greene County, 157
Greenwood, Alfred B., 58, 62, 67, 224n.112
Griffith, Samuel, 147, 248n.103
Gunter, Thomas, 245n.44, 250n.35

Hallum, John, 54, 83, 224n.112
Hamlin, Hannibal, 104
Hanly, Thomas, 138, 144, 145, 148, 156–57
Harrell, John, 85
Hathaway, Gilbert, 10, 11
Helena, Ark., 10, 13, 27, 50, 58, 62, 68, 72, 73, 76, 78, 81, 83, 127, 138, 141, 144, 162, 169
Helper, Hinton R., 96, 142
Hempstead, Samuel, 120, 156, 159, 247n.85
Hempstead County, 111, 120, 139, 144, 160
Herald (Fort Smith), 11, 12, 14, 121, 226n.35
Hilliard, Isaac, 146
Hindman, Sallie Holt, 71
Hindman, Jr., Thomas Carmichael, 3, 61–62, 67–68, 69, 71–83, 86–90, 95, 96, 97, 99, 102, 103–04, 107, 108, 112, 116–21, 123, 125, 129, 130, 141, 150, 151, 160, 162, 167, 168, 169
Hindman, Sr., Thomas Carmichael, 71, 72
Hoadley, F. W., 234nn.59, 63
Hobson, A. H., 154
Holly Springs, Miss., 72
Holt, Michael, 166, 167
Homestead Act of 1862 (U.S.), 21, 54, 105
Hopefield, Ark., 92
Hot Springs, Ark., 62, 81
Houston, Sam, 98
Hubbard, Thomas, 81
Huntsville, Ark., 148

Illinois, 8, 15, 20, 65, 100, 104, 105, 112
Independence County, 110
Independent Balance (Batesville), 23, 36, 85
Indian Territory, 11, 12, 13, 16, 17, 39, 45, 118, 126, 157
Izard, Mark, 22
Izard County, 164

Jackson, Andrew, 34, 37, 41, 70, 71, 125
Jackson, Claiborne F., 158
Jackson, Thomas J. "Stonewall," 168
Jackson County, 110
Jacksonport, Ark., 136, 141
Jefferson County, 47, 75, 110, 120, 123, 138
Jeffersonian Independent (Pine Bluff), 79, 95, 97, 226n.35
Johnson, Benjamin, 43
Johnson, Herschel, 103
Johnson, Jilson, 138, 139, 234nn.59, 63
Johnson, Richard H., 57, 65, 67, 73, 74, 75, 78, 79, 83, 84, 85, 89, 94, 99, 126, 128, 129, 130, 132, 139, 140–41, 147
Johnson, Richard M., 34, 43
Johnson, Robert W., 39, 43–51, 54, 57, 58, 59, 67, 68, 75–79, 84, 89, 93, 94, 96, 101, 102, 103, 106, 107, 117–18, 119, 123, 126, 129, 130, 132, 143, 144, 148, 150, 155, 162, 168
Johnson County, 130, 138, 164
Jordan, John, 234nn.59, 62
Journal of Southern History, 2

Kansas, 157
Kansas-Nebraska Act, 65, 94
Kansas Territory, 65, 66, 67, 93, 94
Kelly, Samuel "Parson," 159–60, 250n.35
Kennard, M. S., 245n.44
Kentucky, 7, 13, 19, 20, 21, 33, 37, 43, 46, 67, 103, 105, 110, 111, 124, 137, 146, 158
Knight, John, 46
Know-Nothings (Arkansas), 42, 60–64, 68, 69, 72, 73, 74; (National), 60, 61, 63, 64
Knoxville, Tenn., 71

Lane, Joseph, 103
Laughinghouse, George, 138
Lay, Bishop Henry, 109, 124, 136
Lecompton Constitution (Kansas Territory), 94
Lewis, Elsie Mae, 2, 52
Lincoln, President Abraham, 3, 29, 104, 105, 106, 109, 110, 113–16, 120, 124, 131, 132, 133, 134–36, 142, 143, 147, 148, 149, 150–51, 152, 153–55, 157
Little Rock, Borland in, 46–47, 51; Conway in, 62; Democratic party in, 70, 78, 99; Douglas in, 105; the Dynasty in, see Dynasty; early economic and cultural development in, 10, 12, 15, 24, 26, 34; early political history in, 37–41; the Family in, see Family; Federal arsenal in,